THE ASIAN CIVILISATIONS MUSEUM A-Z GUIDE

TO ITS COLLECTIONS

To Professor Sarah Harper

welcome to Singapore. Please
visit the Asian Civilizations
Museum and our other museums.

Tommy Koh
chairman
N. H. B.
15 June 06

ASIAN CIVILISATIONS MUSEUM

a National Museum

Managing Editor
Marilyn Seow

Editors
Sharon Ham
Shan Wolody

Project Coordinator
Hairani Hassan

Senior Designer
Annie Teo

Designer
Nelani Jinadasa

Photographers
Kuet Ee Foo
Lee Chee Kheong

Production Manager
Sin Kam Cheong

Published by
Asian Civilisations Museum
National Heritage Board
1 Empress Place
Singapore 179555

Designed and produced by
Editions Didier Millet
121 Telok Ayer Street, #03-01
Singapore 068590

www.edmbooks.com

Colour separation by
Singapore Sang Choy Colour Separation

Printed in Singapore by
UIC Printing

ISBN 981-4068-67-5

Contributors

Liana Chua

Randall Ee

Hairani Hassan

David Alan Henkel

Gauri Parimoo Krishnan

Lee Chor Lin

Heidi Tan

Tan Huism

Szan Tan

Wong Hwei Lian

The Use of Dates in this Guide

The way in which years are numbered differs from calendar to calendar. In the Islamic calendar, year 1 is the year of the Hijrah or 1 AH, which commemorates the migration of Prophet Muhammad from Mecca to Medina. The term 'anno Hegirae' (AH) is Latin for 'Year of the Hjirah'. The first day, month and year of the Hijrah corresponds to 16 July 622 CE. The Islamic year is lunar and consists of about 354 days, which is about 11 days shorter than the Gregorian solar year. This difference means that it is difficult to be accurate when attempting to convert an Islamic year to a Gregorian one, unless the day and month is known.

Unless otherwise stated all dates that appear in this guide use the CE (Common Era) system of dating. In certain (i.e. non-Christian) contexts CE has replaced AD (anno Domini) as the method of denoting the years since the birth of Christ. Islamic dates are included where they are known. Where artefacts date to before the Common Era, BCE (Before Common Era) is used.

Translation

All English translations of the Qur'an come from 'Abdullah Yusuf 'Ali, *The Meaning of the Holy Qur'an*, 5th edition, U.S.A.: Amana Corporation, 1994.

Transliteration

For the sake of simplicity and ease of understanding, the Arabic and Sanskrit words in this guide are generally reproduced without diacritical marks.

Colour Key

Colour coding has been used for the entries in this guide to indicate the region of origin of the objects shown.

China

South Asia

Southeast Asia

West Asia

Contents

This handbook to the collection of the Asian Civilisations Museum reflects an apparent paradox—we are a very young museum with many of the objects featured here having entered the collection only in the past ten years, yet other objects, particularly from our historic Southeast Asian inventory, were acquired one hundred years ago.

The latter are a legacy of the Raffles Library and Museum, the progenitor of the present three national museums of Singapore, of which the Asian Civilisations Museum is one. While the idea for a museum in Singapore was first mooted in the 1820s during Stamford Raffles' day, it was not until 1849 that a collection policy was actually spelt out. A purpose-built structure followed in 1887.

Among the materials identified for collecting were 'implements, cloth or other articles of native art and manufacture', 'figures of deities used in worship', 'instruments of war or other weapons' and 'vessels employed in religious ceremonies'. This policy set the direction for what was to become the ethnological collection of the Raffles Museum, which formed a prominent part of its displays from the outset.

(OPPOSITE) In 2003 the Empress Place Building on the Singapore River became the Asian Civilisations Museum's second home.
(LEFT) Ethnology displays, photographed here in 1931, were an important part of the Raffles Museum collection.

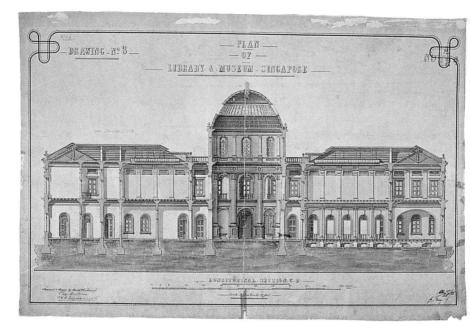

By the time Singapore gained independence in 1965, Library and Museum had become two separate entities. Soon after, the re-named National Museum was to shed its zoological and geological collections and receive a new, more focused, mandate—the history, art and ethnology of Singapore and its neighbours. The museum's ethnological collection therefore continued to grow and was expanded during this period to include material relating to the Peranakans (Chinese, Indian and Eurasian communities that had long settled in Southeast Asia and assimilated aspects of mainstream Malay culture).

At the end of the 1980s momentum was gathering for further changes. Singapore had experienced rapid social and economic

development since independence and investment in cultural resources had inevitably lagged behind. The National Museum was starting to look inadequate as a facility. A bold decision was taken in 1991 by then Minister for Information and the Arts, Brigadier-General George Yeo to devolve the National Museum into three separate institutions. The national collection was accordingly partitioned along the lines of Singapore history, art and ethnology. The ethnological and several other smaller collections came under the care of a newly created Asian Civilisations Museum.

Having inherited a collection focused largely on Southeast Asia, we had to expand the scope of our acquisition policies in order to fulfil a new mission—to highlight the roots of Singapore's different ethnic groups in the various cultures and civilisations of Asia. Government grants were made available through the 1990s to enable us to do this. As a result we have started two new collection areas—South Asia and West Asia/Islamic. We have also judiciously added to our small existing Chinese collection and built on our historic Southeast Asian collection.

At the same time as we were intensively re-shaping and enriching our collections, we embarked on two building projects, to provide homes for our new museum. The first was the former Tao Nan School building in Armenian Street, a historical structure in tropical neo-classical style dating from 1910, which was opened in 1997 after a four-year renovation and rebuilding programme. The permanent galleries were initially installed with thematic displays on China.

Planning work for the conversion of our second home commenced before we opened the first. A ten-minute walk from Armenian Street through Singapore's historic Civic District, the Empress Place Building is a grand colonial pile on the banks of the Singapore River. This was a government office block dating from 1867 that had been progressively added to over the years. We further enlarged the building by adding a basement and two extension wings. At over 14,000 square metres, three and a half times the size of the Armenian Street building, Empress Place provides the space for our growing pan-Asian collections to be comprehensively displayed under one roof for the first time.

(OPPOSITE, TOP) As-built drawing of the Raffles Library and Museum from 1892.
(OPPOSITE, BOTTOM) The Asian Civilisations Museum's Armenian Street premises opened in 1997.
(TOP) The riverside Empress Place Building as it was in the 1920s.

Our collection has been shaped by official mandate over the years. In common with other museums, it has also been enriched by gifts and benefactions. Our purchases have, as a rule, been identified with a view to plugging gaps in the collection, rather than to establish depth in any particular collecting area. Gifts of objects—either single pieces or, sometimes, entire collections—have given both depth and breadth to the collection. And donations of funds have allowed us to acquire some pieces of major significance.

The number of donations has increased in recent years as our new museum developments have caught the imagination of collectors and benefactors. Special tax incentives, in place since the early 1990s, have also played a role in attracting gifts in some cases.

Three separate donations of Southeast Asian gold have created a major collection area where previously there had been none. The large and superb Edmond Chin Gift focuses on gold jewellery. An assortment of classical Indonesian gold objects came to us as part of the Andy Ng Gift, and Annie Wee has given us fine Javanese and Peranakan examples. These objects are the perfect complement to island Southeast Asian textiles—another of the strengths of our collection.

Our Chinese collection has been enriched by donations, particularly of ceramics. The Shaw Foundation has been

our long-time supporter in the acquisition of Chinese ceramics. We have received gifts from the collection of Singapore Leisure Industries and from Frank and Pamela Hickley. The gift of the Hickley Collection has endowed our Museum at a stroke with one of the world's most comprehensive holdings of

blanc de Chine porcelain from the southern Fujian province. Apart from ceramics, the Dr Tan Tsze Chor Family Gift of 19th- and 20th-century Chinese paintings has filled out a collecting area which had been very thinly represented.

The Indian part of our South Asia collection has been regularly assisted by contributions from the Singapore Reinsurance Corporation and India International Insurance, as well as from Hwang Soo Jin, and major acquisitions have been made as a result.

Lenders have made it possible for us to fill gaps in the collection, even if temporarily. Some of the entries in this handbook are therefore objects on long-term loan. The group of Qur'ans, ceramics and other Islamic material from the collection of the Tareq Rajab Museum is the most important of the loans made to us.

While we have naturally chosen to feature many of our best pieces in this handbook—and you will find most of these in the galleries—we have also taken the opportunity to publish here a few objects which we feel merit inclusion simply because they are interesting and unusual.

This handbook celebrates the re-opening of Empress Place in 2003 as the second home of the Asian Civilisations Museum. Thanks to the legacy of the Raffles Museum, we have a fine Southeast Asian ethnology collection. Other areas of our collection have been assembled more recently and are still far from being fully representative of the cultures of origin. A good collection takes generations to form and collection policies need to be constantly tweaked and adjusted to suit changing circumstances and expectations. Museums today do not exist merely to collect— we strive to widen and engage our public and to enhance the museum experience through visitor services, facilities and programmes—but it is ultimately the quality of the collection that gives meaning to this effort.

Kenson Kwok

Director

(OPPOSITE) The new basement area of the Empress Place Building is shown here under construction in 1999.
(TOP) A corner of the Shaw Foundation Foyer; the foundation has been a strong supporter of the museum's Chinese ceramic acquisitions.
(ABOVE) The façade of the museum's newly built extension at Empress Place.

Akha Accessories

to

Zhang Ruitu's Calligraphy

Artefacts
from the Collection

Akha Accessories

Akha women produce some of the most colourful accessories of all the highland communities and their headdresses are particularly distinctive. Akha sub-groups identify themselves by the design of their headgear and the status of the wearer is further differentiated by the extent of decoration. The headdress (BELOW) from the sub-group Loimi Akha (named after a mountain in Burma from where they migrated) is also known as *u bya* or 'flat headdress'. It consists of a cloth cap with a flat tin- or aluminium-wrapped panel attached to the back and rows of silver bosses sewn across the front. Glass beads, silver balls and discs, coins, monkey fur and red-dyed chicken feathers dangle from the sides. Today aluminium is frequently used as a substitute for the silver and other decorative materials which have greater market value.

The jacket and the short pleated skirt (OPPOSITE, RIGHT) are made of indigo-dyed hemp. The jacket is embellished with colourful fabrics sewn on as appliqué combined with colourful stitching and outlined with white seeds and buttons. The same decorative techniques are used on the bag (OPPOSITE, LEFT) which is particularly interesting as it has additional decoration in the form of green beetles threaded together with buttons and colourful wool tassels. Their lasting bright green iridescence must have had great aesthetic appeal.

The Akha originated from Yunnan (1 million live there today) although their ancestors probably migrated there from other parts of China,

(TOP) **HEADDRESS**
North Thailand
Early 20th century
Cloth, silver and feathers
58 x 30 x 13 cm
1993.1327

(OPPOSITE, LEFT) **BAG WITH GREEN BEETLES**
North Thailand
Early 20th century
Embroidered cotton, buttons, wool and dried green beetles
92 x 31 cm
1993.1308

(OPPOSITE, RIGHT) **JACKET AND SKIRT**
North Thailand
Early 20th century
Indigo-dyed cotton with embroidery and appliqué
(JACKET) 64 x 130 cm; (SKIRT) 40 x 69 cm
1993.1333, 11993.1332

Tibet and perhaps even further west several thousand years ago. Economic, political and environmental factors have contributed to profound changes in their nomadic lifestyle of slash-and-burn agriculture. Many were forced to move southwards into mainland Southeast Asia during the 19th century, where they were required to become more settled. As with most hilltribe communities, animism and ancestor worship figure prominently in the Akha belief system. The 'Lord of the Earth' provides bountiful harvests, good health and protection from calamities. The latter are purged from the village by carved wooden gates which purify anyone who may have accidentally acquired evil spirits in the world outside. [HT]

Akshobhya

According to the *Mahayana Sutra Prajnaparamita*, there is a widely accepted belief that different Buddhas exist and teach simultaneously in different world systems. All of them are invisible except for Akshobhya, the Imperturbable One, who is known to us thanks to the special vision of him granted by Shakyamuni. Akshobhya refers to Shakyamuni's calm composure during Mara's attack. Akshobhya is also called the Buddha of the East, referring to the pilgrimage, especially from the Gandhara region, to Bodhgaya.[1]

Seated in *padmasana* (lotus posture), this Pala image of a crowned Buddha strikes a *bhumisparsha mudra* (earth-witnessing gesture). It is identified as Dhyani Buddha Akshobhya. This scene relates to Shakyamuni's encounter with Mara, who tested Shakyamuni's concentration by bringing in his army of demons and sensuous damsels. Buddha called upon Mother Earth to bear witness to this event, called Maravijaya, by the *bhumisparsha* gesture of touching the earth with his right hand. Dhyani Buddha Akshobhya takes on this iconography and is represented here on a throne with a lotus pedestal under the Bodhi Tree and a halo lined with pearls. The iconography is similar to the earlier representations of Buddha from Bihar in the 8th and 9th centuries where Buddha was portrayed with lions and devotees under the seat. As these details are missing here, it indicates that this representation is of a much later date.

Pala sculpture has a certain stylistic form which has become more slender and attenuated over time. The bulkiness of the post-Gupta period was followed by the sensuality of 8th-century sculpture, and by the 12th century it had evolved into a form with highly decorative surfaces and elongated yet stiffened features. Pala style developed at many centres such as Kurkihara, Bodhgaya, Murshidabad, Muzaffarpur, Rajshahi, Nalanda and Dhakka. During the Sena period the style became even more decorative as a result of its confluence with the southern style of the Hoysala period.[2] This sculpture, which probably comes from north Bihar, has a very sombre look: the inner concentration is strongly inspired by Tantrism, while the ornamental details are minimal. This gives the figure a slightly stiff appearance. [GPK]

▶ see RELIEF FRAGMENT DEPICTING THE LIFE OF BUDDHA
▶ see SEATED LOKESHVARA
▶ see SYAMATARA

AKSHOBHYA
East India
Pala period, 12th century
Schist
60 x 35.5 x 12.5 cm
Purchased with funds from Singapore Reinsurance
Corporation Ltd and India International Insurance Pte Ltd
1995.266

Ancestor Portraits

The figures in this pair of portraits are seated in a frontal pose, a conventional feature of Qing ancestor portraits. Their round-backed chairs with footrests have been painted to resemble *huanghuali*, an expensive hardwood. The male figure (FAR RIGHT) wears an official's robe without a rank badge, and a Qing official's hat. He holds a string of vermilion and jade beads in his left hand, while his right hand holds a folding fan inscribed with his name, Mr Shi Chang. In ancestor portraits, both male and female figures were commonly portrayed fingering a string of stone beads or

pearls. The female figure's head (ABOVE, LEFT) is adorned with a pair of gold openwork hairpins and a filigree headdress, which were popular during the late Qing dynasty.

Ancestor portraits were commissioned to commemorate the patrons' ancestors and were hung in lineage halls and homes on special occasions such as death anniversaries and Chinese New Year. Portraits of the recently deceased were sometimes used during funeral marches. The verisimilitude of these portraits was not always guaranteed as they were often commissioned posthumously. Moreover, it was commonplace for the descendant patron to bestow more wealth and status than might have been actually enjoyed by the ancestor in his lifetime. For example, patrons might commission a painting of their ancestors clothed in high-ranking officials' robe, although the latter might not have enjoyed officialdom. This was a gesture of respect on the part of the commissioners and a way to elevate their own social status. Although this might have been considered unacceptable, it was still in accordance with the Confucian virtue of filial piety, for it was one's duty to provide for one's ancestors with the best posthumously.

Ancestor portraits were also called *qiankun xiang,* or portraits of the Heaven and Earth, with the male representing Heaven (*qian*) and the female representing Earth (*kun*). This dichotomy, drawn from *yin-yang* theories, defined the perimeters of behaviour and responsibility for the two sexes (▶ see YIN AND YANG ZODIAC SIGNS). For example, females have to be positioned on the right while males have to be on the left. This is thus the standard for the placement of ancestor portraits. [ST]

A PAIR OF ANCESTOR PORTRAITS
China
Late Qing dynasty
Chinese ink and colour on silk
(EACH) 179.6 x 86.9 cm
1997.737, 1997.738

Ancestral Figurines

These ancestral figurines are carved in boxwood (*huangyang mu*), a softwood generally used for carving statues and figurines in the Qing dynasty. According to the inscriptions found on the back of the figures, the male ancestor (BELOW, RIGHT) is identified as Zhang Zhenglong (b. 1738) and the female (BELOW, LEFT) is identified as Zheng Guanniang (b. 1752). Both figures are seated on round-backed chairs with footstools and chair covers. The female figure holds a string of beads in her left hand while the male figure holds a book in his left hand (the fan originally in his right hand is now missing). They are also dressed in officials' robes with rank badges depicting cranes. From the inscription, the male figure is identified as a ninth-rank civil official. However, this is incongruent with his rank badge of cranes, which was the prerogative of first-rank civil officials.

The portrayal of both figurines—the hieratic postures, formal costumes, furniture and accessories depicted—is similar to that of ancestor portraits painted on silk and paper (▶ see A PAIR OF ANCESTOR PORTRAITS). Ancestral figurines function like ancestor portraits, capturing the likeness, and hence the spirit, of the deceased. Descendants paid respects to these images and offered them joss, flowers and fruit. However, unlike portraits, which were usually only displayed on special occasions such as death anniversaries and Chinese New Year, ancestral figurines were placed on the domestic altar and venerated daily.

As early as the Han dynasty, sculptural images of one's parents were already in existence. Commemorating one's ancestors through sculptural and pictorial forms were conventionally acceptable practices that expressed the Confucian virtue of filial piety (▶ see FILIAL PIETY SCENES ON FUNERARY STELE). However, during the Song and Ming dynasties, Neo-Confucianists argued otherwise. They were against the use of images for ancestor worship as images were believed to be foreign and Buddhist imports. Furthermore, the uncertainty that the images truly resembled the venerated ancestors rendered them ineffective for rituals. Instead, Neo-Confucianists proposed the use of ancestral tablets as the proper and effective medium for worship (▶ see ANCESTRAL TABLET SHRINE). However, for intimate communication with one's ancestors, images were nonetheless more appealing. [ST]

A PAIR OF ANCESTRAL FIGURINES
China
Qing dynasty
Boxwood
(FEMALE) h. 28.5 cm; (MALE) h. 29 cm
1996.673.1, 1996.673.2

Ancestral Tablet Shrine

This tablet shrine has four parallel doors that feature openwork carving and can be opened up like a folding screen. It is made from hardwood from *longyan*, a fruit tree. The use of this rare raw material suggests that the shrine was commissioned by a relatively wealthy patron. Shrines like these were used to house ancestral tablets at home. The recently deceased were usually commemorated with a photograph or portrait while ancestors who had departed this world for more than a year or two were remembered with ancestral tablets. These tablets usually recorded the names, birth and death dates of the deceased, as well as the relationship of the deceased to the patrons. The tablets of the deceased of two to three generations were often kept in the domestic altar and were usually transferred to the ancestral lineage halls from the fourth generation upwards.

A basic domestic altar consisted of an altar table, an ancestral tablet or an image of the ancestor (a photograph, small painted portrait or figurine) and offerings. For wealthier families, a tablet shrine, an altar cloth, candle holders and a censer made from the finest silks, gold, silver and ceramic were also added. Daily offerings included joss sticks, flowers and fruit, while on death anniversaries, and during the Seventh Lunar Month and Chinese New Year, the ancestor enjoyed a feast of cooked food and was offered silver paper money.

Ancestral tablets, rather than images, were preferred by Confucians as they were thought to be better vessels for housing ancestral spirits. The living communicated with their ancestors through visualisation and by invoking their names. Although the spirits of the ancestors were not perceived to be as powerful as gods, they were nevertheless appealed to for blessings of marriages, bearing of sons and other important family matters. [ST]

▶ see ANCESTOR PORTRAITS
▶ see ANCESTRAL FIGURINES

ANCESTRAL TABLET SHRINE
Fujian province, China
Late Qing dynasty
Longyan wood
71.5 x 54 x 24.8 cm
1996.925

Angkor Borei Buddha

This standing Buddha image was an object of veneration in a Khmer temple. It was one of several provincial art styles associated with the early Khmer or pre-Angkor period. Standing images of the unadorned Buddha with hands in various gestures have been found in the lower Mekong Delta at sites perhaps associated with Angkor Borei, one of the important early Khmer centres of Buddhism.[3] Buddhism and Hinduism coexisted during the early centuries of the Common Era, although it is not known whether images such as these were expressions of Theravada or Mahayana Buddhism.

The figure stands with both hands (now restored) in *vitarka mudra* (gesture of argumentation, with the forefinger and thumb forming a circle). The Buddha's features, also known as *lakshana*, are recognisable: the large curls of hair rise to a protuberance or *ushnisha* (which symbolises his enlightenment), where there is a setting, probably for a stone. A gemstone is thought to be more likely in this early period rather than a flame finial which was introduced much later.[4] The unadorned earlobes, which extend almost to the shoulders, are a reminder of the Buddha's past life as a prince and his rejection of the material world.[5]

Indian Buddhist art styles were an important influence during this time. Amaravati in India and Anuradhapura in Sri Lanka were important centres for the earliest Buddhist influences on Southeast Asia.[6] In particular standing images with heavy pleated garments are thought to share stylistic links with these centres (▶ see KEDAH BUDDHA). However, several aspects of this piece indicate that indigenous artists were able to adapt imported styles. For example the Buddha's stance, known as *tribhanga*, is very subtly expressed—a characteristic that has been observed in early Khmer stone images and compared with Indian images.[7] The *urna*, or tuft of hair usually found between the eyebrows on Indian and Indonesian images, is noticeably absent on Khmer images.[8] [HT]

IMAGE OF A STANDING BUDDHA
Lower Mekong Delta, Cambodia
7th–8th centuries
Bronze
43.5 x 12 cm
1999.2602

Ankusha
(Elephant Goad)

A nkusha (elephant goads), which are used by *mahavat* (elephant riders), are also weapons—along with scores of others—that are commonly seen in the multiple arms of Hindu gods such as Ganesha, Durga or Indra. Thus this weapon is primarily associated with Hindu gods. Embellished *ankusha* such as this one seem to have originated in Hindu courts where they were possibly used for religious rituals or other ceremonies of state.

This *ankusha* is ornamental and bears images of animals and vegetation. Its handle is very shapely, with five simple bands surmounted by a pointed but blunt blade and a curved *ankusha*. It ends with a *makara* motif with a flaring mouth and a prancing hound emerging from it. Two rhysomes further flaring upwards and downwards emerge from the mouth of the hound and complete a circular pattern. Its blade bears carvings of animal and plant motifs in a rather abstracted form.

For a weapon that is generally associated with aggression, this *ankusha* has rather curious ornamentation. This subtly suggests the high taste for detailing on the part of the designer as well as the patron. The intricate details on this forged, carved and chased weapon, produced by an ace forger and designer, gives it a high artistic value. Such pieces were also used in Muslim courts in Deccan—one such *ankusha* with Islamic writing was donated by royalty to a Sufi saint. By far, most examples seen in different museum collections are for ceremonial use.[9] [GPK]

ANKUSHA
Mysore or Tanjore, India
17th–18th centuries
Steel and gold
h. 39 cm
1998.1399

Aso Carvings

These Aso figures have been carved from ironwood. The carvings have captured the distinct form of Aso—the powerful Dayak dragon goddess, a chimera-like creature with the elongated body of a crocodile, the head of a dog and the snout of a wild boar with oversized fangs. Dragon imagery in Southeast Asia has often been associated with the lower world (▶ see BATAK CARVED SINGA, ▶ see NAGA MUCHALINDA). The Dayaks believe that this powerful dragon goddess rules the underworld, is the guardian of the dead, and oversees the journeys of the dead from one world to another. They also believe that she is associated with both human and agricultural fertility.

These Aso carvings were used as the legs of a table. Due to her extensive realm of influence, Aso appears in the designs of many other Dayak artefacts. Aso is often invoked as a protective symbol. Aso motifs were painted on Dayak shields to scare and harm enemies during battle as well as to protect the user (▶ see DAYAK SHIELD). The Dayak Aso bears a striking resemblance to Lasara of the Nias (▶ see OSA OSA) and Singa of the Bataks (▶ see BATAK CARVED SINGA). [RE]

DAYAK ASO CARVINGS
Sarawak, Malaysia
c. 1900s
Wood
(EACH) 75 x 35 cm
XX11587, XX11588

Astrolabe

The astrolabe (*asturlab* in Arabic) was an important astronomical instrument used in the Islamic world. The one shown here was very elegantly made in the 17th century by a famous instrument maker living in Isfahan, Iran. His name, 'Abd al-A'immah, can be found engraved at the back of this instrument. Around 30 instruments and three sundials are believed to have survived from his workshop. These instruments are known for their accuracy as well as for their elegance, both of which are characteristics of astrolabes made in Safavid Iran during the second half of the 17th century.

The astrolabe is a Greek invention improved upon by Muslim scientists. This instrument may be said to represent the three-dimensional celestial sphere in two-dimensional form. It is like an analogue computer that enables you to arrive at solutions to astronomical problems. Astrolabes were used for time-keeping, for example it was used to determine the time for the five daily prayers, and for surveying. When in use, the astrolabe was suspended from the ring at its top.

The sun, moon and stars are often mentioned in the Qur'an, and in many verses Muslims are encouraged to use them for guidance. Given the importance of seeking knowledge as a religious duty and the fact that certain Islamic practices are closely linked with astronomy, it is not surprising that this science flourished in the Islamic world. Some knowledge of astronomy is required for the regulation of the Islamic lunar calendar, the times for the five daily prayers as well as to determine the *qiblah* (direction towards the Ka'bah in Mecca). Building on Greek, Persian and Indian traditions, Muslim astronomers further developed the science of mathematical astronomy. These Muslim advances in science were not just limited to astronomy—they laid the foundation for the Renaissance in Europe. [TH]

 see YEMENI MANUSCRIPT

ASTROLABE
Isfahan, Iran
c. 1700
Copper alloy
diam. 15 cm
1999.1562

Ayutthaya Buddha

This figure of a standing Buddha was cast in bronze and finished with gilded lacquer. The gilding was probably re-applied several times since it was made. The image has a flame finial rising from the *ushnisha* (protuberance) at the top of the head, a rounded face with extended earlobes and both hands in *abhaya mudra*. The standing, uncrowned Buddha image with these attributes was introduced during the late Ayutthaya period. The simplicity of such pieces suggests an intentional return to earlier forms that predate the more elaborate crowned Buddha images of the 17th century.[10]

'Abhaya' literally means absence ('a') of fear ('bhaya'). *Abhaya mudra* is a gesture of protection although its earliest use was probably as a gesture of greeting. Images with the right hand in this gesture were known as *ham yat* or 'forbidding the relatives (from fighting)'. When made with both hands the gesture was known as *ham samut*, 'forbidding'[11] or 'subduing the ocean'[12] and this iconography continued throughout the Ayutthaya period.[13]

Although a major entrepôt and one of the wealthiest kingdoms in the region during the 18th century, Ayutthaya is often overshadowed by the cultural legacy of Sukhothai (▶ see SUKHOTHAI WALKING BUDDHA). Ayutthayan culture saw the continued synthesis of Khmer and other mainland cultural influences and the coexistence of Western cultural traditions following the arrival of Europeans in the 16th century.[14] Buddhism flowered under the patronage of the monarchy, especially King Borommakot (reign. 1733–1758), and relations within the Theravada Buddhist world were significantly strengthened. During the mid 18th century Ayutthaya assisted Sri Lanka with the revival of monastic traditions such as the *upasampada* (higher ordination) which had been lost during the long period of European occupation of that country.[15] [HT]

FIGURE OF STANDING BUDDHA IN *ABHAYA MUDRA*
Thailand
Late Ayutthaya period, second half of 18th century
Gilt bronze
h. 112 cm
1996.161

Badik

The *badik* is a dagger that is common across much of the Malay Archipelago, particularly among the Bugis and Bugis-influenced peoples. *Badik* come in a variety of shapes and sizes though the larger varieties are referred to as *golok*.

This particular *badik* is a large example. It is believed to have come from the island of Sumbawa although it is fairly typical of high status *badik* from across the east Nusa Tenggara islands of present-day Indonesia. The highly elaborate silver oversheath is decorated with repoussé and chased floral and geometric designs dominated by a pair of intertwined *naga* (mythical serpents). Two rows of openwork panels provide windows to show the hardwood sheath underneath the silverwork. The pattern welded blade is a fine example of Bugis forging, showing layers of metal of differing composition which create a watered pattern known as *pamor*. The water buffalo horn hilt is a simple but elegant design that highlights the functional refinement of weapons craftsmanship in the Malay world.

The islands of east Nusa Tenggara were of great importance during the height of the trade in spices, particularly nutmeg, mace and cloves from Ambon and Maluku. For much of the 17th century this trade was dominated by the Bugis rulers of Makassar who used Sumbawa as an important outpost to dominate the trade route that passed through the Flores Sea. Later, the Dutch drove the Bugis out of the spice trade. However, Bugis influence in Sumbawa can still be seen in the material culture of the island. [DAH]

BADIK
Sumbawa, east Nusa Tenggara, Indonesia
19th century
Iron, silver, wood, horn
35.1 x 8.4 cm
K1132

Baju and Seluar Melayu

(Malay Tunic and Trousers)

This set of *baju* and *seluar Melayu* comes from the Riau-Lingga Archipelago. It is said to have been the property of Sultan Abdul Rahman, the last sovereign of the Sultanate of Riau-Lingga, who ruled from 1883 to 1911. It is believed that the Sultan wore this at his wedding to Tengku Zabidah bte Tengku Yahha sometime during the 1860s or 1870s. The garments are sewn from imported Indian satin, with a silk weft over a cotton warp, and are decorated with a hand-stitched brocade of silk and silver thread. These form a pattern of floral blossoms, and blue and pink dots on a white field. The brocade devices are typical of Mughal design. It is also interesting that the dark pink and blue dots that intersperse the design are not typical of north Indian fabrics and hence it is likely that the material was originally intended for the export market—in this case Southeast Asia.

The trade in imported fabrics from India to Southeast Asia goes deep into the region's early past. Since the early years of the Common Era, Southeast Asia has been an important gathering point for trade between the Indian Ocean and the South China Sea. Perhaps the most popular trade goods imported into Southeast Asia were Indian textiles. Southeast Asians valued these textiles both for their beauty as well as their high value. These textiles were seen as stores of wealth that were both portable and easily exchanged for other goods. [DAH]

▶ see BAJU KURUNG

BAJU AND *SELUAR MELAYU*
Riau-Lingga Archipelago, Indonesia
c. 1860–1870
Silk, cotton, gold thread
(TUNIC) 160 x 60 cm;
(TROUSERS) 140 x 110 cm
G0007ab

Baju Kurung
(Malay Ladies' Tunic)

This silk *songket*, known as a *baju kurung*, is patterned in stripes of red, blue, yellow and gold. It was reportedly worn by Tengku Fatimah bte Sultan Mahmud, the daughter of a Malay Sultan and a Bugis princess, at her wedding to Raja Muhammad Yusoff of Riau. Tengku Fatimah was the mother of Sultan Abdul Rahman, the last royal ruler of the Riau-Lingga Empire prior to the Dutch annexation in 1911. The *baju kurung* was presented to the Raffles Museum by Tengku Fatimah's daughter, Tengku Zabidah bte Muhammad Yusoff, who, along with her family, lived in exile in Singapore.

The exile of Sultan Abdul Rahman in 1911 marked the end of an important empire first formed some 200 years earlier at the end of the 17th century. In 1699 Sultan Abdul Jalil of Johor, a descendant of the old Malacca sultans, was deposed by a Minangkabau usurper from Siak named Raja Kecik. Sultan Abdul Jalil sought assistance from a group of five minor Bugis princes, mercenary chiefs who had migrated into the region among the large Bugis diaspora driven out of Celebes by the Dutch. In 1722 these five Bugis princes, or *opu* as they were known, succeeded in driving Raja Kecik out of Johor and installing Abdul Jalil's son, Sulaiman, as the new sultan. The Bugis *opu* in return were given the hereditary office of Yang Dipertuan Muda, a position that, while ostensibly subordinate to that of the Malay Sultan, was used by the Bugis to maintain effective control of the Riau Archipelago and much of the area around the Straits of Malacca. From Riau, the Bugis Yang Dipertuan Muda played the role of king-maker, influencing the course of political power in the Malay world until the European consolidation of colonial control in the area in the early 19th century. [DAH]

▶ see BAJU AND SELUAR MELAYU
▶ see SONGKET

BAJU KURUNG
Riau-Lingga Archipelago, Indonesia
19th century
Silk, gold thread
150 x 103 cm
G0008

A Section from a **Baluster**

This upright pillar or baluster, carved on the front and back in shallow relief, bears three roundels interspersed with hexagonal planes. There are lenticular niches on either side to allow the horizontal beams of the railing to slot in. This post-and-rail structure is called *stambha* and *suchi*. It is commonly found in the traditional architecture of stupa sites—usually on the *vedica* (circumambulatory paths) and the *sopana* (staircases)—profusely adorned with decorative and religious motifs. The two roundels on this pillar bear stylised lotuses while the central roundel depicts a mythical aquatic animal. It has a fish tail with scales, hooves and mane, and a crocodile mouth. The origin of many motifs can be found in folklore which have then been absorbed into Buddhist art. There are features from Achaemenid art that can be seen on Mauryan and Sunga architecture, pointing to possible Persian and Greek links.

The importance of nature in early Indian art has been identified by many scholars. They identify the seamless and sensuous manner in which artists handled human and plant forms alike, revealing the same life sap that flows through both forms. Elements of nature were then absorbed into religious monuments, symbolising prosperity and abundance, and enhancing the concept of nature worship. This imagery possibly has its origins in early wooden structures decorated with flowers and garlands which later evolved into decorative motifs. [GPK]

A SECTION FROM A BALUSTER
Mathura area, Uttar Pradesh, north India
Kushana period, c. 2nd century
Red spotted sandstone
h. 102.2 cm
1996.677

Bamboo Brush Holder

The carver of this exquisite bamboo brush holder, Wu Zhifan (or Ruzhen), was regarded by connoisseurs as one of China's last master bamboo carvers. Wu was born in Jiading, an area where carving was a traditional occupation. Before him Zhu Songlin and his immediate heirs—son Zhu Xiaosong and grandson Zhu Sansong—had made bamboo carving a new art form and earned themselves the reputation of the Three Pines (*song*) in Bamboo Carving (*zhu sansong*). In this context, Wu may be seen as the successor of the Jiading school founded by the Zhu family.

However, Wu's fame seems to be engraved only in his art, for not much is known of his life except that he was active during the reign of Emperor Kangxi of the Qing dynasty. Wu specialised in three-dimensional carving—a genre institutionalised by the Zhus—and shallow relief carving (*bodi yangwen*), a style which Wu himself established.

The portrait of a monk depicted on this brush holder is a classic example of Wu's skill in shallow relief carving. Here the plasticity of the monk's image is achieved through carefully calculated strokes used to depict the monk's robe, contrasted with the minute details of the weave on his huge straw hat, and the starkness of the background, left deliberately void to heighten the sense of Zen detachment.

It is very unlikely that this brush holder was a utilitarian object. Signed and in pristine condition, this was an *objet d'art*, collected to be admired and to inspire. The subject matter reveals the owner's aspiration for detachment. Not only is the monk a symbol of detachment and spiritual liberation, the choice of the dried-up lotus stem walking stick and the fisherman's hat are all part of the language of spontaneity and denouncement of worldliness. The fisherman's hat alludes to the poignant image of a lone angler in vast waters awaiting an occasional, and hence surprise, catch which in Zen Buddhist practice may be likened to the sudden realisation of enlightenment (*dunwu chengfo*). [LCL]

BAMBOO BRUSH HOLDER WITH MONK FIGURE IN RELIEF
Jiading, China
17th century
Bamboo
h. 15 cm, diam. 8.3 cm
1999.2652

Ban Chiang Earthenware

This piece of pottery from northern Thailand is popularly known as 'red-on-buff'. The vessel is globular with a flared mouth rim. The scrolls, spiral and curvilinear motifs were painted freehand and the vessel was moulded by the paddle and anvil technique. In this technique the potter forms the body of a pot by beating the exterior with a wooden paddle while supporting the interior with a baked clay anvil. This closes the base and shapes the globular contours of the pot. Red-on-buff pottery was the signature style of pottery from the late Ban Chiang period and exhibits the characteristic freehand application of abstract motifs.

This vessel was probably made for use as a burial jar to contain either food or objects for the deceased's afterlife. The burial style of the late Ban Chiang period was to place intact vessels in the grave—generally directly on top of the body—for reasons which are still not known. Life during the late Ban Chiang period was probably relatively good, judging from the range, diversity and elaborateness of the other burial goods such as bronze artefacts, jewellery and beads. Some graves contained more elaborate artefacts in greater

BAN CHIANG EARTHENWARE
Khorat Plateau, northeast Thailand
300 BCE–200 CE
Earthenware
38 x 25.5 cm
C0765

(OPPOSITE) **DETAIL**
Curvilinear motif on the body of the vessel

quantities, indicating that social stratification was already taking place in the communities of the time. On the whole, however, the burials suggest overall prosperity rather than the existence of elite classes.

The excavations of burial sites at Ban Chiang and other archaeological sites in northern Thailand uncovered a previously unknown and aesthetically distinctive pottery tradition. The pottery exhibits an elegance, sophistication and attention to decorative detail that far exceeds mere utilitarian needs. The funerary ware thus clearly served as an art medium for the potter. The freehand application of abstract designs was a key feature of Ban Chiang pottery, while the depiction of human, animal and other natural forms was rare.

Early pottery in Southeast Asia in general indicates a transition from nomadic hunter-gatherer societies that carried few material possessions to sedentary farmers with more material possessions. This vessel is an excellent example to illustrate the evolving social complexity that was already beginning to arise in the communities of early Southeast Asia. [RE]

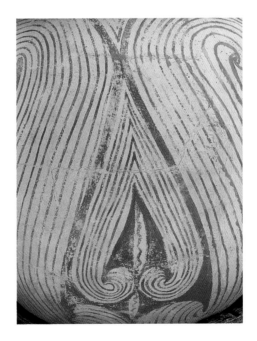

Batak Carved Singa

This pair of Batak *singa* has been carved out of solid blocks of wood. They were lacquered black and red and outlined in white. These *singa* heads were used as architectural adornments that framed each end of a Batak house façade giving the impression that the house was supported by a *singa* body. The lacquer has suffered from weathering.

Singa used on house façades were also associated with warfare as the heads of victims were wrapped in grass and hung from them. One of these carved *singa* heads (BELOW, RIGHT) has seven deep holes punctured into its face which may have held hooks used to display heads.

The basic form of the traditional Batak communal house is said to represent the cosmos. The three levels of the house correspond to the three spheres of the cosmos. The space for animals below the living level symbolises the underworld. The living level, raised on pillars above the underworld, is where humans dwell. Above this is the high roof, the abode of the gods and ancestors. The Bataks believe that the *singa* is a being of the underworld that bears the world of man on its back, hence its use as an adornment to the main structure of the Batak house. [RE]

BATAK CARVED *SINGA*
North Sumatra, Indonesia
c.1930s
Wood
80 x 35 x 63 cm
W0697

Batak Ritual Buffalo Bones

These two pieces of ritual buffalo bones are inscribed on both sides. The concave face (BELOW, LEFT) is etched with symbols of fish, seven-pointed stars, stylised lizards and human motifs while the convex face (BELOW, RIGHT) is inscribed with Batak script. The script and symbols on these bones were most likely engraved with the point of a knife and the fine etchings blackened with soot. The etched script on one of the bones has largely worn off. There is a hole at the end of each bone with lengths of string left, indicating that these bones were probably worn.

These ritual buffalo bones were most likely amulets, made by the *datu* himself and probably worn for protection. '*Datu*' is a Toba Batak word for the magician-priest, an expert in the traditional Batak religion. The basic instructions to make such amulets were contained in a special book, the *pustaha* (▶ see PUSTAHA), a kind of instruction manual for the *datu*.

The *datu* was the only member of the Batak community who could write this archaic form of the Batak script. This script was primarily used to record myths, legends and magic spells. Besides bone, Batak writings are also found on bark, bamboo strips and leather. This monopoly on literacy and knowledge was the key to the power and influence of the *datu* within the Batak communities. [RE]

RITUAL BUFFALO BONES
North Sumatra, Indonesia
c.1930s
Bone
18 x 2.5 cm
XX11755

Batik

Java has long been known for its batik, a resist dye technique of colouring textiles using molten wax to draw designs on the cloth prior to dyeing. Shown here are two examples of Javanese batik. The first (BELOW) is a batik *kain panjang*, an unsewn sarong from Yogyakarta in central Java that dates to about 1935. It has an interesting combination of motifs including winged *naga* (mythical serpent), *wayang* figures and circular medallions with a *parang rusak* motif. These are all presented on a background known as the *geringsing* (fish-scale) motif. The *naga* represents a powerful protective deity in Javanese cosmology and is preferred above all other Javanese decorative themes. The *wayang* figures, drawn

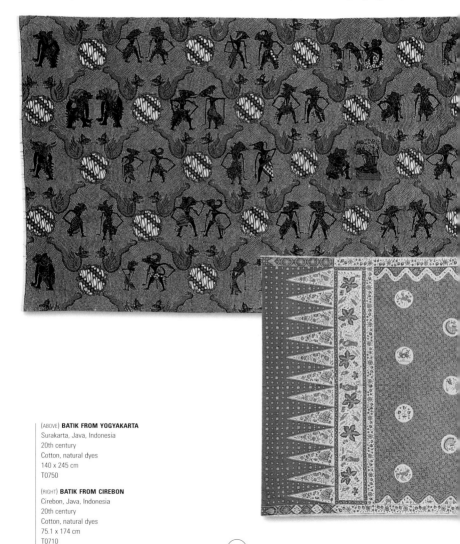

(ABOVE) **BATIK FROM YOGYAKARTA**
Surakarta, Java, Indonesia
20th century
Cotton, natural dyes
140 x 245 cm
T0750

(RIGHT) **BATIK FROM CIREBON**
Cirebon, Java, Indonesia
20th century
Cotton, natural dyes
75.1 x 174 cm
T0710

from the shadow puppets of *wayang kulit* (▶ see WAYANG KULIT), an age-old drama based on the Hindu epics the *Ramayana* and *Mahabharata*, contain important symbolic social messages centred on the various characters in the story. Taken together this textile not only communicates symbolic messages but also has a protective effect for the wearer.

The second piece (BOTTOM) is a *kain panjang* from Cirebon, one of the Pasisir or northern coastal cities of Java. Cirebon had a large Peranakan-Chinese community, which is clearly evident in the motifs and designs on this batik. Mythical animal motifs derived from Chinese embroidery, such as the phoenix and *qilin*, are readily apparent, while the *songket*-

derived layout and motifs give the piece a uniquely Indonesian flavour.

It is generally believed that batik first came to Java from India although the exact date for this is unclear. However, most experts accept that batik had more or less taken its modern form by the 17th-century Javanese kingdom of Mataram. Since then an enormous variety of batik styles have developed on the island; from the classical court styles of central Java to the Chinese-inspired, rainbow-hued batik of the northern coast to the European-influenced batik of colonial Batavia. [DAH]

▶ see SARUNG FEATURING CAMELS AND TENTS

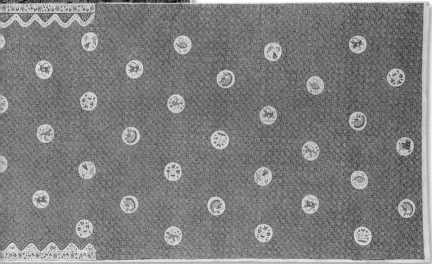

Bhairava

Bhairava is Shiva in his most terrifying aspect. Here he is shown in a standing position with a *kapala* (skull cup) and a broken *trishula* (trident) in his lower arms, while holding a *damaru* (kettledrum) in his upper right arm; his upper left arm is broken. What looks like the staff of the *trishula* could also be a *kankala* (bone weapon). The sculpture is broken below the knees, which makes it difficult to visualise the standing posture. It is clear from the slight bend in the waist that the standing posture had a slight *dehanchment*, shifting the weight onto the left hip and creating a kinesthetically interesting body posture. At the back of the upper arm is a representation of a seated goddess—probably Durga or Parvati—holding a spear, showing the sectarian affiliation of the two cults.

The coiled beard, double stranded cord tied in a knot around the chest, serpentine earrings, *jatamukuta* (crown of matted hair) and *rudraksha* (berries) adornment clearly indicate an ascetic aspect of Shiva's personality which, unlike Vishnu's, is not *alamkarapriya*. He throngs the *smashana* (burning grounds) and smears *vibhuti* (ash) on his body.

As Bhairava, Shiva is perceived in his *aghora* (terrible form). There is a myth that refers to Shiva killing two Brahmins—Vishwaksena and Brahma—from whose bones he created his *kankala*. To atone for this sin, he was banished by Vishnu, and forced to live like a beggar. This image, referred to as Bhikshatanamurti, is found in great profusion in south India.

Stylistically, this sculpture shows a relationship with the guild from the Khajuraho region which exercised strong influence in the surrounding areas. A close observation of the eyebrows and the flexions of the body, including the beaded rendering of the hair on either side of the forehead, suggests a strong Khajuraho influence, although the layout of the sculpture with subsidiary figures on either side suggests it originates from the Surasena region. The stylistic interaction is therefore very significant in the case of this sculpture.[1]

Bhairava is known in Hindustani classical music as a male *raga* (musical composition) that incorporates all the seven notes and is sung at the crack of dawn. [GPK]

BHAIRAVA
Uttar Pradesh, Haryana area, India
c. 10th century
Red sandstone
h. 61.6 cm
1997.4796

Standing Bhairava

This figure is a more complete representation of Bhairava (an aspect of Shiva) than the north Indian one (▶ see BHAIRAVA). It is seen standing with a dog, an animal commonly associated with Bhairava. This four-armed deity carries a *trishula* (trident) and *kapala* (skull cup) in his lower two hands, and a *damaru* (kettledrum) and snake in the upper two. The hair of this deity is matted and tied up, while the flame-like locks adorn a crescent moon. The eyes are wide open, almost popping out, while the mouth has two canine teeth. Although Shiva is associated with scant ornamentation, this figure is adorned with jewels around the neck, ears and arms, with small snakes twined around the chest, waist and thighs. Bhairava also wears bells and anklets on his feet.

This image of Shiva as Bhairava is totally naked, and as a mendicant he is seen begging for food from the *rishipatni* (wives of the seers). Thus this image is also known as Bhikshatanamurti of Shiva as Bhairava. The myth associated with this deity narrates how the *rishipatni* were seduced by his handsomeness and almost forgot their marital vows. In an elaborate sculptural representation on this theme at the sculpture gallery in Tanjore, the *rishipatni* can be seen adoring Bhairava and standing around him in a state of disorientation. [GPK]

STANDING BHAIRAVA
Chola, Tamil Nadu, south India
Late 11th century
Granite
108.5 x 59 cm, diam. 20.5 cm
Purchased with funds from Singapore Reinsurance
Corporation Ltd and India International Insurance Pte Ltd
2000.3945

Black and White Faces of Impermanence

This is a pair of procession idols of the Black and White Faces of Impermanence (Heibai Wuchang), also known as General Xie (BELOW, RIGHT) and General Fan (BELOW, LEFT) respectively. They are also popularly known as Seventh Lord and Eighth Lord respectively or the Tall and Short One when they are distinguished by their height. Sometimes they are depicted as two tall black- and white-faced figures, rather than with one taller than the other. This is especially so in hell scrolls (▶ see TEN COURTS OF HELL). Here, as procession idols, they are both depicted with black faces instead.

The Black and White Faces of Impermanence are identified by their terrifying countenance and long tongues due to their tragic deaths. It is believed that General Fan drowned in a flood underneath a bridge while waiting for General Xie, who arrived late. The latter, in his extreme remorse and grief over his friend's death, committed suicide.

The pair plays several roles in Chinese popular religion. Here they are idols used during the annual procession in the City God Festival, which falls on the 13th day of the fifth lunar month in Taiwan, Republic of China. They are the City God's key assistants, maintaining peace and prosperity in his area of jurisdiction. In the courts of hell, they play a more generalised role of bringing sinners to face charges and meting out the appropriate punishments for their various sins, similar to the roles carried out by the Cow- and Horse-Face Generals (Niutou Mamian), another pair of underworld guardians. It is believed that when your final moment arrives, both pairs of generals will appear together before you to guide you through the journey of purgatory. Interestingly and ironically, the Black and White Faces of Impermanence are also widely popular as gods of wealth. Their characters lend easily to spirit-mediumship and they are often consulted by gamblers for lucky numbers. [ST]

BLACK AND WHITE FACES OF IMPERMANENCE
(RIGHT) General Fan; (FAR RIGHT) General Xie
Taiwan, Republic of China
Contemporary
Silk, satin, metal and wood
(GENERAL FAN) 220 x 93 x 68 cm; (GENERAL XIE) 298 x 108 x 70 cm
Gift of the Xiahai City God Temple, Taiwan
2002.418, 2002.426

Blue and White Stemcup

This stemcup was first made in two parts, then luted together. Inspired by metalwork in Central Asia, the ceramic equivalent here gained popularity with the Mongols around the 13th century. The decoration on this stemcup comprises classic scrolls, moulded floral designs, underglazed blue pearl in flames, and a two-horned and three-clawed dragon chasing a pearl. The cobalt blue pigments used on this stemcup were imported from central and west Asia, possibly Persia (Iran). Kashan potters had worked with these pigments, but were not quite able to produce a defined and non-smeared effect which the potters at Jingdezhen could. The latter's achievement was partly due to the use of a less fluid glaze that prevented a smeared effect during firing. This bluish-green-toned glaze is similar in composition and appearance to that of *qingbai* wares (◗ see QINGBAI PORCELAIN). It is clearly visible in the recessed areas where the glaze had pooled to highlight moulded chrysanthemums and peonies in the stemcup.

Besides this wreath of moulded floral designs, the interior of the stemcup is painted with a central motif of a pearl in flames. This motif is also depicted on the outer wall of the stemcup, but with a serpent-like dragon chasing it, characteristic of the Yuan style. This stemcup would not have qualified as an imperial ware as *Yuan Shi* (Yuan History) states that only two-horned and five-clawed dragons were used at court. It is most likely that this stemcup served as a drinking vessel for daily domestic use. Numerous pieces uncovered in the Yuan capital, Dadu (Beijing), and in Inner Mongolia attest to the popularity of such stemcups. [WHL]

STEMCUP WITH MOULDED FLORAL DESIGNS,
UNDERGLAZED BLUE FLAMING PEARL AND
UNDERGLAZED BLUE DRAGON CHASING FLAMING PEARL
China
Yuan dynasty
Ceramic
h. 9.7 cm, diam. 10.8 cm
1997.4802

(TOP) **DETAIL**
Underglazed blue pearl in flames on the interior of the
stemcup and classic scrolls along the rim

Bowl with Foliated Kufic-Abbasid Script

The decoration around the rim of this bowl is an inscription, written in foliated Kufic-Abbasid script where the vertical shafts of the letters tie themselves into knots and split palmettes. Such inscriptions are difficult to read, especially as the letters do not have any diacritical marks. This style of Kufic-Abbasid script was not used for copying Qur'ans as it possibly would have resulted in the Holy Message being misread. The four dots help by indicating where to begin to read the inscription, and it is done clockwise. The inscription is a proverb which reads, 'He who believes in recompense is generous to the offer.'

This bowl is a fine example of the 'black on white' epigraphic ceramics, produced during the 9th and 11th centuries in the Khurasan area of Iran, which scholars have labelled as Samanid epigraphic pottery. These ceramics seems to have been produced during the Samanid period and have been found in the Samanid capital of Samarqand (Uzbekistan) and in cities that were under their control. Calligraphy is the main decorative motif on such wares and they are perhaps the most beautiful examples of the use of calligraphy on ceramics that has ever been produced.

The majority of inscriptions found on Samanid vessels are proverbs. A scholar[2] has compiled a list of these proverbs and made the observation that most of these have the theme of generosity[3] thus suggesting that such bowls were used during parties. They would have certainly made exciting dinnerware. These bowls can also be seen in the context of the dining etiquette of the time— generous hospitality on the part of the host, reasonable consumption by the guest and educated conversation with fellow diners. [TH]

▶ see KUFIC-ABBASID QUR'AN FOLIO
▶ see SLIP-PAINTED BOWL

BOWL WITH FOLIATED KUFIC-ABBASID SCRIPT
Khurasan, northwest Iran
10th century
Earthenware
h. 10 cm, diam. 34 cm
On loan from the Tareq Rajab Museum, Kuwait
TR131

Dehua Circular Covered **Box**

This circular covered box is one of the earliest pieces of Dehua porcelain produced and was most probably used as a cosmetic box. The box is ivory-glazed, except for the base which is left unglazed to reveal a white clay body. Due to the low iron oxide content in Dehua porcelain, potters were able to produce a pure white body at a firing temperature of about 1,280 degrees Celsius. The thread-like relief scrolls on this covered box are typical of its period, and were most likely inspired by classic scrolls on lacquerware of the same period. The designs were first carved onto a mould and then impressed onto the wet clay. Not only did this method save time, it also proved less laborious than carving.

The Dehua kilns, located in Fujian province, were already operating in the Northern Song period although production only peaked in the 17th century. As early as the 13th century, Dehua wares were not only produced for domestic use, but were also exported to the Philippines and other parts of Southeast Asia. Trade during this period was given an impetus with the opening of more shipping routes from Quanzhou and the reduction of trade controls. Popular trade items include covered boxes, vases, ewers, *kendi*, jars and bowls, mostly for utilitarian purposes. [WHL]

▶ see DEHUA ENAMELLED WARES
▶ see DEHUA FIGURINES
▶ see KRAAK PORCELAIN
▶ see QINGBAI PORCELAIN
▶ see YAOZHOU BOWL

CIRCULAR COVERED BOX WITH
THREAD-LIKE SCROLLS IN RELIEF
Dehua, China
12th–14th centuries
Ceramic
diam. 15 cm
Gift of Frank and Pamela Hickley
2000.3439.1–2

Brahma

Brahma is identified by the *kamandalu* (water vessel) he carries in one of his hands. He is often shown with three heads, with the fourth head (behind) not depicted. His arms are sometimes shown with an *akshamala* (rosary) and the sacrificial implements, *sruk* (large wooden ladle) and *sruva* (small wooden ladle). He is often accompanied by his consorts, Savitri and Saraswati, on a chariot drawn by a swan. He wears jewelled earrings, white garments, and has a *jatamukuta* (crown of matted hair).[4] The *abhaya* and *katisama hasta* poses held by Brahma in this sculpture represent typical features of south Indian deities. This sculpture would have come from a cardinal niche on the walls of a Vishnu or Shiva *gopuram* (temple gate).

In orthodox Brahmanical Hinduism, Brahma, Vishnu and Shiva represent the trinity that is responsible for maintaining the balance between the Creation, Preservation and Dissolution of the Universe, with each God presiding over a designated function in controlling the cosmos. Brahma is attributed the function of the Creation of all the creatures of the world from birds and animals to human beings. He was, himself, created by Vishnu from his navel and stirred into animation by Yoganidra. The representation of Brahma seated on the lotus that grows out of Vishnu's navel when he opens his eyes while reclining on a bed of *naga* coils can be seen on Sheshashayi Vishnu (Vatapatrashayi Krishna in this guide) images all over India (▶ see VATAPATRASHAYI).

Brahma is variously known in different texts. The *Rgveda* mentions him as Prajapati, Vishvakarman and Brahma who produced the sky and the earth and shaped them with his own hands. Another verse of the same text mentions him as a blacksmith, while as Hiranyagarbha he is visualised as the first-born who established the sky and the earth in their proper positions. He also performs some functions attributed to Vishnu in the *Puranas* as Prajapati, the supporter of this universe. The forms assumed by Vishnu—fish, tortoise and boar—were first attributed to Brahma Prajapati in ancient texts such as the *Satapatha Brahmana.*[5]

There is no popular Brahma cult today. Myths related to Lingodbhavamurti Shiva and Sheshashayi Vishnu explain Brahma's subsidiary position to the rising cultic importance of these gods. There are stray examples of temples dedicated to Brahma: Pushkar in Rajasthan and Khed Brahma in Gujarat are cases in point where Hindus of different affiliations offer worship. The earliest references to temples dedicated to Brahma come from the *panchayatana* group mainly from central India and rarely from south India. In temple iconography, Brahma is usually depicted as one of the directional deities, or in conjunction with Vishnu as a god related to Vaishnava Cosmology. [GPK]

▶ see STANDING VISHNU AS TRIVIKRAMA

BRAHMA
Tamil Nadu, south India
12th century
Granite
h. 105 cm
Purchased with funds from Singapore Reinsurance
Corporation Ltd and India International Insurance Pte Ltd
1996.675

Bronze Blade

This asymmetric axe blade with a slightly flared handle was most likely cast using the *cire perdue* (lost-wax) method. The geometric concentric lozenges motifs on the blade are common motifs of the Dong Son bronze culture. The surface of the axe is partially covered with cobalt blue residue.

East Java and the island of Bali had a tradition of bronze making that dated to the period between 600 BCE and 100 CE which was contemporary with the Dong Son bronze period on mainland Southeast Asia. It was unlikely that bronze-making technology was invented independently in Java as there were striking similarities between Dong Son bronzes and those from Java. This may indicate a transmission of both technology and styles from mainland to island Southeast Asia through a network of ancient coastal and overland trade routes in the region.

Bronze artefacts in island Southeast Asia during the Dong Son period reflected the evolving complexity of these early cultures. The production of bronzes required a sophisticated division of labour. This was largely thought to have evolved as a result of the specialisation of labour that was parallelled in wet rice cultivation. During this time technological adaptations and innovations in bronze were already laying the foundations for the Hindu-Buddhist kingdoms of Java and Bali that were to follow. [RE]

▌see DONG SON DRUM

BRONZE CURVED BLADE
Probably east Java or Bali, Indonesia
600–300 BCE
Bronze
28 x 19 cm
1995.1834

Bronze Drum in Pejeng Style

This hourglass-shaped bronze Pejeng-style drum is one of two main styles of early bronze drums found in Southeast Asia. The other is the Heger-type drum (▶ see DONG SON DRUM). The drum shown here has been extensively reconstructed to its present state. Motifs on this drum include an eight-petal flower on the flat face (RIGHT) or tympanum, and a pair of stylised faces with bulging eyes between the drum handles. Horizontal bands of saw-tooth motifs (BELOW, RIGHT) are also present, similar to those found on Dong Son drums.

This drum takes its name from the 'Moon of Pejeng', the largest drum of its kind known, measuring 186 cm high and 160 cm in diameter. The 'Moon of Pejeng' is displayed in the village temple of Bedulu, Pejeng in central Bali. Moulds for casting the stylised face motifs have been found on Bali. Most Pejeng-style drums unearthed so far have been found on Bali and east Java.

Unlike the Dong Son-type drums of north Vietnam that were cast in one piece, this drum has been cast in pieces. However, its surface decorations—the concentric abstract motifs—bear certain similarities to mainland Dong Son bronze motifs. This strongly suggests that the island bronze workshops were greatly influenced by those on the mainland. [RE]

PEJENG-STYLE DRUM
East Java, Indonesia
600 BCE–300 CE
Bronze
h. 161 cm, diam. 81 cm
1999.1402

DETAILS
(TOP) Eight-petal flower on the tympanum
(ABOVE) Stylised faces with bulging eyes

Bronze Silkworm

Cast in bronze and gilded, this is a rare representation of the silkworm, which is more commonly made in another medium, nephrite. The worm, in its caterpillar state, is depicted here in a stylised and stick-like manner as the artists chose to use grooves to represent the segmented body.

The worship of the silkworm spirit can be traced to the Shang period, when it seemed common to make human sacrifices during ceremonies. The spirit was associated with the domestication of the silkworm and hence the science of silk-rearing and silk-reeling, which was considered an activity as primordial as rice-planting. Eventually, during the 3rd century, the spirit of the silkworm became personified in the form of the Empress Xiling, wife of the Yellow Emperor, who was considered China's first sericulturist with her husband as China's first agriculturist. These were the two activities which the Chinese saw as the symbolic roots of their civilisation. Subsequent rulers of China took the roles of the First Couple, and as part of their duty as rulers, the agricultural and sericultural rites had to be observed and carried out personally by them. By then the spirit of the silkworm was worshipped in a special ceremony officiated by the Empress each year during the second half of the third lunar month with offerings of mulberry leaves and woven silk at a special altar set up in the silkworm temple or palace. [LCL]

GILT BRONZE SILKWORM
China
Han dynasty
Gilt bronze
7 x 21.6 x 1 cm
1995.295

Limestone Stele Depicting
Buddha, Avalokiteshvara and Maitreya

The youthfulness of the three Buddhist figures portrayed here—Buddha, Avalokiteshvara and Maitreya—reflects a general spirit of escapism that pervaded the Six Dynasties. Together with the celestial beings who are dancing and presenting the stupa above, this composition represents the resplendent pageantry celebrating the revelation of the eternal Buddha who preached the great Mahayana scripture, the *Lotus Sutra* (▶ see LOTUS SUTRA). This stele probably came from a niche in a cave temple.

Flanking the Buddha are two bodhisattvas, proportionately smaller, dressed in their prescribed princely and bejewelled attire. Buddha, however, looks very much like a member of the Chinese literati of the time, whose main preoccupation was to indulge in idle discourse (*qingtan*) on current philosophical ideas, in particular Buddhism and Taoism. Such activities were escapist acts to avoid the persecution that usually came with a career in politics or the civil service. Dressed in garments with layers of drapery, this voluminous image suggests a spiritual loftiness which the literati associated with themselves. In fact Buddha was the ideal self-image of the literati. Ironically, the nomadic ruling houses that established the Northern Wei polity in northern China promoted Buddhism, a foreign religion, as a counter-balance to the existing Han Chinese scheme of things. Although it was intended as an institution to marginalise the Chinese, the fundamental concept of salvation in Buddhism nevertheless gained a wide following, in particular among the literati. [LCL]

MANDOLA STELE WITH THE TRIAD OF BUDDHA, AVALOKITESHVARA AND MAITREYA
China
Eastern Wei dynasty, 534–550
Limestone
84.5 x 47.7 cm
1995.3901

Seated Buddha

The Buddha is seen seated in *dhyanasana* (meditation posture) with legs folded in *padmasana* (lotus posture) and a *samghati* (monk's robe) covering his left shoulder. The stylistic features are similar to the Andhra style from south India. During the Gupta period the 'wet drapery' look became quite well known all over India and spread beyond India's shores to Sri Lanka, China and Southeast Asia. The *ushnisha* (protuberance) is represented as a *shiraspata* (halo) and may have contained a precious stone. This bump on Buddha's head actually signifies his enlightenment and in artistic convention is represented by a tuft of curly hair tied up in a bun. In other Sri Lankan sculptures the *ushnisha* may also be represented by a flame, a representation found only in Sri Lanka and Thailand. The expression on Buddha's face conveys meditative calmness and inwardness.

Hundreds of similar sculptures have been found and this suggests that they were mass-produced for donation to monasteries and temples as acts of religious merit by pilgrims.[6]

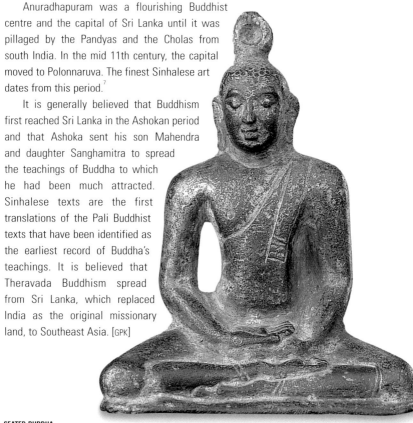

Anuradhapuram was a flourishing Buddhist centre and the capital of Sri Lanka until it was pillaged by the Pandyas and the Cholas from south India. In the mid 11th century, the capital moved to Polonnaruva. The finest Sinhalese art dates from this period.[7]

It is generally believed that Buddhism first reached Sri Lanka in the Ashokan period and that Ashoka sent his son Mahendra and daughter Sanghamitra to spread the teachings of Buddha to which he had been much attracted. Sinhalese texts are the first translations of the Pali Buddhist texts that have been identified as the earliest record of Buddha's teachings. It is believed that Theravada Buddhism spread from Sri Lanka, which replaced India as the original missionary land, to Southeast Asia. [GPK]

SEATED BUDDHA
Sri Lanka
Late Anuradhapura period, 10th century
Bronze with traces of gilding
(SHOWN IN ACTUAL SIZE) 10.5 x 9 x 5 cm
1996.2170

Buddhist Vajra and Ghanta
(Buddhist Tantric Symbols)

V*ajra* (thunderbolts) and *ghanta* (bells) are Tantric symbols used in Vajrayana Buddhism for rituals by the adepts. They can also be seen carried by Vajrasattva or Vajradhara, their arms crossed, with *vajra* held in the right hand and *ghanta* in the left hand.

This *vajra* (RIGHT) is bipolar and decorated with eight pronged spokes joined together at the centre. The beaded tracery marks a decorative elegance. This *ghanta* (BELOW) has a gilded surmount with a Buddha head and six pronged spokes. The *ghanta* itself is decorated with festoons and bears an inscription of the Qianlong period. It may have been donated to one of the monasteries in Tibet by the Chinese imperial court.

The use of these ritual objects symbolises the permanent and adamantine nature of the Universe as well as of Buddha. All Buddhist deities are considered as *vajra*, or *vajra* beings, and *vajra* also has connotations of masculinity, whereas *ghanta* represents femininity. When these two implements are used together they invoke compassion (*vajra*) and wisdom (*ghanta*) in enlightenment.[8]

The *vajra* was adopted from Hinduism by Indian Buddhism as an emblem for Vajrapani, one of the bodhisattvas. It is also the weapon of Indra, who himself was adopted into Buddhism as Shakra. *Vajra* originally symbolised invincibility and enormous power, and represented the strength and hardness of diamond.[9] [GPK]

BUDDHIST *VAJRA* AND *GHANTA*
(ABOVE) *Vajra*; (LEFT) *Ghanta*
Tibet
15th century
Cast and gilt bronze
(VAJRA) 18 x 4.5 cm; (GHANTA) h. 23 cm, diam. 10 cm
Purchased with funds from The Shaw Foundation
1997.3453, 1997.3452

Burial Bronze Bangles

This is a pair of bronze bangles in open form, each with six spherical knobs on one side. These bangles provide some evidence that the Bronze Age cultures of mainland Southeast Asia produced not only drums, oil lamps and other ornaments, but also well-crafted jewellery items. The provenance of these items is not well documented but it has been reported that bronze jewellery was a common burial item. This is perhaps true in this case as they were found in pairs—most burial bronze bangles come in pairs as they are found on each wrist when excavated.

Bronzes appeared in the context of mainland Southeast Asia around 1500 BCE, but it is unclear if they were introduced from China or independently invented in Southeast Asia. The improvements in bronze technology in Southeast Asia eventually led to the rise of its most significant Bronze Age culture in Southeast Asia, the Dong Son culture. Many burial bronzes included personal ornaments such as these bangles and socketed axe blades, with some graves having many bronze items and others having none. The differential wealth between graves of the same communities is a clear indication that there were already different classes of people in early Southeast Asian communities. [RE]

BURIAL BRONZE BANGLES
Northeast Thailand
300 BCE–200 CE
Bronze
h. 6 cm, diam. 10 cm
1998.1364

Burmese Buddha

This image of Buddha is seated on a double lotus base in the *bhumisparsha mudra* (earth-witnessing gesture). The fingers of the right hand extend towards the ground as the Buddha calls the Earth Goddess to witness the power of his undisturbed concentration despite the forces of evil exerted by the demon Mara. Traces of pigment are evident in the shallow incised delineations of the face, robes and throne on this piece. Marble increasingly replaced carved sandstone images around the 17th century, or late Ava Period (1364–1752), and continued to be produced from that time onwards.[10] The merit-making practice of donating images to the temple continues today and carved marble images finished with lacquer, gilding and paint are still produced in Mandalay.

A more localised Burmese style developed during the late Pagan period, following the decline of Buddhism in India, which was to lay the foundations for the later 18th-century style of this piece. Images were increasingly carved in the round without any supporting back slab and the *bhumisparsha mudra* became popular. The anatomical features changed too. The torso became heavier in appearance and features such as the hair were reduced to a simple line which framed the face, while the mouth became bow-shaped. The ears were heavier too, with lobes extending down to touch the shoulders. Hands and feet as seen here were more stylised— fingers were of equal length and feet assumed slab-like forms. The robes are delineated with lightly incised double lines with a flap hanging down the left shoulder. The propensity for flatter surfaces, especially in later images, also saw the use of paint to highlight areas such as the facial features. [HT]

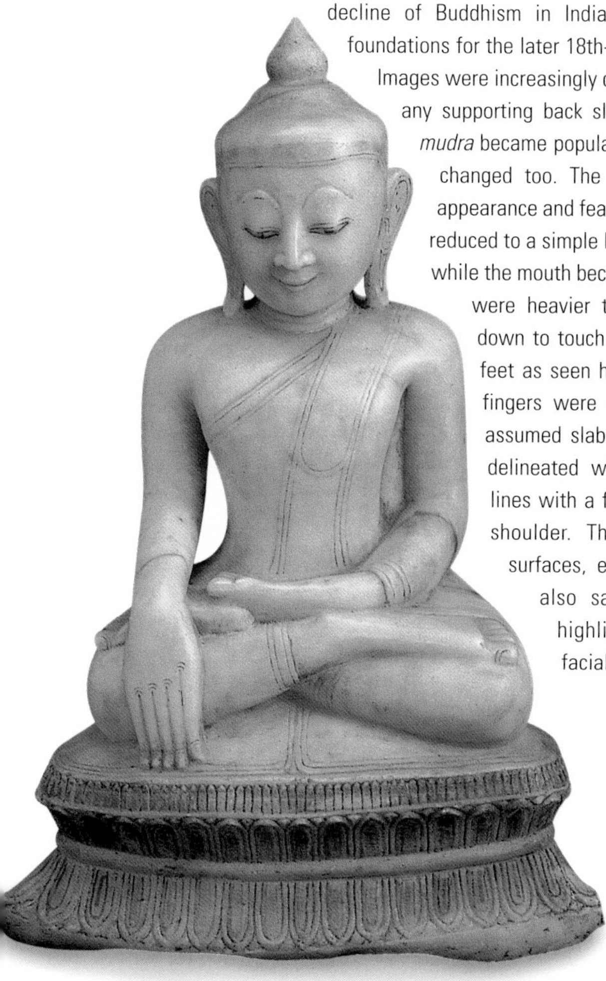

FIGURE OF A SEATED BUDDHA
Shan State, Burma
c. 18th century
Alabaster
64 x 44 cm
Gift of Mr Hwang Soo Jin
2000.1545

Burmese Qur'an Box

This box is decorated with relief-moulded designs known as *thayò*. It is also highlighted with fragments of coloured glass cut into geometric shapes which are arranged into a floral pattern and laid on the *thayò*, a process known as *hman-zi shwei chá*. The presence of gold leaf on the box is notable. This process of embellishing lacquerware with gold leaf designs is known as *shwei-zawa* and the technique requires great skill on the part of the craftsman.

All four sides of the box are decorated with an openwork metal panel of Islamic calligraphy containing the *shahadah* (profession of faith in Islam). The *shahadah* is the acknowledgement that there is only one God, Allah, and that Muhammad is His Prophet; it is a fundamental belief in Islam. The presence of an Islamic motif on the box suggests it was made for a Muslim. This box may have been used to store the Qur'an, which is a holy book and is usually stored away in a box or carefully wrapped in cloth when not in use.

The earliest Qur'an boxes were developed in Mamluk Egypt during the early 14th century. These boxes were often made of brass inlaid with silver and gold. It is unusual to find Burmese lacquerware with Islamic motifs as the majority of Burmese are Theravada Buddhists, and most lacquerware are usually used to offer gifts to monasteries. [HH]

▶ see QUR'AN STANDS

BURMESE QUR'AN BOX
Myanmar
Late 19th century or early 20th century
Wood
33 x 33 x 25 cm
1996.218

Calligraphic Lion

The shape and body of this golden lion is made up of a prayer or invocation to 'Ali (the son-in-law of the Prophet Muhammad) known as *nadi 'aliyyan*. This has been wonderfully done with the skilful and imaginative arrangement of the various letters. Close observation of this lion will reveal tiny pinpricks on the surface of the gold, which adds a subtle interest and shine to the whole composition.

The *nadi 'aliyyan*, which asks for 'Ali's intercession before God, reads:

Call upon 'Ali, through whom miracles are made manifest
You will find him a help to you when misfortunes occur.
All grief and sorrow will be dispelled.
Through your prophethood O Muhammad
Through your closeness [to God] O 'Ali, O 'Ali, O 'Ali.

The lion is often depicted as a symbol of 'Ali, for due to his fearless nature, he was known as Asadullah, the Lion of God. The symbol of the lion and the *nadi 'aliyyan* is part of Shi'ite piety. While the lion and prayer composition is generally associated with Shi'ism, scholars have pointed out that this is not necessarily the case in Ottoman Turkey, as similar lion compositions made for Sunni patrons have also been found.[1]

The use of pious formulae to form various compositions became popular in the 19th century. Aside from animals, shapes of flowers, fruit and even inanimate objects such as boats, ewers and buildings were also formed out of calligraphy. [TH]

▶ see QAJAR STANDARD

CALLIGRAPHIC LION
Probably from Iran
19th century
Gold ink on paper
27.4 x 38 cm
1996.19

Cards for Drinking Game

Entitled *Immortals Drinking Cards* (*liexian jiupai*), these two albums are a compilation of 48 leaves of portrait-sized drinking cards which the late Qing painter Ren Xiong (1820–1857) from Hangzhou illustrated, possibly for a client. The format and concept of such cards came from Chen Hongshou, a Wanli period Hangzhou painter, who in the early 17th century provided illustrations for the *Water Margin* and *In Veneration of the Past* series of cards. Together these three sets became the classic works of the drinking cards. All were made into woodblocks and reproduced in multiple sets for circulation.

In this set the Taoist immortals are the subject matter. Ren Xiong illustrated 48 of them, which were then carved by Cai Zhao as woodblocks for printing. As an indirect descendant of the Hangzhou school, the talented Ren Xiong was able to emulate the eccentric but unique Chen style of portraiture. The immortals are depicted with grotesque or comical facial expressions, while the voluminous garments accentuate their presence in the illustrations. Each is accompanied by a descriptor of the immortal, which ends in an instruction for a drink forfeit.

TWO-ALBUM SET OF *LIEXIAN JIUPAI*
(OPPOSITE, TOP) Title page;
(OPPOSITE, BELOW, LEFT) Laozi card;
(OPPOSITE, BELOW, RIGHT) Zhang Daoling card
China
1854
Paper, woodblock print
17.3 x 7.1 cm
1999.2642, 1999.2643

Made popular at drink parties since the late Tang dynasty, illustrated drinking cards eventually became a favourite among the literati in metropolitan Jiangnan cities such as Hangzhou. A drink party was essentially a dinner party during which wine was consumed in large quantities. Card games were a way to add fun to the drinking. Drinkers took turns to draw a card from the main pile which was placed on the table and read out the descriptor with the forfeit instruction for fellow drinkers. For instance, the Laozi card (BELOW, LEFT) instructs a forfeit for the drinker who was celebrating his birthday, while the Zhang Daoling card (BELOW, RIGHT) forfeits the drinker who lived in the mountains. [LCL]

Cenotaph Cover

This silk fragment comes from a larger textile which was probably draped over a cenotaph in a funerary monument. The design on this textile consists of repeats of four chevron bands of cream inscriptions against a green background. The chevron pattern echoes the triangular-shaped tops of cenotaphs found in Turkey.

The inscriptions, which are done in elegant *thulth* script, ask for peace and blessings for Prophet Muhammad, and that God will be pleased with the four Orthodox caliphs and other companions. The second broad band from the top states that 'Allah is my God and there is none but He, Muhammad is a friend of God'. Cenotaph covers usually do not mention the name of the deceased, but rather that of Prophet Muhammad. This reflects the belief that on the day of judgement, the Prophet will intercede on behalf of his community. There is a practical benefit to not specifying the name of the deceased: it enables such fabric to be woven in large quantities.

Islam requires the dead to be buried in the ground—in other words, the cenotaph is empty. When the deceased is in the grave, it is believed that the two black angels of death, Munkar and Nakir, will appear to interrogate the deceased on his/her faith. The inscriptions on the textile appropriately affirm the deceased's religious affiliation.

The use of green silk for this cover is also interesting, as it alludes to the gardens of paradise. There is a verse in the Qur'an—from verse 21 of *Surat al-Insan* (Humankind)—which states that for the faithful in paradise, 'Upon them will be green garments of fine silk and heavy brocade, And they will be adorned with bracelets of silver ...'. [TH]

▶ see OTTOMAN STELE
▶ see QASIDAT AL-BURDAH

OTTOMAN CENOTAPH COVER
Turkey
18th century
Silk
93.7 x 64.8 cm
1995.3910

Chamunda in Dancing Pose

This ten-armed representation of the goddess Chamunda is seen standing in a dance-like pose called *lalita*, where the right foot is bent at the toes with the heel lifted up while bending both the knees in a *demi plié* position.

Kali, in her *aghora* (terrible form), killed the demons Chanda and Munda, and thus came to be known as Chamunda, according to the *Durga Saptashati*. She was created to kill the demons and thus she carries the weapons of Shiva and Durga— notice the *khanjara* (dagger), *trishula* (trident), *kapala* (skull cup), *ghanta* (bell) and *damaru* (kettledrum) in five of her arms. In two of her upper arms she carries the flayed skin of an elephant, and in her two lower ones she carries a *kapala*, from which she licks the blood of the demons. Her teeth are large and distinct, and her body is emaciated; a scorpion adorns the deep cavity of her abdomen; her sagging breasts and earlobes droop low. She is standing in front of a supine human body and a barking hound, which create the atmosphere of a cremation ground. A retinue of attendants, dancers and musicians surrounds her. [GPK]

CHAMUNDA IN DANCING POSE
Rajasthan or Madhya Pradesh, India
c. 10th century
Sandstone
86.5 x 45 x 23 cm
1997.4795

Chedi

This model of a *chedi* (stupa) has unusually elaborately moulded images of the Buddha on each side and finely incised decoration. One side (BELOW, LEFT) has a crowned Buddha seated on a double-lotus base on a stepped pedestal. His right hand is in *bhumisparsha mudra* (earth-witnessing gesture). The figure is framed by a mandorla with *naga* (mythical serpent) finials, above which is a stylised Bodhi Tree[2] and three Buddha images in relief above.[2] The gesture and the Bodhi Tree represent the episode when Buddha overcame Mara, who tried to put obstacles in his path to enlightenment. The other side has an image of Buddha Shakyamuni standing on a lotus with his feet turned outwards and his right hand closed in a fist against his chest, surrounded by a flaming mandorla (BELOW, RIGHT). Buddha Shakyamuni is uncrowned but wears earrings, a necklace and other adornments. Above and below him are three images of seated Buddhas in relief.

Lopburi was an important Khmer outpost in Thailand during the 11th and 12th centuries and Lopburi-style images such as these were most likely inspired by Cambodian sculptures of the 12th and 13th centuries. Crowned Buddha images originated much earlier in India during the 9th to 11th centuries and these could also have been the prototypes for later Southeast Asian examples such as this.[3] [HT]

ALTARPIECE IN THE FORM OF A *CHEDI*
Central Thailand
Lopburi style, 12th–13th centuries
Bronze
38.4 cm
1999.1713

Chettiar Documents

The museum's collection of documents related to Chettiar moneylenders and their clients in Singapore includes promissory slips, indentures and a lawsuit verdict. They date from 1924 to 1941, and consist of both typed and handwritten documents. Many documents are good indicators of the day-to-day business transactions between different ethnic groups that took place in Singapore throughout its history. Some promissory notes contain Chinese chops and signatures, while an indenture of statutory mortgage records an advance of a hefty $10,000 to two Chinese clients. Of added interest are the receipt stamps attached to each document, which were then used within the Straits Settlements to validate monetary and commercial transactions.

Members of this traditional moneylending caste arrived in Singapore in the 19th century from South India, often bringing with them large sums of money. A large proportion of Chettiars conducted their business along Market Street by the Singapore River, with several of them often occupying a single building. Apart from being a constant presence in the area up to the time of the Second World War, they were important to many small businesses and ordinary people as alternatives to large European and Chinese banks which pursued more stringent loan policies.

These documents illustrate the extent of the Chettiars' activities in Singapore: they issued loans of all sizes—even large mortgages—and catered to more than just the Indian community. The Market Street address of the Chettiar is also clearly marked on each document, thus providing an explicit link to the Singapore River. The Chettiar trade was a dying one after the Japanese Occupation of Singapore (1942–1945), which makes these documents valuable relics of an age past. [LC]

CHETTIAR DOCUMENT
Singapore
1920s–1940s
Paper
25 x 19 cm
2002.11.18

A Section from a **Chinese Qur'an**

This particular Qur'an section is part four of a 30-part Qur'an. One section of a 30-part Qur'an is known as a *juz'*. In this *juz'* there are two illuminated double pages. The opening pages (BELOW, TOP) have been decorated with borders of gold and colour, and feature geometric as well as floral designs, while the endpages (BELOW, BOTTOM) have borders of peonies and chrysanthemums. Just by looking at the endpages, it is possible to guess that this Qur'an comes from China.

This Qur'an *juz'* is written in a script developed by Chinese Muslim calligraphers which has generally been labelled as *sini. Sini* script, with shallow downward strokes, look like, or may be considered a variation of, the *muhaqqaq* script.

Muslims arrived at a very early period in China. There are legends which say that Prophet Muhammad's maternal uncle, Sa'ad ibn Abi Waqqas, arrived in Guangzhou in the early 7th century. By the mid 7th century Arab and Chinese sources mention large Muslim populations settled in Chinese ports such as Guangzhou and Quanzhou. Besides the sea route Muslims also arrived in China overland by the Silk Road. Over time there were intermarriages between Muslims and the local Han Chinese population, and their descendants assimilated aspects of Chinese culture and language. These Muslims are known as Hui.[4] Today in China, the Huis make up the largest Muslim minority,[5] numbering around 8.6 million. [TH]

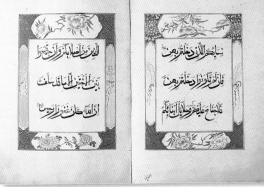

▶ see INDONESIAN QUR'AN
▶ see FRAGMENTS FROM A
   MUHAQQAQ QUR'AN

**A SECTION FROM A
CHINESE QUR'AN**
China
17th century
Ink, colours and gold on paper
(FOLIO) 29.7 x 21.5 cm
1996.187

Cizhou Pillow

This *ruyi*-shaped Cizhou pillow demonstrates the use of polychrome lead glaze, and was probably made in the kilns of Henan. The buff-coloured body is first coated with a white slip before a thin layer of transparent glaze is applied. After firing, decoration is incised over the pillow.

Green and amber glazes are then brushed over the relevant areas, followed by re-firing to a lower temperature of about 1,000 degrees Celsius. The Chinese characters are finally incised to reveal the buff-coloured body beneath.

This Chinese poem (SEE DETAIL, RIGHT), filled with sorrow, bitterness and pain, is contained within a yellow border. A heartbroken lady from a rich family laments the 'heartlessness' of her husband or lover as she waits for him in vain. The predominant green glaze lends a sombre and heavy mood to the poem. Surrounding the poem are incised peonies and scrolling leafy stems, a popular design on Cizhou wares. These floral decorations are bordered by combed lines that follow the *ruyi* shape of the pillow. More combed lines decorate the sides of the pillow to frame stylised leafy stems.

The production of Cizhou wares, mainly folk ceramics, spans over a wide geographical area to include kilns in Hebei and other parts of China, such as Henan and Shaanxi. These kilns produced coarse wares, mostly jars, vases and pillows that were meant for daily use. Pillows made in many forms, including this, were used as headrests for the living and accompanied the dead in their eternal rest. This *ruyi*-shaped pillow would not just be favoured for its utilitarian purpose, but probably blessing its user with good luck, as suggested by the shape of this pillow. [WHL]

▶ see TANG SANCAI TOMB GUARDIANS

***CIZHOU* PILLOW WITH POEM**
China
Song dynasty
Ceramic
22 x 34 x 11 cm
Gift of Singapore Leisure Industries (Pte) Ltd
1995.2391

(TOP) **DETAIL**
Poem on the pillow

Ancient Indian Gold Coins

Royalty generally issued coins in order to demonstrate the endorsement of their rule by a divine power, and to perpetuate it. On most ancient Indian coins one side has the representation of the king with his name inscribed while the reverse has the image of a Hindu deity—Shiva, Vishnu, Durga and others—or indeed deities from other religions and cultures with which the dynasty was affiliated. The coins depicted here show images of Lakshmi seated on a lotus (BELOW, SECOND FROM TOP LEFT) while another depicts her standing holding a lotus and a diadem (BELOW, SECOND FROM TOP RIGHT). The image of Lakshmi is based on the Kushana goddess Ardochsho, the Greek goddess Tyche and the Roman goddess Fortuna, who always carried a cornucopia representing abundance and good fortune.[6] On one of the coins, the Kushana king Kanishka I is depicted with long robes, riding trousers and boots, holding a bow or a sword (BELOW, BOTTOM RIGHT). There are two coins showing Kartikeya (God of War, generally thought to be the son of Shiva and Parvati) seated on a peacock (BELOW, TOP LEFT AND SECOND FROM BOTTOM LEFT). The style and deities depicted on some of these coins can be traced to Achaemenid (Persian), Iranian, Greek and Roman coins.

The Kushanas—who were of Iranian race, and who migrated from western China to Afghanistan and later to northwest India—followed Roman design and denominations for

their coins, but the language of inscription was Bactrian written in Greek script. The Mauryas, indigenous to India, used Brahmi language for their inscriptions. In contrast, the Guptas, also indigenous to India, used Sanskrit language and Devanagari script. The collection includes coins of such famous rulers as Roman emperor Hadrian (reign. 117–138), Mauryan king Ashoka (reign. 273–232 BCE), Kushana king Kanishka I (reign. 127–150) and Gupta king Samudragupta (reign. 330–380).

Coins were valued for accuracy of weight, purity of metal and, above all, the authority and guarantee they bore during transaction. People respected their king and recognised him by the gold coins issued in his name. Thus a systematic collection of coins tells the history of a dynasty and the personalities of the various rulers. Coins are also useful in researching the evolution of Hinduism and the iconography of certain major gods through the ages. Furthermore, coins illustrate the evolution of art and language and greatly assist in the study of interdisciplinary arts. [GPK]

ANCIENT INDIAN GOLD COINS
India
Mauryan, Sunga, Kushana and Gupta periods
Gold
Av. diam. 1.5 cm, weight (CLOCKWISE FROM TOP LEFT) 8.07 g; 4.08 g;
7.89 g; 4.08 g; 7.92 g; 7.97 g; 8.07 g; 7.96 g
On loan from the Chand Collection, Singapore
3.01.16, 4.99.83, 1.9.07, 4.99.83, 1.1.14, 2.3.06, 3.01.16, 2.1.04

Colonial Palanquin

This dark-coloured palanquin has cane panels and flooring, sliding doors with ceramic knobs and louvred windows for air circulation. The shape of the roof resembles Bengali architecture and is made of cloth for filtered light. In the 19th century such palanquins were used for transportation. Four men would lift the bars on each end and a parasol carrier and another attendant would walk along as well. There were different types of palanquins, some like open chairs and others like wheel-less caravans. They were very lightweight and could easily be manoeuvred within narrow and crowded streets. The interiors were decorated with cushions and thin mattresses for additional comfort. Many representations of such palanquins could be seen in Company period paintings.

Palanquins were used by wealthy men and women, including European colonial officers, as a mode of urban transport. In many ways this artefact signifies an era of colonisation and slavery when a wealthier class dominated other classes of society. It suggests an era of oppression and forced labour by India's colonisers and by wealthier Indians themselves. This feudal order continues in some forms even today. [GPK]

COLONIAL PALANQUIN
Bengal, India
1820s
Wood, cane floor and iron attachments
l. 506 cm; (CABIN) 97 x 174 x 76 cm
1999.417.1–4

Cornelis Pronk Dishes

These pieces were commissioned by the Dutch East India Company (*Vereenigde Oostindische Compagnie*) in the late 1730s to capture the domestic market for luxury goods. As part of *chine de commande*, both dishes were designed by the Dutch artist Cornelis Pronk. They were then sent as prints to Jingdezhen and Canton, in China for Chinese potters who successfully copied the shapes and decorations onto their porcelain. It is quite likely that they transferred the design onto the dishes by pricking along the outline of the design, then rubbing charcoal powder through the holes to create an impression of the design on porcelain.[7] The details were only filled in later. Of the five designs supplied by Cornelis Pronk, four have been preserved in the Rijksmuseum in Amsterdam.

Decorated in underglaze blue, the first dish featured here (BELOW) bears the first of five designs by Pronk. Known as 'The Lady with the Parasol', the central scene of this design features a lady feeding three birds—two of which have been identified by scholars as a ruff and a spoonbill[8]—and her servant. A wreath of flowers, different from the usual floral scroll seen on Chinese porcelain, decorates the surrounding narrow concentric band. The details of the central scene are repeated in the cartouches against a honeycomb border. Apart from the

BLUE AND WHITE CORNELIS PRONK DISH
China
18th century
Ceramic
h. 2.9 cm, diam. 23.4 cm
C1210

Western-inspired motifs, an attempt at depicting Orientalism is evident from the 'Chinese' garb worn by the two ladies. Such a fusion of Oriental and Western designs was popular with the Europeans, who perceived the Orient as exotic. It is also indicative of the style adopted by other Pronk porcelain, such as the enamelled dish with 'The Arbour' design.

'The Arbour' (BELOW) is the fourth design out of Pronk's five, and is executed in predominantly pastel turquoise enamels. The central design is that of a lady seated in a garden pavilion, accompanied by two maids and three children, all dressed in Chinese costumes as perceived by the Europeans. In the foreground is a pond with three ducks and flowering plants on each side. Surrounding this scene are 12 cartouches—each containing motifs taken from nature, such as insects, flowers and fruit—on a mosaic-like ground and interspersed with shell motifs. A spearhead border encircles the rim on the reverse side of the dish.

These dishes were used in dinner services in Europe. Despite their popularity, they were discontinued around 1741 due to the high costs incurred and the large amount of time needed to reproduce such intricate designs on porcelain. [WHL]

ENAMELLED CORNELIS PRONK DISH
China
18th century
Ceramic
h. 2.7 cm, diam. 25.9 cm
1998.308

Cosmic Being

This is a *patachitra* (cloth painting) depicting the Jaina cosmology and the results of *karma* (actions of this life and their repercussions on the next birth) including the experiences in purgatory. The Lokapurusha, or Cosmic Being, is portrayed as a standing man, with hands akimbo, his garments broadest at the bottom and narrow around the waist. The artist attempts to blend the microcosm and macrocosm, the relationship between man and nature, in a very organic manner. The section around the chest clearly suggests the celestial zone while the one below is hell. The iconography is relatively fixed but the artists take liberty with the details such as the tortures in hell.

Around the head and neck there are some celestial figures holding lotuses, while around the chest area there are more crowned figures seated in pairs and interspersed with trees. The stomach area depicts a cityscape with trees, boulders and buildings suggesting a kingdom on the earth. Purgatory begins at the hip level and continues into hell at the feet. In horizontal registers scenes of torture unfold: snakes and tigers devouring human beings, figures deep inside wells or boiling in a huge wok over a fire. There are more groups of male figures seated on the sides, watching the gory ordeals the humans are experiencing. Such scenes are also found in the *Sangrahani Sutra* and thus the purpose of this Lokapurusha may also be instructional—to educate the devoted about the virtues of life and the benefits of good *karma*.

An inscription in *nagari* script on the sides suggests that the *patachitra* was painted using an earlier one written by a monk, *sadhu* Baradichanda, as a reference. The artist identifies his lineage and refers to himself as the *shishya* (student) of Jayachand and Gyanamal; the patron is twice referred to as the revered Sitaljimaharaj; there is a repeated mention of *sadhu* Baradichanda from Mewar of Nimach *thikana*, who was probably the religious instructor. This inscription throws a lot of light on the context and the making of the artefact, and helps to explain how religious art and donations to temples and monasteries were implemented. [GPK]

COSMIC BEING
Mewar, Rajasthan, west India
Painted cotton cloth
19th century
183 x 94.5 cm
1999.653

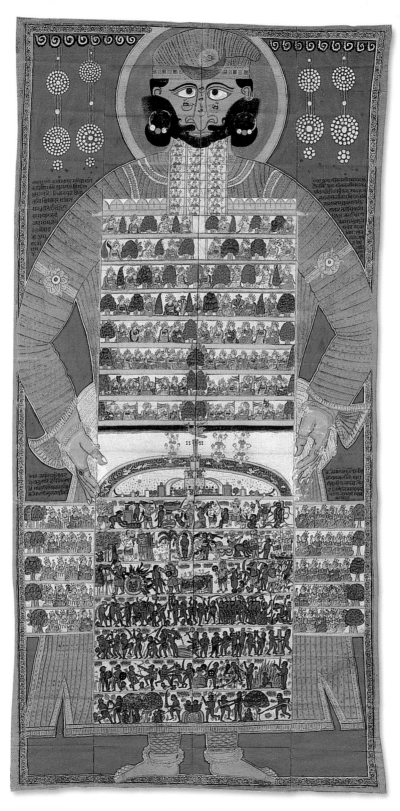

Crowned Buddha

This crowned Buddha is seated in *dhyanasana* (meditation posture) with his hands in *abhaya mudra* (gesture of fearlessness). He wears an elaborate tiara with five peaks and ribbons flowing down both sides of his shoulders. The ribbons are incised with eight auspicious Buddhist emblems, namely the parasol, a pair of golden fish, a vase, a lotus, a conch, an endless knot, a banner of victory and a golden wheel. Buddha also wears a monk's robe with incised floral and foliage designs. On his chest is a swastika which further confirms his identity as a buddha rather than a bodhisattva, who is usually depicted with jewellery.

The depiction of Buddha with a crown is uncommon as he is perceived to have forsaken all earthly materials with the attainment of nirvana (enlightenment). As such, bodily adornments generally do not appear on him as they represent worldliness. The crown, however, is an exception as it represents Buddha's former existence as a royalty. (Buddha was born as Shakyamuni Gautama, a prince of the Shakya clan.)

This statue of Buddha is typical of the Ming dynasty with its outer garment and an inner robe tied around the waist with a ribbon. During the Ming and Qing dynasties, Tibetan Buddhism (also known as Lamaism) yielded a strong influence in the imperial courts of China and consequently permeated the religious lives of the commoners. Imperial patronage of Lamaism was motivated not only by search for personal salvation but also by political motives, of which the most significant was that of control of the borders over the Tibetans and Mongols. [ST]

CROWNED BUDDHA
China
Ming dynasty
Gilt bronze
40 x 27.5 x 25.5 cm
1993.200

Daggers and Hilts

The hilted dagger with a rounded pistol-grip pommel and scroll quillons decorated with vegetal motifs (BELOW, LEFT) has a smooth 'S' shape which allows for an efficient grip and dynamic movement. The jade inlaid dagger hilt (BELOW, RIGHT) has a missing blade, thus it looks more like an ornament than a weapon. It is ornate and richly decorated. It was possibly used by women—judging from the size of the hilt—or offered as a ceremonial dagger. The use of vines and flowers inlaid with special rubies and emeralds is a popular motif in Mughal art. Animal-headed hilts became popular only after the Shah Jahan period, and indeed, animal-headed dagger hilts are known only from the post-Shah Jahan period.[1] Horse-, neel gay-, camel-, ram- and goat-headed hilts, which were preferred by the Mughal princes, are widely found. The ram-headed hilt inlaid with rubies (BELOW, CENTRE) has a delicate flavour that displays a connoisseur's high taste and love for delicate details and the artist's obsessive passion for realism.

Daggers are weapons used for aggression and self-defence, as well as for ceremonial purposes. Such daggers were also given as gifts by nobles to the emperor, or by the emperor to his favourite commanders. Many royal and noble personages may be seen wearing or using such weapons in Mughal period paintings. Art inspired by flora and fauna—including portraiture—were developed during the Mughal period despite Islamic injunctions against representational art. The Mughal flourish in decorative patterns with details and their grandiose scale in planning buildings made them visionaries. Embellishment is a part of the Indian tradition which touched every aspect of Mughal art and has remained as a benchmark of Mughal artistic tradition. Mughal emperors, especially Akbar and some of his successors, are known to have spent their time in the *farashkhana* (royal art studio) actively involved in design discussions with their master artists. [GPK]

(LEFT) **JADE DAGGER HILT (*KHANJAR*)**
India
Aurangzeb period (1659–1707)
White nephrite jade with silver inlay hilt and
steel watered blade with silver inlay
36.6 x 6 cm
1998.1397

(CENTRE) **JADE HILTED DAGGER WITH
RAM-HEADED POMMEL**
India
Aurangzeb period (1659–1707)
Spinach-green jade inlaid with rubies
37.5 x 6.4 cm
1997.4829

(RIGHT) **JADE INLAID DAGGER HILT**
India
19th century
White nephrite jade inlaid with
semi-precious stones and gold
13 x 6 cm
Purchased with funds from the Indian Bank
1993.1750

Dala'il al-Khayrat
(Guide to Goodness)

The *Dala'il al-Khayrat* (Guide to Goodness) was written by 'Abd Allah Muhammad ibn Sulaiman al-Jazuli, a Sufi from North Africa (d. AH 870/1465 CE). Born in Sus, Morocco, he spent about 40 years in the three important Islamic cities of Mecca, Medina and Jerusalem before returning to Fez, where he studied, to write this book.

This prayer book contains a collection of *salawat* (prayers of blessings) for the Prophet Muhammad, the sayings of the Prophet and other information about his life. It is a tremendously popular devotional book, and is often used as a talisman.

The illustrations that usually accompany this prayer book are those of the two most important mosques of Islam—Masjid al-Haram in Mecca and Masjid al-Nabawi (Prophet's Mosque) in Medina. Here are three copies of this prayer book from India, Turkey and North Africa.

The decoration and colours used on the illustrations in the *Dala'il al-Khayrat* from Kashmir (BELOW) are very similar to the lacquerwork produced in the same area. The illustrations are schematic aerial views of the two mosques, with every space available decorated with various floral motifs. The Arabic text is written in black *naskh* script while the accompanying Persian translations are written in small red *nasta'liq*. The words 'Allah' and 'Muhammad' are consistently highlighted throughout the book in red ink.

In the Ottoman copy of the *Dala'il al-Khayrat* (OPPOSITE, BOTTOM), the illustrations of the two mosques are rendered in perspective. The use of perspective was influenced by European art. Interestingly, except for the Ka'bah, all the buildings and even the mountains in the illustrations are depicted in white. The manuscript is copied in *naskh* by a great Ottoman calligrapher, Hasan Riza Efendi (1849–1920), who was known for this script.

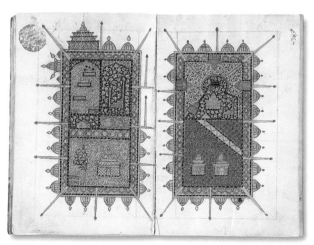

***DALA'IL AL-KHAYRAT* FROM INDIA**
Kashmir, India
18th–19th centuries
Ink, colours and gold on paper
(FOLIO) 21.2 x 14 cm
On loan from the Collection of the Tareq Rajab Museum, Kuwait
TR5

The illustration shown in the copy of the prayer book from North Africa (BELOW) features the Prophet's mosque in Medina in a stylised manner. The Prophet's *minbar* (stepped pulpit) is depicted on the left while the *mihrab* (prayer niche) containing the name of the Prophet—

Muhammad—is on the right. The preceding page, which is not shown here, features the tombs of the Prophet and his two companions, Abu Bakr and 'Umar. The tombs are also found in the Masjid al-Nabawi. The text in this manuscript is written in black Maghribi, the name of the Prophet is highlighted in blue or red ink, and the phrase 'O God' is done in gold.

Up to this day, more than 500 years later, Sulaiman al-Jazuli's book is still popular and read all over the Islamic world. [TH]

▶ see FRAGMENTS FROM A MINBAR
▶ see MIHRAB TILE

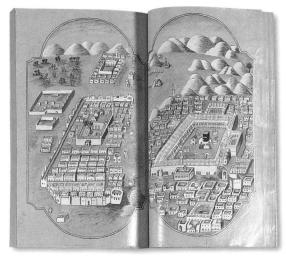

(TOP) *DALA'IL AL-KHAYRAT* FROM NORTH AFRICA
North Africa
18th century
Ink, colours and gold on paper
(FOLIO) 11.8 x 11 cm
1999.1029

(ABOVE) *DALA'IL AL-KHAYRAT* FROM TURKEY
Turkey
Ottoman period, AH 1294/1880 CE
Ink, colours and gold on paper
(FOLIO) 22 x 14 cm
On loan from the Collection of the Tareq Rajab Museum, Kuwait
TR4

Dancing Ganesha

This sculpture of Ganesha comes from the exterior wall of a temple in *nagara* style where niches faced the cardinal directions. Such sculptures were carved and placed in a direction that is iconographically prescribed and symbolically potent to invoke the deity's power. In the South Asia gallery, this sculpture is displayed on a pilastered wall simulating the placement of sculptures in niches and on ledges so that their spatial relationship can be easily perceived.

Standing in a warrior's pose called *alidha*, this six-armed image of Ganesha represents a lighter and humorous aspect of his nature and personality. Standing in between a cymbal player and a drummer, he gently balances his swaying body while his *vahana* (mount), a mouse, squeezes between his feet. This dancing pose suffused with verve and agility reminds us of his passion for dance.[2] Although the trunk and most of the multiple arms are broken, the sculpture retains its inherent dynamism. The arms would have held weapons in them. Ganesha usually holds in his four arms a broken tusk, a *modaka* (sweetmeat), an *ankusha* (elephant goad) and an *akshamala* (rosary). The number of weapons may increase or decrease depending on the number of hands he has. His delicately yet realistically carved head and pot-bellied torso are bejewelled with beaded ornaments that include a pearl-festooned head ornament. He even wears a serpent *yagnopavita* (sacred thread) around his torso that clings on while his dhoti hangs down due to his excessive swaying.

When incarnated as Vignesha, Ganesha is often worshipped as a remover of obstacles before any auspicious ceremony; as Siddhivinayaka he is invoked as a harbinger of good luck, prosperity and success. He is also known as a leader of the *gana* (dwarf soldiers) army of Shiva and hence is seen here imitating Shiva's dancing form. He is variously identified as the son of Parvati and Shiva individually and conjugally according to different texts, and is often called Gajanana, the one with an elephant face. The iconography of Ganesha is also absorbed in Jainism and Buddhism. In Indonesia, he is worshipped in a Tantric context, and his representation is variously depicted with skulls and esoteric iconography. [GPK]

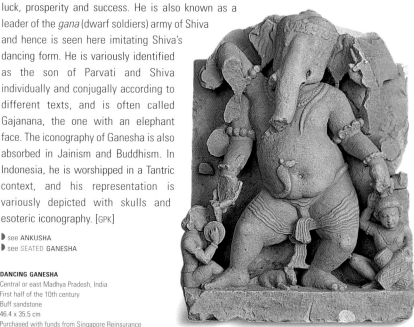

▶ see ANKUSHA
▶ see SEATED GANESHA

DANCING GANESHA
Central or east Madhya Pradesh, India
First half of the 10th century
Buff sandstone
46.4 x 35.5 cm
Purchased with funds from Singapore Reinsurance
Corporation Ltd and India International Insurance Pte Ltd
1996.676

Daoist Pantheon on Robe

This is a robe worn by a Daoist high priest when conducting liturgies. The robe is seamless, without fastenings and depicts the basic structure of the Daoist pantheon. On the front of the robe are Daoist immortals and deities riding on a montage of clouds. On the reverse is an illustration of a special occasion, possibly the Jade Emperor's (Yu Huang) birthday celebrations. This illustration is somewhat unconventional as it is asymmetrical. Seated in the centre is the emperor, who is entertained with a sword dance and presented with a mythical beast resembling a *qilin* (dragon). On his left and right are two entourages of Daoist gods who greet him in their most splendid and formal attire. This heavenly scene is an imperial analogy of the emperor holding court and receiving his officials on earth. The pantheon depicted here reflects Henri Maspero's bureaucratic model of the Daoist pantheon.[3]

Above the Jade Emperor are the Sanqing (Three Pure Ones) and the sun and moon discs, symbols commonly found on Daoist robes. The Three Pure Ones form the apex of the Daoist pantheon and consist of the Yuanshi Tianzun (Celestial Worthy of Primordial Beginnings), the Lingbao Tianzun (Celestial Worthy of Numinous Treasure) and the Daode Tianzun (Celestial Worthy of the Way and its Power), with the last being the deified Laozi. The sun and moon discs with the three-legged rooster and the white rabbit are symbols of *yin* and *yang* respectively, two key principles in cosmology adopted into the mainstream of Daoist philosophy. Dispersed throughout the robe are Daoist symbols of longevity and immortality, such as cranes and mountain shafts respectively. [ST]

▶ see YIN AND YANG ZODIAC SIGNS

ROBE WITH DAOIST PANTHEON (BACK VIEW)
China
Late Ming dynasty, 17th century
Embroidery on silk
130 x 206 cm
On loan from the Collection of Christopher J. Hall
CH 82 (S2)

Dayak Baskets

This is a group of three baskets made by the Dayak people of Borneo. All are tightly woven in an interlocking fashion and are lightweight, with two layers of weaving. The two layers are obvious in the largest basket (BELOW) as the four corners on its base are worn, exposing both layers. The two smaller baskets (OPPOSITE) do not appear to have any handles for carrying and may have been used as containers for storing grain and fruit. The largest basket has two rings attached to it and was apparently worn strapped to a person's back. The motifs on all three baskets appear to be abstract spirals. Wood has been used on two of the baskets, one for a base and the other as reinforced rings for the opening of the basket.

The origin of many of the techniques of basketry remains a mystery but the variety originates partly from necessity—the type of material available in a particular area and the purpose of the basket. For example, these baskets have a close-textured weave that can hold small seeds, while others would be strong yet lightweight for carrying heavy loads. Different Dayak groups make and use very different baskets for the same purpose. This suggests that even if there was an original prototype for

DAYAK BASKETS
Sarawak, Malaysia
Early 20th century
Plant fibre and wood
(ABOVE) h. 23 cm, diam. 18 cm;
(OPPOSITE, LEFT) h. 20.5 cm, diam. 13.5 cm;
(OPPOSITE, RIGHT) h. 17.5 cm, diam. 13.5 cm
WA0331

a particular type of basket, it would have changed over time with the evolution of new basketry techniques and styles.

Archaeologists believe that the peoples of Borneo have been using baskets for a long period of time. Late Stone-Age burial sites in Sarawak confirm the antiquity of basketwork. An excavated basket-holder was dated to 500 BCE. During the same period, pandan (*Pandanus* species) matting was also found to have been used for wrapping corpses. One of the main problems for researching the origins of baskets is the perishable organic material from which they are made. It seems unlikely that very old specimens would ever be found, even though it is widely believed that baskets were one of the first items used in early Southeast Asia. One can only speculate that some kind of containers to gather food or carry goods, and mats for protection from the elements or to sleep or sit on, were used.

There is little written evidence on basketry in the reports of travellers and traders who visited Borneo in the early centuries of the Common Era. Though other items of material culture, such as *pua kumbu* (sacred cloth), weapons and heirloom jars were sometimes described in detail, baskets went unnoticed and were mentioned only in passing. [RE]

Dayak Carved Human Skull

This skull is reportedly from a Kayan Dayak community on the island of Borneo. Swirl patterns have been elaborately incised on its cranium. The practice of incising patterns on skulls is unique to the Kayan Dayak tribe. However, it is not fully understood why these skulls were incised in such a manner.

The ritual life of some Dayak groups required human sacrifice to ensure fertility and to appease demonic spirits believed to cause illness, disease or crop failure. Headhunting, a practice fairly widespread throughout Borneo before the 20th century, was part of the warfare between enemy groups, in which the goal was to enslave the captured and take the heads of certain individuals for ritual purposes. The heads were trophies to the Dayak headhunters and reflected on their prowess as warriors. At the same time, the heads captured were honoured and used in rituals by the community to improve the fertility and prosperity of the community as a whole.

Heads were not taken frivolously. When misfortunes affected a Dayak community, the men would plan a headhunting expedition. A human head was believed to contain a powerful spiritual essence that could be harnessed to improve the community's well-being. It was important for the community that had lost heads to replenish the diminished essence—also through headhunting—and a vicious cycle ensued. Yet, as reprehensible as the custom of headhunting is to us today, it should be seen in context. A head was only taken after its owner had departed from this world. The head was treated with great respect and honoured within its new communal group. The preservation of the head was also carried out with great skill and care.

Among some Dayak groups, headhunting was a rite of passage for men. There was no higher honour than being a renowned headhunter. A bachelor needed to have taken at least one head to be eligible for marriage. An ambitious man could gain influence and prestige by being a successful headhunter.

DAYAK CARVED HUMAN SKULL
Sarawak, Malaysia
c. 1900s
Human bone
h. 16 cm, diam. 17.5 cm
Z0396

(OPPOSITE) **DETAIL**
Incised patterns on the cranium

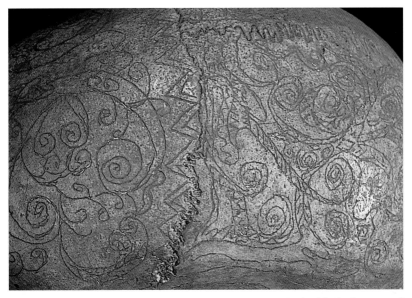

The successful acquisition of enemy heads was equated in ritual with the increase of community fertility. Major rituals that followed headhunting expeditions were believed to restore balance and harmony to the cosmos, thereby promoting the prosperity of the community. The captured heads were treated respectfully and were proudly displayed in a central location in the longhouse. Offerings such as eggs and rice-wine were made regularly to the heads to appease the spirits.

When the British and Dutch colonised Borneo in the 19th century, headhunting was actively discouraged as it was disruptive to trade and expansion. Today, the Malaysian and Indonesian governments have made headhunting punishable by law. [RE]

Dayak Shield

This wooden shield is carved entirely from a solid elongated piece of softwood. It has been painted using red and black natural pigments. The motif on the shield was designed to ward off evil spirits. This motif has been created by two coiled, mirror-image figures that have been aligned back to back to create a fanged face with bulging eyes in the centre of the shield. The design is typical of most Dayak shields.

This shield does not seem suitable for self-defence and was probably used as a ceremonial dance accessory for a male warrior. It does not have tufts of hair attached to it—a common practice among Dayak warriors to indicate that the male owner was a proven headhunter.

Dayak shields, together with *mandau* (ceremonial swords), were the standard equipment for the Dayak warrior. As with *mandau* hilts, well-made shields were highly prized by Dayak warriors who often collected them as war trophies. It is therefore difficult to pinpoint an exact style and design of shield for any particular Dayak group. Today, many Dayak children play with miniature shields decorated with the fierce image of Aso, similar to the one shown here. [RE]

▌ see **MANDAU HILT**

DAYAK SHIELD
Sarawak, Malaysia
c. 1900s
Wood
123 x 39 cm
AA0100

(ABOVE) **DETAIL**
Stylised face of Aso on the shield

Deepalakshmi
(Lady Holding a Lamp)

The image of Deepalakshmi (lady holding a lamp) is metaphorical. It does not merely depict a woman holding a lamp, but is a symbolic representation of a lamp in the form of an auspicious woman, who is seen as a bestower of good luck, happiness and peace.

This lamp bears a donatory inscription, probably referring to the donor's name or the occasion for the donation. Depicted standing with the right knee bent, the lady holds the lamp with her right hand while her left rests by the hip, which is flexed to form a curvaceous bend in the waist in a classical dance-like stance. Her jewellery consists of bangles and bracelets, shoulder bands, earrings, a *thali* (marriage necklace) and necklaces, head ornaments, *payal* (anklets) and bells. The most important ornament is the *thali* which signifies that the woman is married and therefore auspicious. The entire appearance of this Deepalakshmi is similar to that of the *devadasi* (ancient temple dancers); even classical *bharatnatyam* dancers today dress up in a similar manner.

Lamps—utilitarian objects made from materials as simple as clay, to metals such as brass and bronze, or even silver and gold—are perceived metaphorically as a source of life, soul, purity and vision. In every culture lamps are designed in many unusual ways. The imagery of Deepalakshmi is special to India and it is found in only a few parts of India and the world. During temple rituals in Singapore, it is common to find the stems of a lamp dressed up as a woman and wearing a sari and jewellery—a reversal of symbolism. [GPK]

DEEPALAKSHMI
Vijayanagara, India
15th century
Bronze
h. 34 cm
1994.5384

Dehua Enamelled Wares

Dehua enamelled wares were exported to Europe and Southeast Asia around the 18th and 19th centuries. They were especially popular in Europe in the 18th century, evident from the 400 Dehua pieces in the collection of Augustus the Strong (1670–1733), also King Augustus II of Poland, and many others in the European collections. The European preference for ornate things is also reflected in the number of European copies, albeit unsuccessful, of Dehua enamelled wares made during the 18th century.

The first two pieces—the teapot (BELOW, LEFT) and vase (BELOW, RIGHT)—are good examples of Dehua enamelled wares that were exported to Southeast Asia. They were decorated with polychrome enamels resembling those used on Zhangzhou or Swatow wares for export to Japan and Southeast Asia. It is likely that Dehua wares produced around the 17th century were sent to Zhangzhou for enamelling before they were exported to similar destinations. The enamels were applied onto the fired body and then re-fired. Both vessels share similar motifs of birds and chrysanthemums that were executed in a painterly and lively manner, suggesting that these were likely to be decorated in the same kiln. The birds on the teapot are painted with a translucent turquoise wash and black for details, while red and green enamels are used for the chrysanthemums and leaves respectively on both the teapot and vase.

(ABOVE) **TEAPOT WITH ZHANGZHOU-STYLE ENAMELS**
Dehua, China
17th century
Ceramic
h. 8.5 cm
1994.5082

(RIGHT) **VASE WITH ZHANGZHOU-STYLE ENAMELS**
Dehua, China
17th century
Ceramic
h. 17.8 cm
Gift of Frank and Pamela Hickley
2000.3391.2

The third piece, Guanyin seated on a lion, is a good example of a Dehua enamelled ware with unfired overglaze decoration. It is decorated with cold paints of black, green, brown and red, colours most likely chosen to enhance the appeal of this roughly modelled figurine. Cold paints were applied onto the fired body without a second firing, thus leaving the figurine susceptible to damage.

Cold-painted figurines were some of the Dehua wares exported to Europe around the 18th century. However, it is postulated that cold paints were only added in Holland as the ships of the Dutch East India Company (*Vereenigde Oostindische Compagnie*) would pass Holland before they reached their European destinations. Furthermore, cold paints were also used in Europe to embellish plain white figurines, in order to match the opulence of the Baroque period (17th–18th centuries). [WHL]

▶ see DEHUA CIRCULAR COVERED BOX
▶ see DEHUA FIGURINES

GUANYIN SEATED ON A LION
Dehua, China
17th century
Ceramic
h. 22.5 cm
1996.220

Dehua Figurines

Dehua, located on the southeast coast of Fujian province, is well known for its production of white porcelain, known to the Europeans as *'blanc de chine'*. The earliest Dehua porcelain dates to the Northern Song period but the production and quality of these porcelain peaked around the 17th and 18th centuries. Figurines were produced around the 17th century, evident from early dated examples such as Caishen (God of Wealth)[4] dated to 1610.

The pieces featured here are all religious figurines of fine quality. Each figurine is formed from various press-moulded parts. The potter had to work on both the interior and the exterior to ensure that the parts were joined properly. The head and neck were usually luted to the torso, as in the case of Wenchang (BELOW). A sharp tool would then be used to trim the interior so as to reduce the thickness and heaviness of the piece and to prevent warping. This method of construction continued into the 19th century but by the early 20th century another method, known as slip-casting, had taken over the bulk of the production.

This fine example of Wenchang bears an incised square mark of the potter, He Chaozong (16th–17th centuries), known for producing religious figurines such as popular Daoist deities. Seated on a rocky pedestal with a *ruyi* sceptre in his right hand, this dignified figurine is dressed in a civil official's robe with beautifully carved drapes and folds. The rank badge on his robe has incised cranes indicating the highest rank held by Wenchang in officialdom. A cream glaze, typical of Dehua porcelain of this period, covers the pure white body. Wenchang, also known as the God of Literature, was worshipped by scholars—and even by present-day students who want good academic results.

The second figurine featured here (OPPOSITE, TOP) is a rare piece for two reasons—there are not many *blanc de chine* Shakyamuni figurines around and the iconography of this piece is interesting as Shakyamuni is portrayed in deep meditation. He is seated on a rocky pedestal, as is common with religious figurines. The realism and austerity of this piece can be attributed to the sculptor's skill, evident from the protruding ribs on the figurine's body, the folds of the trousers, the *ushnisha* (protuberance) on his head, and a facial expression that emanates calmness.

Another important religious figure in the Dehua figurine repertoire is Guanyin (BELOW). She was depicted by Dehua potters in various forms, each corresponding to one of the 33 manifestations described in the *Lotus Sutra* (▶ see LOTUS SUTRA).[5] Here, Guanyin is seated in *mahārājalīlāsana* (posture of royal ease) with both hands hidden in her long sleeves. As with the previous two figurines, the folds of her robe are beautifully carved. She is adorned with a pendant and a *ruyi*-shaped headpiece.[6] The massive production of Guanyin figurines suggests their popularity as objects of devotion or for offerings.

These figurines are merely a small selection from a large range of excellent Dehua sculptural pieces in the museum's collection, but they reflect the sculptural heights attained by the potter and the spiritual climate of the 17th and 18th centuries. [WHL]

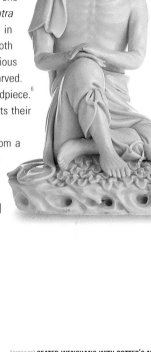

(OPPOSITE) **SEATED WENCHANG WITH POTTER'S MARK**
Dehua, China
Early 17th century
Ceramic
h. 34 cm
Gift of Frank and Pamela Hickley
2000.3335

(ABOVE) **SHAKYAMUNI SEATED IN MEDITATION**
Dehua, China
Early 17th century
Ceramic
h. 21.3 cm
Gift of Frank and Pamela Hickley
2000.3336

(LEFT) **SEATED GUANYIN**
Dehua, China
Late 18th century or later
Ceramic
h. 20.6 cm
Gift of Frank and Pamela Hickley
2000.3387

Dharani Mantra

This scripture in concertina folds contains the 15th chapter of the *dharani* (incantational) text and is part of the collection of Chinese Buddhist canons (*tripitaka*) commissioned for printing under the Mongol patronage between 1228 and 1322. The project was carried out under the supervision of the Yansheng Monastery of Qisha, an island in Lake Chen of present-day Wuxian of Jiangsu province. A total of eight frontispiece illustrations were made by Chen Sheng, and the woodblocks were carved by at least three master carvers. These woodblocks depict Buddha's teaching sessions in similar settings but each with a slightly different audience. The eight frontispieces adorn the 591 volumes of scriptures in this collection.

This volume itself opens with a magnificent frontispiece (BELOW) depicting Buddha preaching to a full audience of bodhisattvas, monks, *arhat* (great adepts), *lokapala* (heavenly guardians), as well as what seem to be Taoist personnel, who are men in Chinese-style dress. Buddha is depicted as a large central figure in *dharmachakra mudra* (teaching gesture) while seated on a gigantic lotus plinth with a body aureole embellished with a

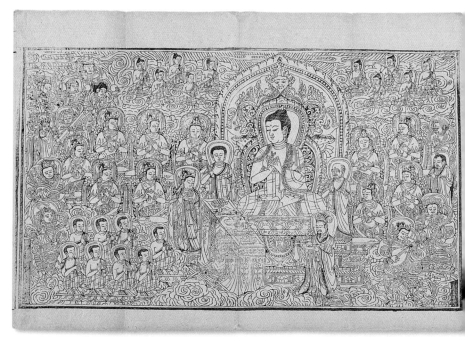

YAMANTAKA *DHARANI* FROM THE QISHA *TRIPITAKA*
Jiangsu, China
Yuan dynasty, early 14th century
Paper, woodblock print
(FOLIO) l. 975 cm; (FRONTISPIECE) 11.5 x 30.2 cm
1998.607

makara and a *kala* head. An altar draped with silk brocade is presented before Buddha with offerings and symbols, such as the conch and water vase. The aura of the preaching is enhanced by the unison *dharmachakra mudra* which is also gestured by the bejewelled bodhisattvas and the cosmic buddhas seen in the topmost register of the scene.

Based on the Sui dynasty translation, this *dharani* is devoted to Yamantaka or Daweide mingwang, the wrathful manifestation of Amitabha, the Buddha of the West, also one of the five cosmic Buddhas. As a Vidyaraja, or king of powerful knowledge that overcomes obstacles of passions and desires, Yamantaka is often portrayed as multi-headed, multi-armed, and equipped with weaponry attributes. His overwhelming appearance is but a representation of the attitude, immense power and knowledge he must command to control and subdue one's passions and desires—both of which are regarded as the causes of sufferings and hence an obstacle to realising detachment and enlightenment. By chanting the *dharani*, devotees of the Yamantaka teaching can invoke the power of the god so as to overcome their weaknesses. [LCL]

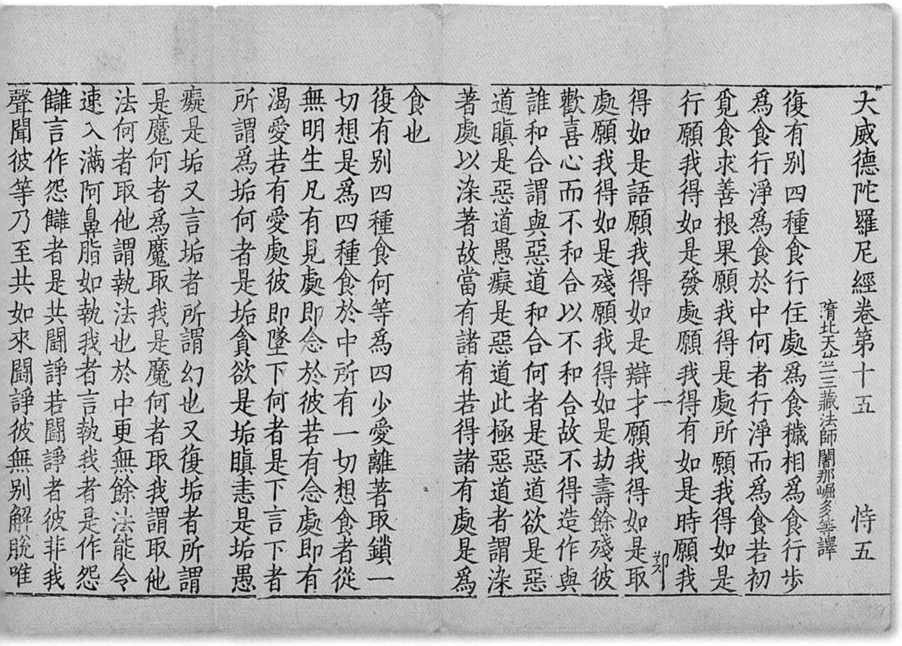

大威德陀羅尼經卷第十五

隋北天竺三藏法師闍那崛多等譯

怡五

復有別四種食行住處為食藏相為食行步
為食行淨為食於中何者行淨而為食若初
覺食求善根果願我得是處所願我得如是
行願我得如是發處願我得有如是時願我

得如是語願我得如是辯才願我得一
處願我得如是殘願我得如是劫壽餘殘彼
歡喜心而不和合以不和合故不得造作與
誰和合謂與惡道和合何者是惡道欲是惡
道瞋是惡道愚癡是惡道和合此極惡道者謂涤
著處以涤著故當有諸有若得諸有處是為

食也
復有別四種食何等為四少愛離著取鎖一
切想是為四種食於中所有一切想食者從
無明生兒有見處即念於彼若有念處即有
渴愛若有愛處彼即墮下何者是下言下者
所謂為垢何者是垢食欲是垢瞋恚是垢愚

癡是垢又言垢者所謂幻也又復垢者所謂
是魔何者為魔取我是魔何者取我謂取他
法何者取他謂執法也於中更無餘法能令
速入滿阿鼻脂如執我者言執我者是作怨
讎言作怨讎者是共闘諍若闘諍者彼非我
聲聞彼等乃至共如來闘諍彼無別解脫唯

Ding Dishes

This group of Ding dishes represents the fine whiteware of the Song dynasty. Ding kilns in Quyang county, Hebei, started production during the Tang dynasty. They closely followed Xing kilns in Lincheng and Neiqiu counties in Hebei in the production of white stoneware. However, these never quite surpassed those produced by the Xing kilns until the Xuanhe and Zhenghe periods (1111–1125), according to the *Ge Gu Yao Lun (The Essential Criteria for Chinese Antiquities)*.[7] The use of coal as kiln fuel provided the oxidising atmosphere and allowed an increased firing temperature which gave Ding wares their much-prized ivory tone. The Ding kilns peaked in the 11th and 12th centuries and produced what connoisseurs of the Southern Song, Ming and Qing dynasties claimed was 'one of the five great wares'.

All three Ding dishes share the common characteristics of a copper rim and 'tear drops'. More thinly potted than other earlier whiteware such as that of the Xing, this stoneware was stacked in saggars with stepped sides and fired upside down to prevent warping. The glaze around the rim was wiped off so that the wares would not adhere to one another. This resulted in a coarse rim, also known as *mang kou*. A copper band was then used on the rim. This reflected the popular practice of decorating other materials, such as ivory, with metal. For this reason Ding wares were favoured and used at court. Tear drops that formed on the exterior walls of the dishes were a result of the warm ivory-tone glaze thickening after the wares were dipped. They add to the naturalism of this fine whiteware and fortunately did not deter the use of Ding wares at court.

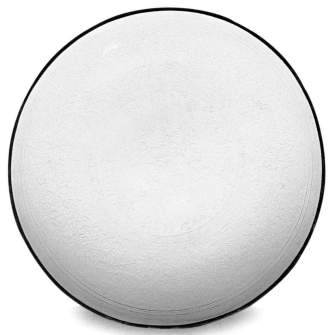

Of these Ding dishes, the largest dish (OPPOSITE) combines both throwing and moulding methods. The leather-hard thrown dish was beaten onto a pottery mould with beautifully carved floral design intaglio on the interior. The central design comprised lotus, mallow, sagittaria and a sedge-like plant that resembles a corncob.[8] This is separated from the peony scrolls in the well by a concentric band of key-fret patterns.

Such elaborate and crowded design is absent on the other two dishes. These smaller dishes offer an organic feel as the motifs are derived from nature. The peony and the butterfly come alive through the gracefully incised lines that follow the shape of the second dish (ABOVE). Double incised lines further add beauty and calm to this natural scene. The decoration on the third dish (RIGHT) is of two incised fish among waves. The glaze filled and deepened the grooves to highlight a sense of fluidity. Both dishes have an incised ring—to confine the decoration to the centre—and undecorated walls.

Ding wares with incised decorations were overtaken by the increased production of wares with elaborate moulded decorations during the 12th and 13th centuries. Production continued right up to the Jin dynasty and thereafter the kilns declined. [WHL]

(OPPOSITE) **DING DISH WITH MOULDED FLORAL DECORATION**
China
Song dynasty
Ceramic
h. 6 cm, diam. 30 cm
Gift of Jurong Town Corporation
1995.2384

(TOP) **DING DISH WITH INCISED FLORAL DECORATION**
China
Song dynasty
Ceramic
h. 3.5 cm, diam. 17.3 cm
1995.2408

(ABOVE) **DING DISH WITH INCISED TWIN FISH DECORATION**
China
Song dynasty
Ceramic
h. 5.8 cm, diam. 20.9 cm
Purchased with funds from The Shaw Foundation
C1382

Divination Manual

(Primbon)

T he pages shown here are from a divination manual written in *jawi*[9], or Malay in Arabic script. Written on European paper, this manual contains 12 pages of illustrations and 27 pages of text, and is not complete. The front page of the manual contains a small note in Dutch written in brown ink stating, 'Semarang 15 May 1824'. Semarang is on the north coast of Java.

The opening pages (BELOW) begin with praises to Allah and continue with instructions on what you should do before using the manual. The first thing to do is to perform ablutions, then recite some Qur'anic verses and invocations, beginning with the first verse in the Qur'an, *Surat al-Fatihah* (The Opening). At the bottom of the first page (the right page—Arabic is read from right to left) is a table of numbers, from which you pick a number—from 1 to 15—that you fancy. The facing page contains a circle divided into 30 segments, each containing the names (in red) of the first 30 *surah* (excluding the first *surah* or chapter) in the Qur'an.

DIVINATION MANUAL
North coast of Java, Indonesia
c. 1824
Ink and colours on paper
(FOLIO) 33.1 x 20.8 cm
1996.525

These *surah* are associated with decisions that need to be made or questions whose answers you seek, such as 'Should I set sail today?' or 'Will I be successful?'. Identify a *surah* that corresponds best to your need. In the text that follows, 15 options are given for each *surah*. The answer you seek is found in the option whose number tallies with the number you chose earlier.

The other page in this manuscript (BELOW) shows a table that indicates the various prophets associated with the days of the week as well as the auspicious and inauspicious times during the day which are ruled by the sun, moon and the planets.

Divination manuals are generally known as *primbon* in Java. They are consulted when guidance is sought, especially for important life events such as marriage, or even when one prepares to shift into a new home. [TH]

▶ see INDONESIAN QUR'AN

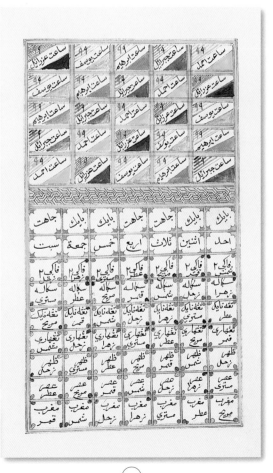

Dizang

The imposing aura of this fragmentary torso of Dizang, or Kshitigarbha, is demonstrative of the power this bodhisattva commands in the realm of purgatory hell. The bodhisattva is far more popularly revered in East Asia—China and Japan—than elsewhere. Often depicted in sculpture as a traveller with hood and staff, Dizang appears as a physically formidable monk. This sculpture of Dizang was carved during the peak of the Tang dynasty, when a mature style of Buddhist sculpture had emerged from a long tutelage of Indian and Central Asian schools. Dressed plainly as a monk, his shoulders bare, Dizang holds a wish-granting jewel (*cintamani*) in one hand while the other missing hand would have held a staff. Both objects are the common attributes of Dizang.

The popularity of Dizang in China is associated with the parallel rise in popularity of the notion of purgatory hell, which came with Buddhism. Dizang, like other bodhisattvas, had vowed to deliver all beings to the ultimate salvation by freeing them from the sufferings of the multiple courts of hell (▶ see TEN COURTS OF HELL). The deeds of Dizang, much applauded by Buddha and the other great bodhisattvas, are recounted in the *Dizang Pusa Benyuan Jing* (*Original Vow of the Bodhisattva Kshitigarbha Sutra*). In this *sutra* we are told that during his previous incarnation as a filial young daughter of a Brahman, Dizang was moved to embrace universal compassion by learning of the horrifying sufferings to which her mother was subjected, and how, due to the greatness of his compassion, the calling of Dizang's name efficaciously transports the souls of the deceased from the excruciating pain of hell.

Emerging as a cult deity in China during the Tang dynasty, Dizang's popularity was comparable to that commanded by Guanyin. This phenomenon is also closely associated with the wide acceptance by the Chinese of purgatory Hell which did not take root in the Chinese psyche until then. Now that the visually overwhelming and physically painful experience of hell had been envisaged for Buddhists, Dizang's role gained an unprecedented importance. Indeed, in Shakyamuni Buddha's own words, the act of chanting Dizang's name, praising and admiring the bodhisattva could exonerate one from sins committed as far back as 30 *kalpa* (eons). In the same *Dizang Sutra*, in which those words were pronounced, Shakyamuni prescribed the ways to venerate the bodhisattva and the many good consequences that could result from the devotion to Dizang, including those on one's subsequent rebirths. Specifically, one's ugliness in this life could even be transformed into great beauty in the next lives by looking at the image of Dizang in veneration. Dizang's popularity is celebrated at the Jiuhua Mountains in Anhui, where pilgrims pay their homage to the bodhisattva during the seventh lunar month. [LCL]

TORSO OF DIZANG
China
Tang dynasty, 7th–8th centuries
Stone
104.7 x 52 x 30.5 cm
2000.3530

Dokoh

These two Malay necklaces made of *suasa*—an alloy of gold, silver and copper that has a distinctive reddish colour—are fine examples of the distinctive jewellery of Pattani Kelantan and Terengganu. These necklaces, known as *dokoh,* consist of a central pendant and additional small pendants, usually five in total, which are arranged together on a chain. The central ornaments on these pieces are made from a hard resin core that has been covered with gold sheet. The first pendant (BELOW, LEFT) is rectangular and has a central arrangement of precious stones surrounded in wire filigree decorations. On the second *dokoh* (BELOW, RIGHT) the central gold pendant is made in the form of a *daun sukun* (breadfruit leaf), a motif said to symbolise the creative fusion of male and female cosmic energies.[10] The pendant is decorated with a row of faceted gold granules and an array of rough-cut diamonds.

It is clear from the way *dokoh* are made that they were intended as charms or amulets to protect the wearer. On both *dokoh* there are two small fluted containers that resemble special containers traditionally used by Malays for keeping written charms. In the case of these *dokoh* however, the containers are resin-filled and were clearly intended to be symbolic. Two coin-like ornaments are also attached to each chain, both of which are decorated, one with gold granulation and the other with wire filigree. These most likely also functioned as or were symbolic of protective amulets.

Today goldsmiths from northeast Malay Peninsula are still well-known for their use of wire filigree and faceted gold granulation, skills that were passed down from generation to generation for centuries. They are particularly noted for their use of *suasa*. Malay goldsmiths enhanced this reddish colour by staining their works a pinkish red colour. They accomplished this using a complicated process that involved alternately soaking the item in various caustic solutions containing sulphur, salt and lime juice and then heating it.[11] [DAH]

DOKOH
Kelantan, Malaysia
Late 19th–early 20th centuries
Gold, *suasa*, diamonds
(LEFT) circ. 42 cm; (RIGHT) circ. 34 cm
GL0001, GL0020

Doucai Cup

This cup was reconstructed from shards found at the imperial kiln sites of Jingdezhen. It is one of many examples of flawed ceramics from the Chenghua period. Such pieces failed to pass the strict quality controls of the imperial court and were broken, usually in the middle, to prevent them from being used or copied without permission.

'Doucai' (fitted colours) is used to describe porcelain that combines the practice of using cobalt blue as an outline and overglaze enamels to fill the spaces. After the cobalt blue pigment was applied and fired, enamels such as red, green, yellow and purplish-brown were applied to fill the spaces and re-fired at a lower temperature of around 900 degrees Celsius.

The cobalt blue on this thinly potted *doucai* wine cup differs from that of the Yuan (▶ see BLUE AND WHITE STEMCUP). It is of a lighter shade and appears more transparent due to its combination of native and imported cobalt blue. Most of the enamels on this cup have worn off as they were painted over the glaze. A six-character reign mark in a double square, *'Da Ming Chenghua Nianzhi'* (Made during the Ming dynasty, Chenghua's reign), typical of its period, can be seen on the base (TOP). Two figural scenes framed by blue lines form the main decoration on this cup. These scenes probably correspond to two paintings—*Xizhi Watching the Geese* and *Bringing a Qin (Zither) to a Friend*. The former is suggested by the depiction of a scholar, possibly Wang Xizhi (active during the 4th century), seated leisurely on the ground and watching the geese in the pond, while his attendant waits for him with his books. The other scene depicts a scholar dressed in green, followed by his attendant carrying a zither. Both scenes are separated by a willow and a pine, which are painted in green enamels and blue outlines. The painting of this period is regarded as one of the finest and was much emulated during the reigns of the Qing emperors Kangxi and Yongzheng. [WHL]

DOUCAI CUP WITH SCHOLARS AND BOY ATTENDANTS
Jingdezhen, China
Ming dynasty, Chenghua period
Ceramic
h. 3.8 cm, diam. 6 cm
1999.2655

(TOP) **DETAIL**
Six-character reign mark on the base of the cup

Drinking Vessels

The *jia* and *gu* were drinking vessels used in the Shang and Zhou dynasties. This *jia* (BELOW) is typical of those found in the Erlitou period (c. 2000–1500 BCE) as distinguished by its larger, flared mouth and simple *wo* (fireball) design. This *gu* (OPPOSITE), with its trumpet-like silhouette, horizontal flanges, and 'two-eyed'[12] and spear motifs, is an archetype of late Shang *gu* beakers. If you compare the two bronzes, it is evident that great improvements were made in bronze casting technology during the Shang dynasty—the *gu* is finely cast and filled with motifs and patterns that are more intricate than those of the *jia*. The widespread appearance of the two-eyed motif and its complexity during the late Shang dynasty, for example, also attests to the development of the bronze culture during this time. (The two-eyed motif is a mysterious mask-like face of a beast in frontal view. It is divided into two symmetrical halves and has a pair of horns or ears. The earliest forms of the two-eyed motif were simple and abstract. By the late Shang dynasty, it had evolved into a flexible, complex design comprising various units that could be taken apart and read individually to form new motifs such as a dragon or a bird.)

The *jia* was used for warming and drinking wine while the *gu* functioned mainly as a serving and pouring vessel during rituals or feasts. However, at times, it was also used by the upper class during ablutions. In burials, it

JIA
China
Early Shang dynasty, Erlitou period, c. 2000–1500 BCE
Bronze
h. 22.7 cm, diam. 15.6 cm
1996.471

was common to find both vessels together with a *jue*, a similarly shaped tripod drinking vessel. These three vessels constituted a basic set for wine drinking. Examples of all three vessels were discovered in ceramic form during the Erlitou period, indicating, perhaps, the beginnings of wine drinking in early civilisation.

From the simplest drinking vessels described above, medium and large-sized wine containers such as the *zun*, *hu*, *fou* or *lei* and *fang yi* were developed (❿ see WINE CONTAINER). The increase in the variety of wine vessels by the late Shang dynasty and the general abundance of wine vessels found during excavations of ancient Shang sites reflected the Shang people's obsession with alcohol. According to Ma Chengyuan, the leading expert on Chinese bronzes, this in turn meant that large quantities of grain were harvested to manufacture fermented wine and hence showed that the Shang had a well-developed agriculture.[13] The Shang's indulgence in alcohol was cited as a major cause of their downfall by the Zhou kings. They did not ban alcohol altogether, but moderation was instead advocated. Consequently, there was a decline in the number of wine vessels made and a proportionate increase in the number of food vessels, especially the *ding* and *gui*, during the Zhou dynasty. [ST]

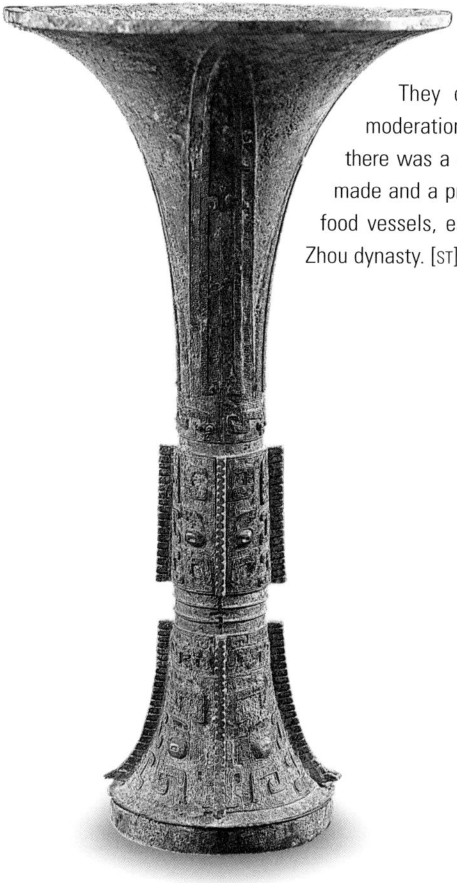

GU
China
Late Shang dynasty
Bronze
h. 30.3 cm, diam. 16.4 cm
2000.8201

Dong Son Drum

This unique artefact is known as a Dong Son drum. A 12-ray star appears on the flat face, or tympanum, as a central motif, with stylised herons flying in a concentric circle around it. Boats with people on them are depicted on the drum shoulder below the tympanum. Water buffalo motifs are present on the body of the drum. These motifs on the tympanum, shoulder and body (SEE DETAILS, BELOW) are framed by abstract designs of saw-tooth and dotted circles. All these motifs are highly consistent with those on other drums found in north Vietnam.

One explanation for these motifs is their depiction of Heaven and Earth and the position of people between these two realms. The central star (SEE DETAIL, LEFT) symbolised the sun, the centre of Heaven around which everything else revolved. Herons were symbols of the Hung kings, the hereditary rulers of north Vietnam during the Dong Son period. The boats represented man and such activities as trade, warfare and water festivals. The water buffalo symbolised the sacred Earth and also its pivotal role in wet rice cultivation.

Dong Son culture was an agricultural one based on wet rice cultivation with a high degree of social stratification. Bronze drums were precious and rare objects, symbols of wealth and power, and only buried with certain individuals. A person buried with three drums may have been a king or someone of very high status.

It is still unclear as to whether there was an exact use for the Dong Son drum. It appears to be a musical instrument, as it has been depicted on friezes being played. It was certainly a funerary item, accompanying the burial of important members of society at the time. Excavated examples were found to have been used as storage containers for other burial artefacts.

Dong Son drums have been discovered in mountainous areas, in mountain caves, along

DONG SON DRUM
North Vietnam
180–100 BCE
Bronze
h. 36 cm, diam. 55 cm
1999.246

(ABOVE, FROM TOP) **DETAILS**
12-ray star, boat and water buffalo motifs

coastal plains and on remote islands in Southeast Asia and south China. The plains and the highlands of north Vietnam, one of the most important original sites of the Dong Son culture, is also the area that Dong Son drums have been discovered in greatest quantity and density. The widespread distribution of these drums in Southeast Asia suggests trading networks yet to be fully understood and the transfer of technology among cultures of the region that still has to be researched.

Dong Son drums exhibit the advanced techniques and great skill that were needed to cast large objects by the *cire perdue* (lost-wax) method. Some drums required one to seven tons of smelted copper ore used in conjunction with up to ten large casting crucibles to manufacture. These drums display an artistic level that few cultures of the time could rival. [RE]

▷ see BRONZE BLADE
▷ see TRIPOD VESSEL

Earrings

This pair of earrings in gold is an unusual reminder of a design and custom of adornment around the beginning of the Common Era.

The earrings are made with sheet gold, embossed and granulated, and the two sides have been soldered together at the inner and outer edges. There are no hinges, thus the wearer must have slid them through wide openings in the earlobes.

As can be observed from Sunga and Kushana period sculptures, many *yaksha* (male vegetation spirits) and *yakshi* (female vegetation spirits) are adorned with ornaments for the ears, neck and wrists. The use of beads and pearls, along with precious metals such as gold and silver, suggests the importance of jewellery in the fashion of the day, and the symbolic meaning and uses of some of these ornaments. They were not simply decorative in purpose but had a social, religious and economic significance.

Stylistically, these earrings have parallels with sculptural art in which detailed jewellery and drapery are depicted. We can connect these pairs to Sunga and Kushana sculptures as well as to those found on stupas such as Sanchi and Mathura of the Buddhist period (▶ see YAKSHI CAPITAL DEPICTING FOUR SHALABHANJIKA). Since ancient gold objects are rare, as they are often melted to fashion new ornaments, this pair fortunately gives us an understanding of the design and technology in jewellery making and the use of ornaments in ancient societies on the Indian subcontinent.[1] [GPK]

A PAIR OF EARRINGS
Kushana, northwest India
1st century
Gold
3.5 x 3.5 cm
2000.350

Eight Immortals on Hanging

This hanging depicts the Eight Immortals in the Kunlun mountains. Seven of the immortals are standing on the terrace, with the eighth, the lame beggar immortal, Iron Crutch Li or Li Tieguai, on the bridge with a crutch in his hand and a tiger near him. The seven immortals on the terrace are (FROM TOP TO BOTTOM) Lü Dongbin, with a sword on his back; the young boy Lan Caihe holding a basket of flowers; pot-bellied Han Zhongli holding a fan; Zhang Guolao holding a unique musical instrument; Han Xiangzi blowing a flute; Cao Guojiu holding castanets; and the female immortal, He Xiangu, standing next to the God of Longevity with his oversized cranium. In the upper left hand corner, the Queen Mother of the West is flying on a phoenix. Another Daoist and folk saint, Liu Haichan, is on the lower left of the hanging with his toad.

This hanging is filled with auspicious symbols, mostly alluding to longevity: the Queen Mother of the West, immortals, cranes, the stylised *shou* (longevity) character (the top central medallion), peaches and the Kunlun mountains. The appearance of Liu Haichan and a deer, both representing wealth, adds to the auspicious meanings contained in this hanging. Hence the hanging could have been used for birthday celebrations.

Immortality is the ultimate aspiration in the Daoist tradition. Immortals are beings who defy the natural process of ageing and are believed to possess other supernatural powers which allow them to heal the sick, predict the future, and transform themselves, others and

the objects around them. The individual legends of the Eight Immortals appeared in literati sources in the Tang and Song dynasties, but they only appeared as a single collective group in the Yuan dynasty. Even then, the composition of the group was volatile and it was only in the late Ming dynasty that the Eight Immortals as we know them now came to be. The popularity of the Eight Immortals cuts across social strata and age, and is based largely on their colourful characters as well as acts of upholding justice and rescuing the distressed. [ST]

EIGHT IMMORTALS ON HANGING
China
Ming dynasty, c. 1600
Silk, *kesi* (tapestry textile)
224 x 172 cm
On loan from Mr Christopher J. Hall
CH 47

Europeans Visiting the Vishnupada Temple

This painting depicts the famous Vishnupada temple in Gaya, an important Hindu pilgrimage centre associated with last rites (conducted at the time of death) and *shraddha* (death rituals conducted annually). Most Hindus will visit this pilgrimage centre at least once in their lifetime to perform death rites for their ancestors, particularly for their parents. This painting illustrates the renovated temple during the reign of Ahilyabai Holkar (reign. 1766–1795) who commemorated and renovated many dilapidated temples all over India; the Vishnupada temple is one of those associated with her.

The juxtaposition of the curious visiting European community and this important pilgrimage site is particularly strange. Interestingly, the India Office Library (now part of The British Library in London) refers to an almost identical painting in which the Europeans are excluded. The Vishnupada temple is also mentioned in another painting from our collection (◗ see PAINTING DEPICTING SHRINES TO LORD SHIVA). That painting, which is about 200 years older, represents Vishnupada in a schematic manner and refers also to a *shraddha* ceremony.

Colonial paintings contain a highly eclectic blend of Indian and European styles, revealing an element of realism adapted from European paintings. Many Indian artists flourished at centres such as Patna, Murshidabad and Lucknow, and painted subject matters requested by their European patrons. These subject matters usually related to important sites, professions and costumes of people of India, their festivals and their flora and fauna. The paintings were bound in portfolio albums which were then either seen as they were or published in the form of a book when sent back to Europe. [GPK]

EUROPEANS VISITING THE VISHNUPADA TEMPLE
Patna or Murshidabad, India
Colonial period, 19th century
Paper and pigment
(WITH FRAME) 74.8 x 66.5 cm, (WITHOUT FRAME) 52.2 x 45.2 cm
2000.5586

Famille Noire Dish

This dish, dated to the Guangxu period with its six-character reign mark on its base, is painted with polychrome enamels against a black ground, hence the term 'famille noire'. The black enamel was obtained by applying a copper-green lead-based enamel over an unfired layer of Chinese cobalt[1] and then fired. Black dots and lines are used to distinguish between the darker and lighter areas, and also to outline the birds and plants. Other enamels used are green, white and yellow. The green enamels range from lime green to pastel green and emerald green, and are used to highlight different parts of the plants. Emerald green is also blended with yellow to give the birds a more three-dimensional effect. The main decorative motifs seen here are the pine, prunus and bamboo, which form the 'Three Friends of Winter' (suihan sanyou). These evergreen plants are celebrated for their immutability and strength.

Famille noire porcelain was first produced during Kangxi's reign, although a similar black enamel was already in use during Chenghua's reign. The popularity of famille noire porcelain grew during the 18th and 19th centuries—not only did it gain favour with Empress Dowager Cixi (1835–1908), it was also much sought after in America and Europe. [WHL]

FAMILLE NOIRE DISH WITH
THE THREE FRIENDS OF WINTER
Jingdezhen, China
Qing dynasty, Guangxu period
Ceramic
h. 5.3 cm, diam. 28 cm
1998.52

(TOP) **DETAIL**
Guangxu six-character reign mark on the base of the dish

Famille Rose Dish

This fine large dish with a six-character Yongzheng reign mark in a double circle is decorated in the *famille rose* or *'fencai'* style. The term *famille rose* was coined by Europeans, and refers to an enamel palette in which opaque pink is the predominant colour among a palette of colours. Opaque pink is the result of mixing translucent pink, made from dispersing crushed rubies in a clear enamel base, with opaque white.[2]

This dish owes its beauty to the effective combination of soft and delicate hues, and the bright and bold colours of the chrysanthemums and leaves. A combination of overglaze blue, opaque yellow[3] and white enamels painted on two small butterflies complements the flowers, while the biggest butterfly, painted in subtle brown tones, dominates this tranquil scene.

Another feature of this dish that is noteworthy and interesting is the continuation of decoration—the flowering chrysanthemums sprout from the foot ring and extend over the rim to the centre of the dish.

The technical virtuosity of the *famille rose* palette was achieved in Jingdezhen, towards the end of Kangxi's reign. However, most of the delicately painted *famille rose* porcelain were produced during Yongzheng's reign.

It has been suggested that Jesuit missionaries introduced the pink enamel used in Europe to the Chinese potters in the early 18th century, for Western glassmakers were already familiar with the technique of creating it. While the Chinese potters might have borrowed this pink enamel, scientific analysis showed that they readapted by reducing the gold and tin contents in the enamel. It is also believed that the Chinese potters borrowed both the opaque white and opaque yellow from the Chinese cloisonné enamels. The 18th century was definitely a period of experimentation for the kilns in Jingdezhen. [WHL]

FAMILLE ROSE DISH WITH BUTTERFLIES AND
FLOWERING CHRYSANTHEMUMS
Jingdezhen, China
Qing dynasty, Yongzheng period
Ceramic
h. 8.8 cm, diam. 50 cm
Gift of Mr Saiman Ernawan
1999.448

Festival Badge

Court servants of the imperial palace were decreed to wear uniforms of prescribed materials with specific badges to mark the change of season. However, during the Ming and Qing dynasties the emperor's birthday was probably the only time the courtiers were allowed to wear clothes of their own choice. This squarish badge *(buzi)*, featuring a mirror-image of a lone peach tree endowed with an abundance of blossoms and the character *shou* (longevity), was therefore very likely part of a festive garment worn by a member of the imperial family for a birthday celebration.

All the images here are auspicious symbols, specially assembled to mark the occasion: the peach blossoms signify the arrival of spring, as well as the fruit of longevity which the tree bears; the cloud scrolls mark the realm of heaven and promises of rain and moisture for the beginning of the agricultural cycle; the waves are a symbol of the dragon's abode, and hence the imperial power; and the seaweed is an aspiration for stability and continuity of the ruler's reign. The peach blossoms suggest that the celebration was very likely for a female imperial member. On the other hand, it was customary for a deceased person to be buried with, or clothed in, garments embellished with auspicious symbols associated with longevity to indicate the good life that had been enjoyed.

A palette rich in gold and warm hues had been deliberately chosen to give the various auspicious motifs on the badge a lovely shimmer, while the polychrome features sprinkled around the badge added texture to the entire garment, which was likely to be heavily embellished with gold materials. [LCL]

EMBROIDERED FESTIVAL BADGE WITH THE CHARACTER *SHOU*
China
Ming dynasty, Wanli period
Silk, gold thread, embroidery
34.5 x 36.5 cm
On loan from the Collection of Jobrenco Trust
CH18 (S2)

Filial Piety Scenes on Funerary Stele

This is a funerary stele with four scenes illustrating filial piety and ancestor worship. The narratives are carved in intaglio, suggesting the stele was probably found in the tomb of a nobleman. The first scene (BELOW, LEFT), depicts the story of a filial son, Guo Ju, who tries to save his mother from starvation by burying his only son alive. A tree divides the pictorial schema, allowing two consecutive scenes to be depicted within one frame. On the right appears Guo Ju's aged mother who sits with a bowl in her hand. Guo Ju kneels before her to pay his respects while his wife and son stand between them. On the left, Guo Ju stands before the grave he has dug for his son and discovers gold bestowed upon him by the Heavens, who have been moved by his filial act. One of the earliest mentions of the story of Guo Ju was by a Han scholar, Liu Xiang (77–6 BCE) in his *Book on Filial Sons* (▶ see LIENÜZHUAN). This story was later canonised as one of the Twenty-Four Paragons of Filial Piety. The same story of Guo Ju appears on two similar slabs belonging to the Nelson-Atkins Museum of Art, Kansas City and the Minneapolis Institute of Art.

The second scene (BELOW, RIGHT) is of a nobleman riding a horse that is led by a groom. Two servants shelter the nobleman with a parasol. The third scene (OPPOSITE, LEFT) shows a gentleman seated on a canopied throne, enjoying a small feast laid before him. He

FUNERARY STELE ILLUSTRATING FILIAL PIETY
China
Six Dynasties
Stone
(ENTIRE PANEL OF FOUR SCENES) 76 x 163 x 2.7 cm
1995.2507

is flanked by four attendants, two on each side. An inscription identifies the scene as a banquet dedicated to the deceased, who is most probably the figure depicted here and to whom this funerary stele is dedicated. The last scene (BELOW, RIGHT) illustrates a scene from the daily life of the nobility with four female attendants holding either a fan or a lotus in their hands.

All four scenes depicted in this funerary stele allude to the wealth and status of the deceased—the servants and horse he possessed, the banquet and the canopied throne suggest he was most probably not of common birth. On the other hand, they could also suggest the commissioner's princely bestowment on the deceased in the afterlife. Regardless, both express the patron's filial piety in honouring his ancestor with an idealised construction of the latter's posthumous world.

This emphasis on filial piety reflects the stronghold of Confucian values in Chinese society since the Han dynasty. Described by Confucius (551–479 BCE) as the foundation of all virtues and the fountainhead from which all moral teachings spring, the application of filial piety was expanded to become a key regulating principle in social and political relationships throughout Chinese history. [ST]

Finger Bowls

These two silver bowls come from the Riau-Lingga Archipelago and what was once the Johor-Riau Sultanate. The first bowl (BELOW, LEFT) has an interesting ten-sided design and a round base. The bowl is decorated with a repoussé floral border and has a large central figure on the bottom. This bowl is reported to have been the property of a Raja Nong from Riau. The second bowl (BELOW, RIGHT) is of a somewhat simpler design, again with floral and vegetal decorations. Both bowls were probably used for a variety of purposes although their primary use was most likely as finger bowls.

Historically, Southeast Asia had very limited natural sources of silver so trade was an important way in which silver was acquired. At the peak of the trade boom of the 16th century, well over 100 tons of silver a year, mostly from Japan and the New World, were brought to Southeast Asia in exchange for the exotic spices and jungle products that made the region famous. Much of this silver became an important store of wealth for Southeast Asian rulers who had it made into luxury items such as jewellery and decorative items. The ability of individual rulers to tap into the very valuable Southeast Asian trade could lead to the control of great wealth and prestige.

Like many of the important historical centres of Southeast Asia, Riau produced few commodities of its own. However, Riau's location at the entrance to the Straits of Malacca made it a key trade location particularly during the 18th century. The rulers of Riau generated extraordinary wealth by providing harbour facilities and a safe haven for traders doing business in Southeast Asia. The traders in turn transformed this wealth into a rich material heritage of which these two bowls are a small reminder. [DAH]

FINGER BOWLS
Riau-Lingga Archipelago, Indonesia
19th century
Silver
(ABOVE) h. 4.3 cm, diam. 8.5 cm;
(RIGHT) h. 4.5 cm, diam. 9.9 cm
S0114, S0371

Finial

This bronze finial depicts a *makara* issuing forth a *naga* (mythical serpent) whose head and tail are grasped by the mythical Garuda. Garuda supports on his shoulders the four-armed figure of Vishnu. Vishnu's attributes, though unclear, appear to include the conch which he holds in his upper left hand, and a mace held in the lower right hand. The pair also appear in carved stone monuments such as the lintels of the Angkor period, in which Vishnu is usually seen crouching or seated on the shoulders of Garuda, surrounded by *naga* and foliage. Images of this type have been interpreted as Vishnu advancing with his left leg forward, into battle, and Garuda with the torso of a man and arms with wings spread out, taking flight.[4]

Vishnu, one of the three main Hindu gods, was reincarnated to save the world. He became the patron deity during the reign of Suryavarman II from 1113 to 1145, whose temple, Angkor Wat, was dedicated to Vishnu. The dynamic image of Vishnu on Garuda (also known as Garudasanamurti) became popular during this period, when it is thought that small images were made for use on domestic altars.[5] Bronzes also served among the metalware fittings employed on chariots, flagstaffs and other accessories for royal processions.[6]

The 13th-century Chinese emissary Zhou Daguan, who was sent to live in Angkor by the Mongols, observed the use of many ornamental metalware accessories for palanquins and parasols during royal processions.[7] They can also be seen on the carved reliefs at Angkor Wat. [HT]

CHARIOT FINIAL OF VISHNU RIDING ON GARUDA
Cambodia
Bayon period, 12th–13th centuries
Bronze
7.1 x 3.4 x 3.4 cm
1997.3353

Firman of Sultan Abdülhamid II

This document is a *firman* (*ferman* in Turkish, imperial decree) of Ottoman Sultan Abdülhamid II (reign. 1876–1909) and is beautifully written in *celi divani* script. This script was developed in the 16th century by the Ottoman administration for official documents. *Celi divani* (*jali diwani* in Arabic) is not easy to read or write—letters are linked and the spaces between them ornamented with dots and markings. It was believed that the script, being tightly written, would make it difficult for words to be inserted into the official documents or for documents to be forged.

Above the main text of this *firman* is the *tuğra* (calligraphic emblem) of Abdülhamid II which is rendered in gold ink. The *tuğra* is composed of the names of the sultan and his father—thus, Sultan Abdülhamid, son of Abdülmecid—followed by the set phrase, 'the ever victorious'. It serves as a state seal confirming that the sultan has issued this document. By the side of the *tuğra* is the word *alghazi* (Champion of Islam), which is an epithet used by Abdülhamid. It is possible that the *tuğra* here was designed by the great calligrapher, Sami Efendi (1838–1912), who lived through the reign of six sultans and designed the *tuğra* of three. It was not usual for calligraphers to sign off their work on state documents.

The *firman* was issued to recognise the promotion of Mehmed Tawfiq Pasha on the 13th day of the month of Safr (tenth month in the Islamic calendar) in the year AH 1311/July 1893 CE. The text is written in alternating lines of black and gold *celi divani* which have been done in such a way that they resemble galleons. The use of gold and the overall elegance and impressiveness of the document indicate that the recipient holds an important post. The leaf-like inscription at the bottom indicates the place in which the *firman* was issued—'written in the protected and guarded city of Constantinople'. Constantinople (Istanbul) was the capital of the Ottoman Empire since 1453, when Mehmed II captured the city from the Byzantines. [TH]

FIRMAN OF SULTAN ABDÜLHAMID II
Turkey
AH 1311/July 1893 CE
Ink and gold on paper
131.5 x 68 cm
On loan from the Tareq Rajab Museum, Kuwait
TR43

Folio from a Maghribi Qur'an

This leaf comes from a 20-part Qur'an, and is written in large brown Maghribi script with illuminated verse endings. On this page, the end of the verses are indicated by three gold dots and the verse count is indicated by a medallion containing the *abjad* letters. The *abjad* system is one where each Arabic letter is given a numerical value. The top right medallion of this page, for example, contains the letter *'alif'*, which has the numerical value of 1, to indicate that this is the first verse of a chapter. The Qur'anic text shown on this page features verses 1 to 4 of *Surat Al-Takwir* (The Folding Up).

What is unusual about this Qur'an is that it is written on paper. Why would the use of paper be unusual? As early as the 11th century, paper was the main writing material used for copying Qur'ans in the eastern part of the Islamic world. Calligraphers in North Africa and Al-Andalus (Islamic Spain), however, were more conservative and continued using parchment to copy the Divine Word until the 14th century.

This peachy pink paper is believed to have been dyed in Jativa, a town known for paper production, located south of Valencia. The use of dyed paper, the high quality of the writing and the elaborate verse ornaments indicate to us that this luxurious Qur'an was probably made for an official or for a member of a princely family from one of the Spanish cities such as Granada or Valencia. [TH]

▶ see KITAB AL-SHIHAB
▶ see KUFIC-ABBASID QUR'AN FOLIO

MAGHRIBI QUR'AN FOLIO
Islamic Spain
13th century
Ink, colours and gold on paper
33.8 x 26.2 cm
1999.797

Foundation Stone

Three lines of elegant *thulth* script with long verticals and star designs are carved on this marble foundation stone, which also has traces of coloured paint surrounding the borders of the inscription. The inscription on the stone records the building of a mosque in India during the reign of the Tughluq ruler Firuz Shah in the Muslim month of Muharram in AH 775/July 1373 CE. The inscription begins with the *basmalah* (In the Name of God, The Gracious and the Merciful) followed by a Qur'anic verse from the *Surat al-Jinn* (The Spirits), which reads, 'And the places of worship are for Allah [alone]; So invoke not anyone along with Allah'. This is an appropriate verse to commemorate the building of a mosque, particularly as Muslims were ruling a predominantly Hindu population in India.

The Tughluq rulers were known for their building activities, especially during the rule of Firuz Shah, who did so as an expression of his devotion to Islam. During the period of his reign, there was overall prosperity in the land, which enabled other wealthy patrons such as his viziers, and also merchants to endow the building of religious institutions.

All over the Islamic world, the building of mosques is considered a particularly pious and meritorious act. Usually the mosques were built as *waqf* (endowments) and it was usual for various estates to be part of the endowments so that the revenue generated from these estates would go towards the maintenance of the mosques. [TH]

▶ see MIHRAB TILE
▶ see QASIDAT AL-BURDAH

FOUNDATION STONE
Probably Gujarat, west India
15 Muharram AH 775/7 July 1373 CE
Marble
61 x 137 cm
2000.5626

Fragments from a Minbar

These wooden panels are fragments from one side of a *minbar*, which is the stepped pulpit found in a mosque. The pieces shown here are carved in very bold curvilinear designs. The panel on the left shows traces of green paint, while the other panels have some elements highlighted in silver and gold paint.

Performing the *salat* (five obligatory prayers) is one of the pillars of Islam. While this act of worship can be fulfilled at home or anywhere that is clean, Muslims are encouraged to pray together. The Qur'an also enjoins all male Muslims to perform the Friday midday prayers in congregation. Such prayers have been held in mosques from the earliest times in the Islamic world. During the Friday prayers, a *khutbah* (sermon) would be read from the *minbar*, which is usually placed to the right of the *mihrab* (prayer niche).

The *minbar* is thus an important feature of mosque architecture. This feature has existed since the time of Prophet Muhammad. The Prophet had a *minbar* made of wood, with two steps and a chair so that his sermons could be heard easily by the congregation.

Some scholars have also suggested that the *minbar* possibly served as a seat of honour for the Prophet, as the leader of the Muslim community. After the death of the Prophet, the *minbar* was used by rulers as a symbol of authority. Indeed, formal mention of their names during the *khutbah* was important to legitimise their claim to leadership.

Most *minbar*, like the one here, are made of wood, perhaps recalling the Prophet's choice of material. There are, however, examples of *minbar* made from stone, brick and even mud. [TH]

▶ see MIHRAB TILE

***MINBAR* FRAGMENTS**
Turkey
19th–20th centuries
Walnut wood
290 x 320 cm
1997.3490

Funan Female Deity

This carved image of a standing female deity is extremely weathered, probably the result of having lain in the wet plains of the Mekong Delta for many centuries. However the still visible upper torso, facial features and hair in a knot at the top of the head suggest that this was once an elegantly carved form. Carbon dating indicates that the piece was made around the 5th century.

The kingdom of Funan was one of the earliest wet rice kingdoms in Southeast Asia. Local legends recount the intermarriage of a visiting Brahman named Kaundinya with a local *naga* (mythical serpent) princess, and their child became the first king of Funan. Chinese chronicles suggest that Funan emerged during the 1st century.[8] Situated in the Mekong Delta, it thrived on the entrepôt trade at the port of Oc Eo, which was brought into the region by Indian and other merchants. They travelled overland across the Isthmus of Kra during the early centuries. However by the 5th century Oc Eo began to decline as the Malacca Straits became the main trade route.

It is unclear whether Hinduism or Buddhism was first adopted in the region. A Chinese text from the 3rd century mentions that there was a population of around 1,000 Brahmans living in a kingdom in the Malay Peninsula who were vassals to Funan.[9] By the 5th and 6th centuries, inscriptions, religious iconography and Chinese annals point to the coexistence of Hinduism and Buddhism. Chinese texts describe Funan as a centre for Buddhism which received Indian missionaries with religious texts. Funanese monks also travelled to China where they translated Sanskrit texts into Chinese.[10] Paramartha was one such Indian missionary who travelled to China via Funan in 546. He was a follower of the Yogacara school, a branch of Mahayana Buddhism.[11]

It is thought that Hinayana Buddhism prevailed at Funan, in which homage to the Three Jewels (the Buddha, the Dharma and the Sangha), images of the Buddha and holy relics were of prime importance. However Funan royalty also worshipped Vishnu and Shiva, and Hinduism together with indigenous beliefs became the state religion.[12] Today Theravada is the main form of Buddhism practised in south Vietnam while Mahayana Buddhism predominates in the north. [HT]

CARVED FIGURE OF A DEITY
Reportedly from the Mekong Delta, Vietnam
c. 5th century
Wood
79 x 19.5 x 9 cm
1999.122

Gamelan

A gamelan is a percussive ensemble of bronze gongs and drums, as well as several other types of instruments which are all tuned to the same tones. The name 'gamelan' literally refers to the action ('*an*') of hammering ('*gamel*') by striking the bronze instruments with beaters. This large gamelan comprises two groups of instruments which are tuned according to the seven-tone *pelog* scale and the five-tone *slendro* scale.

The gongs include the most important and the largest, *gong ageng*, the smaller *kempul*, and sets of kettle-gongs known as *kenong* and *bonang*. Instruments with keys, such as the *saron*, have bronze keys mounted on wooden resonators. These play the main melody and are accompanied by softer instruments such as the *celempung* (zither), the *suling* (bamboo flute) and the *rebab* (two-stringed violin). Percussion is provided by several *kendhang* (drums) of varying size and pitch.

The history of the Javanese court arts can be traced back to at least the time of the early Hindu Buddhist kingdoms of central Java. The origins of bronze instruments are obscure although the Dong Son style bronze drums that may have been introduced from the mainland are the earliest evidence of bronze instruments in Indonesia. Many similar types of instruments can be found depicted in wall reliefs of temples and other religious monuments of the 8th century and onwards.[1]

JAVANESE GAMELAN INSTRUMENTS
(ABOVE) *Gong ageng*
(NEXT PAGE, FROM TOP) *Saron, gender* and *bonang*
(FOLLOWING PAGE, FROM TOP) *Suling, celempung* and *kendhang*
Yogyakarta, Java, Indonesia
Probably mid 20th century
Bronze, wood
2000.8148.1–6, 2000.8167.1–8, 2000.8154, 2000.8168.1–11
2000.8196.1–4, 2000.8185.1–2, 2000.8194.1–3

Belief in the spiritual potency of the gamelan produces great respect for the instruments, particularly the gongs which are made by the most experienced of forgers, who undertake the spiritually dangerous work of forging molten bronze into instruments. Many gamelans have a name and are honoured with offerings from time to time. The name of this set, 'Ngambar Arum' or 'Golden Fragrance', is inscribed inside the *gong ageng*. Respect is also expressed through the musicians' etiquette, such as the removal of footwear and the avoidance of stepping over the instruments. It is also believed that greater refinement of character develops through the process of playing in the correct manner.

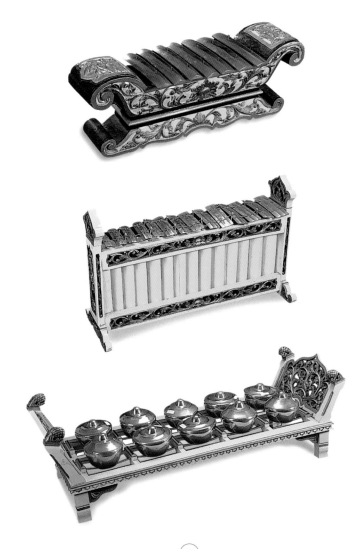

The sonorous quality of gamelan music contributes to the *halus* (refined) nature of Javanese court culture, where the gamelan remains part of the *pusaka* (heirlooms) to be played by court musicians. Although gamelan music also remains very much a part of village life, the wide-reaching effects of the music-recording industry has resulted in the use of recorded music in many areas, as well as the development of new compositions and modern electronic pop adaptations that have popular appeal. [HT]

Gandhara Stupa

This stupa is set on a square base with three circular tiers surmounted by an *anda* (hemispherical dome). The tiers are delineated in a lattice pattern with supporting brackets, while the centre of the dome supports a five-tiered *chatra* (umbrella). This is a miniature votive stupa dedicated by a Buddhist monk, nun or lay worshipper to a monastery or a *chaitya* (worship hall).[2] Some miniature stupas also contain relics in small caskets under the dome. This stupa contains carvings of Buddha in *dhyanasana* (meditation posture) flanked by a disciple on either side (SEE DETAIL, OPPOSITE). Both the style of carving and the inclusion of the disciples indicate that this stupa was constructed in the late Kushana period when the iconography of the Buddha image was well defined.

When Gautama Buddha died, he was cremated and his ashes and relics were distributed among his disciples. With a few relics as the core, commemorative mounds were constructed at places such as Kushinagara, Kapisa, Vaishali and Sarnath. At Sanchi the relics of Buddha's foremost disciples, Sariputra and Maudaglayana, were kept. In Peshawar stupas were built over Buddha's begging bowl and other articles he used. Thus stupas can be of many types: *sharirika* are built over his relics; *paribhogika* are built over articles he used; *uddeshika* are those that commemorate his nirvana. Votives such as this artefact were dedicated by pilgrims when visiting sacred sites to attain religious merit.[3] In west Indian Buddhist cave temples, as well as in the Gandhara region, innumerable stupas which contained the holy relics of Buddhist teachers were constructed or carved in different shapes.

GANDHARA STUPA
Gandhara or Mathura, India
Kushana period, 3rd–4th centuries
Sandstone
56.6 x 30 x 29.5 cm
1994.508

(OPPOSITE) **DETAIL**
Carving of Buddha in *dhyanasana*

Worshippers generally circumambulate architectural stupas contemplating the *parinirvana* (Great Demise of Buddha). There were many stupas erected in the open air or under wooden structures that have now disappeared. Stupas are generally placed at the end of the nave in the centre of a *chaitya*, with a path to enable people to walk around it. They are often decorated with relief sculptures depicting flowers, garlands, dance and music which suggest rejoicing and veneration. Many Buddhist sites built during the Ashokan (c. 272–231 BCE) and later Mauryan periods have survived and were carried on through the Sunga, Kushana, Satavahana, Gandhara and Gupta periods. A typical Buddhist architecture had developed by the Gupta period: *chaitya* enshrined the stupas and *vihara* (living quarters for monks) were attached to them, and together they formed centres of monastic learning. Ajanta and Ellora are two famous sites (4th–9th centuries) in Maharashtra which have self-contained clusters of Buddhist monastic architecture located close to the *dakshinapatha* (southern trade route) that attracted many students and visitors in the ancient and medieval periods. [GPK]

Seated Ganesha

This seated image of the elephant-headed pot-bellied deity, Ganesha, from Halebid, originally comes from a Hindu temple where it was placed near the entrance. Ganesha is believed to be a remover of obstacles, so he is offered worship before one embarks on any new task. Here, he is shown carrying his attributes: an axe, a tooth, a tender plant and a bowl of sweetmeats (Ganesha is particularly fond of sweets). A serpent adorns Ganesha as a girdle while beaded ornaments bejewel his body. The figure of Ganesha is very bulky and he is precariously balanced on his two short legs.

This sculpture is carved in schist and has very intricate carvings of jewels, necklaces, a garland, crown and *jatabhara*. Paying great attention to decorative elements is a feature of sculptures of the Hoysala period (12th–14th centuries).

The cult of Ganesha, or Ganapati, came to be known only in the later part of the Gupta period, around the 6th century. As Vighnaraja (King of Obstacles), Vighna-vinasha (Remover of Obstacles) and Siddhidata (Bestower of Success), he is to be propitiated as is mentioned in the Vedic literature. Subsequently Ganesha became associated with Shiva: as the leader of Shiva's *gana* (host of warriors) and as the son of Shiva and Parvati, although another view holds that he is the son of Parvati alone.

Texts such as the *Vishnudharmottara* and *Rupamandana*[4] mention many iconographic representations of Ganesha with his *vahana* (mount)—a mouse—and with his consorts Saraswati (Goddess of Learning), Sri (Goddess of Wealth), Buddhi and Kubuddhi (Goddesses of Good and Evil Intentions). Many forms of Ganesha are known such as Bala (Infant) Ganesha, Taruna (Youthful) Ganesha, Shakti (Consort) Ganesha and Nrtya (Dancing) Ganesha. There is an image of Dancing Ganesha in our collection (▶ see DANCING GANESHA). An amusing aspect of Ganesha's imagery is the fact that he is represented as a rotund and endearing God even though he is feared and propitiated to mitigate his wrath. [GPK]

SEATED GANESHA
Halebid, Karnataka, south India
12th century
Schist
105 x 55 x 35 cm
On loan from the Archaeological Survey of India, Government of India
346

Garuda Headdress

This Garuda headdress from Kutai in Borneo dates to the 1920s and is crafted from gold repoussé panels fashioned together to form a crown. It was worn with complementary ornaments suspended at the sides and back. This headdress was most likely a part of the wedding costume for an aristocratic lady or one of high status in Kutai.

This headdress also reflects the strong influence of Indianised culture in Southeast Asia. In Hindu cosmology, Garuda is the mount (*vahana* in Sanskrit) of the deity Vishnu and is referred to as the Bird of Life. Garuda's continued popularity as a symbol across Southeast Asia gives some indication of the popularity of Vishnu during the Indianised period.

An inscription found on a *yupa* (sacrificial pole) dated to about the year 400 suggests that the state of Kutai was perhaps the site of Southeast Asia's earliest Indianised kingdoms. It is no wonder then that Hindu deities such as Garuda are an important part of Kutai's material culture even after its conversion to Islam in the 16th century. [DAH]

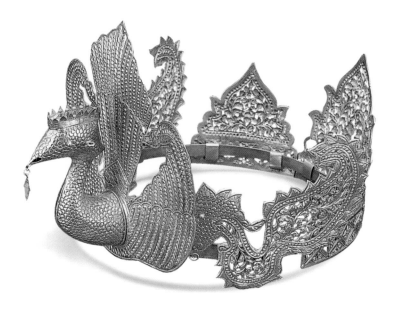

GARUDA HEADDRESS
Kutai, east coast of Borneo
1920s
Gold
15 x 17 cm
Gift of Mr Edmond Chin
EC139A

The Gateway

On entering the Medieval India gallery, you will encounter a large gateway which is as tall as it is wide. The gateway was specially assembled after hours of careful study, discussion and conservation, and when walking through it, you will experience the spatial feel of a traditional arched entrance to a 250-year-old building in a town in north India.

This structure, which is almost square, is made of different blocks of stone. There are two arches arranged one in front of the other, with the cusped outer arch, held together by two floral piers and a lintel made from several blocks of stone, on the inner single point arch. The style of this façade was developed in post-Shah Jahan period architecture.[5] The floral spandrels of the cusped outer arch form the biggest part of the arch. They support

each other by abutments, one on either side. This is not a true arch and there is no keystone holding the arch in place; it is, instead, supported by an interlocking system, and according to Dr R. Nath, 'The stones were chiseled like sculpture and assembled in situ.'[6] Traditional engineering still prevails in India, and the local masons applied their traditional knowledge of stone masonry and building construction to the buildings in Agra and Delhi constructed by the mighty Mughals. It is amazing how mortar-less architecture has withstood the ravages of time for centuries. A case in point is the Fatehpur Sikri buildings from the Akbar period (1572–1585).

The pinkish stone from which this gateway is constructed was quarried at Tantpur, Bansi-Paharpur, Karauli and Fatehpur Sikri, or what is also known as the Vraja area between east Rajasthan and west Uttar Pradesh, according to Dr Nath. The colour and texture of this stone is characteristic of the stone from this region, and many buildings from the Akbar period, such as the Fatehpur Sikri, have been built there with similar stones.

The gateway is decorated with a repeating *guldasta* motif (flower vases with floral plants). The lintel has a blank central panel. The two piers also bear blank *alaya* (niches) on either side that were used for special occasions, such as the birth of a son or a marriage, when *thape* (handprints) were placed in them. Lighted lamps were placed in them during festivals such as Deepavali. All this strongly suggests that this gate comes from the *haveli* (mansion) of a Hindu nobleman from the Vraja region, and not from an Islamic building, as believed by the museum for a long time. [GPK]

THE GATEWAY
West Uttar Pradesh or east Rajasthan, Vraja area, north India
Post-Shah Jahan period, late 17th to early 18th century
Pink sandstone
Purchased with funds donated by Ronald Ooi
350 x 365 x 70 cm
1995.11097

Gauri Mask

This mask depicts the face of Gauri, another name for Parvati. Her headgear and ear ornaments clearly indicate that the sculpture is depicted in the Marathi style. Such a mask is perhaps used for the Ganesh Chaturthi Festival. This festival is celebrated for a period of ten days from August to September. During the festival women perform a fertility rite by installing images of Gauri similar to this one on mounds of grain which are dressed up as married women.

Parvati is the mother of Lord Ganesha and in several parts of India—especially Maharashtra and Karnataka—she is worshipped during the Ganesh Chaturthi Festival. She is associated with fertility and prosperity and women worship her to ensure the longevity of their husbands.

This mask is made with a mould casting and engraving technique and is hollow from the back. [GPK]

▶ see SEATED GANESHA

GAURI MASK
Maharashtra, India
19th century
Brass
40 x 23 cm
1995.899

Gem-set Chinese Porcelain for Turkish Market

What is interesting about this porcelain bowl is that the bowl is of Chinese origin while the jewelled decoration on its body is of Turkish origin, having only been added on in Ottoman Turkey. The interior of the bowl has underglazed cobalt blue decorations while the exterior has gilded floral designs on a dark brownish-red glaze which has since rubbed off. There are four characters at the foot of this bowl: *chang ming fu gui*, which means 'long life and wealth'. This bowl is an example of a ware exported from China known as *kinrande* or 'gold brocade' in Japanese. These wares were highly prized in Japan.

For the exterior decoration, emeralds are set on gilt copper mounts, which are connected by thin gold wires to form a design. A ring-shaped groove is cut into the bowl's surface, scraping off the glaze within the circle in the process before the copper mounts are forced into the recess. This is evidently not a very lasting arrangement as some stones have fallen off.

Chinese porcelain was very much admired in the Islamic world and was imported in large quantities to the Ottoman palace from the 16th century onwards.[7] Today the majority of porcelain with jewelled mounts is found only in the Topkapı Palace in Istanbul.[8] It is believed that this style of decorating porcelain was done by palace artisans and was derived from the mounting of jewels onto metals such as zinc as well as hard stones such as jade. Porcelain was probably considered a hard stone—the majority of the Chinese porcelain with jewelled mounts in the Topkapı Palace Collection date from the second half of the 16th century, and are mostly blue and white ware. There is, however, a very small group of jewelled mounted *kinrande* ware, like the piece shown here. [TH]

▶ see KRAAK PORCELAIN

GEM-SET CHINESE PORCELAIN FOR TURKISH MARKET
(BOWL) China; (MOUNT) Turkey
Late 16th century
Emerald, gilt copper on porcelain
h. 6 cm, diam. 11.7 cm
1999.1405

Guangong

This figure of Guangong wears an asymmetrical robe which exposes his right arm. The robe is an official attire for military generals attending formal functions. The figure sits in a forbidding pose on a horseshoe-backed chair. The details on his attire, accessories and chair show the finest workmanship of the Ming dynasty.

'Guangong' is actually an honorific title given to a historical figure who lived in the Three Kingdoms period (220–280). Guangong was born in Jie county in Hedong province as Guan Yunchang, and is also known as Guanyu. Guanyu was said to have been deified as early as the Southern dynasties (317–589). As a god, he is loved by all levels of society, throughout the centuries, with his cult reaching a peak in the late Ming and early Qing dynasties. The popular appeal of Guangong was enough reason for both Buddhism and Daoism to appropriate and incorporate him into their traditions and pantheon. His functions thus varied through time and according to context.

The figure here represents a Buddhist manifestation of Guangong. Here he is known as Qie Lanshen, or Bodhisattva Sangharama, a protector of the dharma (Buddhist law) since the Sui-Tang dynasties (589–907). In the Buddhist tradition he plays a guardian role with his military counterpart, Wei Tuo (Skanda), usually protecting Guanyin (Avalokiteshvara).

During the Wanli period, Guangong was

known as Guan Sanlang, and was considered a terrifying spirit who ensured the incorruptibility of monks, albeit a strange and limited role. Guangong was still very much feared in the Tang dynasty; it was recorded that a visit by him would result in a high fever. His influence took a turn in the Song dynasty when he became regarded as a wealth god because he was believed to bring rain when there was a drought and sunshine when there was incessant rain—he protected the livelihood of the farmers. It was also at this time that he became affiliated with Daoism as the 30th descendant of the Daoist master, Zhang Tianshi, who summoned his help to exterminate the plague in the salt lakes, which were considered the rice bowls of the Song dynasty.

By the Yuan dynasty, temples dedicated to the god were common. He was highly regarded as the personification of loyalty, integrity and courage. With the appearance of the *Sanguo Yanyi* (*Romance of the Three Kingdoms*) in the Ming dynasty by novelist Luo Guanzhong, the cult of Guangong ascended to a new level. The novel highlighted Guangong's virtues, thereby systematically concretising his character and further fuelling his popularity. Imperial endorsement added impetus to the cult as well. Emperor Yongle (reign. 1402–1424), for example, chose Guangong as his patron deity during his northern expeditions. By the Wanli period his status became elevated to that of *di* (emperor) due to imperial patronage. Thus by the Qing dynasty, Guangong had been assigned with a multitude of functions by his devotees: protector of the country, god of war, god of wealth, protector of the dharma and so on.

Today Guangong's cult is still very much alive and strong. His integrity, a virtue necessary in any economic transaction, is respected among businessmen, who venerate him as a wealth god. Today, because of his loyalty, integrity and courage, he is, interestingly, also popular among both policemen and triads, who value bravery and brotherhood. [ST]

GUANGONG
China
Late Ming to early Qing dynasties
Gilt bronze
32 x 22 x 15 cm
1996.1507

Guanyin

Guanyin, or Guanshiyin, is the Chinese name of the Bodhisattva Avalokiteshvara and literally means the 'Observer of Sound', in which the sounds are the cries and pleas for help from the millions of beings. This miniature sculpture of a bodhisattva is represented as a Tang dynasty court lady in resplendent attire of high-waisted court dress and elaborate jewellery. She stands on a lotus plinth in *tribhanga*, while holding in her left hand one of the many attributes of Guanyin, the water vase. The small image in a niche at the nape of her coiffure represents Amitabha, her guiding Buddha. However, the slightly inclined posture of this Guanyin also indicates that the image was originally made as an attending figure to a more important image, such as that of Buddha.

The cult of Guanyin grew in popularity with the wide acceptance in China of the *Lotus Sutra* (*Saddharmapundarika Sutra*) (▶ see LOTUS SUTRA). This was an important scripture that singled out the bodhisattva as the embodiment of compassion, one who would not only deliver all beings to salvation, but who is also the personification of protection and would avail herself to dispel troubles and save lives. The most interesting and intriguing issue about this bodhisattva is the female form in which he is invariably depicted in the Mahayana Buddhist world of China, Japan, Korea and Vietnam. In China, the transformation from the male to female probably began during the Tang dynasty, as this sculpture shows, but Guanyin became a popular goddess, rather than a Buddhist saviour, after the 10th century as devotees began to venerate Guanyin together with local deities such as Princess Miaoshan of Hangzhou, South Sea goddess of Putuo and other legendary goddesses who performed great deeds. [LCL]

▶ see GUANYIN WITH ACOLYTES
▶ see QUAN AM

BODHISATTVA GUANYIN
China
Tang dynasty, 7th–8th centuries
Limestone carving
43 x 19 cm
1994.5612

Guanyin with Acolytes

Avalokiteshvara (Bodhisattva of Compassion), or Guanyin as she is more commonly known in China, is seated here in *mahārājalīlāsana* (posture of royal ease)—with one leg pendent and another folded horizontally—on a lotus throne mounted on a lion. This is a typical pose of Guanyin statues dating from the Ming and Qing dynasties. Here both hands of Guanyin assume the *vitarka mudra* (gesture of argumentation) symbolising the preaching of dharma, the Buddhist Law.

Guanyin is flanked by four acolytes with a fifth one steering the lion. The acolytes on the lotus base don officials' robes and hats, and are probably Daoist inspired (▶ see DAOIST PANTHEON ON ROBE). The two acolytes flanking Guanyin on the higher level are identified as child guardians Shancai Tongzi, who wears a triangular loin cloth, and Long Nü, who is holding a tael. They are believed to be Manjusri's former disciples and are actually popular figures adopted into the Buddhist pantheon. The incorporation of folk and Daoist figures betrays the religious flexibility and the resulting synthesis prevalent during the Ming dynasty. Buddhism was fully sinicised then, co-opting many indigenous historical, mythical and even Daoist gods as minor guardians.

This gilded figurine is intricately cast with meticulous detailing achieved through the *cire perdue* (lost-wax) method, commonly used to produce small- and medium-sized votive statues. Bronze figurines such as these were commercially available and popular among prosperous Ming patrons and devotees. By the Ming dynasty, the reproduction of religious figurines was no longer confined to devotees wishing to accumulate merit (▶ see RELIQUARY BOX). Wealthy patrons were known to commission such votive figures as *objets d'art* during the Ming and Qing dynasties. [ST]

▶ see GUANYIN

GUANYIN WITH ACOLYTES
China
13th–14th centuries
Gilt bronze with silver inlay
48 x 29 cm
2000.1226

Hanuman

According to Hindu belief, Hanuman is an ape god who is powerful, erudite and highly philosophic—an unusual imagery for a deity who is unparalleled in any mythology. Hanuman is an exemplary devotee of Rama and his exploits are elaborated in the great Sanskrit epic, the *Ramayana*, and its many vernacular versions.

Cast in the elegant mould of Chola period bronzes, this masculine sculpture of Hanuman is very slender and shows him ornamented with jewels and wearing a crown and a short dhoti with intricate pleats. The sculpture is part of a larger group that includes Rama, Sita and Lakshmana, Hanuman's masters; thus Hanuman's gesture is characteristic of a servant. All four sculptures are included in the iconic representation of Ramapattabhishekam (Rama's coronation), which is generally placed in the sanctum of Rama temples in south India. In this representation, the images are usually arranged such that Hanuman is seated by Rama's feet.

There are many divergent views of Hanuman's birth in the myths found in the *Puranas*[1] although the most common ones are associated with Vayu and Anjana. For example, one version claims Vayu is but the carrier of Shiva's semen, so Shiva is considered the real progenitor of Hanuman, while in another version, Hanuman is the son of Dasharatha and therefore is Rama's brother. Hanuman is also known by many names: as the son of Vayu he is addressed as Pavanaputra while as the son of the she-monkey Anjana he is known as Anjaneya. It is said that as a child Hanuman mistook the sun for a fruit and leapt to grab it even though it dazzled him. When Indra (God of the Celestial World) learnt of this, he grew jealous, as Hanuman was merely a child and yet possessed such strength. Thus Indra threw his *vajra* (thunderbolt) at him, and although he only managed to wound him with his *vajra*, Hanuman was left with a deep scar on his chin. As a result, the *deva* (gods) gave him the name Hanuman, which means 'one who has a scar on his jaw'.

The presence of many *sindoor*-smeared (orange-coloured) monolithic sculptures all over rural and urban India underscores the widespread cult of Hanuman, who is worshipped as a bestower of health, strength, fearlessness, success in exams and longevity. As a celibate deity, Hanuman is popularly venerated by young *brahmachari* (celibate brahman students) and bachelors; as a powerful deity he is worshipped by wrestlers and body-builders. [GPK]

▶ see LAKHAOUN KHAOL
▶ see THOLUBOMALATTAM
▶ see RAMAYANA MANUSCRIPT

HANUMAN
Tamil Nadu, south India
Late Chola period, c. 1200
Bronze
63.5 x 22 x 19 cm
1998.702

Heart Sutra

The Qing calligrapher Liu Yong copied this *sutra* when he was 76. The *Heart Sutra* is the shortest version of the otherwise long *Perfection of the Great Wisdom Sutra* (*Prajnaparamita Sutra*). An Indian text completed around the year 350, the *Heart Sutra* was probably translated shortly after for the Chinese audience, as it was one of the most discussed texts among the literati. A little more than 200 words, this *sutra* was of a perfect length for calligraphy practice and as a form of mental exercise. For some calligraphers, the act of copying it, sometimes from memory, was a way of inducing concentration, and for others, to realise detachment. The act of copying the *Heart Sutra* became an interesting secular ritual for the Yuan literati painters and calligraphers. By the late Ming and Qing dynasties, it was almost part of the curriculum for calligraphers.

In this copy, master calligrapher Liu Yong, who was also a member of the imperial academy, has chosen to use gold ink on blue-dyed paper, an exclusive material used for Buddhist scriptures and illustrations. The tranquil and even quality of Liu's calligraphy shows the meditative mood he must have cultivated during this exercise. As a process towards a state of concentration, such an exercise is always done in private. The cabinet minister of the Tongzhi and Guangxu emperors, Weng Tonghe, was known to have practised calligraphy with the *Heart Sutra* during the three-year mourning period for his father. [LCL]

HEART SUTRA IN GOLD CALLIGRAPHY BY LIU YONG
China
Jiaqing period, 1796
Blue-dyed paper, gold paint
22.2 x 11.3 cm
1998.608

Ten Courts of Hell

This is a set of ten hanging scrolls illustrating the Chinese concept of hell and purgatory. They depict the passageway of the deceased immediately after death before reincarnation. Paintings such as these were hung during funerary rites when prayers were recited to the ten kings of the courts of hell. These prayers were believed to help the deceased successfully negotiate the arduous journey of purgatory. The paintings were also hung during the Hungry Ghosts month to alleviate the sufferings of wandering souls and to facilitate their reincarnation. As the illustrations graphically portrayed specific punishments for sins committed, they also served as strong visual aids for moral education.

The Chinese believe that when a person dies, his/her soul undergoes a series of seven trials by underworld bureaucrats every seventh day until the 49th day after death. On the 100th day, the deceased is tried again at the eighth court. Then on the first and third year anniversaries, he/she is judged at the ninth and tenth courts of hell respectively. According

TEN COURTS OF HELL
Taiwan, Republic of China
Late Qing dynasty
Chinese ink and colour on paper, mounted
(EACH) Approx. 135.7 x 66.9 cm
On loan from Mr Christopher Frape
CF 20.1–10

to strict customs, it is only after the last trial on the third year anniversary that the mourning period is considered fully completed. This practice of the 'seven-seven' rites was a Buddhist practice prevalent in China since the Southern and Northern dynasties (420–589) although it is not known whether such scrolls were utilised then. However, they were undoubtedly popular in Taiwan until the early 1960s.

Different crimes are tried at each of the ten courts of hell. For instance, the deceased is made to peer into a mirror of sins and reflect upon past sins at the first court of hell. At the second court, those who have done others bodily harm, such as rape and murder, are tried. The second court is also known as the Freezing Hell as sinners are thrown into a frozen pool of piercing ice. The second to ninth courts are also further divided into different levels of hell where punishments for different sins are meted out. Finally in the tenth court of hell, the deceased is given a potion to consume before embarking on the wheel of

reincarnation. This is to ensure he/she forgets his/her previous life and the torture suffered in the ten courts of hell. This sequence of trials and punishments is depicted in the hell scrolls, although it is usually mixed up by the end of the 20th century. For instance, in this set of scrolls, the Freezing Hell is illustrated in the first scroll instead of the second.

Among the more popularly known hell official is King Yan Lo, also known as Yama raja, who resides in the fifth court of hell. As he is always depicted with a black face, he is sometimes mistaken as Justice Bao. Other popular characters of hell include the Cow- and Horse-Face Generals (Niutou Mamian) and the Black and White Faces of Impermanence, as distinguished by their high hats and long tongues (▶ see BLACK AND WHITE FACES OF IMPERMANENCE). They assist the ten kings in leading sinners to their various stations of torture. Although not depicted in later hell scrolls such as this one, Kshitigarbha, a bodhisattva also known as Dizang wang (▶ see DIZANG), is in fact the real ruler of hell. He is, however, not concerned with the day-to-day administration of the ten courts, which he entrusts to the ten kings.

The Chinese concept of the underworld was largely borrowed from Indian Buddhism. The illustrations of the Chinese ten courts of hell were based heavily on *The Scriptures of the Ten Kings*. However, it also reflected the syncretic tendencies of Chinese religions and philosophical traditions as it borrowed heavily from Buddhism, Confucianism, Daoism, popular beliefs and the administrative bureaucracy. This indigenous concept of the *yin* (underworld) realm thus mirrored the *yang* (earthly) realm to a large extent (▶ see YIN AND YANG ZODIAC SIGNS). [ST]

Hilltribe Silver

This group of silver jewellery is the work of nomadic highland communities including the Hmong, Yao, Lahu, Akha, Karen and others. It represents a fraction of the wide repertoire of silver jewellery made, worn and exchanged by these communities. Large neckrings (RIGHT) were worn in tiered sets or with a chain and pendant known as a 'soul lock', as illustrated here. The soul lock (see detail, BELOW), with applied decoration, is based on the Hmong cross motif that can be found on embroidered collars (▶ see HMONG ACCESSORIES). These silver pendants were often embellished with colourful enamels. Several types of bracelets of coiled, plaited and twisted forms (OPPOSITE) were worn by

(RIGHT) **NECKRING, CHAIN AND SOUL LOCK**
Hmong and Yao people, north Thailand
Early 20th century
Silver
diam. 15.4 cm
1993.776

(ABOVE) **DETAIL**
Soul lock
93.742

(OPPOSITE, TOP AND BOTTOM RIGHT) **BRACELETS**
Lahu and Akha people, north Thailand
Early 20th century
Silver
diam. 6–8.8 cm
1993.554, 1993.539, 1993.549

(OPPOSITE, BOTTOM LEFT) **EARRINGS**
Hmong and Yao people, north Thailand
Early 20th century
Silver
diam. 3.4 cm
93.736.1–2

Lahu and Akha men and the flat engraved earrings (BELOW, BOTTOM, LEFT) were worn by several different groups.

Silver jewellery was a way of investing a family's wealth so that it could be passed down as heirlooms. Hmong girls were given silver jewellery by their parents as *phij cuab* (bride wealth) which ensured them of some independence and status in their new home.[2] Silver is also regarded as having protective properties. Young children wear a silver neckring with a soul lock to protect them against illness. The pendant, or soul lock, is believed to prevent the soul from leaving the body. Today, where security may be a problem, silver is kept locked away while aluminium is used as a substitute.

Silver was valued more highly than gold by many highland communities, who also used it as currency for trade. Old silver coins from Burma, French Indochina and China were often melted down or incorporated to make jewellery, tobacco boxes and other accessories. Yao silversmiths have a reputation for good quality craftsmanship and today many of them produce a wide range of designs for Thai jewellery retailers.[3] [HT]

Hmong Accessories

These colourful accessories are an important part of the Hmong cultural identity and their designs, though difficult to interpret, probably had great significance. The indigo baby-carrier with geometric batik designs (BELOW) was used to secure a baby on the mother's back.[4] The red wool pompoms arranged to form two crosses probably served as protective talismans, like the red pompoms on Yao childrens' hats (▶ see YAO ACCESSORIES). The cross is also found on embroidered collars and on silver soul locks (▶ see HILLTRIBE SILVER). It has been suggested that the cross or 'X' motif in a wide range of configurations essentially served as protection against evil spirits.[5] The collars (OPPOSITE) are decorated with a variety of designs embroidered with cross-stitch and appliqué in bright colours. The collars were sewn onto the neckline of jackets and were worn hanging down the wearer's back, thus they were only visible when the wearer's back was turned.

BABY CARRIER
North Thailand
Early 20th century
Batik and cotton embroidery
69 x 64 cm
1993.1186

The Hmong were originally highlanders from southern China, although their origin myths speak of a land of snow and ice, suggesting that their ancestors came from further north in Mongolia, Tibet or even Lappland. Periodic suppression by the Chinese meant continued migration over the centuries for many tribal groups. By the mid 19th century, the Hmong had begun to move into northern areas of Thailand, Laos and Vietnam.[6] Regional warfare in recent years has resulted in the resettlement of many Hmong communities and cultural adaptation has become an important attribute, whether in the coexistence of ancestor worship and Christianity, or the re-created embroidery designs of Hmong women now living in America. [HT]

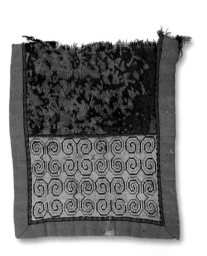

EMBROIDERED COLLARS
North Thailand
Early 20th century
Batik and cotton embroidery
9–12 x 5–7 cm
1993.1127, 1993.1156, 1993.1133

Hornbill Carving

This is a stylised carving of the hornbill, the most revered bird of the Dayak people of Borneo. The carving is painted in red, green, blue, yellow and white. The hornbill's oversized beak swirls upwards into a flower-tipped spiral. According to Dayak legend, the designs that appear on elaborate hornbill carvings are divinely inspired. This was a revered item that was used on ceremonial occasions.

Many Dayak objects were originally made for religious rituals. According to the Dayaks, the rhinoceros hornbill is the chief of the birds. The Dayaks believe that hornbills are the messengers of the deities and are good omens. Hornbill carvings similar to this one were

DAYAK HORNBILL CARVING
Sarawak, Malaysia
Early 20th century
Wood
100 x 20 x 80 cm
W0744

Hsun Ok
(Lacquer Offering Vessel)

This large black and red vessel is a type of container known as *hsun ok*, although this squat form is also known as an *ok-kwet* or *hsun gwet*. There are many types of *hsun ok*, some as tall as two metres. They function as votive food containers for the Buddhist merit-making task of carrying food to the monasteries as offerings to the monks. This example comprises several compartments which fit like trays on top of each other, creating a tiered form. The trays could be used as dishes and the cover as a drinking cup. The base would have held rice, fruit and eggs while the smaller trays above would have held curry, condiments, quids of betel and cheroots.

The simple but striking ribbed base with six feet was formed by building layers of *thayo* ('flesh and bones'), or lacquer mixed with sawdust, clay or ash, over a bamboo structure. The red colour is derived from cinnabar mixed with mercuric sulphide and tung oil.[7]

An inscription on the lid (TOP) records the maker's name, 'Ma Chit Ohn', and the village of Kyaukka, one of the most important centres for lacquerware in upper Burma. It is thought that such inscriptions were introduced by Kyaukka producers around the early 20th century. The names of the owners—a husband and wife from the village of Kyun Date—are also mentioned here as well as on the inner trays and the base, to ensure that these could easily be retrieved from among the many hundreds of similar offering vessels used during special occasions. Although most households have at least one *hsun ok* for carrying food to the temple, stately households would have employed servants to carry several human-sized vessels to the temples. [HT]

LACQUER OFFERING VESSEL
(TOP) Inscription on lid
Burma
Early 20th century
Bamboo, wood, lacquer
h. 20 cm, diam. 36.6 cm
1992.731

Hudoq
(Mask)

This painted wooden *hudoq* (mask) is probably from a Kayan Dayak group. It is carved out of softwood in separate pieces and held together with natural fibres. It has typical Dayak mask features such as big bulging eyes, wide stylised ears, bold markings, exaggerated facial features and fangs. The mask probably depicts Aso—the powerful Dayak dragon goddess, a chimera-like creature with the elongated body of a crocodile, the head of a dog and the snout of a wild boar with oversized fangs. These mythical creatures are associated with the underworld.

Almost all Dayak groups produce wooden *hudoq* of gods, mythical creatures, human ancestors and animals. These groups use *hudoq* in various ways. *Hudoq* are used in performances in longhouses put on by masked dancers during special occasions to repel evil spirits and attract guardian spirits. They are also used to alleviate sadness on solemn funeral ceremonies, to elicit laughter on festive occasions and to attract rice spirits to bless the padi-planting season. Dayak women often don these masks to scare children into obeying their parents. [RE]

▶ see ASO CARVINGS
▶ see DAYAK SHIELD

DAYAK *HUDOQ*
Sarawak, Malaysia
c. 1900s
Wood
33 x 39 cm
W0015

Huqqa

This *huqqa*, or hubble-bubble, is made of silver using repoussé, carving, moulding and gilding techniques. It comes apart into eight pieces and when assembled integrates like a well-engineered mechanism. The smoking pipe can be moved from side to side suggesting that more than one smoker would share the same *huqqa*. The main elements of this *huqqa* are the water container, the tobacco container, the container for burning embers, the pipes which take the vapour over the burning embers and tobacco, and the decorative chains which add charm and elegance to the artefact. The decorative patterns of vegetation motifs, birds and animals are quite animated and add brilliance to the *huqqa*. For a connoisseur it is the coming together of water, fire, smoke and tobacco in the right balance which makes smoking *huqqa* a favourite pastime.

Simple *huqqa* made from terracotta and wood are found in rural India even today but the most artistic ones were made during the Mughal and Sultanate periods across north India and Deccan. They were made of silver, glass, *bidri* and other metals, and often enamelled or decorated with repoussé or *bidri* work. *Huqqa* bases from many collections bespeak the workmanship that went into the making of these artefacts. Generally royalty and nobility would use these in their courts and homes, and many sets were kept for special formal occasions. In Hindu and Muslim traditions it was a sign of good hospitality to offer a guest a smoke on a *huqqa*. Both men and women smoked *huqqa*. [GPK]

HUQQA
North India
19th century
Silver
h. 66 cm
On loan from the National Museum,
New Delhi, Department of
Numismatics and Epigraphy
61.1284/a–h

Ikat

Ikat, which literally means 'to tie', describes the resist-dye process by which *ikat* textiles are made. Warp (vertical) or weft (horizontal) threads are first tied using strips of palm leaf or other similar material to prevent the dye from colouring certain reserved areas of the thread. By removing or re-tying the resists in between dyeing, multi-coloured patterns of great complexity can be achieved. Once the dyeing is completed, the threads are ready for weaving.[1]

The first piece (LEFT) is a warp *ikat* made from abaca cloth, which is made from the hard fibres of a wild banana plant. It is particularly interesting in its use of over-dyeing, where different-coloured dyes are used consecutively to create darker and more complex colours. This *ikat* was made by the T'boli, a tribal people who inhabit the mountainous areas of South Central Mindanao in the southern Philippines. Warp *ikat* is common among many tribal groups in Southeast Asia, suggesting its great antiquity.

T'BOLI WARP *IKAT*
South Central Mindanao, the Philippines
20th century
Abaca
168 x 50 cm
1999.0441

The second textile (BELOW) is a much more complicated piece that uses a double *ikat* technique in which both the warp and weft threads are dyed prior to weaving. As well can be imagined, this process is much more difficult as the weft threads must be carefully placed to keep them aligned with the overall pattern. This piece is an Indian textile that was made for the Indonesian market. It features a very rare pattern with elephants in full livery bearing presumably royal figures (SEE DETAIL, ABOVE). The scene suggests a hunt with various attendants—horsemen, charioteers, foot soldiers and standard bearers—as well as wild animals such as peacocks and tigers.[2] [DAH]

GUJARATI DOUBLE *IKAT* (*PATOLU*)
Gujarat, India
Probably 19th century
Silk
99 x 400 cm
1996.472

(TOP) **DETAIL**
In double *ikat* pre-dyed warp and weft threads must be very carefully aligned in order for the design to emerge

Indonesian Qur'an

While most Qur'ans from Southeast Asia are relatively plain, this particular *mushaf* (single volume Qur'an) has been elaborately illuminated. Instead of having just one double page of illuminations at the front, the norm for most Qur'ans, this *mushaf* has three in total—at the beginning, in the middle and at the end—and all three double-pages have been painted with varying designs. The pages you see here feature the end pages of the Qur'an.

For those who want to finish reading the Qur'an within a given period, the Qur'anic text may be conveniently divided into several parts. For example, the text could be divided equally into 30 parts to correspond to the days in a month. One-thirtieth of the text, known as a *juz'* in Arabic, is usually indicated in a single volume Qur'an with the help of a margin decoration.[3] In this Qur'an, the double pages where one finds the *juz'* division are framed with a decorative border.

INDONESIAN QUR'AN
Indonesia
AH 1237–1238/1822–1823 CE
Ink, colours and gold on paper
(FOLIO) 40.4 x 25.8 cm
2001.1152

The Qur'an contains an inscription which states that this Qur'an was copied by Haji Muhammad Salih bin War'iy in early Ramadan (9th Islamic month) AH 1237/May 1822 CE and completed in the month of Ramadan AH 1238/May 1823 CE.

The art of calligraphy and illumination in the Malay world did not develop to the extent that was found in the central Islamic lands such as Iran and Turkey. The most common script used is the cursive *naskh* and even for Qur'ans, the hand is generally scribal and not as elegant (▶ see QUR'AN IN NASKH). Judging from the care and attention that have been lavished on decorating this Qur'an and its relatively large size, it might be possible that this particular *mushaf* was made for use in a mosque. [TH]

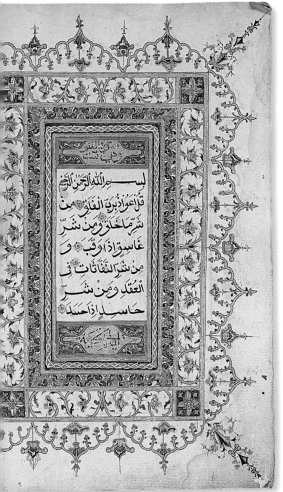

▶ see A SECTION FROM A CHINESE QUR'AN
▶ see PANEL CARVED WITH THE SHAHADAH

Ink Cake by Cao Sugong

This round ink cake has a *bayan jueju* (eight-character quartet) about *Nanji laoren* (God of the South Pole) (BELOW, LEFT). In intaglio and gilt, the inscription is rendered in classic Ming regular *kai* script. Two seal marks, one of Shexian ink master Cao Sugong (owner of the ink studio) and the other of his studio named Yishu, end this inscription.

The reverse of the cake (BELOW, RIGHT) is a pictorial depiction of the elderly deity sitting under an ancient pine tree in the company of a deer and a crane, both celestial signs of longevity and good fortune. This scene is composed in a painterly style by the mould carvers who depicted, with masterful precision, tiny details such as the pine needles, spots of the deer, feathers of the crane and the drapery of the deity's garments. Indeed, ink cakes made at the studio of Cao Sugong often demonstrated such near-painting quality. This high quality and perhaps Cao's good social connections made his products some of the most sought-after by the Qing literati circle during the 17th century.

The life of Cao Sugong spanned the late Ming dynasty and the early part of the Kangxi reign of the Qing dynasty. Not only was he a family friend of the late Ming king of ink, Cheng Junfang, he was also a keen ink collector and, though little known outside his circle of friends, an accomplished painter and calligrapher. Cao bought over the ink business from Wu Shuda and the Cao family made ink until the fall of the Qing dynasty. The Cao studio, known as Yishu zhai (from the former Xuanshu under Wu Shuda), was admired for its ability to replicate intricate illustrations of the Yellow Mountains. [LCL]

▶ see INK STICKS
▶ see ROUND INK CAKE BY CHENG JUNFANG

ROUND INK CAKE BY CAO SUGONG
Shexian, Anhui province, China
17th century
Ink
h. 1.5 cm, diam. 8.8 cm
On loan from the Collection of Yuan Shaoliang
YSL.A3

Ink Sticks

These four ink sticks form part of a series of ink cakes that was probably commissioned by Emperor Kangxi and produced by Huizhou's ink genius Wang Jinsheng. These ink cakes were made based on a series of paintings entitled *Gengzhi tu* (*Illustrations on Agriculture and Sericulture*) by court painter Jiao Bingzhen and his disciple Leng Mei around 1697.

Only one of the four ink sticks here relates to the process of silk-rearing and reeling. Entitled *fenbo* (BELOW, FAR LEFT), this image describes the task of distributing the silkworms evenly on the large woven mats for feeding. One other ink stick depicts *zhuoji* (the ramie-splicing process) (BELOW, SECOND FROM LEFT); while the other two are about the rice-planting process: *guangai* (irrigation) (BELOW, SECOND FROM RIGHT), and *jinzhong* (growing rice in the irrigated fields) (BELOW, FAR RIGHT).

Kangxi was an extremely energetic emperor in the history of China. Not only was he a disciplined administrator who unfailingly attended affairs presented at the court, he also personally conducted four military campaigns, and held numerous hunting expeditions and drills with his banner men. His interest in humanities and sciences was inexhaustible, and while residing in the palace, he supervised the creation of irrigated paddy fields and a silkworm-breeding house. Although these projects were meant for his own learning, they certainly were symbolic gestures signalling his support for economic progress and the well-being of his Chinese subjects, who were largely peasants and workers in cottage industries such as silk-rearing. [LCL]

▶ see INK CAKE BY CAO SUGONG
▶ see ROUND INK CAKE BY CHENG JUNFANG

FOUR INK STICKS WITH ILLUSTRATIONS FROM *GENGZHI TU*
Huizhou, Anhui province, China
Qing dynasty, Kangxi period
Ink
18.2 x 18 x 9 cm
On loan from the Collection of Yuan Shaoliang
YSL-A3

A Pair of **Jali Screens**

Judging from their almost similar dimensions, you could surmise that this pair of *jali* (lattice work) screens hail from the same monument and were probably designed and carved by artists of the same guild. Both rectangular frames consist of double *mihrab* (prayer niches) divided by star-shaped perforations. The interlinked lattice within the inner *mihrab* is carved with hexagonal and octagonal patterns. The spandrels are decorated with rosettes held by scrolling foliage and the point of the *mihrab* is surmounted by a palmette.

Besides allowing light and air into a room, *jali* windows have many functions. They provide an intermediate punctuation that subdivides the architectural space between interior and exterior. In many monuments of the Fatehpur Sikri, *jali* windows or screened walls carved in sandstone and marble allow light and breeze through the building.

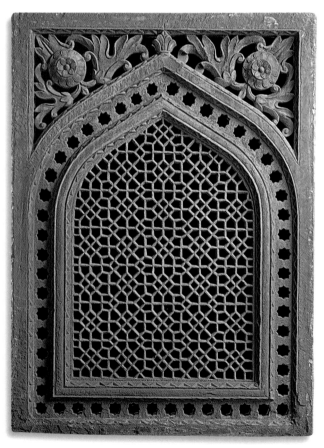

A PAIR OF *JALI* SCREENS
Agra area, Uttar Pradesh, India
Late 17th century
Red sandstone
(ABOVE) 128.5 x 92.5 x 9 cm; (OPPOSITE) 128.5 x 96.5 x 9 cm
1997.2974, 1997.2975

In Indian tradition, both wood and stone were used for carving decorative patterns on lattice windows and the motifs that were carved carried symbolic meaning. The Mughal and Mughal-inspired *jali* also assimilated European and Persian influences in the refinement of the designs and patterns, making the carvings delicate and tender. The workmanship of such carvings can only be spoken of in superlatives.

Decorative designs on Islamic monuments are generally inspired by geometry and relate well to the aesthetics of non-representational art advocated by Islam. The elaboration of patterns bespeaks an interest in embellishment charged by the mathematical pursuit for precision. [GPK]

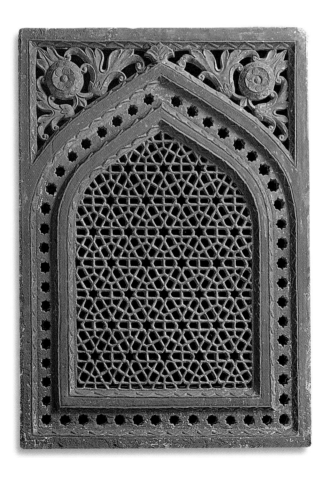

Jataka Stories

This lengthy cotton banner has painted illustrations of the last of the 547 Jatakas, or stories of the previous lives of the Buddha. At first glance, the Jataka appears to have been painted as one continuous narrative. However, the story has 13 parts, each of which is identifiable by a subtitle along the lower register. The story shown here tells of Buddha in his last life, when he was known as Prince Vessantara, and is known as the Maha Chat or 'Great Jataka' in Thailand, where it is the most popular of all Jatakas. The story is portrayed in a lively illustrative painting style, with the narrative conveyed in the manner of a cartoon, through the words spoken by the characters. At the heart of this story is the message that merit can be acquired through acts of great generosity, epitomised by Vessantara. He gives away his white elephant which has the power to bring rain to people in need of water. This causes the king to banish him and his family from the palace. During

TEMPLE BANNER WITH PAINTED JATAKA STORIES
(ABOVE) Vessantara gives away his children
(OPPOSITE) Vessantara reunited with his family
North Thailand
c. 1950s
Painted cotton
l. 33 m
1997.2933

his departure he gives away other possessions (OPPOSITE) and later in the story, even gives away his children and wife, with whom he is later reunited (BELOW).

Banners hung on the walls of the prayer halls of Theravada Buddhist temples in northern Thai villages serve to make the stories more accessible to the laity, as they listen to recitations on special occasions such as Vesak Day (Buddha's Birthday) or Thet Maha Chat at the end of the monks' rainy season retreat in October. The story is usually recited in 13 *kanda* (sections) which are individually 'sponsored' by the laity. It is told in a lively way, drawing on the popular appeal of bawdy humour when necessary and interspersed with more formal doctrinal verses. The sponsors and their offerings are rotated before each new *kanda* is narrated, and the recitation of the whole Jataka therefore takes many hours to complete. [HT]

Javanese Bronzes

The 7th to 16th centuries saw the widespread adaptation of the Hindu Buddhist religion and concepts of kingship from India within Southeast Asia. Bronze and stone images of Hindu and Buddhist deities were produced in Indonesia, not only in association with the kingdoms of central (8th–early 10th centuries) and east Java (early 10th–early 16th centuries), but also in Sumatra, Bali, Kalimantan, Sulawesi and Sumbawa. Local bronzesmiths were quick to adopt new ideas and styles from Indian prototypes, and pieces such as this Kubera and Vajrapani are typical of the localised central Javanese style.

This figure of Kubera (God of Wealth) sits on a high-backed double lotus-shaped throne with a parasol overhead. His right foot rests on a *purnaghata* (pot of overflowing wealth). He holds a lime, which is a symbol of fertility, in his right hand, and the sack of wealth in his left. He is adorned with a crown, earrings, necklace and armbands, and an *upavita* (sacred cord) worn over the left shoulder. Kubera was incorporated into both Hindu and Buddhist pantheons. Images of this deity appeared in Java with two as well as four arms.

SEATED FIGURE OF KUBERA
Central Java, Indonesia
8th–9th centuries
Bronze
11.7 x 5 x 4 cm
1995.297

Vajrapani (Thunderbolt Bearer), was one of the most important bodhisattvas in the Tantric Buddhist pantheon. He is highly adorned and sits in the cross-legged posture of *sattvaparyangka* with his right foot resting on the left thigh, on a lotus throne with a parasol overhead. His attributes are somewhat unclear; he holds a lotus flower in the left hand and a spherical object in the right.

It is thought that Javanese bronze images were made for veneration. They may have been used singly or in larger groups arranged in a mandala formation in temples. However there is no evidence yet of how the figures were used or who their patrons were, although it is thought that the commissioning of an image was considered an act of merit.[1] It also remains unclear why the production of bronze images came to a sudden end sometime during the 10th or 11th century.[2] [HT]

SEATED FIGURE OF VAJRAPANI
Central Java, Indonesia
8th–9th centuries
Bronze
12.5 x 5 x 5 cm
1995.298

Javanese Proto-Classic Jewellery

The gold items pictured here are a representative sample of the many styles of ear ornaments known to have come from the Proto-Classic period (3rd–8th centuries). Most of these are in the shape of an open oval or a loop and vary from simple gold bars to circlets of soldered gold discs and more complex star shapes. Interestingly, despite the very early designs of these pieces, some Southeast Asian societies continue to create jewellery of identical or similar style.

The Proto-Classic period was an important period in the development of gold-working techniques in Southeast Asia. It was during this time that Southeast Asians began using heat to work gold. This included fairly sophisticated techniques such as casting and soldering. Archaeologist John Miksic suggests that the making of gold objects would have become a specialised occupation in Southeast Asia during this period.[3]

The Southeast Asian region was well known to ancient geographers and traders as a source of gold. The Indians referred to Java as Suvarna-dvipa, the 'Isle of Gold', and early Roman writers such as Pliny and Ptolemy refer to a 'Land of Gold' or 'Peninsula of Gold' as far back as the 1st and 2nd centuries. It is not surprising then that, given their reputation, early Southeast Asians were experienced in finding and working with gold. According to Anne Richter, an authority on the arts and crafts of Southeast Asia, the early jewellery of Southeast Asia is remarkable for both its outstanding beauty and technical complexity.[4] [DAH]

JAVANESE PROTO-CLASSIC JEWELLERY
Java, Indonesia
Proto-Classic period (3rd–8th centuries)
Gold
w. 2.5–3 cm
Gift of Mrs Annie Wee
1997.3685, 1997.3686, 1997.4761, 1997.4762, 1997.4763

Jian
(Bronze Basin)

This vessel is known as a *jian*. It is decorated with a robe design amid three registers of *panlong wen* (intertwining dragon motif) or *panchi wen*. The *panlong wen* of the Spring and Autumn period was usually done in low relief, with the intertwining dragons distinguishable, unlike their counterparts in the Warring States period, which resembled a mass of small, highly abstracted swirls with grooves in high relief. (Compare the *panlong wen* here with the motif in the *fou* or *lei* in ▶ WINE CONTAINER.)

The *jian* was a vessel used to contain water during ablutions and for taking baths, depending on its size. On other occasions, it was also used to contain ice, and before the invention of mirrors, the *jian* functioned as a reflector when filled with water. The *jian* had an ancient shape derived from a ceramic basic prototype. However, its bronze counterpart only appeared in the Spring and Autumn period.

This *jian* probably formed part of a larger set of ritual ware. During the Shang and Zhou dynasties, bronze ritual ware played a pivotal role in determining the political and social power of the feudal lords who owned them. The size, number, types and variety of ritual ware used by the feudal lords during their lifetime and buried with them after their death were reflectors of their political and social status. These ritual ware consisted mainly of containers of food, wine and water used during rituals dedicated to gods, spirits and ancestors, or the commemoration of events such as conquests and enfeoffment by the king.

However, by the Warring States period, bronzes assumed new ritual functions during court audiences, weddings and archery contests, reinforcing social relations and in some cases, exhibiting the extravagances of the territorial warlords who owned them. Moreover, weapons, chariot fittings, furniture parts and personal embellishments (seals, weights and garment hooks) supplemented the existing repertoire of ritual vessels and bells as emblems of prestige and power by the mid 5th and 4th centuries BCE. [ST]

JIAN
China
Spring and Autumn period
Bronze
h. 24.3 cm, diam. 56.1 cm
1996.469

Jiaozhi Ceramic

Here are images of He Xiangu (BELOW, LEFT) and Han Xiangzi (BELOW, RIGHT), two of the famous Eight Immortals, made from *jiaozhi* ceramic (▶ see EIGHT IMMORTALS ON HANGING). *Jiaozhi* ceramic is essentially enamelled, low-fired, folk ceramic (*minyao*). It originates from the Guangdong province in south China and can be traced back to Tang *sancai* (Tang dynasty tri-coloured wares, ▶ see TANG SANCAI TOMB GUARDIANS) and Ming *wucai* (Ming dynasty five-coloured wares). It incorporated the influence of low-fired Qing export wares and developed from Jingdezhen's glazing techniques, Shanxi's *liuli* and *fahua* enamelled wares, as well as Western enamels. It was commonly used in religious architecture or in the homes of wealthy patrons. The forms created were usually figurines of folk, Daoist and Buddhist origins, as well as animals, flowers and foliage with auspicious meanings. The art of *jiaozhi* ceramic probably spread to Taiwan in the late Ming and early Qing dynasties with the works of the pioneer master, Ye Wang, being the most famous.

The figurines here are made by Taiwan's top artist-sculptor, Lin Kuang-I. In Lin's hands, folk craft has been elevated to the level of artistic creation. His works exude a hint of archaism and naturalism due to his clever manipulation of enamels and form. Lin's enamelled wares have a muted translucency akin to weathered architectural ceramic. His rendition of the immortals here captures the ethereal quality typical of Daoist saints. [ST]

JIAOZHI CERAMIC
(ABOVE) He Xiangu; (RIGHT) Han Xiangzi
Taiwan, Republic of China
Contemporary
Enamelled pottery
Approx. 36 x 25 x 12 cm
2002.821, 2002.828

Kacip
(Betel Cutters)

The *kacip* is a single-bladed hinged cutter used to cut or pare shavings from the areca nut, one of the principle ingredients in betel, a stimulant widely used in Southeast Asia since at least the start of the Common Era. According to Henry Brownrigg, the primary authority on betel cutters, they invariably had an iron blade although many were made from bronze, brass or other materials.[1] *Kacip* come in an incredible variety of styles, shapes and sizes from all over the region. Some were made to represent animals, deities or even humans while others were simpler geometric forms. Many were lavishly decorated with precious metal oversheaths, inlays or overlays.

The *kacip* displayed here illustrate some of the great variety of forms found in betel cutters. The first cutter is in the form of a winged horse and comes from the island of Bali. It is decorated with silver oversheaths and wings and inlaid with silver in an intricate swastika pattern that confirms the Hindu-Buddhist origins of the piece. Small silver bells add a musical accent to the act of cutting the areca nut.

The second cutter originates from Palembang in south Sumatra and has a peculiar quadrilateral shape that is unique to that area. Highly refined gold *kinatah*, a special form of gilding common to parts of Southeast Asia, accents the iron blade. The oversheaths are made from *suasa* (gold alloy) and have round finial ends.

The third cutter is from Solo in Central Java and demonstrates the very refined workmanship of Javanese iron smiths. It is crafted in the form of a bird with fine openwork cut along the head and back of the cutter. The silver sleeves or oversheaths are decorated with a spiralling design and the small flower-shaped brass hinge represents the eye of the bird. Interestingly, this cutter is from a Malay *sireh* set from Riau, demonstrating the wide popularity and high reputation of Javanese cutters in the 19th and 20th centuries. [DAH]

(TOP) *KACIP* **FROM BALI**
Bali, Indonesia
c. late 19th–early 20th centuries
Silver
17 x 4.7 cm
On loan from the Mariette Collection
BM.48

(CENTRE) *KACIP* **FROM SUMATRA**
Palembang, south Sumatra, Indonesia
c. late 19th–early 20th centuries
Iron, gold, *suasa*
18.5 x 4.3 cm
On loan from the Mariette Collection
BM.49

(BOTTOM) *KACIP* **FROM JAVA**
Solo, central Java, Indonesia
c. late 19th–early 20th centuries
Iron
19 x 6 cm
On loan from the Mariette Collection
BM.67b

Kammavaca Manuscript

This collection of ivory leaves is known as a *kammavaca*. It contains the rules for monastic conduct and ceremonies such as the *upasampada* (higher ordination) of monks. The square script is written in dark brown lacquer known as *magyi zi* ('tamarind seed') due to the heavy brown tone of the lacquer. The margins are decorated with cinnabar and gold leaf.

A complete volume usually consists of one, five or nine *khandaka*—extracts from the monastic code of rules, or Vinaya Pitaka. Different sections refer to Theravada Buddhist ceremonies such as a monk's higher ordination, the presentation of Kathina robes after the rainy season retreat, the purchase of land and the consecration of an area for temple-building, or the releasing of a monk from monastic life. Late 15th century inscriptions refer

KAMMAVACA
Burma
Early 20th century
Ivory, cinnabar and gold leaf
8.9 x 55.7 cm
1998.2

to the reading of *kammavaca* during the momentous re-ordination of monks ordered by the Mon King Ramadhipatiraja (reign. 1472–1492) in response to the fragmentation of Buddhist sects and a decline in monastic discipline.

The earliest *kammavaca*, from the 14th century, were made of lacquered palm leaf. However, by the 18th century new materials were introduced for folios made for royalty. These included the use of cloth—from the robes of royalty or monks—strengthened with lacquer. Another material was ivory, which was difficult to lacquer due to the smooth and slightly oily surface. Materials such as the gold leaf and cinnabar would have been imported from China. [HT]

Kashan Lustre Bowl

The decoration on this bowl glitters in the sun. This is because it has been painted with lustre—a technique which gives ceramics a shimmering surface imitating precious metals. This bowl,[2] with brownish gold lustre, features a central roundel with radiating split palmettes. The side is made up of a band of Kufic-Abbasid script done in reverse on a scrolling background, a band of cursive *naskh* script painted in lustre and another band of *naskh* scratched onto the lustre background.

The lustre technique was first used by potters in Iraq around the 9th century and was probably influenced by the lustre technique used by Egyptian glassmakers. A compound of sulphur with silver and copper oxides is painted onto once-fired vessels, after which they are given a second firing, producing a thin metallic film. The result, as described by a 14th-century historian and tile-master, Abu'l Qasim, 'reflects like red gold and shines like the light of the sun'. Towards the end of the 10th century this technique went to Egypt, probably introduced by immigrant potters from Iraq. After the fall of the Fatimid dynasty, the secret of lustre painting was brought to Iran.

The town of Kashan in central Iran was the centre where beautiful lustre vessels as well as tiles were produced from the late 12th century onwards. Since lustreware require a second firing, they were expensive to produce and were considered luxury goods. Kashan's lustreware was exported to other parts of Iran as well as to places such as Egypt and Syria. The industry, however, came to an end around the middle of the 14th century. [TH]

▶ see LAJVARDINA TILE

KASHAN LUSTRE BOWL
(TOP) The inside of the bowl
Kashan, central Iran
13th century
Stone-paste
h. 10.1 cm, diam. 22 cm
1997.2615

Kavacam
(Breast Plate)

Both these objects entered the collection at different times, but they have been put together to form a set of *kavacam* for a male and a female deity. Their dimensions are quite similar, as is the very intricate and refined workmanship. They bear the classicism of Chola and Vijayanagara style although they are quite late. They have been crafted with a repoussé technique carried out with great finesse and precision. The frontal representation of the female torso (BELOW) has tight breasts and a narrow compact waist. The male torso (RIGHT), which is very muscular and fleshy, stands with a bent waist leaning to one side.

Kavacam such as these were used to decorate the bronze *utsavara* (mobile images) of south Indian Brahminical deities for festive occasions. The deities were specially dressed for each occasion by the priests and *kavacam* were used to define their appearance. Sometimes additional hands and legs were also added to extend the limbs, and dhotis and saris tied around them to make the deities appear larger and more prominent. These *kavacam* are small in size, and probably used inside the sanctum for the small bronzes placed near the *mulavar* (main immobile deity). [GPK]

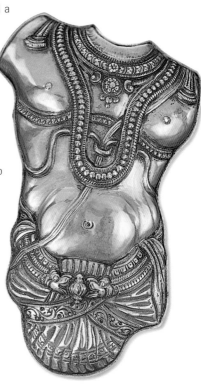

(ABOVE) ***KAVACAM* FOR A MALE DEITY**
Tamil Nadu, south India
18th century
Gold
12.5 x 7.5 cm
1995.897

(LEFT) ***KAVACAM* FOR A FEMALE DEITY**
Tamil Nadu, south India
18th century
Gold
9.7 x 6.8 cm
1994.520

Kazhuththu Uru
(Chettiar Marriage Necklace)

This wedding *thali* (marriage necklace) is used exclusively by the Nagarathar Chettiar community of Tamil Nadu. It is an auspicious ornament used during a typical Hindu marriage ceremony that is sanctified before a sacred fire. Known as *kazhuththu uru* (pronounced *kalutiru*) in Tamil, it is tied by the groom around his bride's neck after they have exchanged their vows. This necklace is unusual as it has an elaborate pattern and is larger than most marriage necklaces.

Marriage necklaces usually comprise 35 pieces: 15 in the lower row, 14 in the upper row plus three central pendants in each row. The pieces are strung by 21 lengths of twisted strings that are smeared with turmeric. In the piece shown here, the most important element—the main pendant representing Mahalakshmi (Goddess of Wealth and Prosperity)—is missing. The central pendant, also called *ethanam*, has four sharp spikes representing the four Vedas (knowledge). This is surmounted by an image of Subrahmanya standing with his parents, Shiva and Parvati, who are seated on a *nandi* (bull) (▶ see SUBRAHMANYA, ▶ see SHIVA, PARVATI AND SKANDA). This motif of Subrahmanya is repeated four times on two pendants on either side of the *ethanam*. These four pendants represent the hands of the bride and the groom. They also suggest wealth, health, fame, progeny, knowledge, beauty, youthfulness, courage and longevity.[3]

The image of Subrahmanya, Shiva and Parvati suggests that the owner of the necklace must have been a great devotee of Subrahmanya—this is corroborated by the fact that the Chettiars are great devotees of Subrahmanya. The owner's initials, '*rukku*', are inscribed at the back of each *padakam* (pendant). All the *padakam* are strung with a black thread and separated by circular, cylindrical and square spacers. The design and craftsmanship of this ornament is rather complex, incorporating repoussé, carving, chasing, granulation and filigree techniques. The sheet gold is filled with lac in the case of the spacers while for the *padakam*, the moulded image of the deities is welded onto a pink backing, creating a three-dimensional effect.

Unlike the simple two-piece *thali* that is usually worn on a daily basis, the ceremonial necklace is worn only once or twice at most during the lifetime of a Nagarathar Chettiar woman, hence its good condition. Besides the wedding day, the ceremonial necklace is also worn on *shashtiabdapurti*, a ceremony celebrating the husband's 60th birthday. This is also when the second marriage ceremony is conducted. The husband usually wears a *rudraksha malai* (ceremonial necklace) while his wife wears the *kazhuththu uru* (▶ see RUDRAKSHA NECKLACE). Interestingly, young Chettiar brides today still wear similar necklaces, albeit hesitatingly. As the necklace forms part of the dowry given to Chettiar women by their parents, it is important that the bride's family be able to afford them.

KAZHUTHTHU URU
Tamil Nadu, south India
19th century
Gold
circ. 94.5 cm
1994.5001

The Chettiars are a Tamil-speaking, rich, merchant-class, money-lending business community who are also staunch devotees of Shiva-Skanda (Subrahmanya). Chettinad is in the Ramanad district and consists of small but plush villages of large mansions near Karaikudi, the largest town in the area. During the late 18th and 19th centuries, many of them travelled to Southeast Asia, especially Malaysia, Burma and Singapore, for business. Many of their descendants are still here although their professions have changed over time. [GPK]

Kedah Buddha

Just months before the Japanese invasion of Malaya in 1941, British archaeologist H. G. Quaritch Wales was digging for artefacts at a site on the Bujang river in Kedah when he discovered this small bronze statue.[4] This beautifully preserved image depicts a serenely smiling Buddha standing in a posture known as *tribangha*, with the hips swayed to the left, and with the right hand in *varada mudra* (boon-bestowing gesture). He wears his robe flung over his left shoulder and gathered up in his left hand. The style of this piece is characteristic of Indian art from the Gupta period, particularly of the Sarnath style.

This figure is a very important archaeological find for a number of reasons. It was found in the ruins of a small brick structure only a few yards from a site that has been dated to around the 9th or 10th centuries. Presumably the brick structure dates to around the same time. However, the same cannot be said for the figure. Indeed it is likely that this Buddha is dated much earlier. Wales argues that this Buddha could be dated to as early as the 5th century as there is evidence of Gupta treatment on it. Furthermore, he points out that there are many examples of ancient religious images being preserved in temple shrines of a much later date.[5] However, Dr Gauri Krishnan points out that this image does not appear to have been done by Gupta craftsmen. In fact, she argues that this image may have actually been a somewhat later copy of a Gupta image by craftsmen in Kedah.[6] Regardless, this figure is almost certainly one of the earliest surviving Buddhist images from the Malay Peninsula and represents a rare glimpse of early Indian influence in Southeast Asia. [DAH]

FIGURE OF STANDING BUDDHA
Kedah, Malaysia
5th–9th centuries
Bronze
h. 20.6 cm
A1354

Keris

The *keris* is an asymmetrical double-edged dagger unique to the islands of Southeast Asia and a very important piece of Malay material culture. It is generally believed that the *keris* originated in Java some time around the 9th century and examples of the *keris* can be found from the old Malay state of Singora in southern Thailand all the way to the island of Sumbawa in eastern Indonesia. Given this wide spread it is no wonder that there is a great variety in the form and style of these intriguing weapons.

Pictured here are two outstanding examples of the *keris*. The first (BELOW, FAR LEFT) is a fine Bugis *keris* that most likely comes from the Riau-Lingga Archipelago or the Malacca Straits. The sturdy, hand-forged blade has nine *luk* (waves) and is decorated with a crowned *naga* (mythical serpent) that acts as a protective spirit. It has a classic Bugis-styled hilt made from *kemuning* wood that is intricately carved with floral, leaf and tendril accents. The finely incised, gilded-brass hilt cup, known in Malay as a *pendokok*, is typical of those of the Bugis style but of extraordinary craftsmanship. This *keris* is sheathed in a scabbard (BELOW, SECOND FROM LEFT) made from highly figured *jati gembol*, a greatly prized wood that comes from the burl of the teak tree.

The second *keris* (BELOW, SECOND FROM RIGHT) is in the classic court style of Yogyakarta, one of the central Javanese kingdoms. Its scabbard (BELOW, FAR RIGHT), fashioned from *pelet* wood, is in the formal dress style known as *warangka branggah*. These are sometimes also referred to as the *ladrangan yogya*, which are characterised by their high, upsweeping shape. The simple planar hilt is also typical of this *keris* type and features intricately carved *cecekan* which are believed to represent the faces of guardian deities. The blade has 13 *luk* and is in a *dapur* (form) known to the Javanese as *sengkelat* or *parungsari*. [DAH]

(FAR LEFT AND SECOND FROM LEFT)
BUGIS *KERIS*
Riau-Lingga Archipelago, Indonesia
Late 19th century
Iron, brass, wood
31.5 cm
K0006

(SECOND FROM RIGHT AND FAR RIGHT)
JAVANESE *KERIS*
Solo, central Java, Indonesia
19th century
Iron, ivory, brass, wood
45 cm
K0114

Keshanistoyakarini
(Lady Drying her Wet Hair)

This sculpture forms part of the temple *mandovara* (wall) display that incorporates images of deities, *dikpala* (directional deities), *apsara-devangana* (celestial beauties) as well as *vyala* and *rishi* (sages). The *apsara-devangana* figures, such as the one shown here, are placed in protruding or receding niches depending on the layout of the temple wall. They are usually placed at a level above human height, and you would have to look up to see them.

This figure, three quarters of which are visible, is shown with her back facing the audience at an angle. This casual pose is an unusual way of depicting a figure. The movement of her feet has been captured, and you can almost feel the celestial figure beginning to stir and turn around. This 'arrested movement' and casualness of pose is characteristic of the medieval period (10th–15th centuries), when sculptors took the liberty of animating figures. The transparency of the lower and the upper garments, as well as the details of the jewellery denote contemporary trends in women's accessories.

KESHANISTOYAKARINI
Madhya Pradesh or Rajasthan, India
11th century
Sandstone
h. 99 cm
1998.1381

The presence of the swan with an uplifted neck is a signifier that helps us to identify the symbolism and meaning of this sculpture. The motif of a lady drying her wet hair is often found on many medieval temple walls all over north India and as far back as the Buddhist monuments of the Kushana period in the form of *yakshi* (female vegetation spirits). It has a long history and was depicted in both Buddhist and Hindu monuments. While it does appear on religious monuments, the inspiration for its depiction originates in Vedic literature.

Apsara are semi-divine spirits who are water and air borne; they appear and disappear at will. They have an ephemeral nature and can take birth even as earthly women. *Apsara* became very popular during the Puranic period (c. 1000–800 BCE), when they were the crown jewels of Indra's court. Famous ones such as Urvashi, Rambha and Menaka have been immortalised by Sanskrit playwrights such as Kalidasa. They are also said to accompany Surya every morning in his chariot, along with Usha-Pratyusha (dispellers of darkness), *rishi*, *gandharva* (celestial youthful male gods), *yaksha* (male vegetation spirits) and *rakshasa* (demons), dispelling darkness.[8] While they were the consorts of the *gandharva*, *apsara* often came in contact with kings and *rishi*, and married them and lived like mortals on earth for a short spell before returning to Indra's abode.

In a philosophical sense, *apsara* are the life principles in matter. They share with the *yakshi* the life-giving force and regenerative power that symbolises fertility in nature, and are also auspicious principles that bestow good luck and happiness.[9] [GPK]

▶ see BHAIRAVA
▶ see CHAMUNDA IN DANCING POSE
▶ see YOGINI

Kesi Fragment

This is a relatively complete back portion of a *chuba* (traditional robe) worn by men in Tibet. Woven in a rich multi-coloured palette, the textile presents a serene tableau of stylised 'Indian' lotuses in persimmon and light pink in a setting of clouds and mountains. Tonality is applied to differentiate the petals as well as to create a three-dimensional feel for the flowers, which would otherwise be dull and flat.

Tapestry weave was first introduced to Chinese weavers by the Uighur, where the technique was used for weaving wool to make such heavy items as carpets and kaftans. As the Chinese weavers applied the weft-faced weaving technique with silk, the result was a range of colourful pictorial and finely patterned silk textiles, often used in the framing or the binding of paintings and Buddhist scriptures. By the Song dynasty, *kesi* (tapestry textile) was a top luxury item reserved for imperial use and tributary purposes. *Kesi* workshops were commissioned to replicate paintings, as the technique allowed for minute detailed work to be copied.

This piece probably represented some of the best-quality *kesi* produced during the Ming dynasty, often thought as a period of decline for this technique. As the technique required long man-hours to produce, *kesi* remained a luxury item which only the very rich and privileged could enjoy. Monasteries in Tibet often received special gifts from the Ming emperors who were devout Vajrayana Buddhists themselves. These gifts usually included generous quantities of imperial silks, which would then be made into hangings or official robes, such as this one. [LCL]

BACK PIECE OF A *KESI* TIBETAN *CHUBA*
China, Tibet
Mid Ming dynasty, 15th century
Silk
124 x 92.2 cm
1998.101

Khmer Crystals

Sites in the lower Mekong Delta area, such as Oc Eo, the port of the Kingdom of Funan (● see FUNAN FEMALE DEITY), have yielded a number of types of hardstones including these quartz crystals with engraved designs. It is thought that these stones were carved in Cambodia as the iconography of certain pieces appear to be of the early Angkor period.[10]

The first piece (LEFT, TOP) is thought to depict the monkey Hanuman from the episode in the *Ramayana* in which he flies from the Himalayas with a special herb to heal the wounded after battle with Ravana's army.[11] The second seal (LEFT, CENTRE) has a standing female figure surrounded by a band with bosses. The elaborate costume and jewellery were skilfully engraved and include a necklace, earrings, anklets, a skirt with concentric designs and a tall hairdo. The third seal (LEFT, BOTTOM) also has a standing female figure with similarly detailed adornment. Her arms are raised above her head and her hips sway to the left as if she is dancing.

These crystals probably served as seals or stamping-dies, although the holes drilled into their convex backs suggest they could have been worn as amulets.[12] It is also thought that the clay impressions taken from the seals may have been used as offerings as they have been found under sema (boundary stones) and the foundations of temples.[13] Most of them have an image of a single figure such as Hanuman, an elephant, a multi-armed deity, or a warrior figure with shield and weapon or bow and arrow.[14] [HT]

(LEFT, TOP) **SEAL WITH IMAGE OF HANUMAN**
Ta Kev region, Cambodia
7th–13th centuries
Crystal
3 x 2.3 x 2 cm
1998.479

(LEFT, CENTRE) **SEAL WITH IMAGE OF A FEMALE FIGURE**
Ta Kev region, Cambodia
7th–13th centuries
Crystal
6.5 x 2.6 x 4.3 cm
1998.482

(LEFT, BOTTOM) **SEAL WITH IMAGE OF A FEMALE FIGURE**
Ta Kev region, Cambodia
7th–13th centuries
Crystal
4.3 x 2.6 x 2.2 cm
1998.480

Khmer Stone Lintel

This lintel depicts Yama, the Brahmanic Guardian of the South and God of Death, whose mount is a water buffalo. He is positioned above a *kala* (face of glory) which disgorges a two-headed *simha* (lion), the Hindu and Buddhist symbol of bravery. The *simha* in turn disgorges two floral garlands, which span the length of the lintel. The deeply carved stylised foliage is typical of Banteay Srei designs.

Banteay Srei (Citadel of Beauty) is the temple dedicated to Shiva and was built during the second half of the 10th century by the Brahman priest Yajnavaraha, a counsellor of King Rajendravarman. The style of carving associated with this temple is a delicate but deeply rendered relief which has the appearance of being almost three-dimensional.

Carved lintels were positioned over doorways; in this case a south-facing doorway, as Yama is associated with the south. Pediments and lintels with the various gods associated with the four directions are found over the doorways to the sanctuary towers at Banteay Srei. Yama appears on the south-facing towers; Varuna, the God of the West, appears on his *hamsa* (goose) on the west-facing towers; Kubera, the God of the North, rides on a *simha* over the northern entrances; and Indra, the God of the East, on his three-headed elephant Airavata faces the East. Yama also carries a mace and noose to secure his victims and can be found in the series of eight large bas-reliefs in the third enclosure at Angkor Wat, where he appears in the south-facing scene of Heaven and Hells, in what is thought to be the persona of King Suryavarman II.[15] [HT]

LINTEL WITH YAMA
Cambodia
Banteay Srei style, 12th–13th centuries
Sandstone
23.5 x 153.5 cm
1999.142

Khurasan Jug

The surface of this brass jug is decorated with silver and copper inlay, most of which has remained intact even after 800 years. There are three bands of inscriptions on the body of the jug—two in cursive *naskh* and one in angular Kufic-Abbasid script. Another band of Kufic-Abbasid script is engraved around the foot. All the inscriptions are supplicatory prayers asking for good fortune, wealth, health, happiness and other good wishes for the owner. The main motifs, which alternate on each facet of the jug, are a stylised vase with tendrils flowing from it and a medallion containing interlacing arabesque (stylised floral motif). The arabesque, which is also found on the cover of the jug, is a popular motif used not only on metalwork, but also on other materials such as ceramic and even manuscripts.

Metalworkers in 12th-century Khurasan were one of the first in the Islamic world to fully exploit the use of inlays as a decorative method. A variety of objects were produced, for example, basins, ewers, candlesticks and penboxes. This jug is a fine example of metalwork produced in this area. In common with many other religions, the use of precious metals for personal use is disapproved of in Islam. This, however, did not prevent the wealthy from using gold and silver. Nevertheless, there was a demand for vessels made from base metals such as brass, with inlays of gold and silver as they were luxurious and yet did not weigh too heavily on the conscience. The inlay industry in Khurasan flourished until the Mongol attack in 1220. The technique, however, continued in the 13th century in other centres which developed in the western part of the Islamic world such as Iraq, west Iran, Anatolia (Turkey) and Syria. [TH]

▶ see MAMLUK BASIN

KHURASAN JUG
Khurasan, northeast Iran
Late 12th century
Silver and copper inlay on copper alloy
h. 27.2 cm
1997.5219

Kiswah Fragments from the Holy Ka'bah

These two silk fragments come from the *kiswah*, which is the curtain used to cover the four walls of the Holy Ka'bah in Mecca. Embroidered in gilt and silver threads, both fragments feature Qur'anic verses in *jali* (monumental) *thulth* script. The circular medallion (OPPOSITE) contains *Surat al-Ikhlas* (Purity of Faith) arranged in a radial manner and the panel features parts of verse 97 to the end of 98 from *Surah Ali Imran* (The Family of Imran). The calligraphy stands out from the background and this three-dimensional effect is achieved by embroidering the letters over cotton wadding. The circular medallion comes from one of the four corners of the Ka'bah while the long panel (BELOW) comes from the *hizam* (band of calligraphy) which goes around the Ka'bah, about two thirds of the way up.

From photographs, most of us are familiar with the *kiswah* being black in colour except for the gold and silver embroidery. This, however, has not always been the case. There are historical records to show that *kiswah* came in various colours such as red, white and green. From the 13th century, however, the colour black became predominant. A close look at the fragments shown here will reveal the remains of green silk fibres near the floral sprays—evidence that they were once embroidered on a green background which has since disintegrated, to reveal a dark blue backing.

The *kiswah* is replaced each year before the *haj* (pilgrimage). The previous year's piece is cut up and sold or distributed as *barakah* (blessings) to pilgrims. Parts of the *hizam* are usually presented to various dignitaries. From the Mamluk period to 1962, the *kiswah* was traditionally made in Egypt, except during periods of political disturbances, for example, during the French occupation of Egypt between 1798 and 1801. A lavish camel caravan would carry the *kiswah* to Mecca, where it was historically presented by the leading Muslim regime. The acceptance of the *kiswah* by the authorities in Mecca was an acknowledgment of the donor's political powers. After 1962 and to this day, the honour of bestowing the *kiswah* belongs to the King of Saudi Arabia, and the *kiswah* is made in a workshop in Mecca.

(ABOVE) **PANEL**
Egypt
Early 20th century
Gilded silver and silver threads on silk
89 x 538 cm
2000.327

The *haj* is one of the five pillars of Islam. This spiritual gathering, which today is the largest such gathering in the world, creates a sense of unity. Every year in the Muslim month of Zu'l Hijah, over 2 million pilgrims from around the world congregate in Mecca to perform the *haj*. A central part of the pilgrimage centres around the Ka`bah, and pilgrims circle Islam's holiest sanctuary. Standing around 16 metres tall, the Ka`bah is a cube-like building made of local bluish-grey stone. It is not only the focus of the *haj* and *umrah* (lesser pilgrimage), it is also the direction of prayer for Muslims all over the world. [TH]

▶ see DALA'IL AL-KHAYRAT
▶ see MIHRAB TILE

(TOP) **CIRCULAR MEDALLION**
Egypt
Early 20th century
Gilded silver and silver threads on silk
87.8 x 74.2 cm
1997.2612

Kitab al-Shihab

(The Book of Luminance)

This manuscript is magnificently written in a script known as *maghribi*, on parchment (dried animal skin). The *maghribi* script is characterised by graceful curving downward strokes, and in this manuscript, the strokes that are close together overlap. Developed by the scribes and calligraphers of North Africa and Al-Andalus (Islamic Spain), this script evolved from the more angular Kufic-Abbasid script. Unlike the Kufic-Abbasid script, *maghribi* was used specifically for copying manuscripts and was not used for inscriptions on objects or architecture.

The beauty of the writing in this manuscript is matched by the ornate medallions illuminated in gold and various colours. This manuscript, which contains various sayings as well as *hadith* (traditions of the Prophet Muhammad), was written in the city of Valencia, by Abi Abd Allah Muhammad ibn Salamah ibn Ja'far al-Quda'i.

KITAB AL-SHIHAB
Valencia, Spain
Dated AH 568/1172–1173 CE
Ink, colours and gold on parchment
(FOLIO) 29 x 17.5 cm
On loan from the Tareq Rajab Museum, Kuwait
TR12

By the beginning of the 8th century, Islam had expanded to North Africa and parts of the Iberian Peninsula (Spain and Portugal). Al-Andalus, the name given by Arabic geographers to Muslim Spain, was a flourishing society known for its scholarship and cultural tolerance during the 10th century. After the fall of the Ummayad dynasty in 1031, Al-Andalus was divided into various rival dynasties. Valencia fell into the hands of the Christian forces led by James I of Aragon in 1238. By the early 14th century, the only Islamic dynasty left was the Nasrid Sultanate at Granada, which held out against Christian forces until 1492.

It is rare to find manuscripts or Qur'ans from Al-Andalus, for after the collapse of Islamic rule in Spain, the production of Qur'ans stopped, and books were also destroyed by the Christians. The manuscripts which survived were probably brought to North Africa by refugees. [TH]

▶ see FOLIO FROM A MAGHRIBI QUR'AN
▶ see KUFIC-ABBASID QUR'AN FOLIO

Kraak Porcelain

The term 'Kraak' probably owes its origins to two terms: the carracks that carried this porcelain to Europe, and the Dutch term *'kraken'* which means the ability to break easily.[16] Kraak porcelain dates from mid to late 16th century, suggested by the shards recovered from excavations on the coast of California. In 1602, the capture of the Portuguese carrack *San Tiago* by the Dutch introduced blue and white porcelain to Holland and generated both public and private interest in Europe.

Kraak porcelain is characterised by its division of decoration into panels and cartouches. Mostly decorated in blue and white, the cobalt blue is often a greyish-blue wash, but the three pieces featured here have a brighter blue, probably due to a higher manganese content. Another typical characteristic of Kraak ware is the 'moth-eaten edges', an apt description of the areas where the glaze has flaked off. This is visible along the rim of the large dish featured here (LEFT). The central medallion on this fine large dish comprises two Persian ladies of the Safavid period, adapted from Persian pottery, textiles and metalwork. These ladies are surrounded by floral motifs alternating with scenes of a farmer at work, a scholar reading in his hut and a man on a boat. The tulip motif on the narrow panels along the rim was probably inspired by decorations on Iznik ceramic tiles from Turkey. Coupled with the tulip craze in Holland in the late 16th century, its repeated use on this dish undoubtedly increased its appeal. In Europe this large dish would have served as a washbasin while in West Asia it would have been a dish used for dining.

This Kraak *kendi* (OPPOSITE, TOP), part of the cargo recovered by Captain Hatcher from a Chinese shipwreck, has a shape derived from the Indian *kundika*. Known to the Dutch as a *'gorgolet'*, this drinking vessel has a bulbous-shaped body with five panels including a bird in a landscape, floral designs, and a panel with scrolls and tassels. Other typical Kraak motifs of peach sprays, diapers and ribbons in panels are used on its spout and shoulder. Plantain leaves encircle the neck.

The third Kraak ware featured here (BELOW) is a *klapmuts*, best described as a bowl with rounded walls and an everted rim. Recognising the increasing popularity of this shape for soup bowls in Europe in the 17th century, the Dutch ordered the production of *klapmuts*. The central decoration shows a bird next to a flower, looking at a butterfly. The bird appears smaller in proportion to the flower and butterfly, a characteristic of Kraak decoration. Cartouches with peach sprays in a large panel alternate with hanging ribbons in a narrow panel. This *klapmuts* has a typical underside with a band of floral motifs under its rim and panelled decoration on its outer walls.

It is little wonder that the Europeans liked Kraak porcelain as it proved its versatility in successful combinations of Chinese and non-Chinese motifs and the arrangement of these various combinations on different vessel forms. Kraak ware not only served as tableware, but also became prized decorative items placed in specially designed cupboards. While production in China decreased around the mid 17th century, its popularity never waned, and imitations continued to be made in Japan, England and other parts of the world. [WHL]

(OPPOSITE) **KRAAK DISH WITH PERSIAN LADIES**
Jingdezhen, China
Mid 17th century
Ceramic
h. 10 cm, diam. 48.3 cm
1995.3897

(TOP) **KRAAK *KENDI***
Jingdezhen, China
Mid 17th century
Ceramic
h. 23.5 cm
Retrieved from the Hatcher Cargo;
Gift of Captain M. Hatcher
C1199

(LEFT) **KRAAK *KLAPMUTS* WITH BIRD MOTIF**
Jingdezhen, China
17th century
Ceramic
h. 4.7 cm, diam. 15 cm
C0957

Krishnalila
(Life of Krishna)

This rectangular five-metre long Kalamkari textile is divided into sections by stylised Ionic pillars and framed by a border of chevron patterns and a motif of parrots and foliage. It hails from Tamil Nadu—the scenes painted are described in Tamil. Although the portrayal of Krishna, *gopi* (cowherdesses) and *gvala* (cowherds) in this painting are inspired by the Tanjore-Mysore and Andhra schools of traditional painting, the influence of European stylisation is also present, which is rather unusual.

Krishnalila is depicted in ten scenes: (BELOW, FROM LEFT TO RIGHT) 1. Krishna killing the serpent Kaliya; 2. Krishna playing the flute; 3. Krishna stealing the robes of the *gopi*; 4. Krishna lifting the Govardhana mountain on his little finger; 5. Krishna killing Arishtasuran the bull demon; 6. Krishna killing the horse demon Kesi; 7. Akrura taking Krishna and Balarama in a chariot to Mathura; 8. Krishna accepting sandalwood paste from a female hunchbacked devotee; 9. Krishna breaking the bow; and 10. Krishna killing Kuvaliyapeeda the elephant. In typical Tamil tradition, Krishna is referred to as Shri Kannan and Swami. A synoptic narrative method is used—only the characters that best capture the essence of each episode are painted.

Kalamkari means 'painting with a pen' and this technique is traditionally used to illustrate Hindu mythology and to create textiles for ritual worship in temples. Shri Kalahasti is a well-known centre from which Kalamkari paintings depicting Vaishnava themes such as

KRISHNALILA
Tamil Nadu, south India
19th century
Kalamkari, cotton painted
and printed
256 x 506 cm
1993.1759

Krishnalila or the *Ramayana* are produced. This tradition of Kalamkari painting has been revived recently. Kalamkari paintings depicting mythological scenes are generally horizontal-shaped, and follow an earlier tradition of scroll paintings, running like a comic strip from left to right.

Kalamkari originated in Andhra Pradesh during the Deccan Sultanate period (14th–18th centuries). Style-wise, it is linked to a much more refined cloth-painting tradition from 17th century Golkonda, Deccan. Golkonda was well known for its exports—cloths which were painted with a pen, stencilled and dyed with vegetable colours—and was patronised by both the Mughal and Deccani rulers. The use of vegetable colours, which included indigo, were popular although they have since been replaced with chemical dyes in recent times. Today this tradition has been revived: Mughal-inspired decorative patterns incorporating elements of Iranian, Chinese and European styles are used in cloth-painting in Masulipattam in Andhra Pradesh and exported. The Kalamkaris from Masulipattam also contain stylistic similarities with Bidriware from the Deccan region. Pulicat, near Madras, was also a famous centre for painted-dyed textile production and export at one time. [GPK]

▶ see PICHHAVAI DEPICTING GOPI UNDER A TREE
▶ see VENUGOPALA

Kufic-Abbasid Qur'an Folio

This Qur'an folio is written in an early bold Kufic-Abbasid script. The amount of care taken to plan and write this Qur'an is evident—the letters are well placed and some of the letter endings are stretched across the page to give this stately script some movement. Such monumental Qur'ans on parchment (dried animal skin) are rare and would have been a very expensive project. As such they were probably only meant for use in a mosque. Parchment was the main writing material used for early Qur'ans.

This particular page features part of verse 85 to part of verse 88 of *Surat al-Anbiya'* (The Prophets). The script on this Qur'an does not have any diacritical (*i'jam*) or vocalisation (*tashkil*) marks. This is quite significant as some letters in Arabic share the same outline so diacritical marks such as dots above or below the outline are used to indicate what letter is intended while vocalisation signs indicate the vowels to use. Hence, unless you are very familiar with the text, it will be very difficult to read a Qur'an like the one shown here. Given the prominence of oral recitation of the Qur'an, it is possible that such Qur'ans would have served as a visual aid. The lack of diacritical and vocalisation signs also suggests that this is a very early Qur'an.[17]

While most of us today might think of the Qur'an as a book, the Divine Revelations were in fact transmitted orally with the help of *huffaz* (people who are able to recite the Qur'an from memory) in the early years of Islam. According to a widely held view, the idea of compiling the Qur'an in written form was prompted by the deaths of *huffaz* during battles in 633, shortly after Prophet Muhammad's death.[18] Qur'ans in the early centuries of Islam were written using a group of angular scripts that has been conveniently labelled as Kufic. This term is derived from the Arabic word '*kufi*', which in historical texts is used to refer to the script that developed in Kufah, an early literary centre in Iraq. Since we do not know what the original Kufic script might have looked like, a scholar[19] has suggested the use of the term 'Abbasid' as a replacement; 'Abbasid being the name of the ruling dynasty during which most Qur'ans written with such angular scripts are found. In this publication, we have chosen to use the hybrid term Kufic-Abbasid to describe the script. The Kufic-Abbasid script was generally used by early calligraphers to copy the Qur'an although it was gradually replaced by other scripts which were more cursive from the 10th century onwards.

Fragments of early Qur'ans survive to this day because of the durability of parchment and the respect accorded to the Word of God, which ensured that Qur'ans were not thrown away but stored.[20] [TH]

▶ see QUR'AN
▶ see QUR'AN LEAF

KUFIC-ABBASID QUR'AN FOLIO
North Africa
Early 8th century
Ink on parchment
55 x 70 cm
1999.214

و كانوا لهم ارض الله و اذ حلفوا
الصبر و اذ ادخلها
في لخمسا اهم
يا الصلوة و اذ الوا
اذ مسا مسا
فطر ار لقصد علي
فا في
لظلم لا لا لا لا
اسسطا ا
كب ما لظلم فا
سعسا و لعيه من
لهو كد لا

Kushana Buddha

Seated in *padmasana* (lotus posture) with crossed legs, this pleasantly smiling image of Buddha Shakyamuni is holding his right hand (now broken) in *abhaya mudra* (gesture of fearlessness) while his left hand with clenched fist is resting on the thigh. The circular halo at the back is partially broken and bears a simple semi-circular border. On the back of the halo is a carving of the Bodhi Tree under which Buddha received his enlightenment. The pleated folds of the drapery cover the right shoulder while the edge of the cloth runs diagonally across the torso. Details of the nipples, seen both bare and through the *sanghati* (monk's robe), demonstrate the level of realism the Kushana artist could achieve. The *mahapurushalakshana*, or signs of a great man, can be identified. There is the *ushnisha*, a protuberance on the head which is a sign of Buddha's enlightenment; the elongated earlobes; the *urna*, the tuft of hair between the two eyebrows; *chakra* and swastika marks on the soles of the feet; and *jalanguli*, fingers joined by a web. The base of the sculpture, which may have contained a small relief with carvings of leogryphs and *dharmachakra* (the wheel of law), is now missing. If intact, this sculpture would have been one of the biggest in the seated Buddha Shakyamuni style found in the Mathura region.

This sculpture is a rare example of dated Buddhas of the Kushana period. It bears a donatory inscription in Brahmi, partially erased, under the seat. What can be read of the inscription says, '[The image was installed] by the monk [follower of Vinaya] on the 8th day of the first fortnight of *hemanta* (winter) of the 19th year of the great king Kanishka.' This corresponds to the era of the Kushana King Kanishka I which is generally agreed to have begun in 78. Thus the year of dedication of the sculpture is most likely 96 or 97. The donation is an act of piety and the monk was probably of a very high order, as inferred from his title.

Buddhas in this iconography are also identified as *kapardin* style, those bearing a topknot. Only five other dated seated *kapardin*-style Buddhas are known and this is a rare and valuable addition to the group.[21] [GPK]

KUSHANA BUDDHA
Mathura, Uttar Pradesh, India
96–97
Red spotted sandstone
84 x 78 cm
2000.5627

Lajvardina Tile

This tile is coated with a cobalt-blue glaze with overglaze decorations in red, white and gold. This technique is known as *'lajvardina'* and is derived from the Persian word *'lajvard'* which means lapis lazuli—a brilliant blue semi-precious stone. Although named after lapis lazuli, the stone does not play a part in this technique, although it is an important ingredient from which painters obtain blue pigment. Potters have to resort to cobalt to achieve the blue colour as lapis lazuli powder turns to grey when fired in the kiln.

The raised inscription on this tile is done in *thulth* script and features part of verse 2 from *Surah Al-Fath* (The Victory). It reads: 'That Allah may forgive thee ...'. This particular *surah* (chapter), which promises victory for believers, is popularly found in mosques or other religious settings such as funerary monuments. While this suggests that the tile probably came from such a context, it could also have come from a secular setting. *Lajvardina* tiles containing Qur'anic verses have been found in the Ilkhanid palace complex at Takht-i Sulaiman in northwest Iran.

The *lajvardina* technique first emerged in Iran in the second half of the 13th century and continued to be used in the 14th century. It is an expensive decorative method, for not only is gold leaf used, the tiles have to be fired in the kiln twice. Aside from producing tiles to decorate interiors, *lajvardina* was also used on vessels such as ewers and plates. [TH]

▶ see KASHAN LUSTRE BOWL
▶ see TILE PANEL CONTAINING THE SHAHADAH

LAJVARDINA **TILE**
Kashan, central Iran
13th century
Stone-paste
33.5 x 32.5 cm
On loan from the Tareq Rajab Museum, Kuwait
TR130

Lakhaoun Khaol Masks

These masks represent a few of the main characters from the *Reamker* story, the Khmer version of the *Ramayana,* which underpins the *lakhaoun khaol* (all-male dance-drama) tradition. Gold headdresses (BELOW, LEFT) are used for the human characters such as Preah Ream (Rama) and Neang Seda (Sita). The ogres and monkey characters which predominate in the all-male *khaol* tradition are seen here in the white-faced Hanuman (BELOW, RIGHT), the multi-headed Krong Reap (Ravana) (OPPOSITE, LEFT) and his assistant, the powerful hermit Eysei Akaneat (OPPOSITE, RIGHT). The masks are made by moulding layers of paper in two halves which are then joined together. Decorative elements are moulded in wax and applied to the mask, which is then painted and gilded with gold leaf. This set was commissioned from the workshop of An Sok, one of the few surviving master mask-makers.

Dance and music have a primordial role in Khmer culture, whose origin myths postulate that the Khmer arose as a result of the union of Kambu and an *aspara* (celestial beauty) known as Mera. Performances are considered as offerings to the gods, hence troupes were associated with the court and village temples across the country—the earliest dated Khmer inscription of the year 611 lists the dancers and musicians who were 'donated' in order to serve the deities of a particular temple.[1] Masks were used in various Khmer dance traditions, including *lakhaoun luong* (court dance) and *lakhaoun khaol.*

(ABOVE) *LAKHAOUN KHAOL* MASK FOR NEANG SEDA
Phnom Penh, Cambodia
1999–2000
Papier-mâché
h. 47 cm, diam. 24 cm
2000.1199

(RIGHT) *LAKHAOUN KHAOL* MASK FOR HANUMAN
Phnom Penh, Cambodia
1999–2000
Papier-mâché
h. 26 cm, diam. 27 cm
2000.1204

The *khaol* tradition is thought to have been revived at the court of King An Duong during the mid 19th century but declined after his death. It was again later revived at Svay Andet village across the river from Phnom Penh during the reign of King Norodom (1859–1904). The dancers were periodically called on to perform at the court and they also performed during religious and festive occasions such as Buddhist novitiation ceremonies and New Year celebrations. The tradition was revived during the 1980s after its near-extinction during the period of rule under the Khmer Rouge. Chanted narration and music produced by a *pin peat* ensemble accompany the dance. The enactment of the *Reamker* is believed to have spiritual significance and is necessary in order to maintain natural forces and social order. It is now performed at New Year festivals in villages to ensure sufficient rain during the monsoon season, as well as to ward off sicknesses such as malaria epidemics. [HT]

(LEFT) *LAKHAOUN KHAOL* **MASK FOR KRONG REAP**
Phnom Penh, Cambodia
1999–2000
Papier-mâché
h. 58 cm, diam. 28.5 cm
2000.1218

(ABOVE) *LAKHAOUN KHAOL* **MASK FOR EYSEI AKANEAT**
Phnom Penh, Cambodia
1999–2000
Papier-mâché
h. 83 cm, diam. 34 cm
2000.1209

Lawon Prada

The *selendang* (shoulder cloth) is a dress item worn by women in the Malay world, particularly on formal occasions. This *selendang* is a ceremonial textile known as a *lawon*, and is dyed using the *tritik* technique. *Tritik* is a stitch-resist procedure where sections of the cloth are tightly sewn up to exclude the dye. As with most *lawon*, it has a central rectangular field; this one is bright green against a deep burgundy background. It is said that *lawon* were worn by widows once they had completed the obligatory mourning period. This was a sign that they were free to re-marry.

This *lawon* is further decorated using the technique of *prada*, that is, the gilding of textiles with gold. This is a well-known technique in many areas of Southeast Asia. In *prada*, also sometimes called *telepok*, glue is applied to the cloth either with a brush or stamp before gold leaf or dust is sprinkled on the cloth and left to dry. The cloth is then burnished to bring out a high shine using a cowry shell. *Prada* creates an effect similar to *songket*, which is a supplementary weft technique that is more labour-intensive. This may have made *prada* a popular and lower-cost alternative.[2] [DAH]

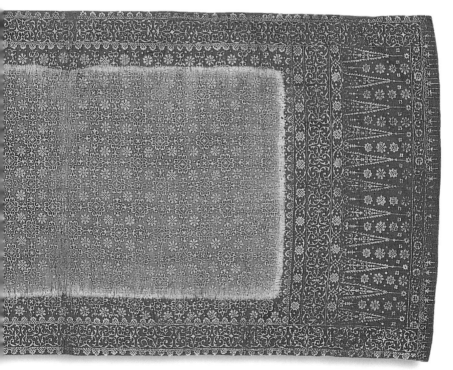

**TEXTILE WITH SEW-AND-DYE
AND GOLD LEAF DESIGN (DETAIL)**
Palembang, south Sumatra, Indonesia
19th century
Silk, gold
83 x 184 cm
1997.3384

Lead-glazed Model Stove

This glazed model stove was fired in an oxidising atmosphere of about 800 degrees Celsius and derived its dark brown colour from iron oxide. The realism of this piece can be attributed to the decorations that were moulded and luted on—a ladle, hooks, prawns, fish, and a figure who appears to be stoking the fire by the fire chamber.

Lead-glazed burial objects were first produced in the Western Han dynasty in shades of green or ochre. Included in the range of objects were earthenware burial figurines, models of domestic animals and kitchen utensils, and architectural and agricultural models, such as watchtowers, houses and granaries. These objects were mainly produced in the kilns of Shaanxi and Henan.

The practice of burying objects with the deceased stems from the belief in life after death. Model stoves are one of the earliest burial objects (*mingqi*) to be produced. They were found in tombs from the late Western Han dynasty and became increasingly popular by the Eastern Han dynasty. Buried with many other ceramic figurines and reproductions of household items in a tomb or a subsidiary pit, the stove served two purposes. It ensured the deceased could continue 'life' in the underworld and served as a proof of his/her identity to underworld officials. [WHL]

LEAD-GLAZED MODEL STOVE
China
Eastern Han dynasty
Ceramic
18 x 18.2 x 9 cm
Gift of Mrs Annie Wee
1992.1277

Liao-Jin Dynasty Silk

Of the published extant fragments of silk brocades woven during the Liao and Jin periods, this particular piece is one of the largest examples. However, this is not a unique fragment for another one exists in the collection of the Metropolitan Museum of Art, New York. Such brocades on monochrome backgrounds emerged as an exclusive luxury textile among the aristocrats of the northern nomadic states of Liao and Jin from the 12th century onwards. It was recorded that the attendants and courtiers serving both the courts of Liao and Jin wore uniforms made of brocade silk on formal occasions and during the spring and autumn hunt outings. Another type of brocade used by the Jin courtiers was woven into red gauze.

While gold had been used to decorate silks, gold threads only became a significant form of embellishment in Chinese workshops after their Liao-Jin overlords began demanding this novelty. Subsequently, when under the Yuan the Mongols became the rulers of China, brocades with gold eventually gained prime status in the imperial silk supply. Until then Chinese imperial silks were characterised by, and famous for, their rich colour palette which required a complicated loom set-up, tedious weaving processes and highly skilled manpower. In fact gold brocade reached unprecedented popularity during the Yuan dynasty, and court

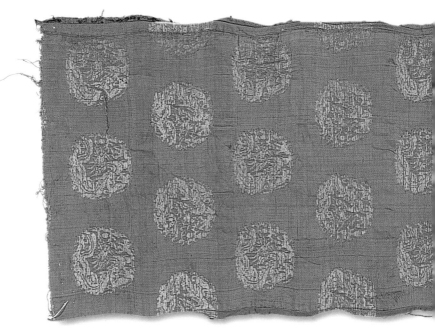

**FRAGMENT OF PERSIMMON SILK WITH COILED
DRAGON MOTIF IN GOLD BROCADE**
Northeast China
12th century
Silk and gold
32.5 x 95.5 cm
1996.167

annals noted that weavers were rounded up from all parts of China, as well as central Asia, to weave for the Yuan court. This tradition persisted through the Ming and the Qing dynasties, during which time the use of gold as decoration on textiles became a common practice.

Most of the similar brocades produced in the Liao-Jin period are woven with animal motifs (swan, gazelle, confronting birds, soaring phoenix) which show central Asian and Persian influences, often composed in geometric shapes such as the tear drop and medallion. This particular fragment, however, features a motif closer to the Chinese repertoire, the dragon coiled in the form of a medallion, called *panlong*. Although the dragon had been a symbol of the emperor since ancient times in China, it only became a widely used symbol on imperial textiles from the Yuan dynasty onwards. The official attire of the Song emperors were still made of plain-coloured silks, in particular crimson red. It was Hongwu, the founding emperor of the Ming dynasty, who instituted robes which were lavishly woven or embroidered with the dragon theme.

Here the dragon motif is woven into a medallion in gold thread as supplementary weft into the tabby-weave persimmon-coloured silk ground. This design was relatively new in 12th-century China and would have been a novel design element from Persia. [LCL]

Lienüzhuan

(Biographies of Exemplary Women)

Lienüzhuan is a collection of stories of virtuous and vicious women first compiled in the Han dynasty by Liu Xiang (c. 79–8 BCE). The original versions of most of the anecdotes compiled by Liu Xiang had previously appeared in *Zuo Zhuan* (*Zuo's Tradition*), *Guo Yu* (*Sayings of the State*) and other Warring States texts. The contents of the *Lienüzhuan* was revised through the dynasties. The original Han version is no longer extant and later editions were mostly based on the Song dynasty version entitled *Gu Lienüzhuan* (*The Ancient Biographies of Exemplary Women*).

The *Lienüzhuan* shown here is a Qing dynasty woodblock printed version originally illustrated by the famous Ming painter, Qiu Ying (c. 1510–1551). In this Qing version, four more volumes were added to the original eight. The organisation of the chapters, however, did not follow the original version which divided the chapters according to the following virtues: maternal rectitude (*muyi*), sagacity (*xianming*), benevolence and wisdom (*renzhi*), chastity and obedience (*zhenshun*), purity and righteousness (*jieyi*), and lastly, argumentative skills (*biantong*). The remaining two volumes of the original version highlighted vicious women and covered supplementary stories. The Qing version was not as systematically laid out, but included stories dating to the Yuan dynasty. In all versions however, the format of the anecdotes did not change. Each anecdote expounded on one virtue or negative trait, and the protagonists comprised daughters, wives, mothers and widows from all walks of life, ranging from empresses and concubines to girls of lowly birth.

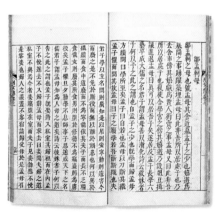

**EXCERPTS FROM 12 VOLUMES OF WOODBLOCK PRINTED BOOKS
ILLUSTRATED BY QIU YING**
(ABOVE) An excerpt from *Lienüzhuan*,
illustrating the story of the Mother of Mencius
(OPPOSITE) An excerpt from *Lienüzhuan*,
illustrating the story of Mulan
China
1779
Paper
(FOLIO) 21.9 x 15.3 cm
1999.2622–34

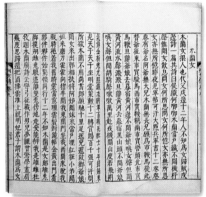

One of the famous stories found in *Lienüzhuan* is that of the Mother of Mencius (c. 371–289 BCE). Mdm Meng was widowed when Mencius was three years old. As a wise and devoted mother, Mdm Meng paid great attention to her son's education. To ensure that Mencius received the right influence, she relocated their residence three times. The third place of residence was near a Confucian school which Mdm Meng found conducive to her son's development. Here Mencius became influenced by the Confucian teachers and learnt about rites and propriety. In the scene illustrated here (OPPOSITE, BELOW, RIGHT), Mdm Meng, extremely disappointed with her son's truancy, admonishes him by cutting off the woven cloth from her loom and comparing her drastic action to Mencius' interruption of his studies: once the cloth was cut, it was rendered useless and could not be sold; similarly, once one stopped schooling, one's future was bleak. Mencius, thus enlightened, turned over a new leaf and applied himself diligently to his studies. He became one of China's greatest philosophers and Confucian scholars.

Another story, about the legendary female warrior, Mulan, whose filial piety and bravery were commended, is also illustrated here (TOP). The story of Mulan did not appear in the early versions of *Lienüzhuan* although she had appeared as early as the Northern dynasties (386–581) in a literary format in the *Ballad of Mulan*. In this scene, Mulan dons military armour, disguising herself as a male to save her aged father from forced conscription. In so doing, she defied conventional expectations of a female's role and place in society. However, as a daughter, she had also observed the highest Confucian virtue of filial piety by protecting her father.

Lienüzhuan served as an instruction text for women for many centuries from the Han to the Qing dynasties. By lauding virtuous behaviour and condemning pernicious women, it reminded women of their roles and positions in society. Women were perceived as agents of virtue and chaos, playing a determining influence on their families and even on the rise and fall of dynasties. [ST]

Relief Fragment Depicting the **Life of Buddha**

This relief in three parts is probably part of an upright pillar with more scenes from the life of Buddha. The lower relief represents Buddha's *mahabhinishkramana* (Great Departure). Prince Siddhartha rides a horse, and a *yaksha* (male vegetation spirit) holds the horse's hooves; Chandaka, the prince's servant, is holding the parasol and Vajrapani, the future bodhisattva, stands in front to welcome the prince. The middle panel shows Buddha seated in meditation touching the earth in *bhumisparsha mudra* (earth-witnessing gesture) surrounded by the retinue of Mara. The top panel represents Buddha in *dharmachakra mudra* (teaching gesture) performing the First Sermon while surrounded by his disciples. This relief encapsulates the most important events from the life of Buddha in a synoptic narrative that is easy to understand.[3]

This relief comes from the Gandhara region of northwest India around the Peshawar valley and bears a confluence of Greco-Roman and Indian styles. The relief is rather worn but the iconography is well preserved. The robes of the man in front of the horse in the lower panel and the woman next to Buddha in the middle panel reflect the Greco-Roman costume while Buddha, his attendants and the disciples are all dressed in the dhoti-style costumes prevalent in India.

Many of the Gandhara-style Buddhist sculptures were produced during the Kushana period from its centre in the Peshawar area and there are sculptures from this region in grey schist up until the 4th century. The other centre of sculpture production was around Mathura in Uttar Pradesh where many stupa sites with sculptures have been excavated. The reliefs adorned stupas and told stories from the life of Buddha; they carried either a moralistic or a religious message. These were the only forms of visual representation that disseminated the teachings of Buddha to lay followers in a lucid and visually appealing manner. The others were texts in Sanskrit and Pali which only monks and the learned could understand. [GPK]

RELIEF FRAGMENT DEPICTING THE LIFE OF BUDDHA
Gandhara, northwest India
3rd–4th centuries
Grey schist
h. 59.4 cm
Gift of Mr Hwang Soo Jin
1998.733

Lintel from Entrance to a Vishnu or Durga Temple

This lintel is part of a doorway which separates the sanctum from the *antarala* and the *mandapam*, thus its iconography and its symbolism are equally important. It also denotes the difference between sacred and profane spaces, which is very important in a temple. The sacred space, which is within the sanctum, can be entered only by priests; devotees may not go past its threshold.

A doorway is made of four parts: *uttaranga* (lintel), *dwarashakha* (door jambs), *udumbara* (threshold) and *pedhya* (lower jambs). Generally, river goddesses such as Ganga and Yamuna are placed on the lower jambs of the doorway, and *makara* and aquatic plants on the threshold; couples, dwarfs, dancers and musicians, and snakes and wines form the jambs. The lintel is the most richly decorated area of a doorway, and has the *navagraha* (nine planets) and the image of the main deity in the *lalatabimba* (central panel). The lintel is to be viewed above eye level so that the *lalatabimba* is above the forehead of the onlooker—that is how it has been displayed in the museum.

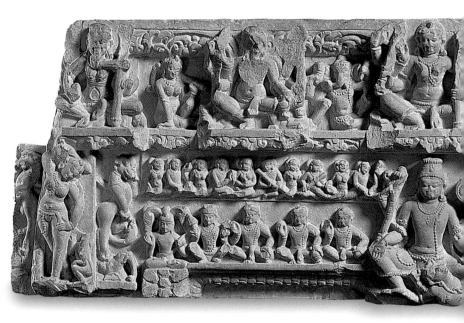

LINTEL FROM ENTRANCE TO A VISHNU OR DURGA TEMPLE (DETAIL)
Central Madhya Pradesh, India
Mid 9th century
Sandstone
40 x 127 cm
Gift of Mr Hwang Soo Jin
1997.3612

This two-tiered lintel has the *navagraha* in the lower level and the *saptamatrika* (seven mothers) in the upper. The central panel contains an image of four-armed Vishnu seated on Garuda. On the extreme two ends are *apsara* (celestial beauties) flanked by *vyala* on either side. One of the *apsara* is being teased by a monkey whom she is hitting with her stick, while the other one is trying to stop her dress from slipping off. In the centre of the upper tier is a representation of a four-armed Durga surrounded by her sons Ganesha and Kartikeya. The other mother goddesses are, from left to right, Chamunda, an unidentified goddess (possibly Maheshvari), Durga, Gauri or Parvati with two lion *vahana* (mounts), and two-ram headed goddesses. It seems that some folk elements have crept into this representation which is based on a local myth or legend. It is possible that this temple was dedicated to Vishnu or to Durga.[4] [GPK]

▶ see STANDING VISHNU AS TRIVIKRAMA
▶ see VATAPATRASHAYI

Lion-shaped Incense Burner

This delightful lion with a tail that ends in a three-lobed semi-palmette design was probably used as an incense burner. Its owner would have placed incense and burning charcoal in the body of the lion by lifting the lion's head, which opens up. The perfumed air would escape through the openwork decorations on the lion's body and its open mouth.

While there was a general orthodox prohibition against the depiction of living things, this rule was not always adhered to in secular settings, as can be seen in surviving metalwork pieces such as this lion incense burner. Nevertheless, this prohibition did have the effect of making the depiction of animals more stylised, and the bodies of the animals are sometimes ornamented with motifs that have nothing to do with the live animal. This incense burner is an excellent example. It is possible to guess that this was meant to be a lion, although the animal has been rendered in an abtract manner. Its body is covered with scrolling floral motifs and there is a band of engraved inscriptions around its neck. The inscriptions in Kufic-Abbasid script—which have become indistinct, probably from use—contain words such as 'glory', 'honour', 'well-being' and 'good fortune'. Metal objects containing inscriptions that ask for blessings and good tidings for their owners are quite commonly found in the Islamic world. [TH]

▶ see KHURASAN JUG

LION-SHAPED INCENSE BURNER
Egypt¹
11th–12th centuries
Copper alloy
h. 22 cm, w. 15 cm
On loan from the Tareq Rajab Museum, Kuwait
TR145

Seated Lokeshvara

okeshvara is shown here seated in *padmasana* (lotus posture) on a double lotus seat supported by a high cushion and a backrest, and his hand is in *vajradhatumudra* (thunderbolt gesture). The throne is elaborately detailed with *makara*, *kinnara* (mythical bird) and leogryphs with riders supporting the backrest on either side. The moulding of the details is very precise and organic. The high backrest is surmounted by an arch-shaped halo. A *makara* with a foliate tail is perched on either side and a Garuda high in the centre of the bronze clasps both tails in his beak. The Garuda in turn has a crescent-shaped surmount with further foliage which resembles plumage. The figure is highly bejewelled and the drapery is inlaid with silver and copper. Below the throne is the representation of a lotus and two lions.

The overall iconography here is clear: Lokeshvara as a bodhisattva is depicted as a teacher and embodies high spiritual powers which he transmits to other teachers in whom he manifests himself. In other instances Lokeshvara embodies the compassion of Avalokiteshvara; and as an aspect of Manjushri he is the protector of the divine law.

This artefact exemplifies the refinement of Pala-Sena sculptural style, decorative motifs and iconography. From the 8th century onwards Pala style spread with Buddhism to China, Tibet, Nepal and as far as Southeast Asia. The hallmarks of Pala bronzes can be seen—with slight variations—in the Buddhist art of these cultures. Much of the Himalayan and Southeast Asian Buddhist and Hindu monuments and votive sculptures have adopted decorative motifs such as the *makara*, *kinnara* and intertwining foliage. This sculpture represents the Sena period artists' mastery of technical skills and detailed vision which allowed them to achieve artistic sophistication. [GPK]

▶ see AKSHOBHYA
▶ see SYAMATARA
▶ see TIBETAN BOOK COVERS

SEATED LOKESHVARA
Northeast India
Sena dynasty, 12th century
Bronze with copper and silver alloy
h. 30 cm
Purchased with funds from Singapore Reinsurance
Corporation Ltd and India International Insurance Pte Ltd
1997.2253

Lolo Garments

This set of garments comprises a jacket (BELOW), headcloth (OPPOSITE, TOP) and trousers (OPPOSITE, BELOW) which were worn by the women of the sub-group of the Lolo known as Flower Lolo (*Rong Me*). A complete outfit includes an additional sash and apron. The geometric patterns in predominantly red, yellow, pink and blue were hand-sewn using an appliqué method of cutting and stitching coloured cloth onto the indigo-dyed garments. The black headcloth is folded and then wrapped around the head like a wide headband. It was tie-dyed with floral and geometric motifs, as well as embroidered and appliquéd with bright fabrics. The beaded tassels are decorated with plastic buttons, glass and bone beads and colourful pompoms.

The Lolo are Tibeto-Burman language speakers and an estimated 3,000 live in the northern provinces of Vietnam today. They live in settled villages farming wet rice and raising cattle. Ancestor worship is predominant and ancient head-hunting rites are sometimes still observed at funerals, when a person carries a cloth bag decorated with the drawing of a head (▶ see DAYAK CARVED HUMAN SKULL). Bronze kettledrums are also still used for

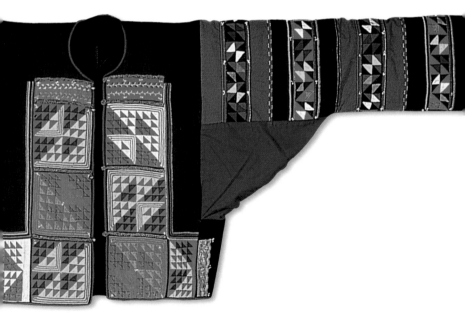

JACKET, HEADCLOTH AND TROUSERS
Ha Giang province, north Vietnam
Early 20th century
Embroidered and appliquéd cotton
(JACKET) 132 x 47 cm;
(HEADCLOTH) 260 x 33 cm;
(TROUSERS) 97 x 87 cm
2000.5618, 2000.5619, 2000.5617

funerary rituals—a male and female drum are hung facing each other near the feet of the deceased, where they are played to help guide the soul back to the ancestors (▶ see DONG SON DRUM). The drums are an essential part of the Lolo origin myth in which their ancestors, a brother and sister, were saved from a flood by keeping afloat in two kettledrums.[6] [HT]

Longyan Wood Day Bed

Called *ta*, the day bed is an informal piece of furniture long favoured by the literati for use in the study, where it had multiple purposes. In the words of the Ming dynasty aesthete Wen Zhenheng, grand-nephew of the Zhejiang school literati painter Wen Zhengming:

> Although the day beds made in the olden days varied widely in size, they simply look elegant and lovely in the study. One can either sit or lean without difficulty. One can spread out books, or calligraphy, or paintings for leisurely inspection. One can also examine antique bronzes on them... (*Zhangwuzhi*, chapter 6)

The day bed performs its various functions best when equipped with certain accoutrements. When the Taoist connoisseur of fine living, Gao Lian, recommended the use of *ta* made of spotted bamboo (*xiangzhu*) in the study for resting when tired, he advised placing a small table (*ji*) on the day bed to lean on, and a small foot stool in front for easy access. For summer comfort Gao advised the use of mats made of bamboo splits, and for winter, mattresses.

These connoisseurs of the Ming dynasty probably had not heard of *longyan* wood and did not know that the fruit tree in its maturity developed a beautiful grain. The *longyan*

LONGYAN **WOOD DAY BED**
Fujian, China
Early 19th century
Longyan wood
203 x 110 x 87.5 cm; (SEAT) h. 51.5 cm
Gift of Richard Loo Leong Chai and family
in memory of their parents
Mr and Mrs Loo Choon Hean
1999.1398

(or, more commonly, '*longan*' in Cantonese) tree was a regional speciality of Fujian province, cultivated for its fruit by Fujianese entrepreneurs during the Ming dynasty, together with tea and other cash crops, such as the lychee. It was only in the Qing dynasty (18th century), when the old *longyan* trees were being felled en masse, that the timber was found to be highly suitable for making furniture. Its aesthetic quality was seen to be comparable to that of the more established hardwoods such as blackwood (*shuanzhi*) and *zitan*.

This Qing day bed is styled in the archaic way that would have won approval from Wen Zhenheng and Gao Lian. All wooden parts are left unadorned but the proportions of the bed lend it a sense of stateliness and make the bed seem larger than it really is. Its simplicity is consistent with the strong, almost single-minded sense of style that characterises most Fujianese furniture of *longyan* wood. The bed exudes a sense of archaism which epitomises literati aesthetics—it is as if *Zhangwuzhi* had been studied as a rule book. Wen Zhenheng had this to say in *Zhangwuzhi*: 'These days the beds are carved with decorations to please the unsophisticated. A bed of vintage commands a magnanimous feeling that makes one exclaim with admiration ...'. [LCL]

Lotus Sutra

This is the third chapter of the famous *Lotus Sutra*, or *Miaofa Lianhua Jing*, printed during the Qianlong period. The frontispiece (OPPOSITE, TOP) is a dramatic scene depicting Buddha preaching the tenets of the *Lotus Sutra* to the bodhisattvas, deities, *arhat* (great adepts) and Virupaksha (Guardian of the West), who is recognised by the pagoda in his hand. Although the setting is the spiritual Vulture Peak, where Buddha taught his thousands of disciples and followers, this 18th-century interpretation renders the scene in an intimate garden setting, which is more akin to the mood captured in paintings of summer literati garden parties.

Completed at the end of the second century and translated into Chinese by the Central Asian monk Kumarajiva around 406, it is the most-read Buddhist scripture in China. The textual section (OPPOSITE, BOTTOM) of the *sutra*, based on Kumarajiva's translation, is executed in elegant regular script (*kaishu*) calligraphy. The basic concepts embraced by Mahayana Buddhism are expounded in this famous *sutra*, in which Buddha reveals the eternity of his enlightenment and compels the appearance of all his previous existence. The *sutra* also testifies to Buddha's recognition of the different qualities, temperaments and levels of intelligence of all beings, and hence the introduction of the compassionate bodhisattvas, enlightened beings who withhold their own enlightenment and selflessly vow to bring into fruition the universal salvation of all beings. One of the most important bodhisattvas, Avalokiteshvara, also known as Guanyin or Guanshiyin (▶ see GUANYIN), is formally introduced to the world for the first time in this *sutra*, specifically in chapter 25. Here the power of Guanyin is described in detail, and her compassion is so great that when her name is called out by any being in distress, the bodhisattva will appear in an appropriate form to deliver the caller from his trouble and peril. The cult of Guanyin grew larger in China as the

LOTUS SUTRA
China
Qianlong period, 18th century
Paper, woodblock printing
h. 26.5 cm
2001.2613

sutra became widely available through printing, and because of the popular appeal of the compassionate and selfless Guanyin. As a result the *Lotus Sutra* is probably the most widely printed and illustrated scripture.

The Central Asian monk Kumarajiva was born to a Brahman sage and a princess of Kucha. Having started his career at the age of seven following his mother who went into nunnery, Kumarajiva was an incredibly learned and widely travelled monk. Fluent in Chinese, he charmed the court of the Jin dynasty and lived for about 12 years in Chang'an, where he supervised a thousand monks on the translation of Buddhist scriptures, among which the *Lotus Sutra* was one. [LCL]

妙法蓮華經卷第三

姚秦三藏法師鳩摩羅什譯

藥草喻品第五

爾時世尊告摩訶迦葉及諸大弟子善哉善哉迦葉善說如來真實功德誠如所言如來復有無量無邊阿僧祇功德汝等若於無量億劫說不能盡迦葉當知如來是諸法之王若有所說皆不虛也於一切法以智方便而演說之其所說法皆到於一切智地如來觀知一切諸法之所歸趣亦知一切眾生深心所行通達無礙又於諸法究盡明了示諸眾生一切智慧世尊譬如三千大千世界山川谿谷土地所生卉木叢林及諸藥草種類若干名色各異密雲彌布遍覆三千大千世界一時等澍其澤普洽卉木叢林及諸藥草小根小莖小枝小葉中根中莖中枝中葉大根大莖大枝大葉諸樹大小隨上中下各有所受一雲所雨稱其種性而得生長華果敷實雖一地所生一雨所潤而諸草木各有差別迦葉當知如來亦復如是出現於世如大雲起以大音聲普徧世界天人阿脩羅如彼大雲徧覆三千大千國土

A Page from the **Mahabharata**

This is a fairly large manuscript painting, now separated from an original set of the epic *Mahabharata*, illustrating the Vana Parva. It may have been commissioned by a royal patron since the format and the finish of the illustration is of a high quality.

The illustration represents the story of the five Pandava brothers who lost a game of dice and were banished for 14 years. The painting illustrates what happened before the game of dice. This scene depicts their encounters in the Panchala region where they went for the *svayamvara* (a wedding procedure) of Draupadi, daughter of King Drupada of Panchal. Arjuna, one of the brothers, won the contest and the hand of Draupadi in marriage. Even though they were princes, the Pandavas were disguised as Brahmans. At the top right of the painting, Draupadi and Kunti, the Pandavas' mother, serve the Pandava brothers food on leaf plates, while below that, they take a nap. The men sleep in one row and Draupadi and Kunti in another. There are several buildings and tents in the foreground which suggests that they are living within the city. There were many princes who came for the *svayamvara* and they are depicted encamped in different tents. Even Krishna and Balarama are seen walking in the street. An interesting element in this narrative is the representation of Draupadi's brother, Dhrshtadyumna, who stealthily observes the behaviour of the Pandavas, to whom his sister Draupadi is recently married. He is represented at least twice watching over the events, then reassures his father that the match between the Pandavas and Draupadi is a good one. King Drupada is also seen with an anxious expression on one of the balconies.

The Pahari region has yielded many beautiful paintings on paper, suffused with a

A PAGE FROM THE *MAHABHARATA*
Kangra, Himachal Pradesh, north India
Late 18th–early 19th centuries
Paper
30.4 x 41.5 cm
2000.3522

grace, lyricism and vigour seldom surpassed by any other style. It is poetry in lines and colour. Generally, they illustrate love poetry, epics and mythological scenes, images of gods and goddesses, historical portraits and court scenes. There were many schools and each one emerged under the patronage of a ruler of the region. Kangra is the foremost and most mature style of the region. This painting style evolved almost parallel with the Mughal style from the Delhi and Agra courts. Many artists travelled across north India, cross-fertilising the various elements of design and style. [GPK]

Mamluk Basin

During the Mamluk period, the increase in the amount of zinc used in the making of brass, a copper alloy, gave the latter a more golden hue. Impressive pieces of silver-inlaid brassware were commissioned and produced for sultans and their *amir* (emirs, or court officials), with many of the brassware showing off the titles of their owners. Little wonder then that of all the types of material culture, metalwork is what the Mamluk period is perhaps best known for. The most magnificent pieces were made in the 14th century.

The large basin shown here (OPPOSITE, BOTTOM) dates from this period. It is decorated with a band of cursive *naskh* inscription on a scrolling background. This inscription is interrupted by four medallions containing, alternately, lotuses (BELOW) and a three-register blazon (OPPOSITE, BOTTOM). If you look carefully at the object, you will find that all four medallions were originally decorated with lotuses, and that the lotuses in two alternate medallions have, curiously, been rubbed off and the blazon added on. The blazon shows a sword in the central register and a duck on the top register. The sword was a symbol of the office of the *silahdar* (armour-bearer), an official in the Mamluk administration. However, this emblem has also been adopted by some *amir* who have not held that post before.

The inscription reads:

The Most Noble Authority, the High, the Lordly, the Masterly, the Learned, the Diligent, the Just, the Responsible, the Supporter, the Marshal, the Helper, the Succour, the Sustaining, the Valiant, the Orderly, the Equitable, the Leader, the Reverend, the Masterful ... [the officer of] al-Malik al-Salih, may his glory be everlasting.

Judging from the quality of the decoration and the amount of silver inlay used, this basin was probably made for a well-to-do patron, an *amir* of Sultan Malik al-Salih, as the inscription indicates. There were two sultans with the title Malik al-Salih—al-Malik al-Salih Ismail (reign. 1342–1345) and al-Malik al Salih Salih (reign. 1351–1354).

MAMLUK BASIN
Egypt
1342–1345 or 1351–1354
Silver inlay on copper alloy
diam. 34.5 cm
2000.5635

DETAILS
(ABOVE) The medallion containing a lotus
(OPPOSITE, TOP) The engraved fish pond motif

From the 14th century, Chinese motifs began appearing on Mamluk metalwork and ceramics. The lotus is one of the Chinese motifs added to the vocabulary of the Islamic artisan. Some scholars have studied the decorations on various Islamic metalwork to try and understand what the decorations might symbolise. It has been postulated that the lotus was more than just decorative, that it might actually be a solar symbol, the meaning of which was not derived from China. Geese, like the lotus, which were often depicted on Mamluk metalwork, could also be seen as solar symbols, with their meanings derived from ancient Egyptian beliefs. On the inside of this bowl (RIGHT), a 'fish pond'

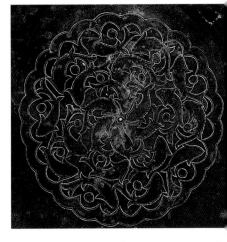

motif[1] is engraved, another motif which could be associated with the sun.[2] By studying metalwork made for Mamluk sultans, a scholar has suggested that the use of solar symbols was intended to associate the sun with the sultan.[3] The use of solar symbols by *amir* was then perhaps to exhibit the glory of the ruler, or for self-glorification. [TH]

▶ see KHURASAN JUG

Mamuli Ornaments

In the Lesser Sunda islands, gift exchange is an important practice during the period leading up to marriage. The bride's family is expected to proffer textiles, which are considered female, to the groom's family in exchange for items made of metal and ivory, which are considered male. One of the most important items of exchange is the *mamuli*, a beautifully crafted, diamond-shaped gold pendant. Some *mamuli* are considered family heirlooms; others that are particularly old and valuable are considered so important they are rarely exchanged. More ordinary ones, however, are often passed on from family to family with each successive marriage ceremony.

Typically, *mamuli* are made from gold or gilded silver and feature granulated and braided wire decorations of sometimes highly intricate design. These decorations often feature animal or even human figures. The Sumbanese say that the shape of *mamuli* represents the female sexual organ[4] and as such is symbolic of fertility.

Three examples of *mamuli* are pictured here. The first example (BELOW, LEFT) features a pair of buffaloes, which in Sumba symbolises wealth. The second *mamuli* (BELOW, RIGHT) is decorated with a pair of curious looking pelicans. The last pendant (BELOW, CENTRE) is adorned with a stylised bird head design that is quite different from the other two examples. [DAH]

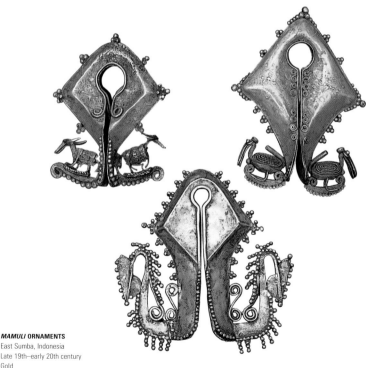

MAMULI ORNAMENTS
East Sumba, Indonesia
Late 19th–early 20th century
Gold
(CLOCKWISE FROM TOP LEFT) 6.5 x 5.7 cm;
7.3 x 6.8 cm; 7.5 x 8 cm
(EC121) Gift of Mr Edmond Chin
EC121, 1999.00220, 1999.00219

Mandau Hilt

This is the carved hilt of a Kayan Dayak *mandau* (ceremonial sword). The deer antler has been elaborately carved in intricate scroll motifs and openwork spirals (SEE DETAIL, BELOW, RIGHT). The effort expanded in the production of this handle is a good indication that it was made for ceremonial use.

Many Dayak groups had sword hilts carved out of the antlers of rusa (sambur deer) or of hardwoods. It is difficult to establish whether a style characterises a particular Dayak group as many Dayak communities were in frequent contact with one another. These contacts were both friendly and hostile. *Mandau* hilts and heads (▶ see DAYAK CARVED HUMAN SKULL) were frequent trophy items in wars and raids on enemy longhouses and communities for Dayak warriors. The origins of most *mandau* hilts in the possession of any one Dayak group are thus ambiguous as these hilts may have been a raided possession of another group.

'Dayak' is the name given to a large number of ethnic groups of interior Borneo, each of which has its own language and separate culture. The major Dayak groups can be classified into three categories: the egalitarian groups such as the Iban and Bidayuh; stratified groups such as the Kayan and Kenyah; and the hunters and gatherers such as the Penans. The various Dayak groups share similarities in material culture, cosmology, social organisation and ecological adaptation. The distribution of these groups is extremely complex, with ethnically related peoples occupying widely separated areas and peoples who are not ethnically related sometimes living in close proximity to one another. [RE]

DAYAK *MANDAU* HILT
Sarawak, Malaysia
c. 1900s
Deer antler
17.5 x 10 cm
2000.00173

(ABOVE) **DETAIL**
Intricate scroll motifs and open spirals on the hilt

Marshall Zhao

This portrait of Marshall Zhao was commissioned by four merchants: Jia Qilüe, Wang Xueceng, Dong Yingke and Guan Yan, as inscribed. Here he is venerated as a god of wealth and identified by his metal headgear, warrior costume and ringed sword. He stands steadfast in an indomitable pose next to his mount, the black tiger.

Marshall Zhao enjoyed a long history of popularity with his cult declining in the mid Qing dynasty. He is, in actual fact, a fictional character who is believed to be named Zhao Gongming or Zhao Lang. The earliest records of him appear in the Jin dynasty, during which he was conceived as a terrifying underworld spirit. In the Liang dynasty, he retained fearsome characteristics as a *Wufang ling* (Five-Directions Spirit), which is similar to an underworld and plague god, and by the Sui-Tang dynasties, he had manifested into one of the five gods of plague. Till then, Marshall Zhao had been perceived as a menacing god.

During the Yuan dynasty, the Daoists sought to incorporate Marshall Zhao into their pantheon by conferring on him the role of a guardian protecting the pot of alchemy created by the Daoist master, Zhang Daoling. It was alleged that the latter took him as a disciple and gave him some alchemical potion to consume, thereby endowing him with the magical ability of self-transformation. Thereafter he became associated with the Daoist altar of alchemy called *xuantan* and was known as Zhao Xuantan. His attributes became more defined and his functions expanded. He also became a more benign god: clearing plague, protecting the people from illnesses and summoning rain and wind when necessary.

It was in *Fengshen yanyi* (*Investiture of the Gods*), a popular novel written in the Ming dynasty that he metamorphosed into a full-fledged wealth god and became popularly venerated as so, especially by the merchant class. During this period, Marshall Zhao was incorporated into the four heavenly generals—together with Generals Ma, Wen and Guan (or Guangong, ▶ see GUANGONG)—who were summoned by Daoists masters during their exorcism rites. Thus Marshall Zhao reached the height of his popularity during the Ming dynasty. He was widely venerated in Sichuan in particular, perhaps due to his association with the Sichuan native, Zhang Daoling. Moreover, due to his association with the black tiger, he also enjoyed immense popularity among ethnic minorities in Sichuan. [ST]

MARSHALL ZHAO
China
Late Ming dynasty
Polychrome and gilt on silk
150.5 x 77.5 cm
1999.69

Relief Fragment of Three Matrika

This relief fragment is part of a larger relief that shows the *saptamatrika* (seven mothers) accompanied by Ganesha and Veerabhadra. The *saptamatrika* are also the *shakti* (female manifestation) of principle Hindu gods. This piece features only three *matrika* (mother goddesses); the other four *matrika*, Ganesha and Veeerabhadra are now missing.

The three *matrika* adopt the typical Indian *ardhaparyankasana* posture on a low seat. On the extreme right is Varahi (*shakti* of Varaha). She has the head of a boar and holds a fish and a bowl. In the centre is Vaishnavi (*shakti* of Vishnu), who is seated on a human figure that probably represents Garuda (Vishnu's eagle mount). Vaishnavi is depicted here wearing a *mala* (garland) around each of her four arms. Her two upper arms hold a *chakra* (discus) and *gada* (mace) each. Her crown is characteristic of the conical caps seen on Pratihara sculptures, especially those from Kannauj in the 10th to 11th centuries (▶ see STANDING VISHNU AS TRIVIKRAMA). On the left is Kaumari, the consort of Kumara, who goes by the name of Subrahmanya in south India (▶ see SUBRAHMANYA). She is seated on a peacock holding a spear in her left hand. The jewels, crowns and hairdo of all three *matrika* are typical of sculptures of the Pratihara style. It can be inferred from the repose of the *matrika's* full-bodied torsos, firm breasts and regal demeanour that they are queens or royal personages.

The *saptamatrika*—Brahmani, Aindri, Maheshwari, Vaishnavi, Kaumari, Varahi and Chamunda—were created to bestow strength on Durga, the primordial Hindu mother goddess.[5] They have an independent cult of their own and are most often associated with water tanks and *yajnashala* (sacrificial halls), such as those at Ellora caves 16 and 21, where they were placed on the southern wall. [GPK]

RELIEF FRAGMENT OF THREE *MATRIKA*
Uttar Pradesh, India
10th century
Buff sandstone
45 x 62.9 cm
1996.679

Mihrab Tile

This *mihrab* (prayer niche) tile would most likely have been set in a wall of a mosque to help indicate the direction of prayer. Made of green-glazed earthenware, the tile has a central panel with a pendant lamp hanging within a horseshoe arch. On either side of the arch is the word 'Allah', done in mirror image on the left. The Qur'anic inscription found around the sides of the tile and in the top two lines at the base is part of verse 18 of *Surat al-Taubah* (The Repentance), which states that 'The mosques of Allah shall be visited and maintained by such as believe in Allah …'.

Mihrab tiles are not found solely in mosques; they are also used in homes to help indicate the *qiblah* (direction of Mecca). The verse inscribed on this tile supports the belief that it was meant for a mosque. The last line contains the name of the maker, Muhammad b. Firuz al- … [the last word cannot be read].

In the prayer hall of any mosque, the *qiblah* wall orientates the prayers of Muslims towards the Ka'bah in Mecca. The *qiblah* wall is usually easy to identify, as it is generally the most decorated wall in the mosque, with the *mihrab* at its centre. Architecturally, the *mihrab* is made up of an arch with supporting columns and it looks like a doorway. The central panel of this tile depicts a *mihrab*.

Mihrab were not found in the earliest mosques of the Islamic world, and the direction of prayer was shown by the *qiblah* wall itself, which was sometimes reinforced by a painted mark or flat stone. From the 8th century onwards, the use of *mihrab* became more widespread and it soon became one of the essential elements of mosque architecture. [TH]

▶ see KISWAH FRAGMENTS FROM THE HOLY KA'BAH
▶ see FRAGMENTS FROM A MINBAR

MIHRAB TILE
Northeast Iran
c. 11th century
Earthenware
43 x 28.3 cm
1999.2704

Minangkabau Jewellery

According to researcher Ann Summerfield, spectacular ceremonial headdresses like this one (OPPOSITE) have been worn by the women of the town of Solok in west Sumatra for centuries.[6] Originally worn draped over the top of a peaked cloth cap, this particular headdress consists of two plates of incised gold hinged at the middle. The front plate is festooned with a profusion of small gold-foil flowers of intricate workmanship while at the back small gold pendants dangle from the back edge of the rear plate.

Decorative bracelets were also worn as part of the Minangkabau woman's ceremonial costume. These dramatic pieces (BELOW), known as *galang gadang*, were the favoured style of the women of Sungei Puar in the heart of the Minangkabau homeland. Measuring just over 24 centimetres in height, this set is very rare due to its good condition as well as its size, although there are even larger ones. The bracelets are made from individual copper plates that have been soldered together and then gilded. They are stained a reddish colour using an acidic solution. Leaf and tendril repoussé patterns decorate these very large, box-like bracelets.

In Minangkabau society, gold jewellery was an important part of a family's *pusaka*, or heirlooms that were passed down from mother to daughter through the matrilineal society. According to Minangkabau tradition, jewellery styles varied considerably according to region, a product of the very close family and regional identification of the Minangkabau people. The motifs and designs of Minangkabau art had specific meaning for the people who used them. Sadly, much of this tradition is no longer followed and armbands of this type are no longer readily available in the region. [DAH]

(ABOVE) **MINANGKABAU BRACELETS**
West Sumatra
1930s
Gold with red staining, gems and copper plate
24 x 18 cm
2000.06701

(OPPOSITE) **HEADDRESS**
West Sumatra
1930s
Gold and copper plate
73 x 48 cm, diam. 14 cm
Gift of Mr Edmond Chin
EC285

Miniature Qur'an

This tiny manuscript contains the entire Qur'an written in a script called *ghubar* (which means 'dust' in Arabic). As its name implies, *ghubar* is a script that is so tiny that it is likened to specks of dust. There are two illuminated double pages in the beginning of this Qur'an, and the pictures you see here show one half of each double page.

The first picture (BELOW, LEFT) features the first *surah* (chapter) in the Qur'an, *Surat al-Fatihah* (The Opening). The text is framed by panels of blue and gold illuminations, and in the top panel, the *surah* heading is written in silver Kufic-Abbasid script on a scrolling ground. Incredibly, the rest of the pages in this manuscript contain 17 lines of text on each page with margins on three sides.

While the *ghubar* script is tiny, the writing has to be legible. To distort the Divine Text is a serious matter, and a calligrapher would thus not only need good eyesight[7] but also a steady hand. While legible, miniature Qur'ans were probably not made to be read. They were most likely kept in a box and worn for protection or for blessings. Ottoman sultans used to commission the production of miniature Qur'ans (known as *sancak* Qur'ans) which would be placed in cases and carried on top of standards during battles.

Miniature Qur'ans are still produced today, although they are printed rather than handwritten. Some are even sold with accompanying magnifiers. The Qur'an shown here is not only handwritten, but is also an early example of miniature Qur'ans produced by Islamic calligraphers. [TH]

▶ see SAFAVID QUR'AN CASE
▶ see QUR'AN SCROLL

LEAVES FROM A MINIATURE QUR'AN
Western Persia (Iran) or Anatolia (Turkey)
14th century
Ink, colours and gold on paper
(FOLIO) 7 x 4.9 cm
1998.1468

Monk's Cap Ewer

This monk's cap ewer has a white body, which is further glazed in white. Under light the transparency of the porcelain body—a result of the low calcium oxide content—is visible. The glaze is not the *tianbai* (sweet white) glaze, for which the Yongle reign was known, but is a bluish glassy glaze rather similar to *yingqing* glaze (◗ see QINGBAI PORCELAIN). This bluish tone is evident on *anhua* decorations, which include a band of lotus scrolls around the rim, on the neck and the body, and the Eight Buddhist Emblems. Encircling the neck are four incised roundels inscribed with the characters '*Yongle Nianzhi*' or 'Made during Yongle's reign' in seal script—one character in each roundel. Below each roundel is a lotus, which forms part of the lotus scroll winding round this unique reign mark. Similarly on the body each lotus from the lotus scroll is incised to correspond to each of the Eight Buddhist Emblems. Lotus petal panels encircle the foot of the ewer. On the top of the handle is a *ruyi* panel which is repeated at the end of the handle.

The monk's cap ewer derives its name from the caps worn by Tibetan monks and this unique shape is attributed to Tibetan metalwork. Further association between Tibet and Emperor Yongle can be traced to 1407 when Yongle conferred the title '*Dabao Fawang*' (Great Precious Dharma King) on the Tibetan hierarch, Halima (1384–1415), after he presided over the Buddhist rituals held in honour of Hongwu, Yongle's father. The preference for white comes from connotations of mourning and filial piety. This is evident in Bao'en Temple where white porcelain bricks were chosen by Yongle to illustrate his filial piety towards Hongwu and his empress in 1412. These acts of filial piety proved Yongle's legitimacy to the throne, which he had usurped from his nephew.

Excavations at the middle section of Zhushan Road in Jingdezhen (the area where the imperial kiln was located) have yielded many monk's cap ewers. This monk's cap ewer might have been one of the gifts presented to Halima or a ceremonial ware for Tibetan rituals at court. [WHL]

WHITE MONOCHROME MONK'S CAP EWER
Jingdezhen, China
Ming dynasty, Yongle period
Ceramic
(WITH LID) h. 20.8 cm
1998.725.1–2

Moroccan Wooden Panels

These three wooden panels, which are probably fragments from a door, are decorated in the same style with only slight variations among them. Each panel is designed with a *mihrab* (prayer niche) arch shape framed by a calligraphic border on three sides. The cursive inscriptions are written over a background of scrolling *arabesque* (stylised plant motif) and are a repetition of benedictory phrases such as

> Mirth, and Joy in all affairs
> Happiness and wholesomeness,
> and the attainment of desires.
> Mirth, and Joy in days and months and at all times.
> Happiness and festivity at night and in the morning
> Mirth, and Joy in all affairs
> Happiness and wholesomeness,
> and the attainment of desires.

Benedictory phrases were quite commonly depicted on objects made for Muslim patrons.

MOROCCAN WOODEN PANELS
North Africa
19th century
Colours and silver on wood
163.2 x 86.3 cm
1999.212.1–3

These panels are decorated with the three most important artistic expressions in Islamic art: calligraphy, geometric and floral motifs. Within the arches are geometric motifs, and the area between the arch and the calligraphic border is filled with floral designs. These three artistic expressions were fully developed by artists in the Islamic world, and which is in keeping with the concept of *tauhid*. *Tauhid*, which encompasses the belief in the absolute power and uniqueness of Allah, is a central concept in Islam and has an important impact on Islamic art. Although the Qur'an does not prohibit it, orthodox Muslims generally frown on the representation of living things. Underlying this is the fear of idolatry, which is especially offensive to a religion that believes in a God which cannot be represented. [TH]

▶ see KHURASAN JUG
▶ see LION-SHAPED INCENSE BURNER

Mosque Candlesticks

These large, bell-shaped candlesticks would most probably have flanked either sides of a *mihrab* (prayer niche) in a mosque. While in the past such lighting equipment undoubtedly provided light in the mosque, there is also perhaps a non-functional reason associated with their use near the *mihrab*. The use of candlesticks and hanging lamps near the *mihrab* allude to a Qur'anic verse which is significant in Islamic spirituality—verse 35 of *Surat an-Nur* (The Light), which reads:

> Allah is the Light of the heavens and the earth. The parable of His light is as if there were a Niche and within it a Lamp: The Lamp enclosed in Glass; The glass as it were a brilliant star; Lit from a blessed Tree, An Olive, neither of the East nor of the West, Whose Oil is well-nigh luminous, Though fire scarce touched it; Light upon Light! Allah doth guide whom He will to His light; Allah doth set forth Parables for men: and Allah doth know all things.

These copper candlesticks have been tinned to give them a silvery finish. It was usual for a thin layer of tin to be applied on to the surface of domestic copper utensils in order to avoid getting metal poisoning from verdigris. However, in the case of these candlesticks, it was perhaps done to emulate silver.

Pairs of monumental candlesticks were often made and given to mosques. Aside from mosques, candlesticks are also found in mausoleums in Turkey. Today, you can still see large candlesticks in use in Turkish mosques. However, instead of holding candles, they have been adapted to hold electric bulbs. [TH]

▶ see MIHRAB TILE

MOSQUE CANDLESTICKS
Turkey
Ottoman period
Tinned copper alloy
h. 76 cm, diam. 51 cm
1996.524.1, 1996.524.2

Mufradat by Hafiz Osman

A *mufradat* is an album which contains pages in which the Arabic letters are written in their various forms. Calligraphers write these pages for practice, and also for use as exemplars for students to study. The usual format for an Ottoman *mufradat* is a horizontal album with two to three lines of *thulth* script with a line or two of *naskh* in between. The two albums shown here are done in this typical style.

The Arabic script contains 17 distinct letter shapes which feature 29 letters of the alphabet; this is done with the help of diacritical dots. What is interesting about the Arabic script is that certain letters of the alphabet take on a different shape depending on their position in the word. For example, in the first album (BELOW) the top line features the initial form of the letter 'ayn, while at the bottom line, the last letter features the 'ayn in its final form. (Note that Arabic is read from right to left.)

The pages in these two albums have been mounted differently. The first (BELOW) has *ebru* (marbled paper) margins, the second (OPPOSITE) has gold-sprinkled paper. Both albums were written by one of the most important Ottoman calligraphers living in the 17th century, Hafiz Osman (1642–1698). At a very young age, Hafiz Osman received the title 'Hafiz' because of his ability to recite the Qur'an by heart—a feat greatly admired in the Islamic world. He was the successor of the calligraphic tradition that was established by Şeyh Hamdullah (1429–1520).

The master-student relationship is an important one in Islamic calligraphy. The use of the *mufradat* as an exemplar for students is a physical manifestation of this relationship. Students have to study their teacher's work and make copies, as accurately as possible, of them. This technique, known as *taklid* (following the model), is an important aspect of their

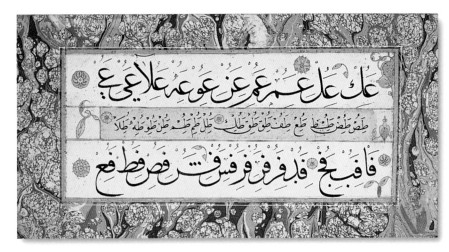

MUFRADAT WITH **EBRU** MARGINS
Turkey
Ottoman period, late 17th century
Ink, colours and gold on paper
(FOLIO) 15.2 x 27 cm
1998.1481

training. Only through close study of various masters' works can one gain an understanding of the art, after which one's artistic abilities can come into play. Hafiz Osman for instance, was taught calligraphy by teachers who studied in the tradition of Şeyh Hamdullah. In order to gain a better understanding of the Şeyh's technique, he then studied Şeyh Hamdullah's original works by doing *taklid*. After this, Hafiz Osman developed his own style, which influenced Ottoman calligraphers for a century. [TH]

▶ see QUR'AN IN NASKH
▶ see PAPER-CUT NASTA'LIQ CALLIGRAPHY

MUFRADAT ON GOLD-SPRINKLED PAPER
Turkey
AH 1095 /1658 CE
Ink, colours and gold on paper
(FOLIO) 17 x 24.5 cm
On loan from the Tareq Rajab Museum, Kuwait
TR49

Mughal Sword Hilt

B eautifully crafted weapons have traditionally been held in high esteem in the Islamic world. This steel hilt, with its silver inscriptions and gold floral motifs, is beautifully decorated, and would likely have been owned by someone of means.

Due to its strength, steel was often used in the Islamic world to make arms and armour. The inscriptions on this hilt, many of which come from the Qur'an, are done in *nasta'liq* script—a script much favoured for copying poetry and epics. The Qur'anic verses chosen for this hilt include 'Help from Allah, and a speedy victory'—from verse 13 of *Surat al-Saff* (The Battle Array)—and 'But Allah is the best to take care [of him], And He is the Most Merciful of those who show mercy!'—from part of verse 64 of *Surah Yusuf* (Joseph). Both are appropriate verses to help ensure military success and protection against injuries. The grip of the hilt is decorated with a Shi'a prayer to 'Ali (▶ see CALLIGRAPHIC LION) which suggests that the owner was of that persuasion. The *Asma al-Husna* (Beautiful Names of God) are also found on the hilt. According to a *hadith* (tradition of the Prophet Muhammad), 'He who memorises them all by heart will enter paradise', so the *Asma al-Husna* was probably inscribed on the hilt for protection.

The blade that came with this hilt would have been a long curved one, and the entire sword a typical length of slightly less than a metre. The ring at the top of the hilt was used to attach a wrist strap. Such a weapon would have been very effective on horseback. [TH]

▶ see DAGGERS AND HILTS
▶ see NASTA'LIQ CALLIGRAPHY BY 'IMAD AL-HASSANI
▶ see TALISMANIC JAMA

MUGHAL SWORD HILT
India
18th century
Gold and silver on steel
17.5 x 8.5 cm
1996.532

Fragments from a **Muhaqqaq Qur'an**

The single folio and the Qur'an fragment shown here both come from the same 30-part Qur'an. The history and origin of this Qur'an, which is written in a distinctive *muhaqqaq* script in an unusual 3-line page format, has fascinated scholars.

If these two pieces come from the same Qur'an, why are the illuminations different? Scholars have noticed that surviving pages of this Qur'an with borders decorated with interlaced medallions and coloured Kufic-Abbasid inscriptions on a gold scrolling ground all come from *juz'* 6 (part 6 of a 30-part Qur'an). Similarly the first folio shown (RIGHT) comes from *juz'* 6, and features part of verse 64 of *Surat al-Maidah* (The Repast). It has been suggested that at one point in its history, this particular section became detached from the rest of the Qur'an, and its pages had border illuminations added to them. Adding illuminations to old Qur'ans was not an uncommon practice in the Islamic world. The second Qur'an fragment (BELOW), which comes from the last *juz'* in the Qur'an, gives an idea of how the Qur'an was originally meant to look. Each *surah* (chapter) heading in the museum's fragment is written in white on an illuminated panel. The pages here are the last two verses of *Surat al-Ma'un* (The Neighbourly Assistance) and the first verse of *Surat al-Kawthar* (The Abundance).

India, Egypt and Iran are some of the places where this Qur'an is thought to have been written. One scholar has, however, put forward a persuasive argument that this Qur'an comes from Anatolia (Turkey). This is based on stylistic similarities to other Anatolian Qur'ans with Persian and Turkic translations. The translations in this Qur'an are Persian and have been written in a small *naskh* script in a zigzag fashion.

This Qur'an is written in a distinctive bold *muhaqqaq* script. *Muhaqqaq*, which means 'accurate' or 'measured', is a rather straight script with flat endings that look like swords. *Muhaqqaq* was a script which was very much favoured for copying Qur'ans from the 14th century onwards, but lost its prominence in the 17th century. [TH]

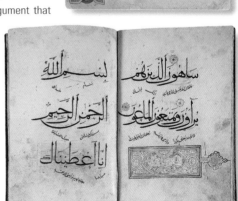

FRAGMENTS FROM A *MUHAQQAQ* QUR'AN
Anatolia (Turkey)
c. 1300–1335
Ink, colours and gold on paper
(TOP) (FOLIO) 28 x 18.5 cm;
(ABOVE) (FOLIO) 28.9 x 18.5 cm
1999.798, 1994.504

see INDONESIAN QUR'AN
see QIT'AH WRITTEN BY AHMET AL-KARAHISARI

Mukhalinga

This piece represents the Hindu deity Shiva with a moustache, a plaited *jatabandha* hairdo and a third eye in the centre of the forehead. It is made of sheet silver with chased details and the ornaments are a mix of silver and gold. The interior has a core of dried clay over which the sheet metal was probably shaped and which presumably helped to maintain its form. It would have been made as a cover (*kosha*) to be placed over the upper section of a Shiva *linga*, thus representing quite literally the face (*mukha*) of the *linga*.

Cham inscriptions mention that *kosha* were the most important gifts made by royal Shaivite devotees to the deity and that many were embellished with jewels.[9] Such practices were rooted in Indian Brahmanical traditions transmitted to Southeast Asia during the early centuries of the Common Era. The kingdom of Champa, situated from Quang Nam province in central Vietnam to Binh Thuan province in the south, was among the earliest kingdoms to have received Indian religious thought. This is indicated by a late-4th-century Sanskrit inscription from Champa, thought to be the earliest in the region.[10]

The royal act of giving a *mukhalinga* probably signified the conferment of power to the deity to protect the kingdom. The worship of a Shiva *linga* adorned with precious metal was probably intended as a means for the Cham kings to increase their territorial powers. This is suggested in literary texts of the time such as the *Ramayana*, which mentions that Ravana carried a gold *linga* which he worshipped.[11] [HT]

MUKHALINGA COVER
Cham, reportedly from south Vietnam
c. 11th–12th centuries
Silver and gold
15.5 x 8 cm
2000.5587

Naga Muchalinda

This image of a serenely smiling Buddha seated in *samadhi* (concentration) on the coils of the seven-headed *naga* Muchalinda relates to the story in which, following Buddha's enlightenment, the serpent Muchalinda sheltered him from the floods. Many such images of the Buddha were adorned with jewellery. However, in this piece, the lack of adornment gives greater emphasis to the expression of detached contemplation and to features typical of the enlightened Buddha, such as the long earlobes, tight curls of hair with the protuberance, or *ushnisha*, at the top of the head. The lack of adornment probably also signifies Buddha's rejection of a wealthy lifestyle.[1]

This iconography enjoyed greater popularity in Cambodia than elsewhere in Southeast Asia. Stone images were placed at the centre of temples such as the Bayon for worship. They were especially popular during the 12th century with the increasing importance of Buddhism and the decline of Hinduism. A more naturalistic style is thought to be characteristic of Baphuon-style images such as this.[2] Note the simple treatment of the nostrils of the *naga*, which in later examples tends to be more stylised.

The significance of this image can be read in several ways. The *naga* symbolised the divine spirit of the earth and in ancient Khmer mythology the king's divine power derived from the mystical union with the *naga* princess Soma. Images of the Buddha were closely associated with the king, or *chakravartin*, and this example perhaps represented the ruler in the likeness of Buddha. Alternatively it may have symbolised aspects of Buddhist doctrine which were referred to in Khmer temple inscriptions. For example, the three coils of the *naga* may be symbolic of the Three Jewels (the Buddha, the Dharma and the Sangha) invoked in an inscription at Preah Khan. Associations have also been made with yogic practices imported from India by Cambodian scholars. The rising *naga* may signify the rising *kundalini* (divine energy) attained through yogic practices for the purpose of achieving spiritual enlightenment. The seven cobra heads may relate to the seven *chakra* (energy centres) in the body.[3] *Chakra* motifs are visible on the chest of each *naga* in this piece, as well as on the back of each hood and along the spine of the *naga*. [HT]

FIGURE OF SEATED BUDDHA SHELTERED BY
***NAGA* MUCHALINDA**
Cambodia
11th–12th centuries
Sandstone
h. 101 cm
1998.102

Nasta'liq Calligraphy by 'Imad al-Hassani

This folio of Persian verses is elegantly written in two lines of *nasta'liq* script, in between which is a line of tiny *nasta'liq*. The calligraphy is framed by gold clouds and the whole piece is mounted on blue margins which have been delicately illuminated with gold. The text is taken from a mystical work[4] titled *Munajat* (*Prayers*) by an 11th-century Sufi named Abu Isma'il Abdullah al-Ansari al-Haravi.

This piece was written by Mir 'Imad al-Hasani (d. 1615), one of the foremost calligraphers of *nasta'liq* script. The *nasta'liq* script is believed to have been invented by a famous calligrapher, Mir 'Ali Tabrizi (d. 1416). Legend has it that 'Ali (Prophet Muhammad's son-in-law), whom calligraphers believe was the founder of their art, appeared in Mir 'Ali's dream, telling him to study the flying geese. Indeed the round and sweeping curves of the *nasta'liq* script does remind you of the wings of a bird. This elegant script is usually used for copying poetry and literary manuscripts and is generally not considered suitable for copying the Qur'an.

Born in Qazvin, Iran around 1553, Mir 'Imad spent some time in Mecca and Turkey before returning to Iran and finally working in Isfahan in the court of the Safavid ruler, Shah Abbas. At court, his greatest rival was 'Ali Reza-i Abasi. In 1615, Mir 'Imad was murdered, possibly due to his having offended the Shah, and also because of court intrigue. Mir 'Imad al-Hassani was one of the greatest masters of *nasta'liq*, and his works were much admired and valued even during his lifetime. He was also a prolific calligrapher, as testified by the survival of many of his works in collections worldwide. [TH]

▶ see PAPER-CUT NASTA'LIQ CALLIGRAPHY

***NASTA'LIQ* CALLIGRAPHY BY 'IMAD AL-HASSANI**
Safavid, Persia
Late 16th century
Ink, colours and gold on paper
16.7 x 26 cm
1999.2801

Nataraja
(Dancing Shiva)

Striking a characteristic *urdhvajanu* dance pose with one bent leg lifted up to the knee, this six-armed sculpture of Nataraja is surrounded by a *makara torana* (arch) overlooked by a *kirtimukha* (leogryph mask). This sculpture would have surmounted the *shukanasa* (pediment above the central entrance) on the exterior of a temple. The six arms of Nataraja carry an *akshamala* (rosary), *trishula* (trident), *damaru* (kettledrum) and flame, and are in *abhaya mudra* (gesture of fearlessness) and *lola hasta mudra* (relaxed gesture). The elaborate jewellery and intricate carving are unique features of Hoysala period sculptures that can also be noticed in the sculpture of Ganesha from Halebid. In this sculpture tiny images of Brahma and Vishnu are placed on either side of Nataraja, completing the trinity yet stressing the supremacy of Shiva in this temple.

Shiva is represented in many forms, in abstract or aniconic *lingam* as well as iconic forms in sculpture and painting. These forms can symbolise philosophical or mythological meanings. A pose such as this one of Nataraja, the cosmic dancer, represents not only the *tandava* (dance of destruction), but may also allude to the story of Ananda Tandava and the episode in the Tillai forest with which the famous Nataraja temple in Chidambaram is connected. Nataraja embodies the progenitive powers of cosmic energy and through him, according to Nandikeshwara's dance treatise, the *Abhinaya Darpana*, the entire phenomenal world is kindled into life.[5] Thus dance is not just a stirring of movement, but of life itself and Shiva embodies both the generative as well as the destructive powers through dance. [GPK]

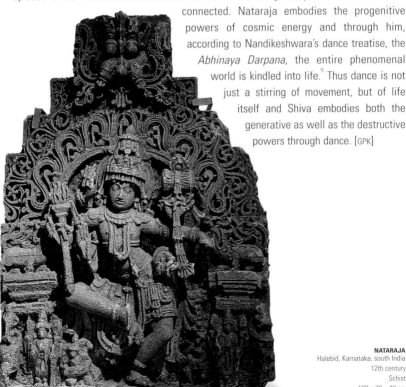

NATARAJA
Halebid, Karnataka, south India
12th century
Schist
102 x 70 x 40 cm
On loan from the
Archaeological Survey of India,
Government of India
NGR 138

Neolithic Black Stemcup

This stemcup from the Shandong Longshan culture (2400–2000 BCE) represents one of the earliest earthenware to be thrown on a wheel, evident from its eggshell-thin body and wheel-turning marks. It was first made in parts then luted together. Its thin body, bulbous stem, and the sharp ridges around the stem and foot attest to the technical achievements of the Longshan potter. This exquisite vessel is decorated with vertical slits, which were made by a sharp implement while the clay was soft. This was then fired in a reducing atmosphere between 700 and 900 degrees Celsius before it was burnished to a shiny finish. Like the other black pottery found in graves of the Longshan culture, this stemcup probably served as a ritual vessel.

The term 'Longshan' is derived from the name of the town of Longshan, near Chengziya in west Shandong. While it was previously believed that this site represented the entire Longshan culture, further excavations revealed that the same culture dominated other parts of China, such as the Middle Yellow River Valley (Henan, Shanxi and Shaanxi), from around 3000 BCE onwards. The Shandong site was the first to be discovered among other Longshan culture sites around the 1930s. Developed from the Dawenkou culture (4300–2400 BCE) in the same area, the Shandong Longshan culture continued the production of grey and fine black pottery, and included a small portion of whiteware. [WHL]

NEOLITHIC BLACK STEMCUP
Shandong province, China
Longshan culture (2400–2000 BCE)
Ceramic
h. 17 cm, diam. (MOUTH) 7.5 cm
1993.1536

Nias Ancestral Carvings

The four carvings featured here are known as *adu zatua*. '*Adu*' means 'image' or 'carving' and '*zatua*' means 'elder'. The term literally translates to 'ancestor carvings'. Three of these carvings are male. The third figure from the left is female. Each of the figures is depicted clasping his/her hands around a bowl. Figures such as these are found in households throughout Nias. Many of these were actually made after a person's death to serve as a reminder of the deceased and act as a charm to protect the household. The features on the carvings are not meant to be clearly defined as they do not represent a particular ancestor. The accessories and some prominent feature on an *adu zatua* is what identifies it.

The *adu zatua* is the standard ancestor image throughout Nias. When a family member dies, a new image is made and lashed together with the other ancestor figures to the right wall of the main room of the house. The *adu zatua* are best thought of as containers for ancestral spirits. The soul is first drawn into a bamboo tube by capturing the last breath of the dying person before transferring it to the *adu zatua*.

Ancestor worship is at the core of traditional Nias belief systems. Throughout Nias wooden ancestor images are used to mediate between the spirit and human realms. There are basically two types of *adu zatua*: those intended to honour the ancestors and secure the co-operation of their spirits for fertility and good fortune, and those intended for protection against disease and other forms of harm. [RE]

ANCESTRAL CARVINGS
Nias Island, Indonesia
c. 1900
Wood
30 x 20 cm
W0029

Osa Osa
(Stone Seat of Honour)

This is an *osa osa si sara mbagi*, meaning literally 'a seat with only one head'. It is carved in the form of a *lasara*—a mythical composite creature with a dragon-like head and a bird-like tail. *Lasara* effigies have a protective role and reinforce the power of the nobility on Nias Island.

Known for the impressive quality of the carving, stone *osa osa* are used by men or women of high honour, or made for an ancestor. An *osa osa* is only carried once, during the feast which is held for its consecration. They serve as seats of honour for the nobility during feasts and are classified according to the number of heads. Those with one head are used to commemorate men who have given feasts. Those with three heads are usually reserved for clan elders. The seats are part of large megalithic plazas that are ritual centres within villages of central Nias.

The culture of Nias has its beginnings in the central part of the island. Nias society is a stratified society consisting of nobles and commoners. The nobility control the wealth of the village and therefore have the finest houses, clothing, ornaments and monuments. They organise the village, control external relations and distribute their wealth in enormous feasts. Their elevated status is given literal as well as metaphorical expression through the use of *osa osa*. At feasts, for example, they are raised to a higher position by sitting on *osa osa*. [RE]

OSA OSA
Nias Island, Indonesia
c. 1900s
Stone
130 x 80 x 115 cm
2000.5576

Ottoman Stele

This stone stele is carved on both sides with inscriptions from the Qur'an. On the side shown here, the top cusped panel features a *tuğra* (calligraphic emblem) with part of verse 185 from *Surah Ali Imran* (Family of Imran) that reads, 'Every soul shall have a taste of death'—this stele served as a grave marker.

If inscribed, grave markers sometimes feature Qur'anic verses which contain the fundamentals of the religion. This stele is carved with three important and popular Qur'anic verses—*Surah al-Fatihah* (The Opening), the first chapter of the Qur'an; *Surat al-Ikhlas* (Purity of Faith), which talks about the unity of God; and *Ayat al-Kursi* (The Throne Verse), which is on the majesty of God. Besides Qur'anic verses, the names of the makers are also found on this stele. According to the inscription, the stele is 'the work of 'Abd al-Halim' [presumably the stone mason] and 'written by 'Abd al-Rahman'.

In Islam, the dead are buried as soon as possible, preferably on the day of death. The body is ritually washed and wrapped, and prayers are said for the deceased. The body is then buried on its right side facing the *qiblah* (direction of Mecca). While the place where the head of the deceased lies can be marked, there is traditional disapproval against erecting elaborately carved and engraved gravestones. What has survived today, however, shows us that in spite of this disapproval, elaborate gravestones were made and funerary monuments built in various parts of the Islamic world. [TH]

▶ see OTTOMAN CENOTAPH COVER
▶ see FIRMAN OF SULTAN ABDÜLHAMID II
▶ see SAFAVID QUR'AN CASE

OTTOMAN STELE
Turkey
Ottoman period, 18th–19th centuries
Stone
161 x 51 cm
1999.2803

Ox-shaped Vessel

This water buffalo- or ox-shaped vessel was made of low-fired earthenware. It was hand-built, perhaps using coils of clay to construct the walls of the vessel, and still bears the fingerprints of its maker. The opening on its back was most likely to contain water. The vessel is heavily potted and the features of the water buffalo have been clearly incised.

The vessel is from a new excavation area in Dong Marum, Lopburi province, central Thailand. It was most likely used during important ceremonies and for burial purposes. The ox was probably symbolic of a deceased farmer's wealth as this was traditionally measured by the number of cattle owned. It could also have been an indication of some sort of animistic worship. Objects and motifs depicting the water buffalo, such as this vessel and also Dong Son drums, were common in the prehistoric communities of Southeast Asia, strongly hinting at cultures in which wet rice cultivation was an integral part.

Like the elephant, the water buffalo is considered by many of the peoples of Southeast Asia to have a soul—a clear representation of a 'higher animal' worthy of worship. The water buffalo is the main agricultural beast of burden in the flooded paddies. Domesticated 4,500 years ago, the water buffalo's natural habitat is the river wetlands of Southeast Asia. Valued for its usefulness and docility, it is also a powerful symbol across the region, representing wealth, status and security. [RE]

▶ see DONG SON DRUM

OX-SHAPED VESSEL
Lopburi, Thailand
300 BCE–200 CE
Earthenware
33.5 x 10.8 x 21.6 cm
1996.120

Padung-padung

The double-spiral motif is an ornamental design of great antiquity in Southeast Asia and examples of its use can be found across the entire region from Assam to New Guinea. In modern times this motif is more prominent in isolated tribal groups which have had limited contact with the larger world. One such group is the Karo Batak people of north Sumatra and their most distinctive piece of jewellery, the *padung-padung*, is a magnificent example of the use of this motif.

The Karo Batak are a sub-group of the Batak people in the Karo Highlands region of north Sumatra. They are unique in that, unlike other Batak groups, they have largely been converted to Islam. The Karo Batak are well known for their use of silver, especially in the making of *padung-padung*, an item of jewellery unique to this tribe.[1] Weighing up to 2 kilograms apiece, *padung-padung* were made with thick silver wire generally between 5 and 10 millimetres thick. While not all *padung-padung* have them, the examples pictured here have small gold and *suasa* (gold alloy) ornaments located at the centres of the spirals.

The *padung-padung* were fashioned by a craftsman and his assistants, who turned the wire into a spiral on a large post, using a long pole for leverage. Amazingly this operation often had to be accomplished after the silver wire had been inserted into the earlobe of the wearer, since many *padung-padung* have no clasp, nor can they be removed. Due to their immense weight the *padung-padung* did not hang directly from the earlobe but were instead attached to the headdress of the wearer. The left piece would be worn pointing to the front while the right would point towards the back. According to anthropological studies of the Karo Batak, this symbolised the shifts of power between husband and wife.[2] [DAH]

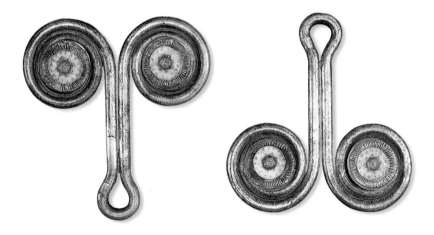

KARO BATAK HEAD ORNAMENT
North Sumatra, Indonesia
c. late 19th–early 20th centuries
Gold, silver and *suasa*
17 x 16.5 cm
Gift of Mr Edmond Chin
EC156

Palembang Lacquerware

Palembang has long been an important centre for trade and has attracted people from both within and outside Southeast Asia. Among them were many Chinese immigrants who intermarried with the local population and contributed to a hybrid culture with Malay, Minangkabau and Chinese features.

These features are very much apparent in the famed lacquerware of Palembang, two examples of which are shown here. Items such as these were reportedly carved by ethnic Malays. However, craftsmen of Chinese descent were the ones who completed the decoration and lacquering. Palembang's craftsmen made an entire range of items, from small wooden containers and woven baskets to *sireh* sets and large ceremonial serving trays. Their wares were widely traded across Sumatra and the Malay Peninsula and were highly prized for their beauty and durability. Even today such lacquerwares are still being produced in Palembang although most are now sold to the tourist market.

(ABOVE, LEFT) *TENONG*
Palembang, south Sumatra, Indonesia
c. 1900
Wood, lacquer, gold leaf and paint
h. 51 cm, diam. 37 cm
LQ0066

The first piece shown is known as a *tenong* (OPPOSITE, LEFT). *Tenong* were special stacked lacquer containers used in marriage ceremonies. They were considered a female contribution to the bridal chamber and would have been used to store food as well as textiles and jewellery. This particular piece is the topmost part of the set and is carved in the style of a lotus flower. It is primarily black with gold gilding in typical Palembang fashion. It would have rested above another flat-topped container that was similar in decoration.

The second piece is a ceremonial paddle (BELOW), painted black with floral decorations and a prominent Chinese phoenix motif in gold gilding (SEE DETAIL, BOTTOM). The reddish colouring of the piece comes from the type of lacquer used. Paddles like this one were used by young, unmarried court ladies on ceremonial boat trips down the Musi river.[3] [DAH]

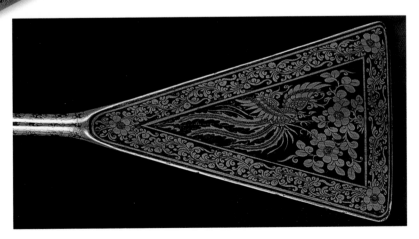

(TOP) **PADDLE**
Palembang, south Sumatra, Indonesia
c. 1900
Wood, lacquer, gold leaf and paint
99.8 x 20 cm
LQ0018

(ABOVE) **DETAIL**
The phoenix on this oar was probably painted by a
Chinese craftsman on an oar carved by a Malay

Palepai
(Ship Cloth)

Like most *palepai*, this piece, which originates from the coastal town of Kalianda in Lampung, south Sumatra, has a central motif of a large ship—hence the name 'ship cloth'. The ship motif dates back to the dawn of civilisation in Southeast Asia and is said to be symbolic of man's journey through life. Surprisingly similar designs are found on Dong Son drums dating to around 400 BCE (▶ see DONG SON DRUM). On board the ship are images of human figures representing ancestors, mythical beasts, birds, fish, elephants and the familiar tree of life. All of these are potent symbols of life, the earth and the afterworld and it is no surprise that these ceremonial hangings were usually displayed at marriages, funerals, investitures or at the presentation of a newborn child.

Palepai were the prerogative of the upper classes and were kept by the families of local chieftains as symbols of wealth and power. Usually they were given as gifts to the maternal in-laws at weddings between members of aristocratic clans. The number of

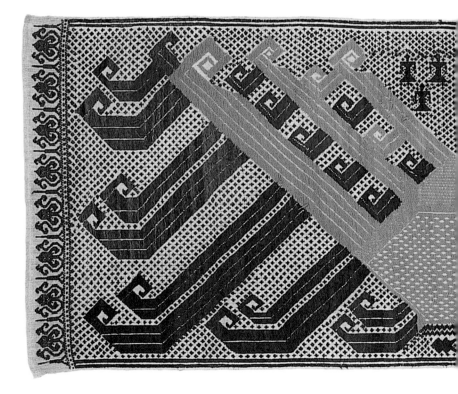

CEREMONIAL SHIP CLOTH
Lampung, south Sumatra, Indonesia
Late 19th century
Cotton and vegetable dyes
50 x 245 cm
T0520

palepai given was dictated by the social status of the bride's family.[4] *Palepai* were woven using a supplementary weft technique similar to that used to make *songket* (▶ see SONGKET). The handspun cotton thread used was coloured with natural dyes: red from the *mengkudu* root, blue from indigo and yellow from turmeric. The designs were sometimes augmented with appliqué, embroidery or beading, and could be quite elaborate indeed. [DAH]

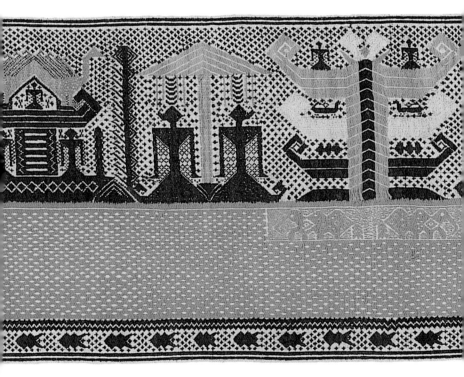

Panakawan

This group known as *panakawan* (literally 'witty friends') represents a fraction of the many important characters depicted in the leather shadow puppet tradition known as *wayang kulit* (▶ see WAYANG KULIT). Semar (BELOW), the father figure, is said to represent the ideal of *halus* (refinement) and is the most important of Javanese deities. The trio shown here (OPPOSITE) includes, from left, the rotund slow-witted Bagong who was created from his father's shadow, sad-eyed Gareng with a lame leg and long-armed clever Petruk. They appear in a wide range of stories and their incorporation into the *Ramayana* and *Mahabharata* reflects a uniquely Javanese adaptation of these Hindu epics.

Despite their disfigured appearance and humorous clowning around they are truly profound in nature. Their *kasar* (crude) behaviour, expressed through bawdy jokes and loud animated chattering, is frequently underscored by words of wisdom. As such they appear to represent ordinary folk, and their appearance at crucial moments in the stories are usually the most popularly attended of the all-night *wayang* performances. The *panakawan* play the role of court servants, although in ancient times their status may have been more elevated. It is thought that they represented indigenous pre-Hindu deities

LEATHER SHADOW PUPPETS
(ABOVE) Semar
(OPPOSITE, FROM LEFT TO RIGHT) Bagong, Gareng and Petruk
Java, Indonesia
20th century
Leather
h. 50–60 cm
X6287, X6268, X6269, 94.3865

who later became subservient to the Hindu gods and Indian epic heroes. In this role, they are free to act without restraint and often mimic the actions of their heroic masters, give advice in times of trouble and provide humorous relief in times of sadness.

The role of the *panakawan*, although provocative, is not satirical or critical of the status quo. Instead, it provides an idealised view of those at the lower end of the social hierarchy, who provide an appropriate contrast to the purer and more ascetically inclined characters at the higher end. This duality is embodied in particular by the two characters Semar and Batara Guru. [HT]

Panel Carved with the Shahadah

This wooden panel from Cirebon features the carved inscription of the *shahadah* (profession of faith in Islam) contained in an oval medallion. The *shahadah* reads, 'There is no God but Allah and Muhammad is his Messenger.'

The carved inscription and motifs are highlighted in gold paint amid the dark red wooden background. The design formed by the motifs found at the top corners of the panel is known as *mega mendung*—a cloud motif that forms a 'canopy' symbolising the sky. The motif found at the bottom of the panel is known as *wadas* (stony soil or rocks)—a motif typical in Cirebon. Both these motifs are found on *batik*, woodcarving and *wayang kulit* (shadow puppet) designs.

Wooden panels such as these are usually hung in Javanese homes not just as decoration, but as a statement of one's religious affiliation. Such panels carved with the *shahadah* or Qur'anic verses were perhaps also hung for protective purposes.

It is not known exactly when Islam first arrived in Java. Islam is believed to have been brought to Cirebon by traders and teachers in the late 15th century. Cirebon, situated in the north coast of Java, was one of the earliest regions in Indonesia to adopt Islam. [HH]

PANEL CARVED WITH THE *SHAHADAH*
Cirebon, north coast Java, Indonesia
Mid 20th century
Wood
51 x 75 x 3.5 cm
2000.5570

Paper-cut Nasta'liq Calligraphy

The writing on this page shown here has not been done with light blue ink. Instead, the shapes of the various letters have been cut out from a sheet of ivory paper and the ivory sheet pasted onto the pale blue background. Cutting out the fine, delicate letter shapes would have required skill. This is a page from a *mufradat*, which is an album that shows how the various Arabic letters are written singularly or in combinations. Apart from blue backgrounds, pale lilac, pink and yellow backgrounds are also used in this album.

The calligraphy in this album is that of a famous Persian calligrapher—Mir 'Ali Haravi (d. 1556). Mir 'Ali is one of the best-known *nasta'liq* calligraphers, and was also a poet. His works were much admired and collected by both Persian and Mughal emperors, and pages of his calligraphy were assembled into albums. Mir 'Ali served in the Timurid court in Herat under the patronage of Sultan Husayn Bayqara (reign. 1470–1506) and his chief minister. Although the end of Timurid rule saw unsettling times in Herat, which changed hands several times between the Uzbeks and Safavids, Mir 'Ali continued to work there. Around 1530, he was taken—apparently against his will—with other calligraphers and painters to Bukhara to work for the Uzbek ruler, 'Ubaydullah Khan. He stayed in Bukhara till his death.

Apart from the name of the calligrapher, this album also contains the name of the *qati'* (paper-cutter), Sangi 'Ali Badakhshi[5]—a master artist in his own right. In the art of paper-cut calligraphy, the aim of the artist is to copy the calligrapher's handwriting exactly. This art is believed to have developed in 15th-century Iran and may have evolved from leather or paper filigree work on bookbinding. [TH]

▶ see MUFRADAT BY HAFIZ OSMAN
▶ see NASTA'LIQ CALLIGRAPHY BY 'IMAD AL-HASSANI

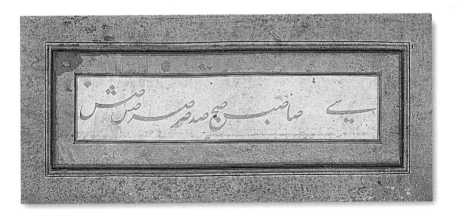

ALBUM OF PAPER-CUT *NASTA'LIQ* CALLIGRAPHY
Iran
Early 16th century
Paper
18.5 x 28 cm
1999.799

Parabaik

This manuscript is made of locally produced paper in the form of a *parabaik* or folded book) with 48 leaves. It is illustrated with brightly coloured pigments of predominantly red, yellow, blue and green. The titles of each scene appear within the lower margin in Burmese script. The scenes depict several types of religious and festive occasions such as donations to temples, the refurbishment of Buddha images, and the novitiation of young monks. These images are interesting for the wealth of information they contain about late-19th-century architecture, *hsun ok* (lacquer offering vessels, ▶ see HSUN OK), rituals, musical instruments and costumes used in dance and other aspects of Burmese material culture.

In addition to colourful works, *parabaik* were also produced using black paper on which white soapstone or steatite was written. They were used to record notes, to make copies of literary works or administrative documents and sometimes for astrological records, maps and tattoo designs. They could extend to as much as 30 metres in length although the average is usually 10 metres. The use of shading and perspective and the inclusion of a horizon were probably the result of European influence during the mid 19th century. The earliest *parabaik* are dated to the Konbaung period (1752–1885) although most are from Mandalay and date to the late 19th century, when they began to be produced for patrons outside the court.[6] Teams of painters worked at royal workshops and produced a wide repertoire of subjects ranging from cosmological scenes to the *Ramayana* (▶ see RAMAYANA MANUSCRIPT) and Jataka stories (▶ see JATAKA STORIES), as well as commemorative royal occasions. [HT]

PARABAIK
Burma
Late 19th century
Paper and water-soluble paints
59.7 cm x 12.65 m
1999.1421

(OPPOSITE) **DETAIL**
Detail of a ball game played at a festive occasion

Penboxes

These three penboxes are fine examples of the variety that can be found in the different parts of the Islamic world. All were made to hold writing implements such as the *qalam* (reed pen), pen rest, scissors and ink or inkwells.

The entire surface of the ivory penbox from India (OPPOSITE, TOP) is finely carved and covered with a dense pattern of floral motifs, except for the bottom. Opening the cover reveals a tray which is divided into three compartments with cusped arched ends which were used to store the pens. There are also three compartments on the side to hold the inkwells.

The lacquer penbox (OPPOSITE, BOTTOM), known as a *qalamdan*, is very finely painted with scrolling floral motifs. Close examination of the cover will reveal tiny animals, such as birds and sheep, among the foliage. The art of lacquer painting was very popular in Qajar, Iran and aside from *qalamdan*, lacquer painting was used to decorate book covers and mirror cases. This penbox has two small cartouches with tiny script which informs us that it was made as a gift for Atabak-i A'zam in the year AH 1318/1900 CE. Interestingly, it is the same year that the title 'Atabak-i A'zam' was bestowed on 'Ali Asghar Khan Amin al-Sultan (1858–1907) by the Qajar king Muzaffar al-Din Shah. 'Ali Asghar Khan was a seasoned politician who was constantly in and out of favour. He served under three Qajar kings, finally becoming Prime Minister in 1907, but was assassinated in the same year.

Of the three penboxes, the Ottoman penbox (OPPOSITE, CENTRE), known as a *divit*, has the most unusual shape. The barrel-like container attached to the rectangular penbox, seen here with its lid open, is the ink well. A *lika*, or wad of raw silk threads, is placed in the inkwell, over which ink is poured. Acting like a sponge, the *lika* prevents ink from spilling should the *divit* be accidentally knocked over. This *divit* is decorated with Qur'anic verses in bold gold *thulth* script and scrolling motifs. The surface of most *divit* are not so elaborately decorated. On the inkwell, the tuğra (calligraphic emblem) of the Ottoman Sultan Murad V, who reigned from May to August 1876, is depicted. The tuğra thus gives us the dating on this piece.

With such beautiful penboxes, it would be hard not to be inspired to try to write beautifully. Indeed, Islamic calligraphers and scribes strive to use the best available materials and tools to produce their works, which explains the care lavished on these three examples. [TH]

▶ see SCRIBE'S TABLE

(OPPOSITE, TOP) **IVORY PENBOX**
India
18th century
Ivory
7.5 x 28 x 11.3 cm
1997.2616

Pending

(Belt Buckle)

The *pending* was typically used by men and women to secure a sash-like textile, or padded belt around the waist. This example is characteristic of the most popular form of *pending*, an eye-shaped design with a stepped edge. This particular *pending* is believed to have come from Riau-Lingga and probably dates from the 19th century. It is decorated with a floral and vegetal design that is representative of Malay repoussé work from Riau-Lingga and southeastern Sumatra. The design is further enhanced with wire filigree, a decorative element that appears to have been introduced to the region by Bugis craftsmen. A ruby, surrounded by 28 diamonds arranged in concentric bands, provides the focal point for the design. Traditionally precious stones of such high quality were quite rare and very highly sought after by aristocratic Malays both as a sign of wealth and for the magical properties they were believed to possess. Burma and the island of Borneo were the two main sources of high-quality gemstones in Southeast Asia and both places were famous in their day for the great wealth of gems they produced.

Given the valuable materials and exquisite craftsmanship needed to execute this piece, it is likely that the buckle belonged to an individual of very high status. Also, its small size and the fact that it is made from gold makes it quite likely that this *pending* was worn by a woman. Islamic law prohibits men from wearing gold so Malay males generally preferred somewhat larger *pending* made from silver or brass.

The *pending* was one of the most recognisable items of Malay material culture. They were popular in traditional dress from Pattani in the northern Malay Peninsula to Jambi in southern Sumatra and were worn in formal dress by all levels of society. They were also popular with the Peranakan Chinese although these *pending* are easily recognised by their use of Chinese motifs and decorations. *Pending* came in a wide range of shapes and sizes—from the well-known ocular shape of this example to cloud-shaped, oval, square or rectangular—and were made using a variety of materials and decorative techniques. [DAH]

PENDING
Riau-Lingga Archipelago, Indonesia
19th century
Gold, diamonds and rubies
19 x 11.5 cm
2001.3805

Picchavai Depicting Gopi under a Tree

This beautiful *picchavai* with a dark blue background has three flowering trees in the upper ground, and a prominent tree in the centre with a slender trunk and white peacocks and peafowls perched on it. The tree probably represents Kadamba, which metaphorically symbolises Krishna. There are three *gopi* (cowherdesses) standing in a row on each side facing the central tree in the middle ground, and a row of three docile-looking cows on each side with a *gvala* (cowherd) in the far corners of both ends in the lower ground. The centrality of this composition is underscored more than once and the air of devotion to Krishna is replete in every nuance of line, colour, shape and design. The eternal fame of Krishna is celebrated here in the venerating gesture of the *gopi* who have gathered here to worship Krishna. They hold beaded necklaces, flowers, *puja* (ritual

PICCHAVAI **DEPICTING** *GOPI* **UNDER A TREE**
Rajasthan, northwest India
19th century
Dyed cotton, painted and gilded
196 x 209 cm
1993.20

worship) materials and food offerings. In the upper ground, divine couples are seated in aerial carriages while the sun and the moon bear witness to Krishna's eternal fame. The lower edge has a lush foliage of lotuses, indicating that the scene is unfolding by the side of a river or a lake.

From the style of the clothes and jewellery worn by the *gopi* and the turbans of the *gvala*, it can be surmised that this *picchavai* was painted in Jodhpur or the Marwar area. This style of dark blue or black background with silver and gold gilding is attributed to the Deccani artists from Hyderabad and Golkonda, who were commissioned by the Rajput princes during their service in Deccan as Mughal commanders. It is a more secular style than the strictly religious ones painted with iconographically accurate details by the Mewari Rajasthani artists. This style then prevailed in Rajasthan as some Deccani artists moved to Rajasthan along with their patrons.[7] The *picchavai* shown here appears to be painted in Rajasthan with a Deccani model, because the *gopi* look more like Rajasthani than Deccani noble women. Even the rather schematic clouds in trefoil semi-circular shape seem to be inspired by the Deccani style.[8]

Picchavai are usually displayed on special festive occasions to mark important days of the Krishna festival cycle among the Vaishnava devotees following Pushti Marga. The *picchavai* would be placed in a Shrinathji shrine in a Rajasthani palace shrine or offered by royalty to one of the Pushti Marga temples in Rajasthan and Gujarat. These devotees refer to Krishna as Shrinathji. Their important cult centres, which include Vrindavan, Gokul, Barsana, Nandgaon and Govardhana, are near Mathura in Uttar Pradesh. One has to visualise the *jhankhi*, or an image of Shrinathji with flowers, fruit and other food offerings, and miniature toys such as silver cows, swings, balls and sticks, placed in front of the *picchavai*. The *picchavai* shown here is probably painted for display on the occasion of Janmashtami, which falls during the rainy season in the month of Shravan. There are different *picchavai* for different occasions and they are taken out for the special *darshana* and kept on view only for a short duration. The following of the Pushti Marga cult is in Gujarat, Rajasthan and Uttar Pradesh. Even today, this tradition of cloth painting is continued by the traditional artists in the temple town of Nathadwara in Rajasthan. [GPK]

Pinggan
(Dish)

This small, shallow silver dish, or *pinggan*, is from the island sultanate of Riau-Lingga. It is a classic illustration of the diverse influences that have inspired Malay art through history. In the middle of the plate we find a simple solar motif surrounded by an intricate pattern of incised tendril and leaf adornments. These are designs that date back far into the ancient, animistic past of the region. The outer edge of the dish is cut in a lotus-flower motif, a design that is a central part of Hindu-Buddhist art, the lotus being, among other things, the seat of gods and of Buddha. The later influence of Islam and the Arab world can also be seen in the *jawi* inscription incised into the dish. *Jawi* is a modified Arabic script adopted by Malay writers with the coming of Islam and commonly used for the Malay language until the early part of the 20th century.

PINGGAN
Riau-Lingga Archipelago, Indonesia
c. 1900
Silver
h. 1.6 cm, diam. 16.3 cm
S0010

(OPPOSITE) **DETAIL**
The *jawi* inscription was likely added at a later date

256

While ceramic and earthenware would have been more common materials for items of daily use, this dish was most likely used for ceremonial occasions or for receiving important guests. Made from silver and carefully crafted, this plate was certainly the property of a person of very high status. A clue to the identity of the original owner of this dish can be found in the *jawi* inscription. While much of the inscription is difficult to read the title 'Tengku Long' is legible. This most probably is a shortened form of 'Tengku Sulong', '*sulong*' being the Malay term used for the eldest child. While the identity of this person remains something of a mystery the fact that he bore the title Tengku means that he was certainly of royal birth.

It is very likely that the dish first came to Singapore around 1911. At that time the last Sultan of Riau, Abdul Rahman, frustrated at the continuing erosion of his powers, refused to cooperate further with the Dutch Governor of Riau. The Dutch Colonial Government of the Netherlands Indies responded by annexing the islands and Sultan Abdul Rahman chose to be banished to Singapore. Many members of the royal family followed the Sultan into exile. They brought with them important items of material culture, some of which have made their way into the museum's collection. [DAH]

Pua Kumbu
(Sacred Cloth)

The *pua kumbu* featured here is an Iban Dayak textile that is woven out of cotton with the *ikat* technique and dyed red using natural dyes. Stylised crocodiles and frog motifs have been employed on this *pua*. *Pua kumbu* are woven by Dayak women, who gain status through the weaving of intricate patterns and the preparation of natural dyes. In Dayak society, women are respected for their weaving skills as much as men are for their hunting skills. A skilled weaver is accorded the same respect as a skilled headhunter within a group.

Pua kumbu are sacred objects as they represent a form of psychic transaction between the gods and man. These textiles are considered spiritually powerful as they contain many potent symbols, and are used during special occasions when powerful spiritual beings are needed for protection and blessings. In the past, young weavers did not attempt to use potent motifs on their *pua* for fear of being overpowered by the spiritual forces present during weaving. Only old and highly respected weavers used powerful anthropomorphic headhunting motifs.

The *pua kumbu* is still used in all the important ceremonies and rituals that mark the life cycle of a Dayak, which include the birth of a child, the coming of age and the receipt of an important item to a longhouse. It is also used to screen a corpse while it is laid out in state on the verandah of a longhouse before burial. When used as a screen, the powerful symbols on the *pua* form a boundary between mortal and sacred space. [RE]

PUA KUMBU
Sarawak, Malaysia
c. 1900s
Cotton
255 x 120 cm
T0703

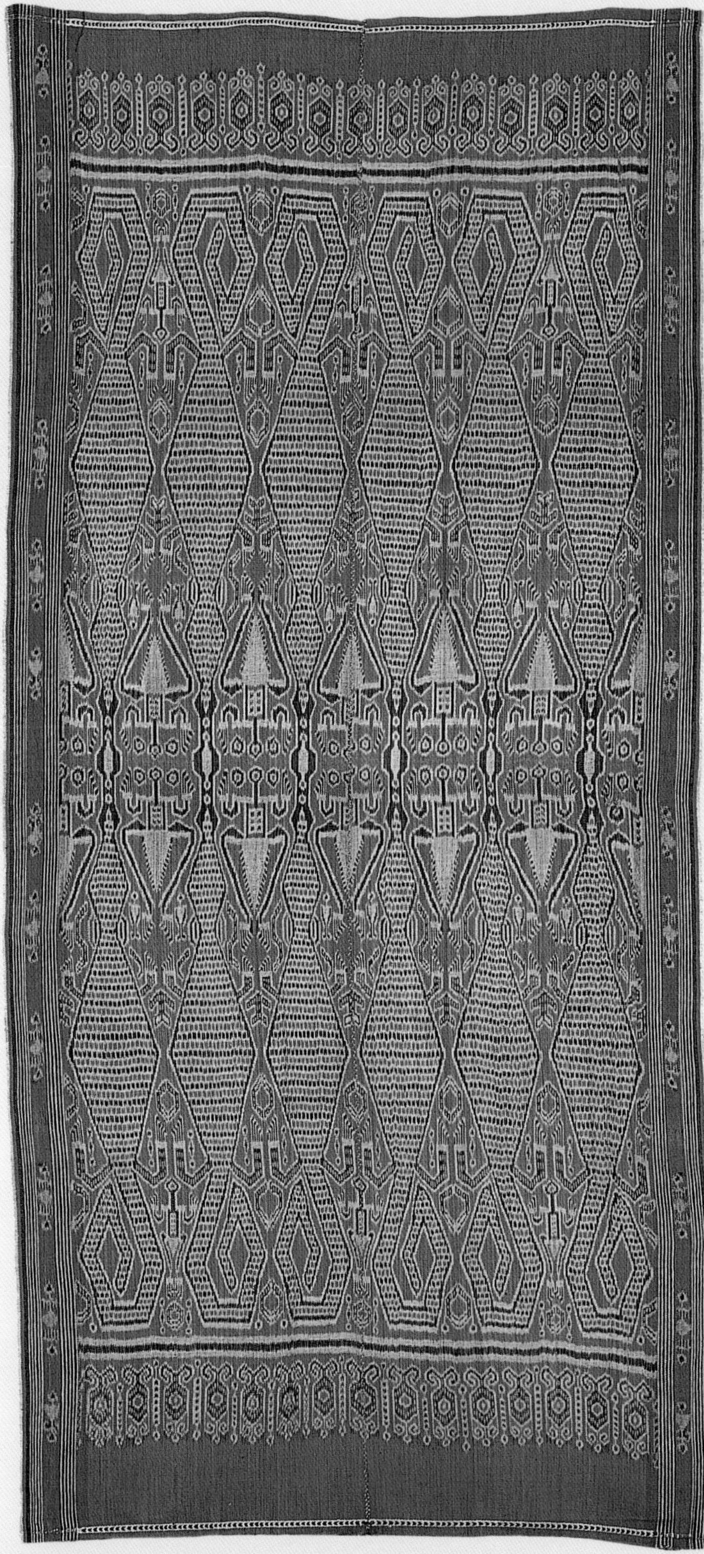

Pustaha

This Toba Batak book is known as a *pustaha*. It was made from the bast of the *alim* tree, which was first removed in long strips, then smoothened and prepared with a rice flour paste. These strips were next cut and folded. The two ends of the bast strips were then attached to wooden decorated panels that also served as the book cover. Plaited rattan cords were used to hold the strips together.

The *pustaha* contains *taba* (magic formulae), oracles, recipes for medicines and instructions for performing rituals and the production of various magic cures. The written language used was one of instruction, an archaic form of the Toba Batak dialect that is no longer used. The knowledge in the *pustaha* can be divided into three categories: the art of preserving life; the art of destroying life; and the art of fortune-telling. The *datu* (magician-priest) was the only member of the Batak community that could write this form of script and it was used to record myths, legends and magical spells.

Towards the end of the 18th century, when the first researchers began to gather ethnographic information about the Bataks, they were surprised to discover that these people had a script and literature of their own. Besides the writings in the *pustaha*, writings were also made on bamboo strips, leather and bone. [RE]

▌ see BATAK RITUAL BUFFALO BONES

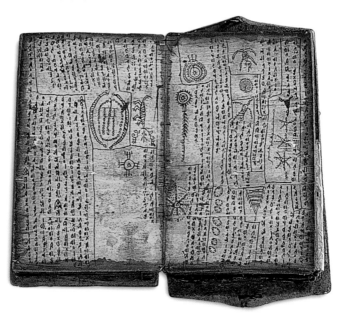

BATAK *PUSTAHA*
North Sumatra, Indonesia
c. 1930s
Bark
32 x 25 x 8 cm
XX3503

Qajar Standard

This cotton standard or flag (*parcham* in Persian) is decorated with a motif of a lion standing in front of a radiant human-faced sun. The motif of a lion with a sun is an ancient and popular symbol in Iran for power and royalty. This particular motif was officially adopted as a Qajar emblem during the reign of Muhammad Shah (reign. 1834–1848). The body of the lion contains an Arabic prayer to 'Ali known as *nadi 'aliyyan*.

In the borders of this flag are cartouches containing Persian verses referring to Imam Husayn (the grandson of the Prophet Muhammad) and his martydom in Karbala (Iraq). This strongly suggests that this flag was made to be carried during the 'Ashurah processions. Muharram, the first month of the Islamic calendar, is considered the month of mourning for Shi'ite Muslims. Throughout this month, gatherings recounting the suffering and martyrdom of Husayn are held in mosques, homes or places known as Husayniyyah. 'Ashurah, the tenth day of Muharram, is the climax of the commemoration of Husayn's tragic fate. On this day, street processions are held, where flags and banners like the one shown here are carried on poles; there would be weeping, lamentations and men performing self-flagellation.

Shi'ites are a group within Islam which regard 'Ali and the descendants of the Prophet as the only legitimate successors to Prophet Muhammad. Today, around 11 per cent of Muslim population around the world are Shi'ites, with the largest number of Shi'ites living in Iran. [TH]

▶ see CALLIGRAPHIC LION

QAJAR STANDARD
Iran
AH 1262/1845–6 CE
Ink and colours on cotton
122 x 191 cm
1998.1471

Qanat
(Tent Panel)

A *qanat* is a large portable screen surrounding a tent complex, and this example is enormous. Its three panels are bound by cusped arches, each of which contain flowering poppy plants or chrysanthemums, with a border of alternating cypress and foliage motifs. This style is attributed to Amer or Jaipur *toshkhana* (workshops).[1]

The Mughal and Rajput princes used *qanat* for long expeditions, during hunting or war, or simply to enjoy the outdoors. They were lavishly designed as reception halls for receiving guests, discharging affairs of State or for organising special meetings. *Qanat* are mobile palaces of princes and were also set up during weddings and special festivals. Walls, canopies and curtains were erected using cloth, bamboo and ropes to create an enclosed space that could be raised and dismantled whenever required. Even today, an Indian wedding is not complete without the *qanat*—which is usually red and white—rented from the *tentwala* or the *farashkhana*. Red is a colour often seen in Rajput and Mughal miniatures depicting festivals or hunting expeditions and in the tents of royalty. The use of velvet, gold foil or embroidery with gold thread was also popular with royalty while today simple cotton is most often used.

It is said that Akbar's Diwan-i-am was actually held under tents; twice a day the emperor sat in state, attended by the nobility and honoured guests, and transacted business. In the Mughal court there is a profuse use of cloths, awnings, carpets, canopies, cushions and spreads. Even the robes, sashes and turbans worn by each courtier were unique and special. The *qanat* usually had two layers, the outer one a strong coarse red cloth while the inner one lined with hand-painted chintz. The kings gave audience under velvet or flowered silk *qanat*. Mughal *qanat* were so well designed that they contained two-storeyed tents and imitated architectural spaces. Shah Jahan was fond of hunting, and tents became most popular and lavish during his reign. The use of cypress and flowering plants alternating in a formal pattern, such as shown in this border, came into vogue from his time.[2] In the collection of the Jodhpur museum there is a whole tent interior that originally belonged to Shah Jahan.[3] [GPK]

▶ see SUMMER CARPET

QANAT
Rajasthan, possibly Jaipur, India
18th century
Velvet, stencilled and painted with gold leaf
439 x 268 cm
1997.2617

Qasidat al-Burdah

(The Mantle of the Prophet)

This manuscript contains one of the most famous classical Arabic poems in praise and honour of the Prophet Muhammad, the *Qasidat al-Burdah* (The Mantle of the Prophet), or 'Glittering Planets in the Praise of the Best of Mankind', its proper title translated into English. The poem is beautifully written in *thulth* script and each verse ending is marked with a gold dot. The colophon of the calligrapher is found on the last page and reads, 'Written by the one needy [for God's favour] Muhammad, also known as Arab Zade, in the year 1121.'

The *Qasidat al-Burdah* was composed by Imam Sharafuddin Muhammad Al-Busiri (1212–1296) in Egypt. Legend has it that while composing this poem, Imam Al-Busiri suffered a stroke which left him half paralysed. One night, he dreamt that he was reciting this *qasidah* (ode) to the Prophet Muhammad. The Prophet touched the paralysed part of his body and threw his *burdah* (mantle) over him. Upon waking, Imam Al-Busiri found that he was miraculously cured. The poem thus became known as *Qasidat al-Burdah*.

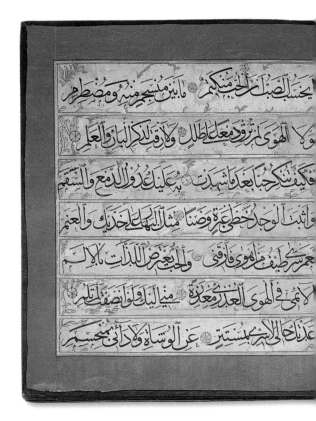

QASIDAT AL-BURDAH
Turkey
AH 1121/1709 CE
Ink, colours and gold on paper
(FOLIO) 31 x 27 cm
On loan from the Tareq Rajab Museum, Kuwait
TR42

This poem extolling the noble qualities and life of the Prophet became quickly known for its auspicious qualities and healing powers. Verses from the poem have been copied, recited by heart and even inscribed on buildings. Many a scholar has written commentaries on the *Qasidat al-Burdah*. To give you a taste of the poem, here is a verse from chapter 3 describing the Prophet:

Like a flower in tenderness and like the full moon in glory,
Like the ocean in generosity and like time in grand intentions. [4]

This particular copy of the poem is special not only because it has been beautifully written but also because it has been written entirely in *thulth*. *Thulth* is one of the most impressive cursive scripts with deep downward sweeping strokes. More commonly used for enormous inscriptions on architecture, it is rarely used for copying entire texts. When found in manuscripts, it is usually used to write chapter headings. [TH]

▶ see OTTOMAN CENOTAPH COVER

Qingbai Porcelain

Qingbai porcelain derives its name from the shadow blue or bluish-green (*yingqing*) glaze that covers its white clay body. Its appearance, which has been compared to clear still water and clear blue sky, is even said to be an imitation of jade. *Qingbai* porcelain is fired upside down in multiple stepped saggars within larger saggars. This method originated from the Ding kilns in Hebei province. Production of *qingbai* porcelain probably began during the Northern Song period—a *qingbai meiping* (vase) was uncovered from a tomb dated 1020 in Nanjing.

Qingbai wares gained greater importance with the increase in maritime trade during the Yuan dynasty. Many *qingbai* vessels, including miniature ones, have been found in Asia, particularly in Southeast Asia. For instance, *qingbai* wares similar to the pieces featured here have been found off the coast of South Korea in a Sinan wreck dated to the early 14th century. As demand for *qingbai* wares increased, incised and carved decorations on early pieces gave way to mass-produced pieces which made use of moulding, applied decoration and painted decoration. Such pieces were not only produced in Jingdezhen but also in Guangdong and Fujian.

The belimbing jarlet (BELOW, LEFT) was one of the many finds from excavations in the Philippines around the 1960s. This eight-panelled vessel derived its name from its starfruit form. It has two lugs by the rim—one is now missing—and an unglazed flat base. The brown iron spots appear to have been made with a design, possibly floral motifs, in mind.

(ABOVE, LEFT) *QINGBAI* BELIMBING JARLET WITH IRON SPOTS
China
Yuan dynasty
Ceramic
h. 6.6 cm, diam. (MOUTH) 6.5 cm
Gift of Dr Stephen Zuellig
2001.9

(ABOVE, RIGHT) WATER DROPPER IN THE FORM
OF A BOY SEATED ON A BUFFALO
China
Yuan dynasty
Ceramic
9.3 x 8.3 cm
On loan from W. & M. Troesch
WT 1

Iron oxide was applied under the glaze to produce brown spots, either as a group or small individual ones, upon firing. This decorative technique was used only on export wares for the Southeast Asian market and mostly on small non-utilitarian pieces.

The range of iron-spotted wares is clearly demonstrated in two other pieces featured here—the water dropper and the miniature ewer. The water dropper (OPPOSITE, RIGHT), in the form of a boy on a buffalo set on a rectangular plinth, has a whimsical and fun appeal. The double gourd-shaped ewer (BELOW, LEFT) recalls a Chinese form, though much smaller in size, and has a curved spout and handle. Iron-spotted miniatures such as these appealed to the Southeast Asian market. More spotted ewers have since been found at excavation sites in the Philippines.

Another popular export ware was the cuboid jarlet (BELOW, RIGHT). Here it is decorated with copper red cloud scrolls on each face and moulded *chi* dragons applied to the shoulders. This particular jarlet is an early piece that used copper oxide before it was fully mastered, as some parts of the scrolls appear grey and hazy.

With its wide variety of forms and decorative techniques, it is hardly surprising that *qingbai* porcelains were in high demand in overseas markets during the 13th and 14th centuries. [WHL]

▶ see DING DISHES

(LEFT) *QINGBAI* EWER WITH IRON SPOTS
China
Yuan dynasty
Ceramic
h. 11 cm, diam. (MOUTH) 2.3 cm
On loan from W. & M. Troesch
WT 5

(ABOVE, RIGHT) *QINGBAI* JARLET WITH COPPER RED MOTIFS
China
Yuan dynasty
Ceramic
6.5 x 6 x 5.8 cm, l. (MOUTH) 1.8 cm
On loan from W. & M. Troesch
WT 18

Qit'ah Written by Ahmet Al-Karahisari

This *qit'ah* (calligraphic piece) is written in two scripts—the top line in very elegant *muhaqqaq* and below that, four smaller lines in *rayhan* (the smaller version of *muhaqqaq*). The text in Arabic records a *hadith* (tradition of the Prophet Muhammad), and here are the first few lines from it:

'O son of Adam,[5] your house in this world is in ruin, and what you own at the day of judgement will be closely accounted for. You start from dust, and you will end in dust. How long will you remain hopeful in this ruin?'

This particular *qit'ah* is the work of one of the most outstanding Ottoman calligraphers, Ahmet Semseddin Karahisari (?1470–1556). Working in the tradition of the great 13th-century calligrapher, Yaqut al-Musta'simi, Al-Karahisari is best known for his *jali thulth* (*celi sü/üs* in Turkish) script. In this *qit'ah* (*kıta* in Turkish), the way he has written the *basmalah* (In the Name of God, the Gracious and the Merciful) on the top line is quite delightful—especially the flourish found at the end of the word 'Al-Rahman' (the Gracious).[6] Compare this with another *basmalah* written in *muhaqqaq* from an early 14th-century Qur'an (▶ see FRAGMENTS FROM A MUHAQQAQ QUR'AN).

The word '*qit'ah*' means 'piece', and it is used to describe a rectangular calligraphic piece which features a few lines of text. Such calligraphic pieces were mounted onto boards, which were then compiled into albums. The design of *qit'ah* is such that there are empty panels on either side of the text area written in the smaller script. These empty panels, known as *koltuklar* (literally 'armpit' or 'armchair' in Turkish), are usually illuminated. Here, the signature of Al-Karahisari is found on the left panel. He had signed off indicating that this work was an exploratory piece. [TH]

▶ see QUR'AN

***QIT'AH* WRITTEN BY AHMET AL-KARAHISARI**
Turkey
16th century
Ink and gold on paper
(TEXT AREA) 11.5 x 23.2 cm
On loan from the Tareq Rajab Museum, Kuwait
TR55

Quan Am

This large bronze figure of Quan Am has 24 arms: two at the front in the prayer gesture, two on her lap in meditation, and five detachable pairs at each shoulder holding many different attributes including a lotus, *chakra* (discus), conch shell, *vajra* (thunderbolt), vase, bell, prayer beads and so on. She wears a tall crown with several detachable hairpins. Her eyes are closed in meditation and her serene expression is further reflected in the symmetry of her body, swathed beneath evenly gathered robes. The figure is heavy in appearance, with a broad face and thick elongated earlobes that extend to the shoulders. The whole figure is covered with lacquer, the face, body and two pairs of hands in gold paint and the rest in an orange-toned gold leaf. An underlying layer of red paint is visible at the edges of the robes and crown.

Quan Am is the Bodhisattva Avalokiteshvara, and is also known as Guanyin in China, where the female form evolved during the Song dynasty. She became highly popular due to her universal powers to help alleviate all kinds of sufferings. This universal quality is expressed in the striking iconography of the multiple arms. Mahayana Buddhism was transmitted from China during the early 1st millennium along with Daoism and Confucianism, and by the 2nd century, Hanoi was a centre for Buddhism. The bodhisattva ideal lent a compassionate image to rulers who associated themselves with Mahayana Buddhism. During the Ly dynasty Buddhism became a state religion, and temples and monasteries received state patronage, to the extent that their power became a threat to the rulers. That and the rise of Confucianism among the elite saw a decline in Buddhism after the 13th century.[7] [HT]

 see GUANYIN

MULTI-ARMED FIGURE OF QUAN AM
North Vietnam
18th century or later
Bronze, painted and gilded lacquer
107 x 135 x 60 cm
1998.54

Qur'an

The pages you see here come from a Qur'an that has been beautifully written in *rayhan* script. On the left page, there is an illuminated panel where the *surah* (chapter) heading has been written in gold *thulth* script over a scrolling background. The *surah* featured here is *Surat al-Anbiya'* (The Prophets). At the end of this Qur'an there is a colophon which reads, 'Written by Yaqut al-Musta'simi during the sixth month of the year 681 in the City of Peace [Baghdad].'

Yaqut al-Musta'simi (d. 1298) is one of the greatest calligraphers of the Islamic world. Born in central Anatolia (Turkey), Yaqut was a eunuch working as an official secretary in the court of the last Abbasid caliph in Baghdad.[8] He is credited with the innovation of cutting the nib of the reed pen at an angle, which made cursive scripts more elegant and flexible. His style of calligraphy greatly influenced calligraphers up until the 16th century.

Traditionally calligraphers were held in high esteem in the Islamic world, for it was they who copied and beautified the Word of God. Apart from professional calligraphers or scribes, rulers and literate persons also copied the Qur'an for it was, and still is, seen as an act of devotion. The pious desire to beautify and propagate God's Word was central to the development of the art of calligraphy in the Islamic world.

Apart from the Qur'an as written scripture, Muslims experience the Qur'an in other ways. The Qur'an is listened to, recited during prayers and from memory, and also serves as a guide for social conduct. [TH]

▶ see KUFIC–ABBASID QUR'AN
▶ see QUR'AN IN NASKH

QUR'AN
Baghdad, Iraq
AH 681/1282 CE
Ink, colours and gold on paper
(FOLIO) 17.4 x 12 cm
On loan from the Tareq Rajab Museum, Kuwait
TR32

Qur'an in Naskh

This wonderful Qur'an was written by one of the most celebrated calligraphers, Şeyh Hamdullah al-Amasi (1429–1520), who has the Turkish epithet *kıbletü'l-küttab* (the focus of calligraphers). Şeyh Hamdullah was born in Amasya, central Anatolia (Turkey). He taught calligraphy to the Ottoman prince Bayezid, during the latter's stay in Amasya as governor. When Bayezid[9] became Sultan in 1481 he invited his teacher to Istanbul to become his chief calligrapher in the palace. Given the importance of calligraphy, it is hardly surprising that rulers were interested in this art form. Rulers did not just commission and collect the works of master calligraphers, they also tried their hand at calligraphy, and some became masters of the art.

This Qur'an is written in a cursive script known as *naskh*. Before the 10th century cursive scripts were only used for copying non-Qur'anic materials. This situation changed after the 10th century when an Abbasid vizier named Abu 'Ali Muhammad ibn Muqlah (886–940) devised a set of rules[10] which enabled cursive scripts to be perfectly proportioned. Only with this breakthrough did cursive scripts gain enough elegance to be considered worthy for copying the Divine Revelations. With this system, Ibn Muqlah established the Six Pens (*al-aqlam al-sittah*)—*muhaqqaq, rayhan, thulth, naskh, riqa'* and *tawqi'*—the six scripts which were to become an important part of a calligrapher's repertoire. By the 13th century the Six Pens were made more elegant by a famous calligrapher, Yaqut al-Musta'simi (▶ see QUR'AN).[11] Şeyh Hamdullah was taught and worked in the tradition established by Yaqut. While Şeyh Hamdullah was in Istanbul, Sultan Bayezid II encouraged him to develop a new interpretation of the Six Pens different from the Yaqut tradition. Şeyh Hamdullah's new styles were to become the calligraphic tradition in Ottoman Turkey. [TH]

▶ see MUFRADAT BY HAFIZ OSMAN

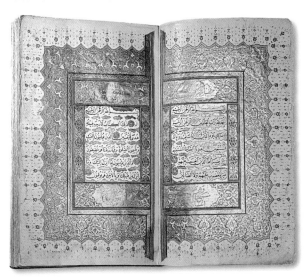

OTTOMAN QUR'AN IN *NASKH*
Turkey
AH 907/1501 CE
Ink, colours and gold on paper
(FOLIO) 35 x 24 cm
On loan from the
Tareq Rajab Museum, Kuwait
TR30

Qur'an Leaf

This Qur'an folio, which features part of verse 55 to verse 64 from *Surah Ya Sin*, is written in a very elegant script on paper. This style of script is generally known as Eastern kufic although a scholar, Décroche, has pointed out that this term is not appropriate (▶ see KUFIC-ABBASID QUR'AN FOLIO) and suggested the term 'New Style' script as a replacement.[12]

New Style script was the main script used for copying non-Qur'anic materials in the 9th century. By the 10th century, it had achieved enough status to be used for copying the Divine Revelations. Being closer to the cursive scripts used in everyday life (thus more easily read and written), New Style scripts gradually replaced Kufic-Abbasid scripts for the copying of the Qur'an and continued to be used until the 13th century, although by this time, Qur'ans were more popularly written in cursive scripts such as *naskh* (▶ see QUR'AN IN NASKH).

The use of New Style script for Qur'ans developed during a period which saw considerable change in the production of books in the Islamic world. The end of the 9th to 11th centuries saw a switch in writing material as well as format. Paper[13] gradually replaced the use of parchment as the main material for the Qur'an from the 10th century onwards—paper was a cheaper material and thus enabled more Qur'ans and other manuscripts to be produced. There was also the preference for a vertical rather than a horizontal page format. [TH]

▶ see BOWL WITH FOLIATED KUFIC-ABBASID SCRIPT
▶ see SLIP-PAINTED BOWL

QUR'AN LEAF
Iran
11th–12th centuries
Ink, colours and gold on paper
(FOLIO) 28.2 x 18.2 cm
2000.03519

Qur'an Scroll

It is quite wonderful to unroll this Qur'an scroll. The entire Qur'an has been written in tiny *ghubar* script, and is done in such a way that it forms a prayer in a larger *thulth* script. While the Qur'anic text is written in black, the *surah* (chapter) headings are written in red ink. The illuminations (found at the beginning of the scroll) as well as the writing on this scroll have both been beautifully done.

The large text on the scroll begins with the calling of Allah's blessings on the Prophet Muhammad, and follows with the names of 12 Shi'ite Imams and a popular invocation to Ali known as *nadi'aliyyan*. This suggests to us that this Qur'anic scroll was probably meant for a patron of Shi'a persuasion. A scholar[14] has proposed a mystical reason for containing a text within a text—that in reading the text in the larger script it is as if you are transmitting the entire contents of the Qur'an.

The *ghubar* (which means 'dust' in Arabic) script was probably first developed for military communication by pigeon post. However it was soon used as a way to display one's calligraphic skills. The *ghubar* script was generally used to produce scrolls and miniature Qur'ans. When copying the Qur'an using *ghubar*, the calligrapher has to ensure that the text is legible because the Qur'anic text should not be distorted.

There is a very charming story about the *ghubar* script. A 15th-century calligrapher, 'Umar Aqta', wrote a miniature *ghubari* Qur'an reputed to be so tiny it could fit under a signet ring. He did so to impress Timur, yet the great conqueror was unimpressed with this feat. It was only when 'Umar Aqta' wrote a Qur'an so large that it needed a cart to be transported was he then suitably rewarded. [TH]

▶ see CALLIGRAPHIC LION
▶ see MINIATURE QUR'AN

QUR'AN SCROLL
Turkey
Ottoman period, 15th century
Ink, colours and gold on paper
14 x 112 cm
1995.1828

Qur'an Stands

As the medium responsible for transmitting God's divine revelations, the Qur'an is highly regarded in Islam and is always treated with great respect. No Qur'an would be left lying unattended on the floor in a Muslim home. When read, the Qur'an is placed on the table or if one is sitting on the floor, on an elevated plane—a pillow or a Qur'an stand. The Qur'an is often kept in a box or wrapped in cloth and placed in a high place when not in use. Pious Muslims usually perform *wudu'* (ablution) before touching the Qur'an and sit facing the *qiblah* (direction of Mecca) when reciting it, taking care not to sit higher than the Qur'an. Qur'an stands, therefore, play an essential role in ensuring that proper treatment is accorded to the Qur'an while it is being recited.

Qur'an stands (*rahil* in Arabic) can come plain or highly decorated. As depictions of human beings or animals are discouraged in Islam, decorations commonly take the form of geometric patterns and floral motifs. The Qur'an stands featured here are fine examples of those found in the museum's collection.

The entire surface of the Qur'an stand from Ottoman Turkey (BELOW) is covered with tortoiseshell and mother-of-pearl inlay to form a geometric pattern. This is a fine piece of work. The early 14th and 15th centuries are known for the start of new techniques and decorative elements such as the inlay found on this stand. Besides this, carving and latticework were also prominent techniques used to produce decorative elements.

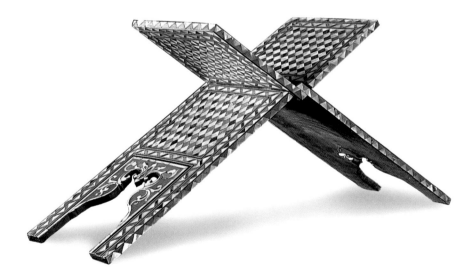

QUR'AN STAND WITH TORTOISESHELL AND MOTHER-OF-PEARL INLAY
Turkey
Ottoman period, 18th century
Wood
(OPEN) h. 56.5 cm, w. (BASE) 61 cm, (TOP) 30 cm
2000.3521

The wooden Qur'an stand from central Anatolia (Turkey) (ABOVE, FRONT) is carved with circular medallions containing star motifs and multi-petalled flowers which resemble the lotus. This stand is not as elaborate as the one from Ottoman Turkey.

The Qur'an stand from North India (ABOVE, BACK) is made of jasper and set in steel frames damascened with gold and silver floral motifs. The top of the upper panels are decorated with steel crenellations while the lower panels are shaped into the form of a *mihrab* (prayer niche). The use of such luxurious materials suggests that this stand was probably a prized possession. The use of stones such as jade and rock crystal in the production of decorative items was very popular during the Mughal period in India.

Most of the Qur'ans you see are of a regular size for personal use. Qur'ans are, in fact, made in different sizes, and Qur'an stands also come in different sizes to accommodate them. Large stands have been given to mosques to hold large Qur'ans. One of the biggest Qur'an stands made was commissioned by Ulughbeg (Timur's grandson) for the Great Mosque in Samarqand in the early 15th century. The metal stand measures a remarkable 2.3 by 2 metres! [HH]

▶ see BURMESE QUR'AN BOX
▶ see SCRIBE'S TABLE

(TOP, FRONT) **WOODEN QUR'AN STAND**
Anatolia (Turkey)
19th century
Wood
(OPEN) h. 24 cm, w. (BASE) 37.5 cm, (TOP) 35.5 cm
1996.180

(TOP, BACK) **JASPER QUR'AN STAND**
North India
Late Mughal period, early 19th century
Jasper
(OPEN) h. 28 cm, w. (BASE) 31.5 cm, (TOP) 27 cm
1994.5221

Qur'an Written by 'Abd Allah Al-Sayrafi

What you see here are the opening pages of a Qur'an luxuriously illuminated in predominantly blue and gold. These pages contain the first *surah* (chapter) in the Qur'an—*Surat al-Fatihah* (The Opening)—written over two pages. From the 14th century onwards, it became increasingly common to devote the right page to the first *surah* and the left page to the first five lines of the second *surah*,[15] with the text written within rectangular panels (▶ see QUR'AN IN NASKH).

As with all other Qur'ans, the opening pages are generally the most decorated[16]—the subsequent pages of this Qur'an are not as elaborately decorated. The pages of this Qur'an feature superb calligraphy written in 11 lines and framed by a gold border. The top and bottom line of each page is written in blue *thulth* and the middle line, between four lines of black *naskh* (a smaller script) on either side, is in gold *thulth*. This style of using two scripts (one large and the other small) for copying the Qur'an was popular from the 12th century onwards.

This Qur'an is the work of a great 14th-century calligrapher named 'Abd Allah Al-Sayrafi. The son of a moneychanger, Al-Sayrafi was born in Shiraz, Iran, but lived most of his life in Tabriz. He was a student of Sayyid Hayder Gandah-navis, who in turn was a student of the great calligrapher Yaqut al-Musta'simi. Al-Sayrafi is believed to have written 36 Qur'ans during his lifetime, and is known for his *naskh* script. Aside from copying Qur'ans, he designed many monumental inscriptions for buildings in Tabriz. [TH]

▶ see QUR'AN

QUR'AN
Iran
14th century
Ink, colours and gold on paper
(FOLIO) 29 x 19 cm
On loan from the Tareq Rajab Museum, Kuwait
TR31

Rabbit Dish

Moulded from roughly levigated clay, and produced for use in Japan, this rabbit dish stands on three unglazed circular feet. The eyes, ears and legs were painted with cobalt pigment under the glaze (BELOW, LEFT). Blue rings and spots decorate its body. Executed in a less controlled manner, these spots were probably achieved either by blowing the cobalt pigment through a tube or flicking it from a brush, a technique also known as *fukizumi* or *bleu soufflé* (blue blows). This dish is also typified by 'moth-eaten' edges where the glaze had fritted, and a thick glaze filled with bubbles. The reverse side (BELOW, RIGHT) has less detail with facial features outlined in blue and fewer blue spots. The Japanese considered these imperfect wares natural and in keeping with the simple and understated Japanese tea ceremony. This dish probably formed part of a set of five or ten, and was used as a *mokuzuke* (sweetmeat dish) during or after the tea ceremony.

Generally known as *ko-sometsuke*, this term given by the Japanese refers to the 'old blue and white' wares exported from China during the early and mid 17th century, that is, the earlier half of the Transitional period (1620–1683). This period marked the end of Chinese imperial patronage for the Jingdezhen kilns and the beginning of more demanding domestic and overseas markets. The Japanese had probably sent sketches to the Chinese potters so that this blue and white porcelain could be custom-made in China for use in Japanese tea ceremonies. Nevertheless, the production of *ko-sometsuke* signified a greater freedom for the Chinese potters to experiment and innovate without having to adhere to imperial regulations. [WHL]

BLUE AND WHITE RABBIT DISH
(ABOVE, RIGHT) Reverse side
Jingdezhen, China
Early to mid 17th century
Ceramic
3.5 x 17.8 x 9.3 cm
1997.2629

Ramayana Manuscript

This manuscript is written in Marathi—a language which originated from Sanskrit—in Nagari script. It is unusually well preserved and has a very graphic and detailed description of the location and the context in which the story is unfolding. Although incomplete, the title of the manuscript can be discerned as *Shri Ramavijaya* and it was based on the original version of the *Ramayana* of Valmiki. The text is in prose with descriptive similes and phrases. Only 12 pages from two *adhyaya* (chapters), one Balakanda and the other Uttarakanda, are available and even then most of the sections are incomplete. Two pages are illustrated, one showing Sitakalyanam, the marriage of Rama and Sita (BELOW AND DETAIL, OPPOSITE), while the other depicts Ramapattabhishekam, Rama's coronation.

The illustrations are particularly noteworthy and belong to the genre of south Indian painting. The resemblance to the Nayaka-period murals and Tanjore-style paintings from the Andhra and Tamil Nadu regions is most obvious. The style of the costume, jewellery and physiognomy are so distinctly south Indian that one could surmise that a Maratha patron commissioned the painting from a Tamil or Andhra painter after the manuscript had been written in Marathi.

Maratha rulers of Tanjore were known to have been great patrons of the arts during the 18th century. Tanjore, in Tamil Nadu, was the capital of the Maratha rulers for some time. [GPK]

RAMAYANA MANUSCRIPT
Maharashtra or Tamil Nadu, India
Maratha period, 18th century
Natural colours on paper
20 x 40 cm
1996.2178

(OPPOSITE) **DETAIL**
Illustration from the manuscript, showing Sitakalyanam

गी ॥ द्वावे सरकरीसावघ ॥९९॥ चौबी

करीद्वारथ ॥२०॥ अंतःपटमधे

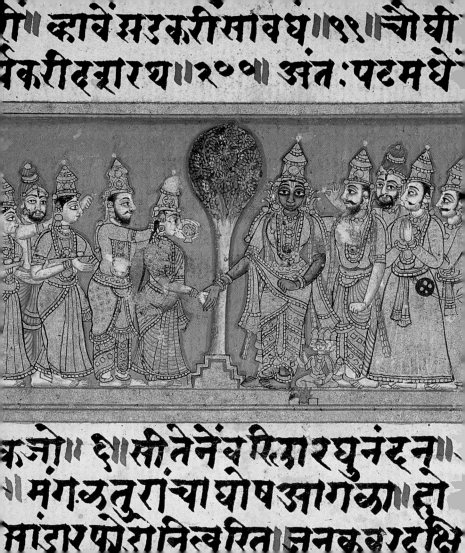

कनो ॥ दासीतेनेंवरिछारघुनंदन

॥ संगळतुरांचा घोष आगळा ॥ हो

सांदार फोरानिव्वखित जनकराटखि

Ranganatha

This painting depicts the Sheshashayi form of Vishnu, who is seen reclining on the *sheshanaga* (coiled serpent). This form of Vishnu is popularly associated with the temple of Shrirangam in Tamil Nadu, where Sheshashayi Vishnu is addressed as Ranganatha and his reclining image seen in the sanctum sanctorum. This painting has many four-armed images of Vishnu standing and holding a *shankha* (conch) and a *chakra* (discus), including the image of Para Vasudeva, who is considered the most absolute and greatest form of Vishnu according to Vaishnava theology. His icon is seen emerging from the dome of the sanctum at Shrirangam, and this is how the artist has depicted him in this painting. There are two images of seated *acharya* (spiritual teachers) flanking the image of Ranganatha and offering lotuses to him. Ritual objects used in daily *puja* (worship) are also placed in front of the deities.

The iconographic text from south India—the *Vaikhanasagama*—refers to many different forms of Vishnu, i.e. standing, seated and reclining, of which the *shayana* (reclining) form of Vishnu is the most important. The earliest reference to Vishnu's reclining form can be seen in the *Rgveda*,[1] which refers to Vishnu-Narayana, who is closely associated with primeval waters and the creation of the universe from the *hiranyagarbha* (primordial egg).

This painting is painted on paper using earth colours and dates from the late 17th to early 18th century. Such paintings were used for ritual worship and were collected by devotees on their visits to temples. This painting is done in the Tanjore style without the gems and gilding. It is rather rare and plays the role of an icon, just like the gem-set Tanjore paintings (▶ see VENUGOPALA), and was sold as souvenirs to pilgrims visiting the temple of Shrirangam. [GPK]

RANGANATHA OR SHESHASHAYI VISHNU
Tamil Nadu, south India
Tanjore style, 18th century
Ink on paper
21.3 x 15.6 cm
1996.496

Reliquary Box

This is a reliquary box with designs of peonies and undulating leaves, a decorative development which began in the Song and Jin dynasties. The box is made of silver and covered with rectangular panels of gold foil. It is most probably part of a set of reliquary boxes made of various materials. The innermost box is usually made of gold, followed by a larger silver or gilded silver box, and both are contained in a bronze or stone container. Sacred Buddhist relics such as *sarira* (Buddha's remains) or representations of it in the form of precious pearls are housed in the gold container.

The innermost reliquary box is usually intricately designed with complex floral or figural schemas and luxuriously encrusted with pearls and turquoise stones. They reflect the commissioners' devotion and desire to shorten or terminate the cycle of rebirth and suffering, thereby attaining nirvana (enlightenment). Devotees believe that merit is accumulated through the making of Buddhist images and relics, and the accumulation of merit not only decreases the amount of suffering in the next life but also shortens the cycle of rebirths.

Reliquary boxes were popular in the high Tang period of the 8th century. Two of the most famous Buddhist sites where sets of nested reliquaries were excavated are the Famen Monastery at Fufeng in Shaanxi Province and the Temple of the Great Clouds (Dayunsi) in Gansu Province. According to Prof Roderick Whitfield, a leading scholar of Chinese painting and Chinese Buddhist art, these nested reliquaries are actually three-dimensional representations of mandalas. [ST]

RELIQUARY BOX
China
8th century
Gold foil on silver
3.8 x 7.2 x 4.6 cm
1998.1395

Ren Bonian's 'Birds, Pine and Prunus'

In *Birds, Pine and Prunus*, Ren Bonian (1840–1895) displays a virtuosity of brushstrokes in a complex scheme of twisted and interweaving branches. The meticulous layering of dark and light tones that articulates the 'knottedness' of the branches, combined with the layering of the branches, suggests space and adds depth. The quaint distortion of the subject matter hints at the influence of Chen Hongshou (1598–1652), who inspired Ren Bonian's uncle and elder brother, Ren Xun (1853–1893) and Ren Xiong (1823–1857) respectively. (Ren himself had studied painting from Ren Xun, his uncle.) In this composition, Ren demonstrates his forte in imbuing a sense of poetic naturalism through his use of calligraphic strokes and smooth washes.

Ren excelled mainly in figure as well as bird and flower paintings. He was also known as Ren Yi or Xiao Lou. Although he was born in Shaoxing, Zhejiang province, Ren became one of the key proponents of the Shanghai school of painting, together with the other three Rens (Ren Xiong, Ren Xun and Ren Yu), Xugu and Qian Hui'an. The Shanghai school breathed new life into the clichéd compositions inherited from literati traditions. They demonstrated a propensity for smooth surfaces and easily comprehensible, popular subject matter and themes (such as bird and flower paintings, and figure paintings of immortals), and veered away from academic topics, such as landscape paintings, which were favoured by the literati class. The support of the emerging mercantile community in the Shanghai area who were the patrons of the Shanghai school, coupled with the artists' innovation, brought about this change in the style of painting. [ST]

REN BONIAN'S *BIRDS, PINE AND PRUNUS*
China
1882
Chinese ink and colours on paper
242 x 121 cm
Gift of the Tan family in memory of
their late father Dr Tan Tsze Chor
2000.7903

Robin's Egg Glazed Vase

This bulbous vase with a broad neck and low foot ring has an incised Qianlong seal mark on its base. The cobalt and copper contents in the glaze were opacified with arsenic (▶ see FAMILLE ROSE DISH). When fired to a low temperature of about 700 degrees Celsius, they culminated in fine specks and streaks of blue. These trickled from the rim to the foot ring of this vase, further enhancing its bulbous form. As one of the technological achievements of Qing ceramics, this glaze, known as robin's egg glaze, developed from the opaque turquoise glaze. It is also a 'transmutation' glaze, or *yaobian*, as the effects are a spontaneous result of glaze designs reacting during firing. This further implies that no two results are the same.

The term 'robin's egg glaze' was derived from its similarity to the appearance of robin's eggs, most likely the American robin. The true robin's egg glaze was introduced to Jingdezhen during Yongzheng's reign.[2] Two types of this glaze have been identified—one with red patterning caused by iron red enamels and the other with dark blue and turquoise streaks, exemplified by this vase. The use of such a dramatic glaze extended beyond the kilns of Jingdezhen to encompass Yixing kilns in Jiangsu province and Shiwan kilns in Guangdong province, a testament to its popularity. [WHL]

ROBIN'S EGG GLAZED VASE
China
Qing dynasty, Qianlong period
Ceramic
h. 17.1 cm, diam. (MOUTH) 10 cm
1998.1074

Roi Nuoc
(Water Puppets)

Water puppetry probably evolved in the Red River Delta as part of village folk rituals connected with fertility and agriculture, and probably also enjoyed periods of court patronage. An inscription dated 1121 at Doi temple in Duy Tien District, Nam Ha province, includes a description of a story enacted by water puppets.[3] It is thought that water puppetry, together with other performing arts, went into decline during the 15th century with the establishment of Confucianism at the court.[4] These examples are made of carved wood decorated with colourful paints or fabrics. The lion (BELOW) consists of a carved head with a series of cane hoops covered in fabric for its body. This enables it to perform various acrobatic movements during the lion dance in which it frolics and plays ball with another lion. The female figure (OPPOSITE, TOP) has moveable arms with fabric wings, controlled by strings, which are levered from the base. The Dance of the Immortals, perhaps associated with the mythical female ancestor Au Co, involves a group of eight such figures who twirl and flap their wings in synchronised fashion. The Boy on a Buffalo (OPPOSITE, BOTTOM) is one of many peasant characters who appear in the vignettes of daily village life enacted by water puppets.

Legends and *hat cheo* stories are often performed. However, the most entertaining are the vignettes of rural life, which are given profound and often humorous expression, as well as the dances with special effects. Farmers plough their fields, fishermen cast their nets, fish jump in and out of the waves and dragons glide through the water shooting sprays of water and fireworks, accompanied by lively music, narration and sound effects. The puppets are brought to life by a series of rods and wires, connected to parts of their anatomy, which are worked underwater by puppeteers standing waist-deep in the water behind a bamboo curtain. The ingenious use of recycled materials adds a life-like quality to the puppets' movements. For example, a dragon puppet in the museum's collection has a segmented body held together by a bicycle chain which produces sinuous movements. The buffalo (OPPOSITE, LEFT) has a piece of rubber inner tubing attached to its neck which adds natural flexibility to the movements of its head.

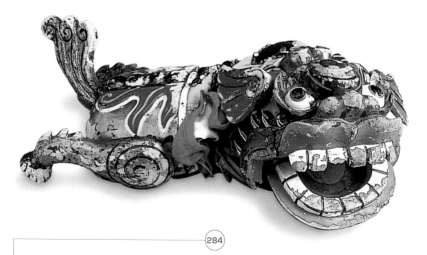

A *thuy dinh* (literally 'Temple of the Water'), or water puppet theatre, on the lake in front of Thay temple is thought to date to the Le Dynasty, and is one of the few village theatres that have survived.[5] Water puppets perform at Chua Thay (Temple of the Master) in Ha Son Binh province around March each year. The festival honours the monk Tu Dao Hanh, who is revered as the reincarnation of a buddha as well as King Ly Nhan Thong (1066–1127). He was also a master puppeteer. There were at least 28 guilds dedicated to water puppetry in 1996, which suggests the art is still very much alive in villages in the Delta region.[6] However, this art form is now most visible as a cultural tourist attraction, performed nightly by troupes in Hanoi and Ho Chi Minh City. [HT]

(OPPOSITE) **LION WATER PUPPET**
Hanoi, Vietnam
c. 1995
Wood
57 x 29 cm
2000.1186

(TOP) **FAIRY WATER PUPPET**
Hanoi, Vietnam
c. 1995
Wood
59 x 21 cm
2000.1188

(ABOVE, LEFT) **BOY ON A BUFFALO WATER PUPPET**
Hanoi, Vietnam
c. 1995
Wood
56 x 25 x 31 cm
2000.1189.1–2

Round Ink Cake by Cheng Junfang

This round ink cake is made with a moulded design of a cluster of moving dragons. All sinuous and slim in form, these dragons demonstrate a style which summarises the general decadent but luxuriant mood of the highly creative period of Emperor Wanli of the late Ming dynasty. Only the centre dragon is gilded; the reverse of the ink cake (BELOW, RIGHT) has an embossed and gilded inscription of *longjiuzi* (nine dragon sons) in pictogram. Produced in the workshop of Cheng Junfang, this ink cake was highly valued, even during its time, by collectors of different social backgrounds including the emperor. Cheng was one of the most influential and prolific ink designer-manufacturers of Huizhou, a centre of ink-making established since the Song dynasty. After being acknowledged by the court as a master ink-maker, Cheng published an extensive illustrated catalogue of 500 ink cakes with accolades from the Huizhou art and literati world.

The traditional ingredient—soot from pine trees—had by the late Ming dynasty been depleted in the region of Huizhou. Cheng's skill and innovation led him to substitute pine with peat and resin as the basic ingredients, improving the quality and eventually surpassing that of the pine-soot-derived ink. Cheng also employed master carvers to replicate on wooden moulds the painterly illustrations drawn by commissioned artists, some handsomely paid. One of the admirers of Cheng ink cakes was the doyen of literati painters, Dong Qichang (1555–1636), whose confidence in the quality of Cheng's ink led him to comment in public that it would still be treasured a thousands years thence! [LCL]

▶ see INK CAKE BY CAO SUGONG
▶ see INK STICKS

ROUND INK CAKE BY CHENG
(RIGHT) Reverse side
Huizhou, Anhui Province, China
Second half of 16th century
Ink
9 x 18 x 18.2 cm
Collection of Yuan Shaoliang
YSL.A1

Roundel

The images on this roundel are embroidered on a yellowish lattice-patterned fabric. The main feature here is the large *kaishu* (regular script) character *'wan'* (ten thousand) embroidered entirely in gold thread. Next to the *'wan'* character, a five-clawed dragon, also in gold with its scales outlined in black and white silk, soars to a cloud-filled sky chasing a pearl in flames. This composition is in mirror image along a central axis that divides the roundel in halves. Other auspicious symbols include the plum blossoms, cloud scroll, stylised bat, coin and the mandatory sea wave and mountain motifs at the base of the composition.

Most certainly this roundel would have been seen or worn together with other roundels of a similar design scheme featuring other characters to make up phrases such as *'wanshou wujiang'* (boundless longevity) and *'wandai jixiang'* (eternal prosperity) which were customary birthday and festival greetings directed to the emperor and his immediate family. Similar birthday and longevity symbols have also been found on textiles and garments in the imperial tomb, in particular in Dingling, where Emperor Wanli and his two empresses, Xiaoduan and Xiaojing, were buried. It is very likely that this roundel was formerly attached to a ceremonial robe worn by a member of the Wanli court. Imperial textiles were also given to significant guests of the court. Among these were high-ranked lamas (religious teachers) from Mongolia and Tibet who were often recipients of such textiles as they were regularly called upon for their liturgical services. [LCL]

Royal Malay Seal

Authentic royal Malay seals are very rare and this is a particularly interesting one because it is double-sided. The two sides of the seal bear dates one year apart—one side (BELOW, LEFT) is dated AH 1310, which corresponds to 1892–1893 CE, while the other side (BELOW, RIGHT) bears the date AH 1311. This suggests that the seal was re-used after it expired in AH 1310. It is made from a copper disc that has been wrapped with a layer of tin.

Official seals were used in the Malay courts for official correspondence or to endorse legal documents. This particular seal was used by Tengku Besar Tuan Long Yusuf ibni al-Marhum Sultan Ahmad, who was also known as Tuan Soh. His title was Tengku Besar Indra Raja in the court of the Sultan of Kelantan and he served for a time as the State Minister for Public Works. He was the sixth son of H. H. Sultan Ahmad ibni al-Marhum Muhammad, the reigning Sultan from 1886 to 1890. [DAH]

ROYAL MALAY SEAL
Kelantan, Malaysia
AH 1310–1311/1892–1893 CE
Tin, copper alloy
h. 1.2 cm, diam. 3.9 cm
2000.5593

Rudraksha Malai
(Rudraksha Necklace)

This necklace with rudraksha berries, otherwise known as Linga Padakka Muthumalai, consists of a pendant with a suspended *lingam* box. This suspended *lingam* box contains a sacred object called the *jangam* (mobile) *lingam* which is worshipped regularly. The necklace is strung with rudraksha berries, a fruit of *Elaeocarpus ganitrus*, and divided by gold spacers.[7] This fruit is considered a most sacred symbol by devout Shaivites, who wear one or many berries around their necks, and never remove them. The *padakam* (pendant) contains an image of Shiva, Parvati and Subrahmanya. Shiva, who stands between Parvati and Subrahmanya, is depicted in his Nataraja (Lord of Dancers) form striking the classic *bhujangatrasita-lola abhaya hasta*. The images are depicted standing under a canopy that suggests the *kanakasabhai*—the golden canopied dance hall in Chidambaram.

This necklace is not an ornament but a sectarian ritualistic emblem. It is worn and worshipped on special occasions by Shaivite priests and Chettiar householders. It has been observed that when Nagarathar Chettiars take the annual *kavadi*—the ritual carrying of milk for Murugan (Tamil name of Subrahmanya)— the veteran Murugan male devotees are seen wearing this necklace. The necklace is referred to as *gaurisangam*, a colloquial term for Gauri-Shankar which in turn refers to the inseparable form of Shiva and Parvati. Just like the Lingayat devotees, these devotees also worship the *jangam lingam* during festivals. Today, many Nagarathar Chettiar families who own such a necklace worship it on the days of ancestor worship.[8] [GPK]

▶ see SOUTH INDIAN LINGAM BOXES

RUDRAKSHA MALAI
Tamil Nadu, south India
19th century
Bronze
circ. 39 cm, h. (LINGAM BOX) 7 cm
1995.896

Safavid Qur'an Case

This Qur'an case was made to contain a miniature octagonal Qur'an. The cover is of pierced steel featuring four lines of cursive calligraphy floating on a slight scrolling background. If a Qur'an was stored inside, the design would become more visible. The pierced decorations featured here are similar to those found on other Safavid items such as *'alam* (standards) and belt plaques. The inscriptions are framed by a scrolling gold border. The eight sides of this case are decorated in gold with alternating floral and calligraphic motifs, while the back is decorated with interlacing tendrils and flowers.

The four lines depicted on the cover make up *Surat al-Ikhlas* (Purity of Faith), one of the most succinct Qur'anic chapters regarding *tauhid* (the unity of God). It reads, 'Say: He is Allah, The One and Only; Allah, the Eternal, Absolute; He begetteth not, Nor is He begotten; And there is none Like unto Him.' The concept of *tauhid* is a fundamental one in Islam. This is reflected in a *hadith* (tradition of the Prophet Muhammad) which states that this short *surah* is 'equivalent to one-third of the Qur'an'. As such, it is one of the most popular Qur'anic verses recited during *salat* (five obligatory prayers) and depicted on objects.

Such tiny Qur'an cases, with the sacred book inside, were carried on one's person for protective reasons. Given the sacred nature of the Qur'an, these cases were worn or carried above the waist, as a sign of respect. [TH]

▶ see KISWAH FRAGMENTS FROM THE HOLY KA'BAH
▶ see MINIATURE QUR'AN

SAFAVID QUR'AN CASE
Iran
17th–18th centuries
Gold on steel
(SHOWN IN ACTUAL SIZE) 5.9 x 4.6 cm
2000.5636

Stele Depicting Shakyamuni and Prabhutaratna

The scene in which the historical Buddha, Prabhutaratna, springs from his stupa and appears in undissipated body to hear Shakyamuni preach the *Lotus Sutra* was a popular theme in Buddhist iconography during the Six Dynasties. On this Northern Qi marble stele the two Buddhas sit side by side in the woods, represented by the interlocked trunks and luxuriant leaves above them. The disc-shaped leaves are also the only element depicted at the back of the stele. Standing next to the Buddhas are probably the disciples Sariputra and Kasyapa. The hand gestures of the Buddhas—*abhaya* (fearlessness) and *varada* (boon-bestowing)—are in mirror image, as in most paired figures of this period. At the top of the stele the Buddha of the Future, Maitreya, is flanked by celestial beings said to have come to witness the greatness of the *Lotus Sutra* being preached.

Prabhutaratna, or *Duobao fo*, is one of the physical representations of the many Buddhas from the past who are visible to humans. His dramatic appearance is depicted in the widely accepted *Lotus Sutra* to illustrate the eternal nature of Buddha across time and space. Since its translation into Chinese by Central Asian monk Kumarajiva in 406, the *Lotus Sutra* has been the main Mahayana Buddhist scripture to capture the imagination of Chinese Buddhists. [LCL]

MARBLE STELE DEPICTING THE
CONVERSATION OF SHAKYAMUNI AND
PRABHUTARATNA
China
Northern Qi dynasty (549–577)
White marble
57 x 35 cm
1998.1462

Sarung Featuring Camels and Tents

The decorations on this *sarung* (tubular skirt) are done using a technique called batik, and in a style associated with the north coast of Java. The main field of this textile depicts a procession, presumably to Mecca, either of the *haj* (pilgrimage) or an *umrah* (lesser pilgrimage). The procession comprises bearded men (presumably Arab) leading camels and carrying flags bearing these words in Romanised Malay: *Bendera Radja Mekkah*, which mean the 'Flag of the Ruler of Mecca'. There are camels carrying a couple in a litter while others carry luggage (or perhaps goods for trade). The front panel or *kepala* (head) of this *sarung* features a tree with a variety of flowers and birds on a purple ground.

This *sarung* is done in a style similar to what is known as *kain kompeni* (cloth of the Company), which usually features marching soldiers. The company referred to is the

SARUNG FEATURING CAMELS AND TENTS
Possibly Pekalongan, north coast of Java, Indonesia
Early 20th century
Cotton
(FOLDED) 107.2 x 88.9 cm
2000.5573

Dutch East India Company (Vereenigde Oostindische Compagnie). It is likely that this *kain* (cloth) was from an Indo-Arabian (Arabs who have settled in Indonesia) workshop. Judging from the theme, the *sarung* was made to be worn by a Muslim, perhaps to commemorate the wearer's or his/her family member's completion of the pilgrimage to Mecca.

Performing the *haj* or pilgrimage to Mecca is a lifetime ambition of all Muslims. For early Southeast Asian Muslims, performing this religious duty would have entailed a long and arduous journey. First they journeyed to Arabia by sea, then to Mecca by caravan. [TH]

▌ see KISWAH FRAGMENTS FROM THE HOLY KA'BAH
▌ see BATIK

Sawankhalok Ceramics

The royal twin cities of Sukhothai and Si Satchanalai in north-central Thailand were at the heart of one of the largest ceramic-producing centres in Southeast Asia during the 14th century. Si Satchanalai was later renamed Sawankhalok and the name became a convenient if somewhat inaccurate term to refer to ceramics that originated from either of these two areas.

A wide range of iron-brown-decorated wares was made, including jars (RIGHT) and pouring vessels (OPPOSITE, TOP, RIGHT), and dishes with the fish motif (BELOW, LEFT). Sculptural pieces were also typical of the Sawankhalok repertoire, such as the small figure of a mother with a baby (OPPOSITE, TOP, CENTRE) made for ritual decapitation to ensure a safe birth. Ceramics offered a substitute for the lack of fine sandstone with which to embellish religious monuments constructed on a large scale particularly at Sukhothai during the 14th century.[1] The *makara*-shaped roof finial (OPPOSITE, LEFT) is heavily potted and was made from moulded parts that were joined together, with a hole through the body to attach it to the roof of the ordination or assembly hall of a temple. The thickly glazed celadon

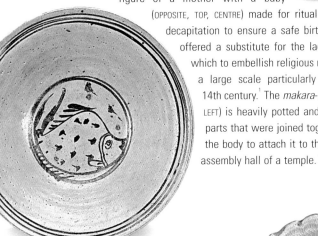

(TOP, RIGHT) **BROWN AND WHITE COVERED JARS**
North-central Thailand
13th–15th centuries
Stoneware
(CLOCKWISE FROM TOP) diam. 9.7; diam. 8.5 cm; diam. 14 cm
(1992.804, 1992.807) Gift of Dr Earl Lu
1992.804, C1092, 1992.807

(ABOVE) **DISH WITH FISH MOTIF**
North-central Thailand
13th–15th centuries
Stoneware
diam. 24.5 cm
C1606

(RIGHT) **CELADON BOWL**
Si Satchanalai, north-central Thailand
Mid 15th century
Stoneware
h. 8.5 cm, diam. 24.5 cm
Excavated from the east coast of Malaysia.
1998.965

bowl (OPPOSITE, BELOW) has a Chinese-style foliate rim, an incised floral medallion at the centre and lotus petals around the exterior.[2] It was salvaged from a shipwreck dating to c. 1450 off the east coast of Malaysia, as part of a group of 21,000 celadon pieces from Si Satchanalai.[3]

Mixed cargoes of Thai, Vietnamese and Chinese wares retrieved from shipwrecks in recent years have confirmed that Thai kilns competed with neighbouring producers for regional export markets. Thai wares have also been found in large quantities in the Philippines, Java and Sulawesi where they were used for ritual purposes, for example as burial wares or as *pusaka* (heirlooms).[4] They were also exported to Japan. The earliest evidence of Thai export wares comes from a mid-14th-century site at a castle in Okinawa where shards from a covered box and other vessels were excavated.[5] Late-17th-century Japanese records of Thai wares used in tea ceremonies suggests a long production period, contrary to the belief that the Burmese sacking of Ayutthaya curtailed production during the 16th century.[6] [HT]

(TOP, RIGHT) **POURING VESSEL IN THE SHAPE OF A KNEELING FIGURE**
North-central Thailand
13th–15th centuries
Stoneware
18 x 8 x 9 cm
Gift of Dr Earl Lu
1998.211

(TOP, LEFT AND CENTRE) **SCULPTURAL FIGURES**
(LEFT) Kneeling figure
(CENTRE) Figure of mother and baby
North-central Thailand
13th–15th centuries
Stoneware
h. 10.3 cm; h. 10.5 cm
(1992.815) Gift of Dr Earl Lu
1992.815, C1093

(LEFT) *MAKARA* **FINIAL**
North-central Thailand
13th–15th centuries
Stoneware
64 x 26 x 27 cm
Gift of Dr Earl Lu
1992.822

Scribe's Table

This scribe's table is a splendid addition to the museum's collection of tools and furniture used by calligraphers. The rectangular table is decorated with tortoiseshell and mother-of-pearl inlay—a technique widespread among the Ottomans after the 15th century. This decorative technique was also used for Qur'an stands, window shutters and cupboards. The inlay on this table has been placed in a decorative geometric pattern. Geometrical designs are often used in Islamic art as they create the impression of unending repetition, which is believed to encourage the contemplation of the infinite nature of God.

This table has a small drawer at the front which is divided into three compartments that were used to store writing implements. These instruments consisted usually of reed pens, penknives (used to trim the nib of the reed pens), scissors (to cut the paper) and inkwells (to store the ink). Calligraphy, or the art of beautiful writing, has always been considered the noblest and most featured art in the world of Islam as it transmits the Divine Revelations of God. [HH]

▶ see PENBOXES

SCRIBE'S TABLE WITH TORTOISESHELL AND
MOTHER-OF-PEARL INLAY
Turkey
Ottoman period, 17th century
Wood
35.5 x 56 x 33 cm
1999.1413

Seurapi
(Acehnese Necklace)

This necklace from Aceh is known as a *seurapi*. It is composed of a series of flower- or leaf-shaped pendants linked with a double chain. These beautifully shaped pendants are decorated with golden wire filigree and faceted granulation in an intricate but effortless style so often characteristic of Acehnese art.

The *seurapi* is an integral part of the Acehnese wedding costume, although they vary from region to region and according to the socio-economic status of the wearer. Barbara Leigh, a prominent researcher of Acehnese art, describes the Acehnese bride as 'dripping with gold', an apt description considering the amount of gold jewellery worn by an Acehnese woman on her wedding day. According to Leigh, wedding professionals were typically hired to dress the bride. The jewellery was owned by these professionals—usually women—and was rented to the families of the bride and groom.

Aceh, in north Sumatra, is a place that has been known for centuries as a source of gold. In 1595 a Dutch traveller described the Acehnese town of Pedir as 'a towne … from whence commeth much pepper and golde'. As a result of its supply of gold, Aceh gained a reputation for goldsmithing, which it retains even until today.[7] [DAH]

SEURAPI
Aceh, north Sumatra, Indonesia
Late 19th century
Gold
35 x 11.3 cm
1997.04791

Sewar

The *sewar* belongs to a class of Malay slashing weapons that includes the *tumbuk lada* and the *rencong*. These three types are often confused with one another and there is significant variation in the regional names for them. *Sewar* were common throughout the island of Sumatra and were also popular among Peninsular Malays. This particular example is a typical *sewar* from the Palembang region in south Sumatra, with its deeply carved water buffalo horn scabbard and hilt as well as a floral and tendril-decorated silver oversheath. The hilt is further embellished with silver ornaments intricately decorated with wire filigree. While most *sewar* are far less ornate, this particular example would most likely have been more for prestige wear.

The *sewar* blade is typically a slightly downward-curving single-edged blade with a sharp point. A distinguishing feature of the *sewar* is the sudden widening, known as a *tampo* (bolster), where the blade meets the hilt. This strengthens the blade at a critical point, and helps support and keep the hilt from splitting.

While not as common as the *keris* (▶ see KERIS), the *sewar* was often carried as an additional sidearm, and in the hands of a skilled fighter would have been a formidable weapon. In fact traditionally, the *sewar* enjoyed a rather gruesome reputation as a weapon of assassins because its relatively small size made it fairly easy to conceal. Smaller examples of the *sewar* are also thought to have been carried by women as a form of self-defence. [DAH]

SEWAR
South Sumatra, Indonesia
19th century
Silver, horn, wood, iron
34 cm
K0221

Shatari
(Vaishnava Ritual Cap)

The Shatari (Vaishnava ritual cap) is a Shri Vaishnava headgear used by priests in Vaishnava temples in Tamil Nadu to transmit Vishnu's blessings to devotees. It is neither worn by a deity nor a priest, but is itself a highly venerable ritual object to which worship is offered, just as icons of Vishnu are offered worship. Considered the most sacred among the ritual objects of the Vaishnava cult, the Shatari is seldom removed from where it is always placed, which is near Vishnu's feet.

The Shatari has an inverted lotus pattern with the slippers of an *alvar* saint named Nammalvar. It was Nammalvar who first began the practice of having a priest place the Shatari on the heads of each and every devotee gathered for the *darshana*. This signifies equality among the devotees as they are all eligible to receive the blessings of Vishnu. As devotees usually do not enter the sanctum but instead gather outside for the *darshana*, the priest brings the Shatari to the door of the sanctum. Receiving the Shatari is an honour and devotees generally bow humbly before the priest as he approaches them with the Shatari and places it individually on their heads.

Alvar are Vaishnava saints who composed great religious literature between the 5th and 9th centuries. There are 12 *alvar*, of which Nammalvar is the fifth. It is said that for the first 16 years of his life he did not touch food and meditated under a tamarind tree. Nammalvar is considered an incarnation of Adi Shesha, the serpent on which Vishnu reclines. He was the guru of Madhura Kavi, a poet who celebrated him in his works, and is also referred to as Sadakopan and Senai Mudaliar (Chief of the Hosts) in Vaishnava literature. Nammalvar is referred to 'our *alvar*', which shows the devotion Vaishnava devotees have for him. Nammalvar is also famous for his *bhakti* poetry: *Thiruvirutam*, *Thiruvasiriyam*, *Thiruvayamoli* and *Periya Tiruvantati*, all of which are celebrated for their theological knowledge and as aesthetic compositions of visionary poetry. [GPK]

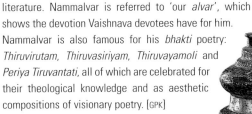

▶ see SHRI CHAKRA
▶ see SHRI YANTRA ON KURMA

SHATARI
Tamil Nadu, south India
19th century
Gilt copper
h. 14 cm, diam. (BASE) 18.4 cm
1996.495

Shiva, Parvati and Skanda

This Somaskanda[8] depiction of Shiva[9] shows the mutual admiration of Shiva and Parvati of their son Skanda, also known as Subrahmanya, or Murugan in south India. Shiva and Parvati are shown in *lalitasana* (relaxed posture) and are each on a lotus seat atop a rectangular throne. Between them is their son Skanda, shown here as a little baby in a dance-like pose holding a flower bud and a ball in each of his arms. Parvati wears a dhoti with detailed patterns, beaded and pearl ornaments, an *ekavali* (single-strand necklace) and a *karandamukuta* (basket crown) on her head. Shiva holds a *parashu* (axe) and a deer with his two upper arms while his two lower arms are in *abhaya mudra* (gesture of fearlessness) and *kapitha mudra* (clasping gesture). He wears a *jatamukuta*—a complex hairdo of matted hair that resembles a crown—and he is elegantly ornamented with a pearl necklace, chest band, waist band, *yagnopavita* (sacred thread), and bangles. His ears are decorated with a *makara* and a circular earring respectively.

This is a very family-oriented representation of the otherwise

SOMASKANDA (SHIVA, PARVATI AND THEIR SON SKANDA)
Tamil Nadu, south India
Late Chola period, c. 1200
Bronze
(SHIVA) h. 54.9 cm, (PARVATI) h. 51.4 cm
2000.777

ferocious deity. Shiva has a unique dichotomy in his personality, combining asceticism with sensualism; ascetics as well as young girls desirous of a good husband invoke him. Shiva is known to be very easy to please, thus earning him the name Bholenath, which means the Easily Appeased One. The Somaskanda depiction of Shiva is generally worshipped during festivals of the Shaiva cycle in south India; no north Indian representation is known.

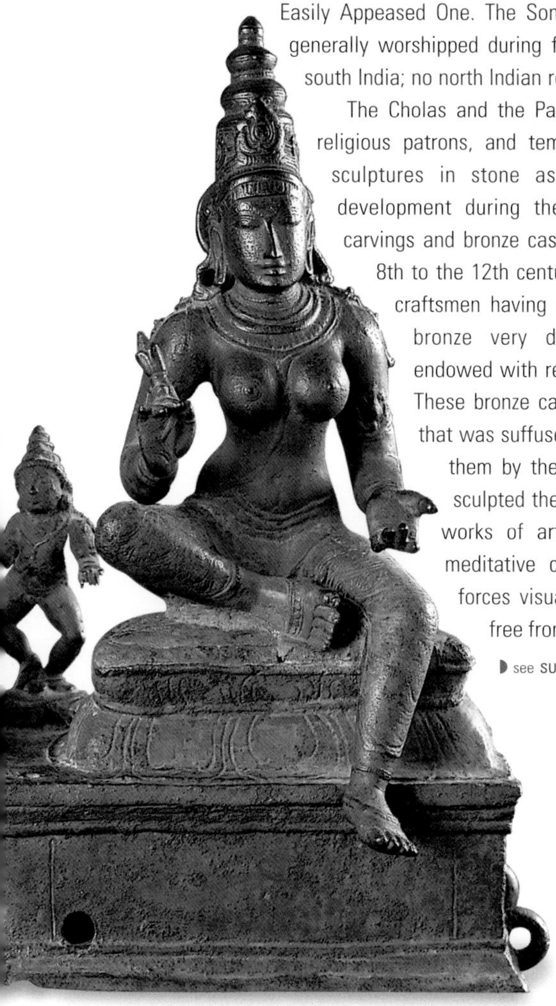

The Cholas and the Pallavas before them were great religious patrons, and temple-building and donations of sculptures in stone as well as bronze saw great development during their time. Some of the finest carvings and bronze casting examples are found in the 8th to the 12th centuries in Tamil Nadu, the master craftsmen having perfected the art of casting in bronze very delicate and slender figures endowed with refinement and aesthetic beauty. These bronze castings represent the classicism that was suffused with devotion endowed upon them by their patrons and the artists who sculpted them. On one hand, they are great works of art but on the other, they are meditative constructs of the great divine forces visualised in a human form that is free from the bondage of humanity. [GPK]

▶ see SUBRAHMANYA

Shri Chakra
(Vishnu's Discus)

The Shri Chakra is one of Vishnu's weapons, and is held in his arms. In most sculptures of Vishnu it is simply clutched while in some south Indian sculptures it is held in *prayoga mudra* (ready to be released). This indicates that Vishnu is about to annihilate an ogre or descend to earth to avert a calamity.

The *chakra* (discus) is also regarded as a deity in south Indian Shri Vaishnava cult philosophy. Conventionally, the *chakra* is represented as a wheel on one side and Narasimha on the other. Both of these are considered to be *ugra* (angry forms of Vishnu). However, this piece is an independent cult icon of Sudarshana or Shri Chakra—Narasimha is not represented. In this piece the *chakra* is placed on a lotus pedestal held up by a pair of addorsed rampant *vyala*, each sprouting a foliate rhysome from its gaping jaws. The *chakra* is formed by two interlocking triangles containing an eight-ray *biju* (seed) and decorated with beads along the inner and the outer edges. Four flaming projections representing the four cardinal directions frame the outer edge of the wheel.

According to the cult of Lakshmi Narasimha—those who worship Narasimha with his consort Lakshmi—Sudarshana or Chakratalvan is seen in combined form with Narasimha. Chakratalvan Sannidhi, the independent cult temple of Chakra, can be seen in many Shri Vaishnava temples in south India and Singapore. The Shrinivasa Perumal temple in Singapore has a shrine dedicated to this deity. Daily ritual worship is offered to the deity and special sacrifices are conducted for devotees seeking his grace for a healthy life. [GPK]

▶ see SHATARI
▶ see SHRI YANTRA ON KURMA

SHRI CHAKRA
Tamil Nadu, probably Thanjavour, south India
c. 1700
Bronze
h. 48.9 cm
1999.2754

Shri Yantra on Kurma

The Shri Yantra is a ritual object representing the goddess Lakshmi, also known as Shri, in a geometric form. It is conceived in tantric form as a tapering seven-tiered pyramidal mountain called Meru. Unlike the anthropomorphic representation of the goddess, in which she is seated on a lotus with two elephants pouring water on her, this is a non-figural conception of the deity. Every facet or corner has a specific form of the goddess ascribed to it as its presiding deity. The base of the pyramid rests on the back of a *kurma* (tortoise), which is an incarnation of Vishnu, the cosmic supporter of the universe. Thus the Shri Yantra on *kurma* suggests the combined forms of Lakshmi and Vishnu.

Devotees invoke the blessings of Lakshmi by performing ritual worship such as chanting, offering flowers and *kumkum* (vermilion powder) to this ritual object. They also pledge the Shri Yantra *puja* (ritual worship) in honour of Lakshmi by joining the priest as he chants her 1001 names. The devotees offers *kumkum* to Lakshmi for every name chanted by the priest.

Interestingly, the making of ritual objects associated with deities has the same iconographic importance as the making of icons of deities themselves. Having such ritual objects in the museum's collection allows us to better understand the role they play in the worship of deities. [GPK]

SHRI YANTRA ON *KURMA*
Tamil Nadu, south India
19th century
Copper
9.5 x 22.8 x 16 cm
1996.494

Painting Depicting Shrines to Lord Shiva

This is an extremely rare cloth painting from the Pahari region depicting an equally rare subject matter—one related to *shraddha* (annual death rituals). Thus, some familiarity with *shraddha* is required in order to fully appreciate the symbolic and schematic composition of this painting.

The painting is divided into three parts. In the middle (SEE DETAIL, OPPOSITE) is a large *yoni* shape containing several *shivalingam*, the aniconic representation of Lord Shiva combining both male (*lingam*) and female (*yoni*) principles. The larger *shivalingam* is inscribed with Vishveshvara while the one above it is inscribed with Shrungareshvara. In the zone on the right are references to *shraddha*-related sites where most devout Hindus perform the last rites for their parents or annual death rites. This customary practice is considered very auspicious among Hindus. The sites mentioned in this painting are Dashashvamedha (also known as Varanasi), Prayag, Bodhagaya and Gaya. Within Gaya there is mention of the Vishnupada temple (▶ see EUROPEANS VISITING THE VISHNUPADA TEMPLE), Akshayavata, Brahmapretashila, Gayasira, Pitamaha and Kagabali, among others. All of them refer to the main sites in Gaya connected with *pitr* (ancestor worship) and annual *shraddha* rituals. There is also mention of the sacred rivers such as Ganga, Yamuna and Saraswati, but Phagu, a sacred river in Gaya, is either absent or has been erased. The celestial world is represented in the zone on the left with the celestial animals Airavata, Ashva, Vasuki and Kamadhenu. Above them two men, Madhava and Venimadho, are shown having a conversation. They are probably chanting some verses from the *shraddha* ritual.[10]

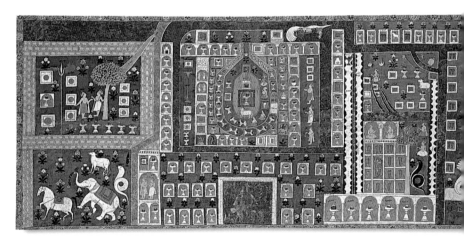

PAINTING DEPICTING SHRINES TO LORD SHIVA
Pahari region, Himachal Pradesh, India
Late 17th–early 18th centuries
Cotton, painted and inscribed
90 x 198 cm
1994.675

(OPPOSITE) **DETAIL**
A section from the central zone

The most striking part of this painting is the presence of nearly 90 *shivalingam*, each referring to either a major *jyotirlinga* (a *linga* that is naturally formed) or a regional Shiva temple. Each *shivalingam* is placed under a shrine-like arched canopy. Another interesting detail can be found at the upper right corner of the middle part of the painting (SEE DETAIL, ABOVE). Vishnu and his divine spouse Lakshmi are depicted sitting on a *sheshanaga* (coiled serpent) in the waters, which in Hindu mythology represents the primeval waters before Vishnu created the world. It is interesting to note that the painter has depicted this significant event albeit in a small area of the painting.

This painting has a grey background with a floral border and shows very little surface damage although there are some signs of repainting. The colour scheme is grey, orange, green, red and black, making the painting very bright and cheerful. Stylistically it bears many similarities to the Basohli and Chamba schools of Pahari painting, which is usually done on paper and in a small horizontal format. However, the format of this painting relates more to Jaina *tirthipata* cloth paintings, which are like topographic renderings of sacred sites. They tend to celebrate a pilgrimage and capture in a diagrammatic manner how a journey was performed or what the pilgrim site might have looked like. In the same way, this painting commemorates a noble family's visit to Gaya for a *shraddha*-related ceremony. It was probably done in the last quarter of the 17th century and it was quite likely that the painter accompanied the family to Gaya. Such paintings are very rare and this painting is a unique one among all known collections. [GPK]

▶ see MUKHALINGA

Sireh Sets

The practice of chewing *sireh* (betel) dates back deep into the prehistory of Southeast Asia and remained popular until the early part of the 20th century. The *sireh* quid is made up of the nut of the areca palm along with lime paste wrapped in the leaves of the piper betel vine. *Sireh* is a mild narcotic that has a calming effect and chewing *sireh* was often a highly ritualised social custom, especially in the Southeast Asian courts.

Sireh was usually presented in a special set that contained all of the necessary ingredients for chewing *sireh*. These two *sireh* sets are typical of sets that are commonly used in the Malay world. The first of these is a lidded container known as a *kotak sireh* (BELOW, TOP). It is a rhomboid-shaped wooden box covered with repoussé silver plates decorated with floral motifs and framed with gilt silver strips. The second is a pedestal tray set known as a *puan sireh* (BELOW, BOTTOM). The tray is cast brass, with floral designs around the bowl and base. The upper and lower rim of the tray are clad in silver strips. The upper strip bears the seal of the State of Kedah, indicating that this set was an official state item or gift. The set contains all of the paraphernalia and containers needed for serving *sireh*. Four small fruit-shaped silver receptacles would have

held the areca nut, lime, tobacco and various spices such as gambier or cloves. The larger, tapered box held the betel leaves used to wrap the *sireh* quid prior to chewing. The set also contains a *kacip* (▶ see KACIP) for cutting areca nuts and a *gobek*, a mortar and pestle used mainly by older, toothless individuals to mash the contents of the quid prior to chewing. [DAH]

(TOP) **KOTAK SIREH**
Riau-Lingga Archipelago, Indonesia
19th century
Silver, gilt silver, lacquer, wood
15 x 32 x 19 cm
S0403

(RIGHT) **PUAN SIREH**
Kedah, Malaysia
1900–1950
Silver, brass, iron
h. 14.5 cm, diam. 23.5 cm
1999.147

Slip-painted Bowl

The interior of this bowl is decorated with Kufic-Abbasid inscriptions which are arranged concentrically, except at the centre of the bowl. The remaining spaces are filled with red dotted grounds with four-petalled motifs in red and manganese. The decorations as well as the background colour of this bowl have been painted on with coloured slips which were then glazed with a transparent and colourless lead glaze.

This bowl is an example of slip-painted pottery with polychrome decorations produced during the 10th and 11th centuries in Iran. Such bowls are generally known as Samanid epigraphic pottery. The Kufic-Abbasid script used here is similar to that found in manuscripts. See ▶ BOWL WITH FOLIATED KUFIC-ABBASID SCRIPT for an example of a more ornate script which is believed to be a later development of this simple script.

This bowl is special as it is perhaps the only known example of such wares that is dated. The date is found in the top line at the centre of the bowl and reads 'three hundred'. This date was inserted into the decoration, perhaps to commemorate the end of the 3rd century of the Muslim era. While most other Samanid bowls are inscribed with proverbs or good wishes and blessings for their owners, this bowl contains an inscription from the Qur'an— verses 51 and 52 of *Surat al-Qalam* (The Pen):

And the Unbelievers
would almost trip thee up,
With their eyes when they
Hear the message; and they
say: 'Surely he is possessed!'
But it is nothing less
Than a Message
To all the worlds.

It is possible that the choice of this verse is a reflection of the situation in Samanid society—which was located on the frontiers of the Islamic world— where there was still a substantial percentage of non-Muslims.[11] [TH]

SLIP-PAINTED BOWL
Samarqand (Uzbekistan)
AH 300/912 CE
Earthenware
diam. 36 cm
On loan from the Tareq Rajab Museum, Kuwait
TR 106

Songhua Inkstone

Of the four major inkstones highly regarded by the Chinese, the green Songhua stone is a northern Chinese speciality mined mainly in the Liaoning province. Like other inkstones, such as the Duan of Guangdong and the She of Anhui, Songhua is derived from sedimentary rock. For a long time this green stone with its horizontal grain had been used by the Tungusic-speaking natives of the northeast as sharpening device for knives. It was not until the 17th century that emperor Kangxi gave instructions for the stone to be made into inkstones, hence making it unique in the Qing imperial collection of studio stationery.

As if a reflection of the emperor's personality, the rectangular inkstone is simple in decoration, carved at the sloping reservoir portion with an elegant design of carp and scroll (BELOW, LEFT). The quiet serenity echoes the steady and fatherly personality of the Qing dynasty's longest reigning emperor. Indeed, attention is focused on the functionality of the object and its natural beauty. This preference for simplicity seemed deliberate, as Kangxi was one of the most diligent emperors, often capable of supervision of political, military, as well as household matters simultaneously. The reverse of the stone (BELOW, RIGHT) is inscribed with the emperor's elegant *kai*-script calligraphy of an eight-character proverb: *yijing weiyong, shiyi yongnian* ('quiet is the quality leading to strength and eternity') which appears on many of his collection of Songhua inkstones at the Taipei Palace Museum. [LCL]

**SONGHUA INKSTONE WITH IMPERIAL INSCRIPTION
OF KANGXI MARK**
(ABOVE, RIGHT) Reverse side
China
Qing dynasty, Kangxi period
Green Songhua stone
16.9 x 12.1 x 1.5 cm
1999.1395

Songket

(Supplementary Weft Textile)

This is a Malay *baju panjang* (long tunic) that is thought to have originated from the Riau Sultanate. The high collar, in *cekap musang* style, is fastened with two buttons and the front opening is trimmed with plaited maroon silk and silver metal thread. The fabric is hand-woven Malay *kain songket*, a fabric made using a supplementary weft of gold-wrapped threads. The threads are woven in such a way that they skip over certain warp threads, thus creating floral and geometric patterns in the cloth. The dark purple cloth is sumptuously decorated with rows of large floral blooms interspersed with decorative horizontal stripes. These stripes are made up of two types of small floral devices and wrapped with intertwining tendrils.

This garment was part of a group of items that originally entered the collection of the Raffles Museum in Singapore early in the 20th century. In the early 1900s the Dutch government of the Netherlands Indies had annexed Riau-Lingga and abolished the royal government, sending the majority of the members of the royal family, including the last Sultan, Abdul Rahman, into exile in Singapore.[12] It is believed that these items were acquired from one of these exiled family members.

Sometimes dubbed the Malay world's 'cloth of gold', *songket* were traditionally strictly reserved for royalty in most societies. Richly woven with gold or silver threads on silk or cotton fabric, *kain songket* were used mainly for ceremonial occasions and weddings. While the origins of *songket* are obscure, it is believed that the art arose as a local effort to imitate imported Indian textiles. It is generally believed that the art first began in the Srivijaya period in Southern Sumatra near present-day Palembang and Jambi. From there it spread to both the Minangkabau and to Malay areas as far as Terengganu and Kelantan. [DAH]

MALAY *SONGKET*
Riau-Lingga Archipelago, Indonesia
Mid to late 19th century
Silk, gold threads
150 x 103 cm
G0097

South Indian Lingam Boxes

*L*ingam boxes contain the cult objects of the Lingayat community. The Lingayat are the staunch Shiva worshippers of Karnataka known as *lingi* who believe in worshipping the portable and abstract form of Shiva, the *lingam* (*linga* in north India). There are three interesting silver *lingam* boxes, also known as *ayigalu*, in the museum's collection. One (BELOW) is in the form of a *chauka* (square shape) from Karnataka. It has an abstracted bull's horn-shaped cover which opens in the middle and contains a small crystal *lingam*. The surface is smooth apart from a repoussé floral pattern on the underside (BELOW, BOTTOM] and it is tied by a silver plaited cord. The second *ayigalu* (OPPOSITE, TOP) is from Andhra Pradesh and has a stupa or shrine shape over the *lingam*, with a *nandi* (bull) in veneration visible through the small opening. It has granulation and punch mark patterns and is quite flat and squarish in shape. The third *lingam* box (OPPOSITE, BOTTOM) is in a cylindrical amulet shape. According to Oppi Untracht, a leading authority on traditional Indian jewellery-making,

CHAUKA *LINGAM* BOX
(ABOVE, BOTTOM) Floral pattern on the underside
Karnataka, south India
18th–19th centuries
Silver
5.9 x 10.5 x 4 cm
1994.516

lingam are bathed and worshipped every day by the *lingi*. The *lingam* box is tied around their head, arm or neck and to lay it down is considered a sacrilege. After being initiated by a priest, the *lingi* will carry his or her *lingam* box until death when it is placed in the left hand of the devotee, who is then buried, not cremated.

The sect is called Vira Shaiva and its leader is Basavanna who popularised it during the 12th century at Kalyana, the capital of west Chalukyas. Basavanna started this sect to counter the narrow ritualism of Brahmanism but was soon expelled from the kingdom. The cult grew and today there are Vira Shaivas in Maharashtra, Andhra Pradesh and Tamil Nadu.

Unlike other Shaivites, the Vira Shaiva philosophy is against temple building, idol worship and pilgrimages to *sthavara* (stationary) *lingam* shrines or temples. Another Shaivite cult covers the *sthavara lingam* with *mukhalinga* (*lingam* with a human head), a cult object created to give a human identity to an otherwise phallic symbol. [GPK]

▶ see MUKHALINGA

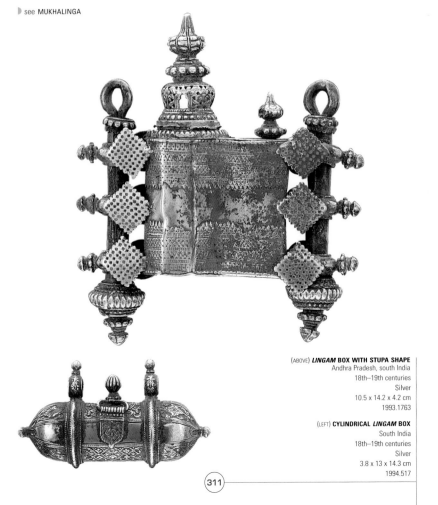

(ABOVE) ***LINGAM* BOX WITH STUPA SHAPE**
Andhra Pradesh, south India
18th–19th centuries
Silver
10.5 x 14.2 x 4.2 cm
1993.1763

(LEFT) **CYLINDRICAL *LINGAM* BOX**
South India
18th–19th centuries
Silver
3.8 x 13 x 14.3 cm
1994.517

Staff of Authority
(Tunggal Panaluan)

This staff is a classic example of a *tunggal panaluan*, a powerful ritual instrument through which the Batak *datu* (magician-priest) protected the village, ensured victory in battle and called forth rain. This piece is highly polished, with human and animal figures carved on top of each other. It is evident that it was once crowned with feathers that have largely broken off.

The motifs on the *tunggal panaluan* are a representation from a particular Batak legend about a pair of incestuous siblings. There are many variations of this myth but the essence of the story remains the same. The siblings incurred the wrath of the gods by their incestuous acts and were cursed and turned into wood. The other figures in the myth were people who tried to help them and in turn were turned to wood as well, and these included family members and *datu*. The animal figures of the snake and lizard were symbols of these *datu*. This legend was chosen and depicted on the *tunggal panaluan* as it was a powerful symbol of the consequences of defying the gods.

The *tunggal panaluan* is the most important ritual object of the *datu* as it acted as his staff of authority. The *datu* always made their staffs themselves as the power of the staff was largely derived from the process in which it was made. This macabre process involved the killing of a kidnapped child, brewing a potion from its corpse, placing the potion in selected parts of the staff, then sealing this in with resins or wooden plugs. It is widely believed that the *tunggal panaluan* has its origins in the Toba region of Batakland and subsequently became used throughout the Batak region. The Toba Bataks are just one of six Batak ethnic groups. The other five are the Mandailing, Angkola, Pakpak-Dairi, Karo and the Simalungun.

'*Datu*' is a Toba Batak word that refers to a magician-priest. The Karo Batak word for a magician-priest is '*guru*'. *Datu* were experts in the traditional Batak religion. Besides holding ritual ceremonies, they determined much of the daily life of the community. *Datu* occupied a very special place in the community group as they possessed an extensive knowledge of the gods and spirits, black and white magic, and of illnesses and the ways of curing them. This made them influential members of society. In most villages, the *datu* held a monopoly on knowledge as they were the only people who could use the Batak script (▶ see PUSTAHA). [RE]

TUNGGAL PANALUAN
North Sumatra, Indonesia
c.1930s
Wood and feathers
l. 106 cm
XX11371

(RIGHT) **DETAIL**
Human figures on the staff

Majapahit-style Statue

The only one of its kind to have been found in Southeast Asia, this tiny lead statue was discovered during archaeological excavations near the mouth of the Singapore River at Empress Place in 1998. Depicting a horse and its male rider, it is almost intact apart from the figure's head and possibly the horse's wings. Together with various other artefacts from the 1998 excavations, this object is an important feature of the precolonial history section of the Singapore River Interpretive Centre.

The statue bears stylistic similarities to Javanese art—although whether it was produced on Java itself is debatable. As Dr John Miksic, who led the excavation, points out, the absence of any precise Javanese equivalents and the paucity of lead on the island raise the possibility that it was made elsewhere in what is now the Indonesian Archipelago.[13]

The Empress Place site dates back to the early Majapahit era (c. 14th century), when the statue was probably made. Singapore, or Temasik as it was then known, appears to have been a tributary of the Java-based Majapahit kingdom in the 14th century, mentioned in the Javanese chronicle *Pararaton* as a potential conquest, and in the *Nagarakrtagama* epic as a dependency. Precious few written sources on the island's existence prior to 1819 are available, and archaeological evidence serves to fill many of the gaps. This statue thus represents a tangible link with an intriguing but murky episode of Singapore's history. That it was found near the mouth of the Singapore River together with numerous fragments of trade ceramics also bolsters the fact that the island and its river were once an integral part of the precolonial maritime trade network which empires such as the Majapahit dominated. [LC]

HORSE AND RIDER FROM THE MAJAPAHIT ERA
Possibly from Java, Indonesia
Majapahit era, c. 14th century
Lead
5.5 x 5.6 x 1.9 cm
1998 excavations at Empress Place site
2002.431

Subrahmanya

Murugan, or Subrahmanya as he is known in south India, is the son of Shiva and Parvati. Just some of the other names by which he is known are Skanda-Kartikeya, Shanmukha, Vishakha, Kumara and Mahasena. As a six-headed infant he was nursed by the six *krittika* maidens and came to be known as Kartikeya. As Mahasena he is commander of the *deva* and was destined to appear as the son of Shiva and Parvati to kill the demon Taraka. As Subrahmanya he is supposed to have enlightened his father, Shiva, on the meaning of Brahman. Skanda and Vishakha originated in the *laukika devata* (folk deities), while Murugan is from the folk cults of Dravidian culture. Over time they have evolved to become associated with mainstream Brahmanical deities such as Shiva and Parvati.

This deity is seen standing with a *vel* (spear) in his right hand, a weapon of great power which devotees worship even today as the representation of the deity himself. In his left hand he carries a *vajra* (thunderbolt). His other two hands hold the gesture of *abhaya* (fearlessness) and *katisama* (waist-resting), a gesture regularly used to indicate deities in south India. The cult of Murugan is very popular in Tamil Nadu and among the Tamil diaspora all over the world. Although as the son of Shiva his cult is absorbed within the larger Shaiva fold, it has its own festival calendar and a following of staunch Murugan devotees.

Thaipusam is the most popular festival celebrated in Malaysia and Singapore in the months of January and February in celebration of Murugan receiving his *vel* from his mother. Thousands of devotees carry *kavadi*, a wooden pole with milk containers, to offer to their beloved deity on this day. They are either performing a vow or simply offering their thanks for good life and happiness. Many other festivals such as Kartikai, Skanda Shashti and Panguni Uttiram are celebrated throughout the year in his honour. The money-lending Chettiar community, who arrived in Singapore in the early 19th century, established the first Murugan temple here and continues to run the Thandayudhapani temple on Tank Road. In Tamil Nadu, six important temples are considered most holy and Murugan devotees will visit these during their lifetime. [GPK]

▌ see CHETTIAR DOCUMENTS
▌ see KAZHUTHTHU URU
▌ see RUDRAKSHA NECKLACE
▌ see SHIVA, PARVATI AND SKANDA

SUBRAHMANYA
Tamil Nadu, south India
Late Chola, 12th century
Granite
116 x 56 x 26 cm
1995.895

Sui Buddhist Triad

Executed in the classical Sui dynasty style, the Buddha stands between two bodhisattvas with his hands in *varada mudra* (boon-bestowing gesture) and *abhaya mudra* (gesture of fearlessness). The figurines reflect a sinicisation in terms of style with their attenuated forms, soft facial features and schematised flow of robes, a schema which began in the Northern Wei dynasty (386–534). However, by the Sui dynasty, precursors of the more voluminous forms typical of Tang figurines had already appeared, as can be seen in the face and body of the central figure in this triad.

According to the inscription on the stand, this image of Wuliangshou Buddha was commissioned in 609. Buddhists believe that reproducing Buddhist sutras and images earn them merit, and an accumulation of merit results in a shorter cycle of rebirth and hence less suffering.

Buddhism first entered China in the 2nd century BCE. As a foreign religion, it was persecuted on many occasions. However, it reached a peak in the Sui-Tang dynasties (581–907) when Emperor Wen of Sui identified himself as the universal monarch in the Buddhist tradition and propagated Buddhism on an extensive scale. By the end of his reign, he had expanded the number of temples and stupas built to 120. By the early Tang dynasty, the foundation had been laid for the spread of Buddhism across all classes of society and all parts of China. [ST]

SUI BUDDHIST TRIAD
China
Sui dynasty
Gilt bronze
25.5 x 13.4 x 10.5 cm
1998.1394

Sukhothai Walking Buddha

This image of the Walking Buddha or *cankrama* (walking back and forth) is conventionally regarded as the quintessential icon of the Sukhothai period.[14] He is depicted in mid-stride with his right foot forward and right hand in *abhaya mudra* (gesture of fearlessness). The left arm is relaxed at his side and its inward curve accentuates the underlying sense of fluidity and movement.[15] The robe is barely visible except for the fine outlines and flowing hemline. The *ushnisha* (protuberance) rises to a *cintamani* (flamed top-knot).

Images of the Buddha were commissioned as an act of merit. Their significance lay not only in their embodiment of what Buddha himself stood for, but also for the dharma and the *sangha*, the other two equally-important constituents of the Triratna (Three Jewels).[16] The image of the Walking Buddha has been interpreted in various ways. It is thought to refer to Buddha's return from Tavatimsa Heaven where he preached the doctrine to his mother.[17] Alternatively, it is associated with meditation and magical powers, as found in stucco reliefs at temples in Sukhothai and the twin town of Si Satchanalai—walking is one of the four meditation postures and a pair of flanking Buddhas depicted with a seated image indicate Buddha's magical ability to duplicate his appearance.[18]

The origins of the Walking Buddha remain unclear and the dating of several images continues to be questioned. There is some evidence for a bronze precursor from Lopburi dating to the 13th and 14th centuries and very few bronze images have been dated by inscription.[19] More recently it was proposed that the city of Sukhothai was not abandoned in 1438 with the rise of Ayutthaya, but instead flourished until 1786, and that many architectural images of the Walking Buddha were probably produced during the 18th century.[20] [HT]

FIGURE OF WALKING BUDDHA
Sukhothai, north-central Thailand
15th–16th centuries
Bronze
h. 117 cm
1999.1714

Summer Carpet

This quilted summer carpet with silk thread embroidery is a typical example of needlework with chain stitch produced in Gujarat during the Mughal period. Besides Lahore, Agra and Fatahpur, the state of Gujarat was a well-known centre for needlework. In this piece the field is covered with crimson-coloured flowers, leaves and tendrils devoid of any shading, all intertwined in an all-over pattern. There is no cartouche in the centre, which is typical of Persian-style carpets, suggesting this carpet is of localised style and patronage. A meandering creeper in yellow and blue forms the border while blue chain stitch is used as the outline for this piece.

The use of quilting, especially for embroidered carpets, was quite popular during the Mughal period and it still is today in parts of rural India. For instance, the *kantha* (quilts) of Bengal is very well known. The use of very fine and dense chain stitch for embroidery is a typical feature of Mughal embroideries. Even the so-called Chinese stitch became very popular in Gujarat, especially among the Parsees. Imperial Mughal embroidered summer

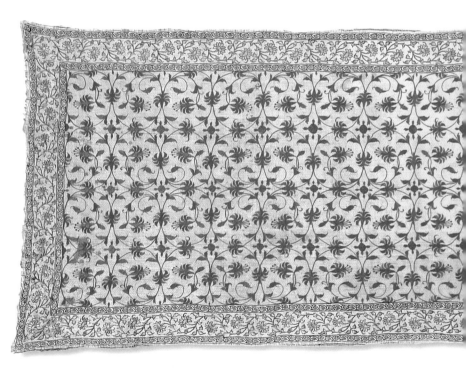

SUMMER CARPET
Gujarat, west India
c. 1800
Quilted cotton with silk thread embroidery
135 x 401 cm
1997.4826

carpets also tended towards a detailed use of shades to create a more realistic rendering of flowering plants in a painterly manner. The borders of many *patka* (sashes) in later Rajasthani courts were designed using this motif of alternating tendril with leaf and flower.

Summer carpets were quite widely used in India, both at courts and in households. A summer carpet combined luxury with practicality—it was usually richly decorated and had a sturdy surface that could last generations. It is not difficult to imagine a prince using a summer carpet just like the one shown here on a hot summer evening, sitting on a marble-floored balcony by the side of a lake enjoying music and wine. Indeed the Mughal Emperor Akbar used *qanat* (tent panels) (▶ see QANAT) and carpets very regularly, even at Fatehpur Sikri, where his court was held in tents. Many Mughal, Pahari and Rajasthani paintings illustrate gorgeously designed carpets and bed spreads. Different carpets were used for different hierarchies of visitors, on different occasions and during different seasons, resulting in a diversity of designs and materials used. [GPK]

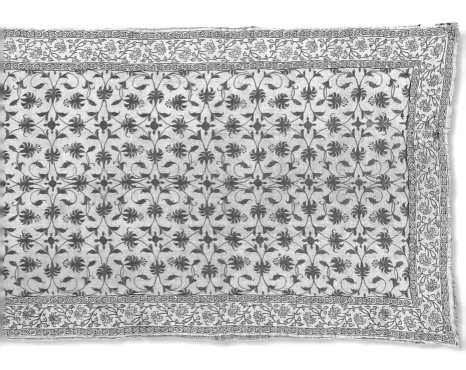

Syair
(Malay Poetry)

It is not surprising that early Malay manuscripts are rare. Southeast Asia's harsh tropical climate, with its dampness and heat, along with its myriad of hungry insects conspired to destroy a lot of what was a surprisingly rich literary heritage. Add to that the fact that until the introduction of movable type printing methods, most manuscripts had to be painstakingly copied by hand.

This rare early Malay manuscript is from Pattani, an old Malay Sultanate that is now a part of Thailand. A line in the text notes that the manuscript was completed on the 15th day of Ramadan in AH 1250, which corresponds to 15 January 1835. Interestingly, while the text clearly states that it was written in Pattani, it also notes that it was copied by Bayu bin Damah Syah and was the property of Fakir Ramli of Burma (Myanmar). This link to Burma is significant because the manuscript is handwritten using white ink on black gatefold paper. This type of text was common to Burma and Thailand but is rare in the Malay world.

The first text included in this manuscript is the *Nyanyi Siti Fatimah* or *Song of Siti Fatimah*. These were poems written in praise of the Prophet Muhammad's daughter Fatimah, her husband Ali, and their sons Hasan and Husain. At 15 pages, this text takes up the majority of the manuscript. The remaining five pages of the manuscript includes two short texts, *Nasihat Kepada Laki dan Perempuan* or *Advice for Men and Women* and *Inilah Syair Anak Anak Muda Berkahwin* or *This is a Syair for Young People Who are Marrying*. The majority of the manuscript is written in verse and most likely would have been recited or sung, perhaps to boys and girls of the Pattani court. [DAH]

SYAIR
Pattani, Thailand
AH 1250/1835 CE
Paper, pigment
(FOLIO) 17.5 x 8.5 cm
1999.2644

أنيله تعبير بهجي كند انق

دكي ليسي الق كامي مولاي

دكي تقدير الهاب ربو

سورع الق جيبنا بيسلام

سورع الق درك برسام

امسو ڤل ميروك كاوي ايزكي

نالي ايوف كامي خلتك

دمكيل كاوي اورع سلطين

كركايو ساء مسم و نماك

نكوروك سالاك تعالي

ميبو حمده جبرايل قول

دمكيل كطلبين قوم نفسي

كل جبرايل ايخلاون ردكن

جاوب ول دكي داتع سلطين

ستمن داتع نبيط كل جلال

ايتله كاوي داتع زبنالو

مقابلون انكو تهدو دكستو

بكر نفعت ممعر مر مسر

واهي

سغاب جعاتي مند دكاي كذو جاوبن

الحمد لله والصلاة النبي

سمحي نفصو دشجهبينا

سلطان علاوي رد ترسبا

كاوي ابونكي برسام

انق دتاورو والم ابونن

امسو لن ميروق كاوي بهلي

اول واهي ايبو بغا امون زوان

ميبال شكر كدن وفي

كرن منداقه ابني بكلا

دكي تقدرن ادسط

طرع طالين هندي زجمايه

سمون ان اتو هو ح بلاه

برن جكيل اككي ان نورن

ستهن رجالي برنامو اون

مغو مخزو انكوشهيلو وزهو

كرم جاحة ايبو بغا امو

جاوب مربك السي اول لهمو

ولهي ياتقلكو فيكبر اولهمو

ايبو بغا امو واربس وزكي

برساء كبس وماكي

ادون انق ماكي كنياث

هندله سبب ماكي عرث

تمجعه ذاهن كجي كران

ايله هند سبح عون زوان

كتيد ايبر محاكي نبري

دمكينله انق كاوي دنكي

جاريله كويت جاعنله نكي

بكسر برهيان مات

حكل علمونا ادله ليت

ومكينله انق لغاب علمو

دكي سبب مكين ايت

جكا تيدق دمكين نرب

يايكد ول جاحت سام دهاني

جلا لا ول مرام و روماكي

بر جاني ايبو وبنا ام سمعو

انق دابو كاوي يابيك

هاف ول دستام كلنلك

طاووم وهي ايبو يقاث

تمجع ذاهن كلن بلاهي

علم انق همو واتسا ون

لغد ايبو بغا امو قدون

غوله ايبو بغا جركلي يسلاغي

انو س وعجب كي لا ون

ايبو بغا سومنتا زميلكي

مليهر الي انق رقملا جرن

احري عالمو اوكام كليت

سركتن عالي مزرن بيتا

يايكد ول جاحة يات كبنو

جاديله يايك سامع لالو

Syamatara

This seated image of one of the most important deities in Mahayana and Vajrayana Buddhism, Syamatara, is represented in *lalitasana* (relaxed posture). She holds a lotus stalk in her left hand while her right is in *varada mudra* (boon-bestowing gesture). Her right foot is placed on a smaller lotus flower, using it like a footrest. The throne has a high backrest with sashes fluttering from the sides and foliage curling around the halo which is large and encircled by twisted strands of pearls. Syamatara wears elaborate jewels over a diaphanous dhoti and an upper garment that partially covers her full breasts. A long pearl strand hangs like a *yagnopavita* (sacred thread), and there are armlets, bangles, anklets, waistband and disc earrings. Her hair is tied up in a high bun secured by a crown with a conical pinnacle. Her face has an inward look with a slight smile on her parted lips, suggesting a Tantric meditative mood.

'Tara' refers to 'one who saves'. Syamatara enjoys a very important place in the Mahayana and Vajrayana schools as the mother of all the buddhas. She is also the feminine concept of Avalokiteshvara (▶ see GUANYIN). Like him, she delivers her devotees from suffering and maintains a benign nature throughout. Primacy of her position can be observed when she is placed right next to Akshobhya Buddha (▶ see AKSHOBHYA) in the Vajradhatu mandala.[21]

The earliest representations of the goddess can be seen in the transition from Mahayana to Vajrayana, and at Ellora, Nasik, Kanheri, Ajanta, Aurangabad and other west Indian Buddhist caves. During the Pala period the concept of Syamatara developed along with that of Prajnaparamita and spread to the Sino-Tibetan areas. Chinese Buddhism is especially influenced by the concepts of Syamatara and Avalokiteshvara, which are manifested in the deity Guanyin. [GPK]

SYAMATARA
Bihar, east India
10th–11th centuries
Schist
h. 49.9 cm
1997.4831

Talismanic Jama
(Talismanic Shirt)

This short-sleeved cotton *jama* is made up of one big rectangular piece with a central opening at the front and two smaller pieces stitched on as sleeves. What is amazing is that time and effort has been put into inscribing the entire Qur'an in black *naskh* script on the *jama*. Qur'anic verses fill up the rectangular compartments ruled in blue and orange as well as the compartments with triangular points found on the lower borders of the *jama*. The *Asma al-Husna* (Beautiful Names of God) are written in gold within the white borders with red speckled ground. The front of this *jama* features two large roundels painted in orange and blue which contain the *shahadah* (profession of faith in Islam). The back of the *jama* (not shown) contains a large central cartouche containing part of verse 64 of *Surah Yusuf* (Joseph), which reads, 'But Allah is the best to take care [of him], And He is the Most Merciful of those who show mercy!' This *jama* is typical of the talismanic *jama* made in Mughal India during the 16th and 17th centuries. The colours and motifs used on these *jama* are reminiscent of the illuminations found on 15th-century Qur'ans from India which were written in *bihari* script.

Talismanic *jama* can also be found in Turkey and Iran. Given the sacred nature of the Qur'an, these *jama* were probably made for protective purposes. Some *jama* feature certain Qur'anic verses which suggest that the *jama* were used to ensure military success or against battle injuries. It is interesting to note that the same verse from *Surah Yusuf* is found depicted on a sword hilt (▶ see MUGHAL SWORD HILT). It is not certain whether these *jama* were meant to be worn as some have been found folded up as one would a talismanic chart, perhaps to be carried about on one's person. [TH]

▶ see QUR'AN IN NASKH

TALISMANIC *JAMA*
India
17th century
Ink and colours on cotton
66 x 96 cm
On loan from the Tareq Rajab Museum, Kuwait
TR178

Tang Sancai Tomb Guardians

The Tang *sancai* (three-coloured palette) used on these tomb guardian figures comprises cream-white, green and amber. Each tomb guardian was made in several press-moulded parts and joined together. The figures are hollow and have holes on the sides of their bases to prevent the figures from warping during firing. They were first slipped with white clay and biscuit-fired to about 1,000 degrees Celsius. Before glazing, a wax medium was probably used on their faces and hands to prevent the glazes from adhering. This was then followed by glazing and low firing at a temperature of 700 to 800 degrees Celsius in an oxidising atmosphere, resulting in the melting and fusing of these tri-coloured glazes.

This retinue of tomb guardians consists of a pair of earth spirits, a pair of Buddhist *lokapala* (heavenly guardians) and a pair of civil officials. Mostly found in the tombs of nobility, their presence in tombs signified the high social status of the deceased. The earth spirits (BELOW), as the Chinese name '*zhenmushou*' (literally 'beasts that guard the tomb') suggests, are beasts that protect the tomb. Placed in niches—one on the east and the other on the west—along the corridor, either midway or near the main chamber of the tomb, these winged beasts help to frighten evil spirits away. One earth spirit has a semi-human face with the body of an animal, wings and hooves. The other more ferocious-looking spirit has an animal face with sprouting horns, wings and hooves. It bares its teeth in fury to warn evil spirits from going near the deceased. The *sancai* glazes were deliberately applied to create decorative effects, particularly on their chests, where they give a streaked appearance. It is possible that resists, such as powdered kaolin resist, were applied on certain parts of their bodies to achieve a different look. The glazes and resists were therefore used to decorate different parts of each figurine in different ways.

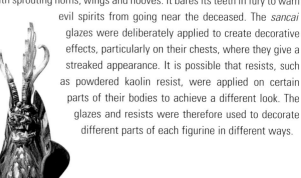

A PAIR OF EARTH SPIRITS
China
Tang Dynasty
Ceramic
(LEFT) h. 76 cm, diam. 20 cm;
(RIGHT) h. 80 cm, diam. 20 cm
Purchased with funds from The Shaw Foundation
1995.957.2, 1995.957.1

The Buddhist *lokapala* (RIGHT), also known as *tianwang* (heavenly kings), help to avert evil. Clad in armour, each *lokapala* stands on one foot while the other tramples on a reclining animal. They would each have held wooden weapons in their hands, but these have decayed over the centuries. Without the weapons, these guardians still instil fear through their posture and the intense look in their eyes. These were also placed in the east and west niches along the corridor with the earth spirits. The large number of *lokapala* uncovered in tombs dated to Xuanzong's reign (713–756) attests to the popularity of these guardians during that period.

The least fearsome of these guardians are the civil officials (BELOW). Dressed in long robes with long flowing sleeves, these stand upright with their hands clasped together, looking solemn. Their hands once held wooden tablets but these are now missing. Placed on each side of the tomb chamber entrance, these figures also serve an apotropaic function.

These tomb guardians were most popular between the 7th and 8th centuries, evident from those uncovered in tombs of nobility or other men of status in Shaanxi province—the seat of Tang power. [WHL]

(TOP) **A PAIR OF BUDDHIST *LOKAPALA***
China
Tang Dynasty
Ceramic
(LEFT) h. 84.5 cm, diam. 14 cm;
(RIGHT) h. 80 cm, diam. 17 cm
Purchased with funds from The Shaw Foundation
1995.294.1, 1995.294.2

(LEFT) **A PAIR OF CIVIL OFFICIALS**
China
Tang Dynasty
Ceramic
(FAR LEFT) h. 76 cm, diam. 13.5 cm;
(LEFT) h. 76 cm, diam. 14 cm
Purchased with funds from The Shaw Foundation
1995.958.1, 1995.958.2

Tangka
(Tibetan Scroll Banner)

Even in its current fragmentary state, this *tangka* features two *lokapala* (heavenly guardians), three Cosmic Buddhas and six *arhat* or *luohan*, great adepts who have achieved enlightenment and are assured of nirvana, freed from the cycle of suffering and rebirths. This iconography of the 18 *arhat* is based on the famous Tibetan Narthang woodblock prints. The *arhat* are arranged along two main tiers, each ending with a *lokapala*, while the Cosmic Buddhas are inserted in a slightly higher half-tier between the *arhat*. All except the Buddhas sit orienting towards their left in veneration of a centrally located icon, which is missing from this portion. The three Cosmic Buddhas are in *padmasana* (lotus posture) and may be identified by their respective *mudra*—Amitabha in *dhyani mudra* (meditation gesture); Akshobhya in *bhumisparsha mudra* (earth-witnessing gesture); and Amoghasiddhi in *abhaya mudra* (gesture of fearlessness). The six *arhat* seen here are Bhadra, Hvashang, Ajita, Kanakabharadvaja, Nagasena and Kalika; the two *lokapala* are Virukpasha (Guardian of the West) and the sword-wielding Virudhaka (Guardian of the South), who is deep blue in colour.

TANGKA WITH SILK APPLIQUÉ *ARHAT*, BUDDHAS AND *LOKAPALA*
China
Qing dynasty, Qianlong period, 18th century;
(SILK FRAGMENTS) Qing dynasty, Wanli period, early 17th century
Silk
265 x 512 cm
1996.2628

All the images are appliquéd with fragments of imperial silks from the Wanli period of the Ming dynasty. The outline and detailed drapery of the heavily embellished and brocaded figures are delineated using piping of a monochrome silk. Along the lower register of the *tangka* is a railing with panels of Indian lotuses (*fanlian*) in rich brocade and embroidered inscriptions which translate roughly thus: 'I prostrate to all the Buddhas of Ten Directions and to Shakyamuni, the supreme owner of Ten powers, blazing with major and minor marks as the crown of Gods and of the entire world; and to the sixteen Arhat, who maintain the teachings of the Buddha until end of Samsara ...'.

Silks woven as imperial commissions were often given away by the Chinese emperors as presents or favours. Like most other foreign dignitaries who visited the imperial court, the Tibetan monks received luxuriously woven brocades, sometimes with special Buddhist symbols, in return for the ritual services they performed for members of the imperial family. Although the textiles on this *tangka* can be dated to the Wanli period, the iconography suggests that the *tangka* was made only after the second half of the 17th century. [LCL]

Tholubomalattam
(Shadow Puppetry)

This is a leather shadow puppet of Hanuman (Veera Anjaneya in southern tradition), the ape hero from the *Ramayana* who is depicted with the *namam* (Vaishnava forehead mark). He has a dark brown and red complexion and a warrior's physique, and wears elaborate jewels, garlands and headgear. The puppet has detachable arms, legs and a tail, and is perforated with a floral motif all over which, when seen against light, lends an exquisitely beautiful appearance to it. Hanuman is usually painted green in south India, white in Indonesia and green in Thailand. He is a highly revered celibate deity in India while in Thailand he is a womaniser who has numerous love affairs with women of the earth, the heaven and the seas.

Shadow puppetry is an art form that is as old as civilisation itself and encompasses both visual and performing arts. Both *patachitra* (religious scroll painting) and *chadma nataka* (shadow puppetry) are accompanied by songs, dialogue and music that enliven mythological tales, creating an experience of emotional exaltation. The famous Indian epics, the *Mahabharata* and the *Ramayana*, were both illustrated through this art form. In shadow puppetry, the characters are classified and codified by colour and iconography into good and evil, a distinction that is rarely lost—the puppets are almost never combined even when they are packed and stored. Once they are painted and have eyes etched onto them, the puppets are treated with reverence. This is especially so for the divine characters, who are believed to possess a spirit potent enough to be propitiated.

Specialists of shadow puppetry performances are from the Killyekatha tribe and the origin of the art form can be traced to Maharashtra. There are six main centres where this art form was practiced and they are known by slightly different names: Pinguli (Maharashtra), Togalu Gombe Atta (Karnataka); Tholu Pava Koothu (Kerala); Ravana Chhaya (Orissa) and Tholu Bomalatta (Tamil Nadu and Andhra Pradesh). The puppeteers are called *sutradhara* and until recently, were invited to perform from village to village during Shivaratri (the spring festival of Shiva) or for celebrations and thanksgiving for a good harvest or birth of a child.

It is said that a family of the Killyekatha tribe migrated to different parts of south India and brought with it the art of shadow puppetry. The art form took root in different states although its form and images were slightly altered. Many kings were patrons, most notably the rulers of Vijayavada and Vijayanagar. King Kona Budha Reddy, ruler of Vijayavada, had the *Ranganatha Ramayana* written exclusively for shadow play during his reign. The appearance of each character and the scenery was described in poetic and literal form. The puppets used were also very large, comparable only to the Thai Nag Yai puppets which are even larger.[1] Depending on which region they are from, shadow puppets differ in the way they are carved—the main differences are noted in single characters that have one or more moveable limbs and scene-based puppets that have no movable parts. Some of the most

THOLUBOMALATTAM
Andhra Pradesh or Karnataka, south India
19th century
Goat or deer skin
(ARM TO ARM) 110.5 x 137 cm
1996.486

fascinating puppets are those which have a movable waist, shoulder and feet, for example the puppet of the dancing girl, which requires two players to manoeuvre.

Shadow puppets are made from goat or buffalo hide, and the divine characters are sometimes made from deer hide. The hide is removed, washed and scraped to remove the hair, and soaked in a solution of salt, alum and water. It is then washed again, beaten and scraped, and stretched on a wooden plank to dry. When dry, its surface is smoothened out before the drawing is etched onto it. The design is traced from old puppets. The puppet is painted with earth and vegetable colours (today synthetic dyes are used) and punched with patterned holes. Finally the eyes are drawn and the puppet is infused with life. Rama and Krishna are painted indigo blue (the colour of Vishnu), female characters are painted yellow, red or brown, while Ravana and Duryodhana are painted red.[2] [GPK]

▶ see PANAKAWAN
▶ see WAYANG KULIT

Thousand Buddha Robe

The centrefield of this rare rectangular garment is made of 49 alternating yellow and green stripes embroidered with images of Buddha seated on a lotus plinth. Each corner of the centrefield is filled with a *lokapala*, the heavenly guardian of the four cardinal directions. On the green stripes the Buddha images are embroidered directly onto the damask silk, but on the yellow stripes the Buddha images are embroidered separately on a reddish fabric. Surrounding this centrefield is a large black border also filled with similar Buddha images. Altogether the 820 Buddhas were meant to represent the eternity of Buddha who, when required, would appear in multiplicity so that humans could visualise the true essence of universal salvation. The composition of the Thousand Buddhas, represented on murals and paintings, is an important theme in Buddhist art.

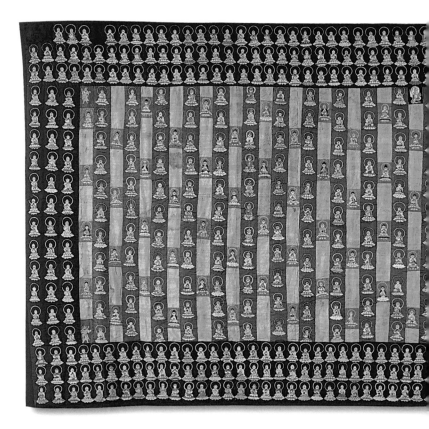

THOUSAND BUDDHA ROBE IN NEEDLELOOP EMBROIDERY
China
Ming dynasty, 15th century
Silk
116.5 x 271.5 cm
On loan from the Collection of Jobrenco Trust
CH103 (S2)

Although this textile is dated to the 15th century, needleloop embroidery (*wangxiu*), used primarily to adorn scriptures or to produce images of Buddhist iconography, already existed in the Yuan dynasty. This technique requires the embroiderer to execute the net-like needlework in such a way that it is detached from, and afloat on, the base fabric.

As the monk's robe is a powerful symbol of the denunciation of the material world, it is made with fabrics of non-primary colours. In fact, most traditional monk's robes in China were made in patchwork style. Although this textile is constructed with fabric fragments, as are most monks' robes, given the rich iconographic presence, it is highly probable that it was used to adorn a Buddhist image. The standing image of Vairochana Buddha at the 5th-century Yungang cave, for instance, is depicted wearing such a cape (or *kashaya*) of the Thousand Buddhas. [LCL]

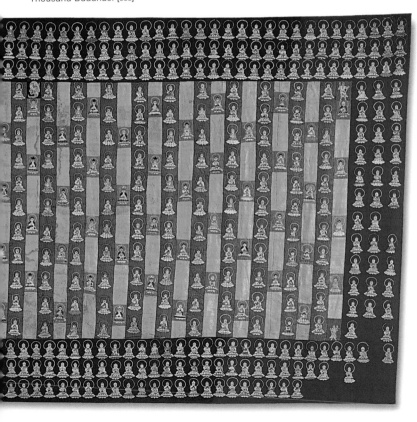

Tibetan Book Covers

This pair of book covers is decorated on both sides. Book covers are used as a firm support for paper or palm leaf manuscripts of several pages that are read by turning the pages horizontally. They were tied together by a cotton cord to keep the pages and the covers intact when stored away. While reading the manuscript, the cord is loosened, the upper cover removed and the read pages placed on its reverse face.

The outer sides are carved and gilded with decorative scrolling patterns. The central motif on the upper cover (BELOW, TOP) is a *kala* head with foliage oozing from its mouth. The lower cover (BELOW, BOTTOM) bears a *purnakalasha*, a pot brimming with foliage, an

TIBETAN BOOK COVERS
Tibet
12th–13th centuries
Painted and gilded wood
10.7 x 61 cm
1997.780

auspicious motif representing abundance. Such imagery has a very long lineage and can be traced back to the Buddhist art of the early centuries BCE. Dwarves and *yaksha* (male vegetation spirits) were depicted with lush and scrolling vegetation spilling from their mouths in architecture of the Sunga and Kushana periods. Even these images stemmed from a yet earlier phase of folk religion which worshipped nature. The survival of these elements after 15 centuries is an amazing phenomenon.

The pictorial representations on the inside of the covers have stronger references to Vajrayana Buddhism—delicately painted images of buddhas and bodhisattvas. Many of

them have faded from the constant rubbing against the pages of the manuscript. Five Vajrayana deities are represented on the inner side of the upper cover (BELOW, TOP), namely Dharmapala Mahakala, the three *tathagata* Buddhas and Sadakshari Lokeshvara. Generally these deities are found in a Vajradhatu mandala, which is a circular rather than linear concept, but here they are placed horizontally, one next to the other. On the inner side of the lower cover (BELOW, BOTTOM) five Buddhas or monks face the seated figure of four-armed Vajrasattva in the centre. [GPK]

Tile Panel Containing the Shahadah

This eight-piece tile panel is decorated in blue, white and turquoise, the typical colour scheme found on tile-work in the Multan area in central Pakistan. The use of these colours was influenced by Persian tiles, which is not surprising given the trading links between the two regions. The inscription and floral motifs on these tiles were painted onto the red earthenware body[3] before being covered with a transparent glaze. This style of decorating ceramics is known as underglaze painting. The technique of painting blue and black designs before glazing was probably first developed in Iran in the 12th century and used for ceramic vessels. The method spread to other parts of the Islamic world and continues to be used today.

This tile panel contains an inscription on a fundamental belief in Islam—the unity of God and the prophethood of Muhammad.

> I bear witness that there is only one God, Allah, with no Associates
> And I bear witness that Muhammad is his Helper and Messenger.

The above statement is a variation of the *shahadah* (profession of faith in Islam). In the Multan area some funerary monuments, such as the shrine of Sufi saint Muhammad Yusuf

TILE PANEL CONTAINING THE *SHAHADAH*
Multan, central Pakistan
18th century
Earthenware
53.5 x 120 cm
1998.1077

Gardezi, have the *shahadah* on their exterior walls. This suggests that these tiles probably came from a funerary monument or a religious institution. The *shahadah* is, understandably, a popular phrase for funerary monuments as it is a testimony of one's faith in the face of death.

While scholars are most fascinated by tiles with inscriptions, such tiles form only a small proportion of the tiles produced by Islamic artisans. The majority of tiles would have been decorated with floral or geometric motifs or glazed in one colour.

The use of glazed tiles to decorate the walls of both secular and religious buildings, either by introducing spots of colour on brick walls or by covering entire walls, has a long tradition in the Islamic world. When used externally, glazed tiles also provided the building with protection against the weather. The use of shimmering tiles to cover entire buildings, while not found on all Islamic monuments, was nevertheless extensively done and is one of the characteristics that people identify with Islamic architecture. [TH]

▶ see LAJVARDINA TILE
▶ see OTTOMAN STELE
▷ see PANEL CARVED WITH THE SHAHADAH
▶ see TIMURID KUFIC-ABBASID TILE

Timurid Kufic-Abbasid Tile

The white, stylised Kufic-Abbasid inscription on this tile resembles a white swan swimming in cobalt blue water. The inscription reads *'al-mulk'*, and is probably part of a common phrase found on architecture, *'al-mulk lillah'*, which means 'Sovereignty [of the visible world] belongs to God'.

The Kufic-Abbasid script was used to copy early Qur'ans, as well as for inscriptions on early Islamic objects and architecture. From the 9th century onwards, artists and calligraphers began developing the script so that the verticals and downward strokes of some letters were plaited, stretched to form leaves or flowers, or even adorned with human and animal heads.[4] On this tile, the Arabic letter *'lam'* has been drawn in such a way that it resembles a swan's neck.

This tile has been decorated with the *cuerda seca* technique, which developed in the latter half of the 14th century in Iran. This technique, which means 'dry cord' in Spanish, involves the painting of different colours which are separated by a substance containing manganese. The substance prevents the colours from running into each other and after firing, it leaves a black outline that looks like a cord. This was one of several decorative techniques employed by Islamic tile-makers.

The use of glazed tiles to decorate entire walls of buildings became very popular from the 14th century in Iran. *Cuerda seca* tiles, together with tile mosaics, were extensively used for cladding the surfaces of buildings during the Timurid period. This particular tile would most likely have come from a funerary monument or a religious building. [TH]

▶ see KUFIC-ABBASID QUR'AN FOLIO
▶ see TILE PANEL CONTAINING THE SHAHADAH

TIMURID KUFIC-ABBASID TILE
Iran
c. 1450
Glaze and gold on stone-paste
15.2 x 14.5 cm
1999.2695

Topeng
(Mask)

These masks represent a fraction of the many characters that appear in the *topeng* dance tradition. The white mask (BELOW, TOP) represents Prince Panji, whose character represents the ideal of the *halus* (refined) hero. It has an Arabic inscription on the interior and a leather strap, which would have been gripped in the mouth of the dancer in order to secure the mask during the dance. It is said that the strap was the means by which the spirit of the character could enter the body of the dancer. The red mask (BELOW, BOTTOM) with eyes wide open, a long nose and real hair for a moustache represents the proud King Klana, thought to have been a foreign king who posed a threat to the 12th century capital of Kediri in East Java.

Wayang topeng (masked dance) is one of the oldest of the Indonesian performing arts, dating back to the early 16th century.[5] Masks were used especially for ritual purposes, funerals, initiation and healing ceremonies, which are still undertaken today. It is believed that the masks enable the wearer to communicate with the spirits and to personify the ancestors and deities. *Topeng* dance origins are believed to have been introduced by one of the nine *wali sanga* (Islamic saints) during the 16th century, along the north coast of Java, where *wayang topeng* retains a strong presence.[6] It was later refined as a court art accompanied by music and narration similar to the court masked dance of Cambodia and Thailand (▶ see LAKHAOUN KHAOL MASKS). *Topeng* dancers included members of the royalty, many of whom also carved their own masks, such as Sultan Pakubuwono IX's son who danced during the late 19th century. The *gedhog* stories of east Java form the core of the *topeng* repertoire, in which Prince Panji features prominently. He is the counterpart of Arjuna, the princely hero figure in the Hindu epic the *Mahabharata*.[7] [HT]

TOPENG
(TOP) Panji
(ABOVE) Klana
Java, Indonesia
Early 20th century
Wood
14–20 x 14–16.5 cm
W643, W422

Tripod Vessel

This tripod vessel depicts stylised deer, birds and abstract motifs that are common on many Dong Son drums. However this vessel shape is seldom seen in the Dong Son bronzes that have been excavated. The tripod shape hints at a distinct Chinese influence in later Dong Son bronzes, which is supported by the fact that north Vietnam was under Chinese Han rule from the 1st century. This piece was cast by the *cire perdue* (lost-wax) method and was possibly commissioned for the burial of a Chinese official although it was made by northern Vietnam Dong Son craftsmen.

There is a definite link between the Dong Son bronzes of mainland Southeast Asia and the early Chinese bronzes of the same period, but it is unclear whether the Dong Son bronzes were introduced from China or were invented independently in the region. The excavated evidence, however, points towards the evolution of a distinct style in north Vietnam that characterised the Dong Son bronzes and their subsequent spread to island Southeast Asia. [RE]

▶ see DRINKING VESSELS
▶ see DONG SON DRUM

TRIPOD VESSEL
North Vietnam
100
Bronze
h. 43 cm, diam. 40 cm
Purchased with funds from
The Shaw Foundation
1999.51

(TOP) **DETAIL**
Anthropomorphic figure with large eyes

(338)

Tung Thieu
(Temple Banner)

This long banner has horizontal bands of motifs woven along the weft axis in green, white, yellow and indigo blue silk on a red cotton ground. The design comprises many stylised elements including zoomorphic motifs such as elephants, buffaloes and horses as well as mythical lions and tigers. The conical motif in the upper register is probably Mount Meru, the cosmological centre of the Buddhist world. Below that appears to be a scene of a temple or celestial palace, with figures, tree motifs and guardian figures at the gates. The lower registers include the names of the donors who funded the making of this banner for a temple by the name of Ban Nong. Above this is a row of repeated motifs of the earth goddess Nang Thoranee wringing out her hair.

Woven banners were donated to temples for use during festivals associated with the agricultural cycle, such as Bun Phraawes. This is the major harvest festival, celebrated by villages in February, to give thanks for a fruitful harvest and to pray for renewed rains and crops.

The name Bun Phraawes refers to Phraa Wes or Prince Vessantara. The Vessantara Jataka (▶ see JATAKA STORIES) is the story of the Buddha during his last birth as Prince Vessantara, whose examples of great generosity are recited as a form of merit-making during the festival. Among the possessions given away by the Prince were his white elephant—which had the power to bring rain—several hundred servants, elephants, horses, buffaloes and chariots. The appearance of the earth goddess symbolises the Buddha's victory over the evil forces imposed by Mara which are washed away by the waters produced as she wrings her hair. Although the motifs on the banner are largely Buddhist, the interweaving of indigenous spirit worship and Buddhist religious ideals in festivals underscore the importance of syncretic belief systems in village life. [HT]

TUNG THIEU
Yasothorn Province, northeast Thailand
c. 1930s
Silk and cotton
384 x 54 cm
1997.2579

Vaishravana

This is a representation of Kubera, the Hindu God of Wealth, as Lokapala Vaishravana, seated on a lion *vahana* (mount). He holds a *nakula* (mongoose) in his left hand and his right hand may have held a spear which is now missing. He wears a breastplate, windswept sash, five-leaf crown, and has a short curly beard, bulging eyes and slanted fiery eyebrows. The lion *vahana* is rather toy-like with a stiff body, a skimpy mane and stunted legs. The bronze is quite large and impressive with gilding, colouration and intricate moulding which is well preserved.

Vaishravana, which means 'offspring of the famous', is a protective divinity who was supposedly appointed as guardian of Khotan by Shakyamuni himself (▶ see STELE DEPICTING SHAKYAMUNI AND PRABHUTARATNA). In origin, he seems to be a *yaksha* (male vegetation spirit) and is identified with Kubera. In Hindu tradition Kubera is the son of a sage, Vishravas. According to Hsuan-tsang—a Chinese Buddhist monk who in the 8th century wrote extensively on his travels through India—Kubera appears as an *arhat* (great adept) capable of miraculous powers. In Tibetan accounts he is recognised as an apparition of Manjushri (Bodhisattva of Wisdom). Vaishravana is a *lokapala* (heavenly guardian) in Tibetan and Chinese traditions where he is known as a protector against invaders.[1] [GPK]

VAISHRAVANA
Tibet
18th century
Gilt bronze and copper repoussé
h. 44.4 cm
1997.4798

Vatapatrashayi

(Krishna Lying on a Banyan Leaf)

Krishna is one of the incarnations of Vishnu. In this piece, Krishna is depicted as a baby sucking his toe, and lying on a banyan leaf—the latter an important detail that is missing in this piece but nevertheless implied by his reclining position. An unusual detail here is the presence of Brahma on the lotus stalk emerging from Vishnu's navel—Brahma is regarded as a God of Creation and was himself created from Vishnu's navel (▶ see BRAHMA). The infant Krishna is represented here naked save for a pair of *makara kundala* (*makara*-shaped earrings), rings, bangles, armlets, waistband, anklets, toe-rings and necklaces; his hair is curled up and meticulous.

This is the story behind this depiction of Krishna:[2] Markandeya, a sage and devotee of Vishnu, was doing penance by a river when the wind began to blow. It gradually became a whirlwind accompanied by thunder and heavy rains. Soon the rivers swelled and there was no place to stand. Markandeya was surrounded by the rising waters when he saw a banyan tree and an infant floating on one of its leaves. When the infant drew near, Markandeya looked at it and was swept off by its inhalation, thus entering the infant. Once inside, Markandeya saw the whole universe, the *deva* (gods) and the *danava* (demons), nature, *yuga* (an age of the world) and *manvantara* (an immense span of time) pass by. This was the vision of *brahmanda*, the cosmos within the being of the infant, who was no ordinary child. Markandeya emerged from the infant when it exhaled and before he realised it, the infant had disappeared. This vision is also known as the vision of Maha Vishnu, the great Hindu God of Creation, as infant Krishna. One can hardly imagine the depth of meaning this cherubic form of Krishna is encapsulating within. [GPK]

▶ see STANDING VISHNU AS
TRIVIKRAMA

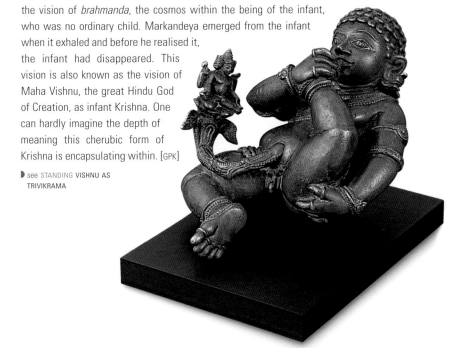

VATAPATRASHAYI
South India
Vijayanagara style (15th–16th centuries)
Bronze
14 x 10 cm
1994.5383

Venugopala
(Krishna Playing the Flute)

In this painting, Krishna, in a characteristic Venugopala pose, is seen flanked by two *gopi* (cowherdesses) and cows. He is standing under a tree that is entwined by a five-hooded *naga* (mythical serpent), which symbolises his brother, Balarama. The whole painting is bound by a multi-arched canopy gilded with semi-precious stones in the typical style of the Tanjore school of painting.

In keeping with the contemporary style of costume and jewellery, the *gopi* are dressed like Tamil women, with saris, jewellery and even hairdo that are unique to 19th-century fashion. The appearance of a violin and a *tanpura* suggests the popularity of these musical instruments and the veneration of the deity through music and dance. The representation of the cows—especially the one behind Krishna—in high relief using silver gesso is remarkable. Gesso is a gilding technique that varies from guild to guild; the guild in Tanjore uses high relief and gold-coated silver leaf.[3] Tanjore paintings are prepared on wood and cloth surfaces which are coated with raw lime powder and a paste made of the powdered seeds of tamarind. Gold and silver are applied after the paste dries.

The iconographic similarity of Krishna in this painting and Tamil Krishnalila Kalamkari is remarkable (▶ see KRISHNALILA). The *kudumi* with a *sarpech*-like ornament, *bulak* (nose ring) as well as ear ornaments look quite similar. The tying of the dhoti, sash and the flower garland that hangs from either shoulder is also remarkably similar, as are the folds of flesh around the neck, cheeks and the waist—which lend a cherubic demeanour to the adorable figure of Krishna—and the cow licking Krishna's feet while he stands in *swastika pada*.

Tanjore paintings were generally used as votive pictures. They were used for worship in homes, for personal shrines as well as for dedication in temples. Their iconography is standard and rather formal; and devotees or patrons are often depicted within the frame. There is an influence of European realism in the depiction of roundness in human figures, perspective for the depth of the room in which a scene is happening, and elements of architecture. The paintings display an eclectic flavour typical of the 19th century. [GPK]

VENUGOPALA
Tamil Nadu, south India
Early 19th century
Painting on wood with semi-precious stones
(INCLUDING FRAME) 118 x 93 x 5.5 cm
1995.892

Vietnamese Blue and White Ware

The tall-necked ewer (BELOW) with an elegant spout and strap handle is a good example of wares that were decorated with a combination of glazed and unglazed designs. The openwork lobed panel at each side is unglazed and has the motif of a parrot among foliage. The underglaze blue motifs of leaves around the neck and lotus petal panels around the lower register are reminiscent of Chinese Yuan blue and white motifs which were also arranged in bands.

Blue and white ceramic production in Vietnam is usually thought to have originated in China. However, exactly when and how Chinese techniques were introduced remain unclear. One theory is that Chinese potters migrated to Vietnam during the early 14th century.[4] Local legends support this view and one pottery in Ha Bac province still honours a Chinese potter as a local deity.[5] However the Chinese porcelain centre of Jingdezhen was highly productive at this time and it is unlikely that potters would have wanted to emigrate. It is more probable that blue and white grew out of the existing monochrome white or white and brown traditions, perhaps by borrowing techniques, materials and inspiration from kilns nearer to home, for example in the southern Chinese province of Guangdong.[6]

Local materials and potting styles are unique to the Vietnamese ceramic tradition. The area of North Vietnam from the Red River delta to Hoanh Son produced some of Southeast Asia's most sophisticated ceramics. Although technically not 'porcelain', which is translucent and pure white, these grey-white stonewares are quite different in appearance and feel from Chinese and other mainland Southeast Asian ceramic wares. In addition, close proximity to China enabled the importation of supplies of cobalt oxide. The availability of these raw materials meant that Vietnamese potters became the only Southeast Asian ceramic producers to make blue and white ware.

The large and heavily potted dish (OPPOSITE, TOP) has a foliate rim, pale underglazed blue decoration arranged in bands around the rim and sides which enclose a central landscape scene, and a wash of chocolate slip on the base. The landscape with rocky outcrops and gnarled trees, executed in a painterly style with generous allowance of space, is a unique 15th-century design with no known Chinese prototype.[7] The poetic use of space and motifs (possibly pine trees) has been remarked on as a quintessentially Chinese convention, which was reinterpreted and employed in the spirit of Vietnamese nationalism.[8]

The origin of the cobalt blue used on this large dish is not easy to ascertain. Imported Middle Eastern cobalt produced various shades from dark to brilliant blue, while unrefined cobalt from Yunnan tended to produce brownish tones due to the high iron-oxide content. The significance of the wash of chocolate-brown slip on the base also requires further research. It is thought that it could be an attempt to emulate the orange-red finish of the bases of Chinese Yuan blue and white ware.[9]

The Hoi An cargo recently recovered off the coast of Central Vietnam comprised an estimated 250,000 pieces. It revealed that high-quality wares, including dishes with a wide range of designs, formed an important part of the growing intra-regional trade of the late 15th century. Large dishes would have been used in Islamic communities for the custom of serving food communally and the quality of the decoration suggests that by this time, Vietnamese potters were catering for a sophisticated clientele.

Vietnam entered the international ceramics trade during the 14th century and produced the greatest volume and variety of wares for Southeast Asia, particularly Indonesia, the Philippines and Malaysia.[10] Sites in Java and Sulawesi have yielded the largest quantities of Vietnamese ware in Indonesia. These shards of architectural tiles (BELOW) were reportedly found at the Majapahit capital of Trowulan. They represent specially commissioned products made to suit the needs of Islamic communities in Javanese towns. Complete tiles can still be found at the mosques of Demak and Kudus where they embellish minarets, walls and gateways.

These examples illustrate some of the various forms that were made, including a stepped-square form, quatrefoil and cartouche. The motifs painted in underglazed blue include mythical beasts such as the *qilin*, cranes, and floral, vegetal and geometric patterns. Enamels and white and brown decoration can also be found on these wares. [HT]

(OPPOSITE) **BLUE AND WHITE EWER**
Vietnam
16th century
Stoneware
h. 23.5 cm, diam. 13.5 cm
1997.2257

(TOP) **DISH WITH UNDERGLAZED BLUE LANDSCAPE DESIGN**
North Vietnam
15th–16th centuries
Stoneware
diam. 33 cm
1996.171

(LEFT) **SHARDS OF ARCHITECTURAL TILES**
Vietnam
15th–16th centuries
Stoneware
l. 9–20 cm, w. 8–12 cm
(99.525) Gift of Loh Teh Soon
1998.90, 1998.82, 1998.80, 1998.75, 99.525

Vietnamese Green-glazed Wares

This dish (BELOW, LEFT), jarlet (BELOW, CENTRE) and cup (BELOW, RIGHT) represent an important style in the repertoire of Vietnamese monochrome-glazed ceramics. The glaze colourant is copper oxide in a lead-based glaze.[11] The variation in tone of these pieces appears to be due to the different thickness of their glazes and different conditions during the firing. The thick dark-green glaze on the dish has run in places, compared to the thinner apple-green glaze on the jarlet which has a beautifully even quality like a fine skin that enhances the lobed form.

Dishes like the one shown here were produced in sizeable quantities, as indicated by the unglazed ring around the centre on which another dish could be stacked and large stacks then fired simultaneously. The base of the dish and lobed jarlet have a wash of rich chocolate-coloured slip, which scholars suggest could have been used as a trademark, or perhaps was a style of finishing that emulated the orange tone found on the base of earlier Chinese porcelains.[12] The ribbed cup is glazed on the exterior as well as the base, and has a contrasting brown wash around the foot rim and white glaze on the interior, perhaps to enhance the colour of the tea or wine.

This celadon jar (OPPOSITE) is a different type of Vietnamese ware. The clay body visible at the unglazed base is of a light

GREEN-GLAZED DISH, JARLET AND CUP
North Vietnam
14th–15th centuries
Stoneware
(DISH) h. 5 cm, diam. 23 cm;
(JARLET) h. 7 cm, diam. 8 cm;
(CUP) h. 5.5 cm, diam. 9.5 cm
(1992.798, 1992.784) Gift of Dr Earl Lu
1992.798, 1996.1760, 1992.784

(OPPOSITE) **CELADON JAR WITH COVER**
North Vietnam
14th century
Stoneware
diam. 15.5 cm
2000.1239

buff colour with very few impurities, which is a sign of good quality.[13] An inscription on the base has three Chinese characters: *tian, chang, kou* (literally 'heaven', 'long', 'mouth'). The squat form with a cover has applied sprig-moulded decoration in the form of floral scrolls and bosses around the outer walls, while the cover has a knop consisting of applied floral motifs with stems. There are several types of beakers and bowls in the Vietnamese repertoire which are decorated with rows of bosses and incised or applied designs. The shape and use of bosses has been compared with the Chinese drum form, on which rows of nails are used to fix a drum-skin.[14]

The thickly applied glaze is very similar to Chinese celadons of the Longquan kilns in Zhejiang province, which are thought to be the prototypes for Vietnamese celadons. Longquan wares were exported to Vietnam during the 13th to 14th centuries and many designs appear to have been adopted by Vietnamese potters.[15] The best Longquan glazes were prized in China by the Song dynasty literati who likened the greenish-blue tone and feel of the glaze to the qualities of jade. Their taste for monochrome wares has also been ascribed to their Neo-Confucianist outlook which valued the understated quality of the naturally coloured glazes and purity of the forms which were used for rituals, as scholars' wares or for refined leisurely pursuits such as tea-drinking. However further research has yet to be done with regards to Vietnamese green-glazed wares, the dating of the wares, the consumers of these wares and the locations of the kilns.[16] [HT]

Vietnamese Whiteware

This parrot-shaped vessel (BELOW) was probably used as an oil lamp. The wood-ash glaze is typically thick and uneven, and fires a natural ivory-white with a fine network of crackles. Iron-brown glaze was used to highlight the bird's beak and eyes, and the base. The superb sculptural qualities of the piece are emphasised by the thinly potted elegant form of the bird, with delicately incised feathers and a deeply carved lotus-petal base. The lotus petal is a Buddhist motif that is another hallmark of many ivory-glazed wares. The motif is also found on vessels such as offering dishes and large covered jars which are thought to have taken their inspiration from Cham gold and silver containers with similar designs.

Although a prototype is difficult to ascertain, the motif of a parrot preening itself appears in other Vietnamese art forms, and metal oil lamps in the shape of a parrot were made in India.[17] It is a good example of ritual and utilitarian whiteware made for use in temples or tombs during the Ly and Tran dynasties. In 1009 the Ly clan came to power in northern Vietnam ending a millennium of Chinese political rule. The flourishing of Vietnamese national identity during this period is recognisable in the development of art styles which moved away from copies of Chinese forms towards adaptations that were more uniquely Vietnamese. The frequent appearance of the lotus motif reflects the rising importance of Buddhism, which was instituted as the state religion in Vietnam during this time.

This conical bowl (OPPOSITE, BELOW) has an inverted rim, a thin finely crackled glaze, a delicately carved flower motif at the centre (SEE DETAIL, OPPOSITE, TOP) and leafy sprays fluidly

OIL LAMP IN THE SHAPE OF A PARROT
Vietnam
11th–12th centuries
Stoneware
11.5 x 18.2 x 8 cm
1996.602

incised around the inner walls. It is difficult to identify the types of plants represented in this piece. There appears to be some similarity to narcissus floral motifs which were used as decoration by Chinese potters.[18] Sketchy stylised floral motifs are incised on the outer wall. Spur marks around the centre suggest that wares were stacked inside each other during firing. The skills required to carve such designs on the interior of these semi-closed forms are remarkable and the results can sometimes appear as if painted in underglaze brown. The conical bowl with inverted rim may have been based on a celadon prototype from the Longquan kilns in China,[19] while the freely incised style of the design was characteristic of earlier Chinese whiteware such as Ding and *qingbai* ware (▶ see DING DISHES, ▶ see QINGBAI PORCELAIN).[20] [HT]

CONICAL BOWL
(TOP) Incised flower motif at the centre of the bowl
Vietnam
13th–14th centuries
Stoneware
h. 9.4 cm, diam. 19.5 cm
Gift of Dr Earl Lu
1998.188

Standing Vishnu as Trivikrama

This formal iconic representation of a four-armed Vishnu from the Surasena[21] area is an excellent example of Pratihara style. It has some unique features, including the depiction of the *gada* (mace) with a foliate end as if combining *padma* (lotus) and *gada* shape in one, and the depiction of Shankha Purusha (conch in human form) and Gada Devi (female representation of a mace) as male and female attendants to the deity. There are also two seated female devotees at the feet of Vishnu while two *maladhara gandharva* (garland-carrying celestial beings) flutter in the air around the large and luminous halo. The lower right hand in *varada mudra* (boon-bestowing gesture) shows the benevolent nature of the deity. The elongated halo, conical cap, delicately rendered chest band and jewels are typical features of Pratihara sculpture. The elongated earlobes with *makara* earrings are also unique to Vishnu. The hourglass-shaped torso, diaphanous drapery and slender fingers gently clutching the weapons suggest the refinements of Pratihara style in the post-Gupta period. A comparison with sculptures from south Uttar Pradesh and west Madhya Pradesh suggests that this sculpture was made in the Uparamala-Surasena region.[22] It was placed either in the sanctum or in one of the cardinal niches of an important Vishnu temple.

Along with Shiva and Brahma, Vishnu is one of the primordial deities of the trinity and is attributed the functions of Creation, Preservation and even Dissolution. Shiva and Vishnu are said to maintain the cosmic balance. Vishnu is a syncretic identity, a coming together of three gods: the man-god Vasudeva-Krishna, the Vedic sun god Surya and the cosmic god Narayana of the Brahmanas. Vishnu was first mentioned in the *Vedas* then continued to evolve over time, rising in importance gradually. He is mentioned as a god who took great strides, and as Trivikrama who took three strides (as represented in this sculpture); the latter developed as a myth from the *Dashavatara* stories, one of his ten incarnations in the Puranic period.[23]

The theologians of the Vaishnava cult found the cult of Vishnu very complex and they divided the cult into philosophical, mythical, spiritual and iconographical categories, for example *para* (the highest) belongs to the philosophical category, *vyuha* (the emanatory) and *vibhava* (the incarnatory) to the mythical, *antaryamin* (the inner controller of all beings) to the spiritual, and *archa* (the image used for worship) to the iconographical categories. Of the *vibhava* category, Krishna and Rama are the most beloved incarnations of Vishnu. [GPK]

▶ see RANGANATHA
▶ see VATAPATRASHAYI
▶ see VENUGOPALA

STANDING VISHNU AS TRIVIKRAMA
Uttar Pradesh, India
9th century
Red-beige sandstone
107 x 55 x 18 cm
1996.98

Votive Paintings of Luohan

These are three of a larger set of 18 portraits of the venerable *luohan* (*arhat* or *arahant* in Sanskrit) painted at the commission of Emperor Qianlong in 1795, the 60th year of his long reign. Emancipated from the cycle of rebirth and hence suffering, the *luohan* are the sages who have realised the Buddhist doctrine (or dharma). A devout Buddhist, Qianlong grew up studying Tibetan Buddhism in the company of the Mongolian incarnate lama Rolpay Dorje, one of the emperor's most trusted friends. This religious devotion found its expression in Qianlong's other passion—art. In fact, he was one of the most significant imperial patrons of the large body of fine paintings which came from the hands of a multi-ethnic group of Chinese, Mongolian, Tibetan and European artists.

Luohan paintings are an important genre of paintings in the tradition of Tibetan—as well as Chinese—Buddhist image-making. These three are accompanied by inscriptions in the four official languages of the Manchu court—Chinese, Manchu, Mongolian and Tibetan. Each describes the commission and the name of the *luohan* in the four languages.

**THREE VOTIVE PAINTINGS OF *LUOHAN*
COMMISSIONED BY EMPEROR QIANLONG**
(RIGHT) Kalika
(OPPOSITE, LEFT) Budai
(OPPOSITE, RIGHT) Nagasena
China
1795
Silk
(WITHOUT FRAME) 122 x 67.5 cm
Purchased with funds from The Shaw Foundation
1997.706, 1997.707, 1997.708

In the portrait of Kalika (OPPOSITE) the *luohan* is placed in the centre, with his left hand holding one gold ring while another pair of earrings features prominently on his ears. The rings are the attributes of this *luohan*, as these were gifts showered on him by the deities when he preached the Buddhist doctrine. A fair-complexioned devotee is seen behind him.

Budai *luohan* or Hvashang (BELOW, LEFT) is depicted here as a dark-faced man seated to the left of the painting and being venerated by gift-bearing children. Two bodhisattvas, Avalokiteshvara and Manjusri, are his guiding spiritual inspirations and are located at the top corners of the painting.

Nagasena *luohan* (BELOW, RIGHT) sits to the right of the portrait, enhanced by the presence of three lotuses in pink (which is reserved for the highest deities), blue (the symbol of wisdom) and white (the symbol of mental purity and spiritual perfection). The attributes in Nagasena's hands were gifts from the Guardian Kings and the Dragon King who were moved by his teaching of the doctrine. [LCL]

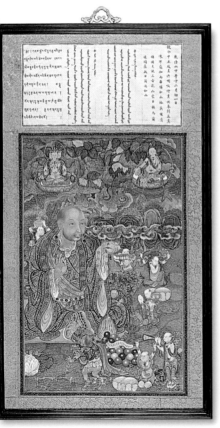

Votive Tablets

These small votive tablets stand as a silent testament to the early importance of Buddhism in Southeast Asia. Dating to the period when Sri Vijaya was a dominant power in the region, many of these terracotta tablets have been found at sites in the central part of the Malay Peninsula, from Kedah in the south to as far north as Chaiya in southern Thailand. Made from soft clay pressed with a stamp, these tablets bear images of Buddha and of bodhisattvas, as well as passages from the dharma.

These tablets are some of the earliest artefacts to enter the museum's collection. In 1901 an English scholar travelling in the peninsula collected a number of these tablets in the vicinity of Trang and had them sent to the Raffles Museum. At around the same time another group of Buddhist votive tablets was unearthed in the floor of a cave in Kedah by a British archaeologist. These also were sent to Singapore where they are now a part of the collection.

Votive tablets have been a tradition in Buddhism since its earliest days. Buddhist monks, often living in secluded hermitages, made these tablets in order to create merit for themselves. These amulets were believed to bring good fortune and protection to their wearers. Votive tablets are said to derive their power to protect the wearer through their association with sacred things. They endow the wearer with a sense of well-being and a desire to behave well towards others.[24] [DAH]

VOTIVE TABLETS
Malay Peninsula
8th–10th centuries
Clay
h. 5–7 cm; w. 3–4 cm
A1575, A1574a, A1573d, A1564c

Water Containers

A great variety of water containers were used by Southeast Asians for drinking. Shown here are two examples: the *kendi* and *labu*. The word '*kendi*' is derived from an old Sanskrit word, suggesting that the *kendi* was probably first introduced from India. It is characterised by a more or less rounded body, a straight neck and a spout set at an angle on the shoulder of the container.[1] The *kendi* shown here (BELOW, RIGHT) is a magnificent example of the *cire perdue* (lost-wax) brass casting technique of the Minangkabau, who were much renowned in their heyday. It was purchased for the museum in Padang Priaman, Sumatra in 1911 and is unusual in that it has three rather than the usual single spout.

The *labu*, an earthenware flask with a rounded body and a long neck, was another popular water container used in Southeast Asia. Its name comes from the gourd, a fleshy fruit of a creeping vine that since ancient times was hollowed out and dried for use as a water container. Thus the *labu* itself is probably derived from these containers and almost certainly has a long history in Southeast Asia. This *labu* (BELOW, LEFT) is believed to come from Kuala Kangsar, Perak in the Malay Peninsula. It is fairly typical of traditional Malay earthenware, although its silver throat and stopper suggest that it belonged to someone of considerable means.

According to historian Anthony Reid, water was the everyday drink of Southeast Asians, much to the surprise of both tea-drinking Chinese and beer- and wine-drinking Europeans. Period accounts from the 16th and 17th centuries report that most Southeast Asians drew their water from freshwater streams and allowed it to settle for a few days before drinking. They seldom boiled their water before drinking because of the high cost of time and fuel.[2] Thus it is quite likely that Southeast Asians developed a natural immunity to bacteria in the water. Europeans who followed suit though, suffered appallingly from waterborne diseases. [DAH]

(ABOVE) *LABU*
Kuala Kangsar, Perak, Malay Peninsula
c. late 19th–early 20th centuries
Earthenware, silver
29 x 55 cm
C0431c

(RIGHT) *KENDI*
West Sumatra, Indonesia
c. 1900
Brass
30 x 21.5 cm
B0022

Water Dropper

This beehive-shaped water dropper is a water vessel for a scholar's use. Its tiny everted rim controls the small amount of water dropped onto the inkstone while the ink is ground. The rim rests on a short and narrow neck that extends to rounded shoulders and a slightly flared base. On its base, a six-character Kangxi reign mark in regular script is written in underglaze blue. A crack runs through the word Kangxi, possibly a result of the tension between the glaze and the body. This vessel is covered in peach bloom glaze (*jiang guo hong*). Resembling the colour of a red apple, the glaze is characterised by blushes and mottles of red set against a rather pinkish-red ground. The effect was probably achieved by applying a copper lime pigment onto the first layer of clear glaze before another clear glaze sealed it.[3] Being an innovation of the Kangxi period, this type of glaze was mostly used on small scholars' objects, probably because it suited the scholarly taste for all things refined and simple (*ya dan*).

From the 7th century onwards water droppers were made from various materials and in different shapes. Clay was favoured over other materials, such as wood or metal, as it was less heavy and more affordable. Water droppers often appeared in myriad forms (▶ see QINGBAI PORCELAIN), such as the beehive shape of this water dropper. This form is attributed to the Kangxi period and continued to be popular during the Qing period. [WHL]

WATER DROPPER WITH PEACH BLOOM GLAZE
China
Qing dynasty, Kangxi period
Ceramic
h. 8.7 cm, diam. (BASE) 12.5 cm, diam. (RIM) 3.5 cm
Gift of Singapore Leisure Industries (Pte) Ltd
1995.2414

Wayang Kulit
(Leather Shadow Puppet Theatre)

Wayang kulit is the general term for the leather shadow puppet theatre of Indonesia and Malaysia. These characters are from the Javanese and Kelantanese traditions of *wayang purwa*, or Hindu epics such as the *Ramayana* and *Mahabharata*. The first puppet (RIGHT) is Batara Guru, which is the Javanese name for the Hindu deity Shiva. He is depicted with four arms and standing on his mount, Nandi the sacred bull. Batara Guru as King of Heaven stands in contrast to the other figure of authority, Semar (▶ see PANAKAWAN).

In Java, shadow puppet theatre is considered the highest of the performing arts, and its history can be traced to the royal courts of the 9th century—inscriptions indicate that female dancers, clowns, masked performers and shadow puppeteers were all resident at the courts and temples of that time.[4] The court arts were part of the ritual apparatus that legitimised the ruler's authority and enhanced his divine status. *Wayang* became a rich source of inspiration for other art forms and is often referred to for metaphorical insights into the meaning of everyday life in Java. The *dhalang* (puppeteer), far from being a mere entertainer, also possesses spiritual power, and puppets are included among the court *pusaka* (sacred heirlooms). However the art form has been adapted for various purposes, including ritual feast days, televised broadcasts, and religious and other forms of mass education. There is also a Chinese version for the Chinese community in Java. The flourishing of the music-recording business has over the years resulted in a decline in live performances. Today, it is not uncommon for a family to rent an 8-hour recording of a traditional *wayang kulit* performance, to be screened on such ritual occasions as weddings or circumcision ceremonies.[5]

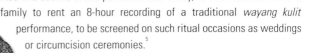

The character Bima (FAR LEFT) is one of the five Pandawa brothers from the epic *Mahabharata*. His father was Batara Bayu (God of Winds) and therefore his appearance—round eyes and a long nose, a large frame and wide stance and a long thumbnail which he uses in battle—is different from that of his refined princely brothers.[6] Bima is known for his great strength and violence in battle. In one episode a youthful Bima embarks on a journey to find the Holy Water that would enable him to become a perfect person. He reaches the depths of the ocean where he meets Dewa Ruci (OPPOSITE, BOTTOM, RIGHT), a personification in miniature of his true self, and to whom he expresses great humility.

Kelantanese puppets (*wayang kulit Siam*) developed in close association with the Javanese *wayang kulit* tradition. Around the turn of the 19th century, Malay *dhalang* travelled to and from Java and among the stories they brought back to north Malaysia were the Panji stories and the Hindu epics. The Malay tradition was, until the mid 20th century, patronised by the courts of Kedah, Kelantan and Pattani in southern Thailand. However, by the 1970s the tradition had already noticeably declined and today is virtually extinct.[7]

Performances of the *Ramayana* serve various social and ritual purposes, one of which is didactic in nature. For example, *Ramayana* characters illustrate the social ideals of *halus* (refinement) and *kasar* (coarseness) through their physique, behaviour and speech. Seri Rama (BELOW, LEFT) and other members of royalty have small refined features and elaborately decorated clothing, while evil rulers such as Ravana, the ogres and the monkey Hanuman (BELOW, RIGHT) (▶ see HANUMAN, ▶ see LAKHAOUN KHAOL MASKS) have broad noses, big eyes and large mouths with teeth.

Ramayana performances also serve to demonstrate the importance of traditional values and codes of conduct.[8] For example, Rama's formal introduction at the beginning of a performance, after offerings have been made to the spirits, illustrates examples of correct behaviour between a prince and his warriors. [HT]

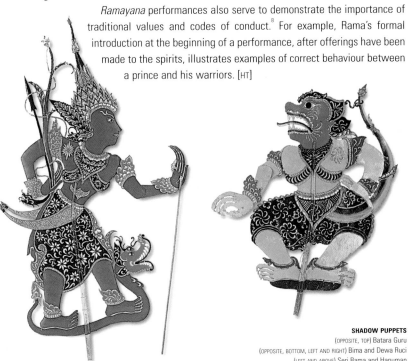

SHADOW PUPPETS
(OPPOSITE, TOP) Batara Guru
(OPPOSITE, BOTTOM, LEFT AND RIGHT) Bima and Dewa Ruci
(LEFT AND ABOVE) Seri Rama and Hanuman
Java, Indonesia
20th century
Leather
h. 50–60 cm
1994.4021, 94.4045, 94.3887, X6275, X5303

Weft Ikat

This *pidan* (temple hanging) (SEE DETAIL, BELOW) is a rare example of Khmer weaving in which the designs are oriented along the weft axis. Silk threads were tied and dyed—a technique known as *ikat*—and then woven across the warp threads. The highly symmetrical design consists of groups of motifs comprising a pair of interlocking *naga* (mythical serpents) with a pair of lions on the left and confronting birds on the right. They are arranged across the width of the textile and repeated throughout the length of the piece.

Weft *ikat* are found throughout Southeast Asia, including Laos, northern Thailand, Cambodia and the Khmer-speaking areas of northeast Thailand as well as northern Burma, the east coast of the Malay Peninsula, coastal Sumatra, Bali and Mindanao Island in the southern Philippines. They were highly valued as objects of beauty and wealth, and were associated with the court, where they were presented as gifts to loyal officials and important visitors. Cambodian *pidan* were used as decoration in the bride's home during a marriage.[9] They were also used as ceremonial coverings for walls and ceilings of temples which housed Buddha images.[10] The weaving and presentation of such pieces to the temple would have been considered as merit-making activities.[11]

Pidan designs include a wide range of motifs—architectural motifs, zoomorphic and anthropomorphic motifs with Buddhist significance, European and Chinese trade motifs such as ships and junks, and the more ancient abstract hook or key motifs as well as *naga*. The designs vary considerably and include narrative scenes or repeated patterns. The *naga* include a swimming form as seen in this piece, as well as a clawed

variety sometimes employed as an intertwined Buddhist swastika, which is similar to the Chinese dragon.

The sources of imported textiles which influenced Cambodian textiles included both India and China, two major trading powers who exchanged textiles for exotic Cambodian forest products.[12] However, Indian textiles

DETAIL FROM A *PIDAN*
Cambodia
19th century
Silk
87 x 230 cm
1995.2038

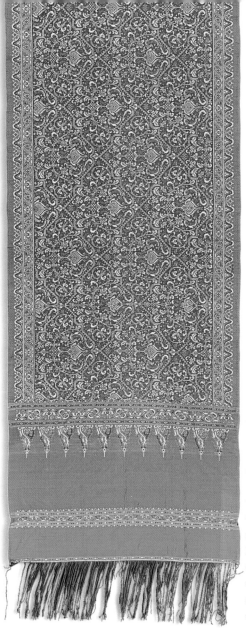

were considered the finest. Weft *ikat* were probably among the earliest types of textiles associated with Indian cultural influence in Southeast Asia and their production can be found along the main trade routes. However it was not until the introduction of silk and new loom technologies that weft-based designs were made in Cambodia. Khmer stone images of the Angkor period and Thai sculptures of the 11th to 14th centuries show figures clad in textiles with stripes running down the length of the body, indicating weft designs.[13]

Silk weaving is thought to have been introduced by the Siamese around this time. Zhou Daguan's 13th-century observations suggest that production was still largely limited to simple woven cotton on backstrap looms, until silk was cultivated by the Siamese who imported silkworms and mulberry trees.[14] Finer threads required new weaving technology. Thus, a comb was added to the loom to separate and better manage the fine silk warp threads. However this made traditional warp *ikat* patterns more difficult to achieve and hence the development of weft *ikat*.[15] [HT]

KAIN LIMAR (WEFT *IKAT* SHOULDER CLOTH)
Bangka Island, south Sumatra, Indonesia
19th century
Silk
500 x 90 cm
T0021

Wine Container

This large vessel, known as a *fou* or *lei*, was used for storing wine. Its most distinctive features are its buffalo-head rings—for hanging ropes—and its swirling and intertwining design. Wine drinking had been a crucial part of early Chinese civilisation since the Shang dynasty (▶ see DRINKING VESSELS). The intertwining design covering the main register of the body is called *panlong wen* (intertwining dragon motif) or *panchi wen*. This is actually a variation of the *kuilong* (dragon) motif and was particularly popular during the Spring and Autumn and Warring States periods.

The ability to reproduce these highly intricate designs in high relief on such large vessels attests to the casting skills and technology of the bronze maker. Chinese bronzes were manufactured using the piece-mould casting method, as opposed to the *cire perdue* (lost-wax) method. The former allowed the Chinese to make larger and much finer objects, but was much more complicated and laborious. It entailed making a solid model of the intended object in clay, then fabricating an inner and outer mould around it. Decorations were carved onto the moulds, after which the clay model was removed and the moulds joined. Lastly, molten bronze was poured into the gap between these two moulds. Once the bronze had cooled, the moulds were removed and discarded. Moulds were not recycled as the craftsmen did not want to compromise on the clarity of the designs by using old moulds. Thus each piece of bronze produced was unique, making it a prized possession. [ST]

FOU OR *LEI*
China
Warring States
Bronze
h. 38 cm, diam. 18.4 cm
1996.470

Woodblock Print

This print is a satire on the state of Confucianism, which was introduced from China during the first millennium and practiced by the ruling elite particularly during the 15th century following the decline of Buddhism as a state religion. The scene depicts the toad teacher, who is described as a '... puffed-up, incompetent creature that places the stress on preparing tea and handing out corporate punishment to the pupils instead of teaching'. Satirical humour perhaps provided the best way of expressing dissatisfaction within a feudal society.[16]

This print was made in the Hang Trong style, named after the street of Hang Trong whose resident printmakers were part of a lively industry up to the 1940s.[17] Unlike the folk prints of Dong Ho village, the other main centre for this art form, Hang Trong-style prints only use the woodblocks to print the outline of the design, which are then hand-coloured with Chinese inks. The colours that result are much brighter and the paper much smoother compared to the village prints, which comprise raw mineral and vegetable colourants and handmade mulberry paper.

It is thought that woodblock printing dates back to the Ly dynasty. Prints with auspicious greetings were used as household decorations on festive occasions such as Tet Nguyen Dan (Vietnamese Lunar New Year). Prints with religious images, such as the Daoist Five Tigers and the syncretic pantheon of local deities together with Quan Am, the Goddess of Mercy (▶ see QUAN AM), were also placed on altars for rituals and worship. However there are many other themes that are still produced at Dong Ho village or in Hanoi today. These include depictions of village occupations and seasonal activities associated with fertility such as wrestling competitions, as well as legendary ancestors and deified heroines such as Lady Trieu Au who defended the nation against the Chinese during the 3rd century. [HT]

WOODBLOCK PRINT OF THE FROG SCHOOL (*THAY DO COC*)
Produced at the workshop of Le Ding Nghien,
Hanoi, Vietnam
Late 20th century
Paper and inks
32 x 65 cm
2001.1766

Woodcarving

Carved wooden architectural panels such as these are common across much of the Malay world and are a key source of artistic expression. The beautiful and diverse motifs were used to communicate special messages and carry important spiritual and cultural meanings for the artists.

The first panel featured here (BELOW) is a Minangkabau piece that is most likely to have adorned a traditional *rumah gadang* (great house). According to Ibenzani Usman each ornamental motif carved on a *rumah gadang* has a name, and traditional teachings associated with that name give each motif a unique meaning.[18] Interestingly the Minangkabau normally paint their architectural panels, a practice that accentuates the various components of the carving, thus making it easier for the observer to understand and appreciate the meaning of the motifs.

The second panel (OPPOSITE, TOP) was made in the northeast of the Malay Peninsula and most likely came from a home of high status. Its extreme depth and openwork carvings are indicative of first-class workmanship, and would have been extremely difficult to make. The fact that it has openwork carvings indicates that this panel was most likely used as interior

(ABOVE) **MINANGKABAU ARCHITECTURAL PANEL**
West Sumatra, Indonesia
20th century
Wood, pigments
50 x 156 cm
2001.1629

decoration. Such panels allowed air to circulate within the house easily, thus keeping the house cool.

Although the panels shown here are of very high quality, most Malay wood-carved panels are not made by professional carvers but by the homeowner himself. Even the humblest of traditional Malay homes would have had some sort of carved decoration as the home would be considered incomplete without them. [DAH]

(TOP) **MALAY ARCHITECTURAL PANEL**
Northeast Malay Peninsula
20th century
Wood
79 x 20 cm
2001.1623

Yakshi Capital Depicting Four Shalabhanjika

This artefact seems to be the capital of a pillar or the stem of a trough from a Buddhist monument. It has four representations of a *yakshi* (female vegetation spirit) as a *shalabhanjika* (woman holding a tree branch). There are two *shalabhanjika* on each side of the capital—one side of the carving is more mutilated than the other and all except for one head are completely chipped off. Two *shalabhanjika* on one side (BELOW) stand under a tree with their opposite legs slightly bent and heels lifted up, while on the other side (OPPOSITE, TOP) they stand with their feet crossed in the *swastika sthana* (posture of good fortune). They bend their opposite arms to form a bow-like bend intertwining with the branches of the flowering plant, which emerges from the mouth of a *makara* head at their feet. The

branches of the tree are bent, presumably from the weight of the flowers and buds. The *shalabhanjika's* diaphanous garments and long flowing sashes create the impression of movement in their stance.

Shalabhanjika are found on Buddhist and Jain monuments of the early centuries of the Common Era. They were absorbed from the prevailing folk cults and practice of worshipping *yaksha* (male vegetation spirit) and *yakshi* as harbingers of good luck, prosperity and happiness. In Jainism each *tirthankara* (holy teacher) has a presiding *yaksha-yakshi* couple taking on a parental role. In Buddhist monuments such as Sanchi, Barhut, Amaravati and many other stupa sites, they are represented as generative vegetation spirits, or they symbolically evoke a fertility ritual. The *yaksha-yakshi* couple are richly ornamented and their sensuous bodies and commanding gait suggest they are in control of themselves. They are generally depicted holding a tree branch and kicking or touching its trunk, a popular fertility ritual in ancient India. There is a famous reference to this ritual in *Malavikagnimitra of Kalidasa*, a Sanskrit play in which the king falls in love with Malavika upon seeing her performing this ritual. The imagery of the *yakshi* evolved over time into *apsara* (celestial beauties) as symbols of fertility, sensuality and valour, and an auspicious feminine principle on later Hindu temple architecture. [GPK]

YAKSHI CAPITAL DEPICTING FOUR *SHALABHANJIKA*
(OPPOSITE) Front
(FROM TOP TO BOTTOM) Back and sides
Northwest India
Kushana period, 2nd century
Red spotted sandstone
50 x 49 cm
1999.120

Yao Accessories

Embroidered clothing is an essential part of the Yao cultural identity. The women embroider colourful geometric patterns on their garments and accessories. The apron (OPPOSITE, CENTRE), which is worn for weddings and other special occasions, has applied motifs, cross-stitch patterns and silver bosses (▶ see HILLTRIBE SILVER). The brightly coloured wool pompoms on the childrens' hats (OPPOSITE, TOP) liken them to flowers, an association seen also in baby carriers (▶ see HMONG ACCESSORIES).

The Yao are thought to have migrated south from central China over the last millennium. The Opium Wars and civil unrest of the 19th century saw increased migration into the region. Today Yao communities still live in southern Chinese provinces as well as in Thailand, Vietnam and Laos. They speak languages from the Sino-Tibetan group of languages and in this respect are related to the Miao and Hmong tribal groups. They also practise a mix of Daoist and animist religions and use the Chinese writing system.

Yao society is organised at the village level with a hierarchy that comprises the headman, priest and elders. There is no land ownership as swidden farming requires them to be temporarily resident in one place before moving on to a new area. However, national boundaries and pressure for more land from mainstream societies have brought about a decline in this nomadic way of life. Today the Yao are just as likely to be market-traders and town-dwellers often catering to the tourist industry in towns such as Chiangmai in northern Thailand. [HT]

TROUSERS (RIGHT)
North Thailand
Early 20th century
Embroidered and appliquéd cotton
80 x 132 cm
G0592

CHILDREN'S HATS (OPPOSITE, TOP)
North Thailand
Early 20th century
Embroidered and appliquéd cotton
h. 13–18 cm, diam. 18–20 cm
93.1187–89

APRON (OPPOSITE, CENTRE)
North Thailand
Early 20th century
Embroidered and appliquéd cotton
79 x 88 cm
93.1192

SHOES (OPPOSITE, BOTTOM)
North Thailand
Early 20th century
Embroidered and appliquéd cotton
24 x 11.5 cm
93.1191

Yaozhou Bowl

This rare example of a Yaozhou bowl—found with gold Cham jewellery in it—was retrieved from a burial site on Cham Island off the northeastern coast of Vietnam. The beauty and uniqueness of this bowl lie in the carved decoration and the gold band. Peony with scrolling stems and leaves were carved in low relief, probably by a piece of sharpened bamboo, such that the thin green glaze pooled in the recessed areas to give depth and fluidity to the decoration. The gold band is possibly a Cham addition since it is rather similar in feel and appearance to the gold jewellery found in the bowl. The floral scroll design on the gold band, which is in relatively good condition, is eye-catching and this repoussé work provides contrast to the low relief carved decoration. This bowl probably served as an heirloom for a Cham family.

Inspired by Yue wares of the south, the Yaozhou kilns at Tongchuan county in Shaanxi started to produce celadons around the 10th century. These were mainly fired in *mantou* kilns (of horseshoe shape) at about 1,300 degrees Celsius. According to *Song Shi* (Song Annals), these good-quality wares were presented to the Song court.

Celadons with crackles and floral decorations, such as this bowl, certainly appealed to the Chams. Copper-glazed Vietnamese celadon was often decorated with moulded floral scrolls. This could have been due to the influence of southern Chinese celadon (made in Guangxi), which was in turn made to imitate Yaozhou celadon. Furthermore, trade flourished during the Song dynasty, with records showing that merchants traded with 50 or more countries, including Champa (Vietnam). However, it is unclear if this bowl was an item of trade or was specially commissioned by the Chams since Yaozhou wares were made primarily for local consumption. [WHL]

YAOZHOU BOWL WITH GOLD BAND
China
Song dynasty
Ceramic
h. 9 cm, diam. 14.5 cm
Purchased with funds from Mr David Zuellig
2001.2611

Yemeni Manuscript

This page comes from a manuscript which features topics on astronomy, astrology and history. It is written in Arabic, and opens with a dedication to the Rasulid Sultan al-Mudjahid 'Ali ibn Da'ud ibn Yusuf ibn 'Umar ibn 'Ali ibn Rasul al-Jafani al-Ghassani (reign. 1321–1363). The Rasulid sultans ruled Yemen from their capital of Ta'izz for about 200 years. Their economy was very much supported by international trade in goods such as spices, perfumes and textiles. This period saw a thriving literary culture and architectural development. Several members of the Rasulid clan were authors of religious and even astronomical texts—it is possible that the author of this work was a member of the clan.

In Islam's sacred geography, the Ka'bah is the centre of the world. It is not only the direction towards which Muslims pray, but also the direction in which various rituals are performed. For example, Muslims are also buried facing the Ka'bah in Mecca.

On this page, the Ka'bah is depicted in the centre with 12 radiating sectors. The sectors inform us of the *qiblah* (direction of Mecca) for various places. Places within the same sector share the same *qiblah*. It has been known from the earliest times that the base of the Ka'bah is astronomically aligned. During the time of Prophet Muhammad, the corners of the Ka'bah were associated with the regions in which they faced. For example, Yemen is associated with the southern corner of the Ka'bah, so the *qiblah* is due north in Yemen. This formed the basis of Ka'bah-centred geography, which is an example of folk astronomy,

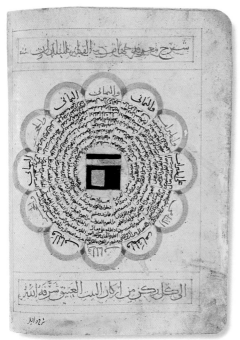

which was particularly popular in Yemen. Given the importance of the *qiblah*, scholars working in mathematical astronomy were also involved in determining through calculations the *qiblah* values for various cities and towns, which they then compiled into tables.[1] [TH]

▶ see ASTROLABE
▶ see KISWAH FRAGMENTS FROM THE HOLY KA'BAH
▶ see MIHRAB TILE

YEMENI MANUSCRIPT
Yemen
Muharram AH 758/
25 December 1356–23 January 1357 CE
Ink and colours on paper
(FOLIO) 26.5 x 17.5 cm
2000.5624

Yin and Yang Zodiac Signs

These wooden plaques depict Tai Yin (BELOW, LEFT) and Fu Xi (BELOW, RIGHT), representations of *yin* and *yang* respectively. They were possibly mounted together with other constellation deities or zodiac signs in the ceiling of a tomb. Such anthropomorphic symbols of *yin* and *yang* are rare.

Traditionally, *yin* represents the absence of sunshine or that which is dark, while *yang* represents the presence of light and sunshine. This interpretation is further expanded into *yin* symbolising femininity, cold and softness, and *yang* symbolising masculinity, heat and hardness. The two forces are interdependent and work in tandem to achieve an equilibrium ideal for human survival. These two correlates are also visualised as primordial cosmic forces by the Daoists. The creation of the universe is believed to be the direct result of their interaction.

According to Lisa Raphals,[2] before the 3rd century, the *yin-yang* polarities were largely cyclical and non-hierarchical. By the end of the Han dynasty, however, *yin* and *yang* began to be associated with gender hierarchy in which *yin* symbolised the female and the weaker sex vis-à-vis *yang* symbolising the male and stronger sex. The *yin-yang* polarity provided an appropriate analogy and explanation for the workings of nature for the Chinese and was applied in the fields of food, medicine, *fengshui* (geomancy), physiognomy, astrology and even ancestral worship. [ST]

YIN AND *YANG* ZODIAC SIGNS
(LEFT) Tai Yin; (RIGHT) Fu Xi
North China
Liao dynasty
Wood
26.5 x 20.5 cm
2001.1784, 2001.1785

Yogini
(Mother Goddess)

This sculpture of ten-armed Yogini, or Mother Goddess, is seated in *lalitasana* (relaxed posture). The missing arms would have once held the weapons and attributes of this goddess. The goddess is bejewelled with exquisite ornaments. Her hair is tied in a *jatamukuta* decorated by the leonine *kirtimukha*. The *ekavali* necklace twists to one side while a pearl necklace flows over her breasts. The waistband, anklets and earrings are carved with remarkable precision. The slight bend at the waist animates the body and lends it an unusual dynamism. The face has retained its crispness of carving especially in the arching brow. The benevolent expression of the face and the stylistic details make this a remarkable example of Paramara period sculpture from Madhya Pradesh.

At the Bijamandal site a mosque built by Aurangzeb (1658–1707) stands on the plinth of a ruined temple of the Paramara period. There is an inscription relating to the temple's donor, Paramara King Naravarman (c. 1094–1133), on one of the pillars while another Sanskrit inscription refers to a temple to the goddess Charchika, a local mother goddess.

Scholars believe these sculptures, pillars and pilasters belong to the demolished temple to Charchika. Paramara-period temples were usually in *bhumija* style and delicately carved. The original temple may have had enormous height as the plinth is very high and sculptures such as this Yogini were placed in niches with large *udgama* (triangular surmounts) on the *adhishthana* (plinth level). To the north of the monument is a *baoli* (stepwell) of the Pratihara period, around the 8th century, which bears carvings depicting Krishna's life (▶ see KRISHNALILA) and exquisitely carved pillars. Thus this site has sacred roots traceable to pre-Paramara dynasties.

The Archaeological Survey of India conducted excavations at this site from 1971 to 1972 and from 1992 to 1995. A site museum is being constructed which will display the sculptures retrieved from the site—Durga-Mahishasuramardini, *apsara* (celestial beauties), *saptamatrika* (seven mothers), Ganesha—and architectural fragments of great quality.[3] [GPK]

YOGINI
Bijamandal, Vidisha district, Madhya Pradesh, India
c. 11th–12th centuries
Pink sandstone
138 x 78 x 40 cm
On loan from the Archaeological Survey of India,
Government of India
BM/II/4/94

Zhang Ruitu's Calligraphy

The album of late Ming Fujian calligrapher Zhang Ruitu (1570–1641), signed Ruitu and containing two seal marks Zhang Ruitu *yin* and Ershui, opens with a regular-script (*kaishu*) transcript of the poems and a colophon by Liu Xiaoyun, dated 1944. Liu, who authenticated the work at the request of its owner, Wang Shaoping, cautioned that the work had been partially tampered with and that some words were also missing.

Nevertheless, this 30-page calligraphy is a classic example of Zhang's strange and *qiyi* (extraordinary) style. There is generous spacing between the columns while the individual characters are tightly packed in a way unique to him. Here, Zhang's brushwork is sharp and blade-like, accentuating not only the oblique strokes but also extending, sometimes threefold, the last vertical stroke of the characters; see pages 1, 4, 14 and 17 (OPPOSITE). Perhaps more than usual, the cursive calligraphy is at times impossible to decipher, and so a regular-script transcript of the poems by Song Zhiwen, Wang Wei and Li Bai, and a preface seemed necessary to help understand and appreciate the work. The album ends with colophons by three other authenticators.

Written in 1626, the year Zhang was promoted from the Imperial Academy to the office of the Grand Secretariat by the notorious eunuch, Wei Zhongxian, this calligraphy perhaps echoed the tension and anxiety that must have clouded Zhang's psyche despite his meteoric rise. Although an outstanding scholar in his own right, it was Zhang's calligraphy that won the admiration of Eunuch Wei. Indeed, by the early 1600s Zhang, together with Dong Qichang, Xing Tong and Mi Wanzhong, were known as the Four Masters of Ming calligraphy.

When Xizong, emperor of the Tianqi reign died in 1627, Eunuch Wei's reign of terror, as well as Zhang's career and reputation ended. In years to come, mainstream critics would either shun or condemn Zhang's work, because of his perceived moral shortcomings and his service to Eunuch Wei. However, his aesthetic achievements were always recognised, and today, it is Zhang's refreshingly strange calligraphy and his Zen Buddhist aesthetic views that exonerate him from the unfortunate circumstances of his own time. This was a calligrapher who was determined to free his art from the constraints of orthodox forms and to abandon himself in the true essence of calligraphy. [LCL]

ALBUM OF CURSIVE CALLIGRAPHY OF THREE TANG POEMS
(OPPOSITE, RIGHT TO LEFT, FROM TOP TO BOTTOM)
Fujian, China
1626 *bingyin* year of Tianqi reign
Ink on paper, hardwood covers
33.5 x 19.9 cm
1998.00756

(RIGHT) **DETAIL**
The seal of Zhang Ruitu

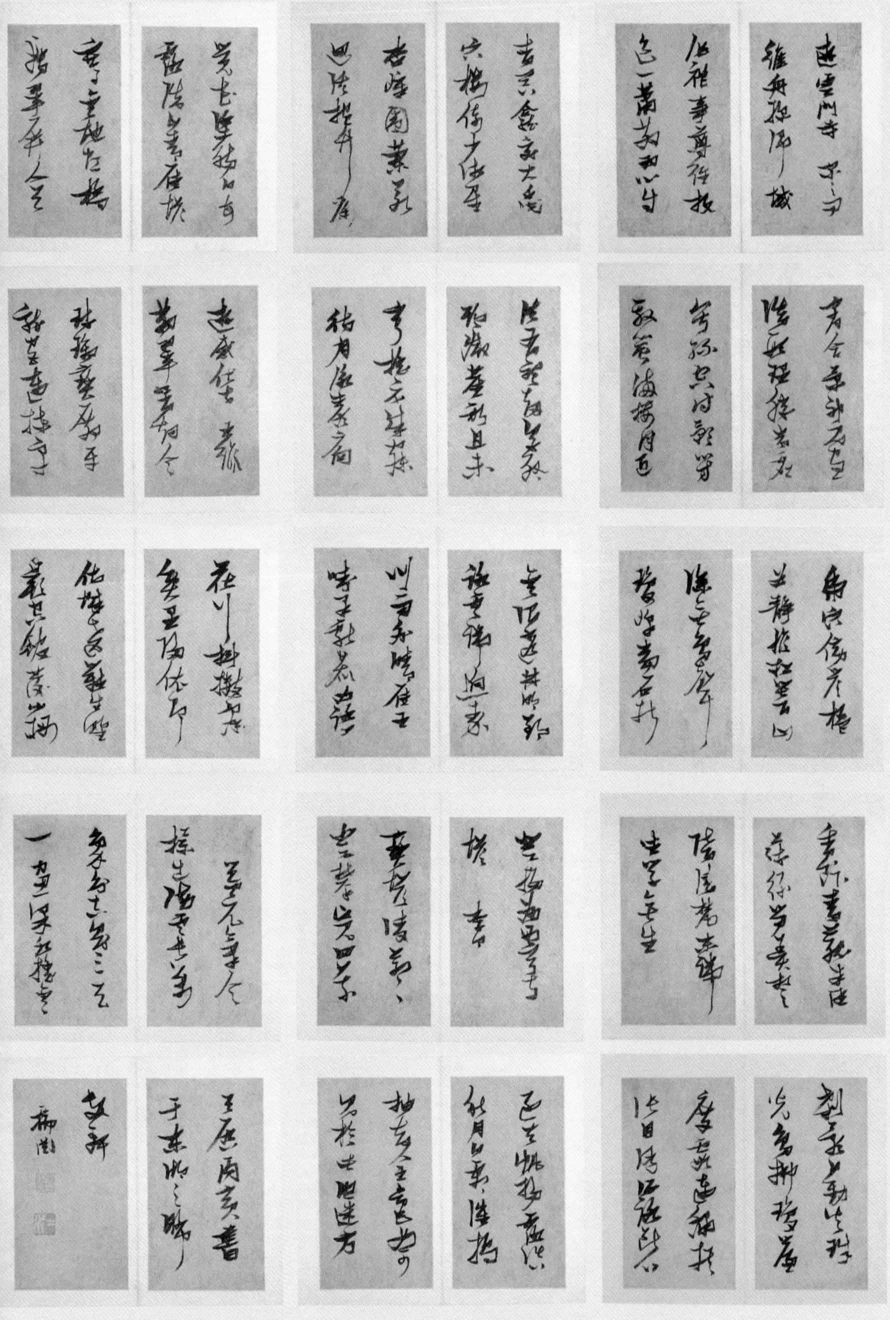

Appendices

Endnotes

A

1. Snellgrove, David, *Indo-Tibetan Buddhism: Indian Buddhists and Their Tibetan Successors*, London: Serindia Publications, 1987, p. 56.
2. Miller, Barbara S. (ed.), 'Pala and Sena Sculpture', *Exploring India's Sacred Art, Selected Writings of Stella Kramrisch*, Philadelphia: University of Pennsylvania Press, 1983.
3. Jessup, Helen Ibbitson & Zephir, Thierry, (eds.), *Millennium of Glory: Sculpture of Angkor and Ancient Cambodia*, Washington D.C.: National Gallery of Art, 1997, p. 147.
4. Ibid., p. 152.
5. The half-closed eyes and youthful appearance of the face is similar to Dvaravati images of this period, although the bare right shoulder is thought to have been a Khmer convention. Thai figures have the left shoulder bare and Amaravati figures typically have both shoulders covered. Ibid., p. 149. The mid 10th century saw many stylistic exchanges between Dvaravati and Cambodia. Woodward, Hiram J., *The Sacred Sculpture of Thailand: The Alexander B. Griswold Collection, The Walters Art Gallery*, London: Thames & Hudson Ltd, 1997, p. 72.
6. Jessup et al., op. cit., p. 147.
7. Ibid., p. 148.
8. Ibid.
9. Welch, Stuart Cary, *India: Art and Culture 1300–1900*, New York: The Metropolitan Museum of Art, 1985, pp. 303–305.
10. Woodward, op. cit., p. 239.
11. Ibid., p. 310.
12. Moore, Elizabeth H. et al., *Ancient Capitals of Thailand*, London: Thames & Hudson Ltd, 1996, p. 246.
13. Woodward, op. cit., p. 259.
14. More recently this cultural diversity has been cited as the basis of modern Thai culture. Moore et al., op. cit., p. 240.
15. Andaya, Barbara Watson & Ishii,

Yoneo, 'Religious Developments in Southeast Asia c. 1500–1800', *The Cambridge History of Southeast Asia*, vol. 1, part 2, *From c.1500 to c.1800*, edited by Nicholas Tarling, Cambridge: Cambridge University Press, 1999, p. 219.

B

1. See similar examples in Desai, Vishakha & Mason, Darielle (eds.), *Gods, Guardians and Lovers: Temple Sculptures from North India AD 800–1200*, New York: Asia Society Galleries, 1993, p. 181, illustration 25.
2. See Panaroglu, O., *Functions of Literary Epigraphy on Medieval Islamic Ceramics* from the website: www.islamicceramicsashmol.ox.ac.uk.
3. Aside from the proverb found on this bowl, here are two more from other vessels that are on the theme of generosity: 'Generosity is a quality of the people of paradise' and 'Generosity does not consume wealth before it is exhausted, and greed will not increase a miser's wealth'. For a list of proverbs visit the website www.islamicceramicsashmol.ox.ac.uk.
4. Banerjea, J. N., *The Development of Hindu Iconography*, New Delhi: Munshiram Manoharlal, 1974, chp. xii, p. 516.
5. Ibid., chp. xii, p. 511.
6. von Schroeder, Ulrich, *Buddhist Sculptures of Sri Lanka*, Hong Kong: Visual Dharma Publications, 1990, pp. 204–207.
7. Lerner, Martin, *The Flame and the Lotus, Indian and Southeast Asian Art from the Kronos Collections*, New York: The Metropolitan Museum of Art, 1984, p. 46.
8. Huntington, Susan & Huntington, John, *Leaves from the Bodhi Tree: The Art of Pala India (8th–12th centuries) and Its International Legacy*, London: Dayton Art Institute, 1990.
9. Reynolds, Valrae, *From the Sacred*

Realm: Treasures of Tibetan Art from the Newark Museum, London: Laurence King Publishing, 1999, p. 255.

10. Fraser-Lu, Sylvia, 'Buddha Images from Burma', *Arts of Asia*, vol. 11, no. 2, January–February 1981, p. 78.

C

1. Rogers, J. Michael, *Empire of the Sultans: Ottoman Art from the Collection of Nasser D. Khalili*, U.K.: The Nour Foundation, 1996, pp. 258–259.

2. The smaller relief images are probably Akshobya Buddha or 'Immovable' who guards against the passion and temptation.

3. Pal, Pratapaditya, *The Sensuous Immortals: A Selection of Sculptures from the Pan-Asian Collection*, Los Angeles: Los Angeles County Museum of Art, 1978, p. 216.

4. The word 'Hui' has been used at different times to refer to all Muslims living in China, or specifically to Muslims who are culturally and linguistically similar to the Han Chinese. The latter is how the People's Republic of China uses the term and the Huis in this case are seen as an ethnic nationality. One should note that there is great diversity among the Huis.

5. Other Muslim minorities include the Uighurs and Kazaks. The Uighurs are the second-largest group and live mainly in Xinjiang province. The Huis on the other hand, are found in all provinces of China, but especially Gansu and Ningxia.

6. These interpretations have been adapted from an unpublished catalogue by Joe Cribb from the Coins and Medals Department of the British Museum, London.

7. Jörg, C. J. A., *Chinese Export Porcelain*, Hong Kong: Urban Council, 1989, p. 106.

8. Howard, David S., *The Choice of the Private Trader*, Minneapolis: The Minneapolis Institute of Art, 1994, p. 73.

D

1. For similar examples see Welch, Stuart Cary, *India: Art and Culture: 1300–1900*, New York: The Metropolitan Museum of Art, 1985, pp. 257–259, illustration 168; Skelton, Robert, *The Indian Heritage: Court Life and Arts under Mughal Rule*, London: Victoria & Albert Museum, 1982, p. 129, illustrations 363, 409 & 411.

2. For similar examples see Desai, Vishakha & Mason, Darielle (eds.), *Gods, Guardians and Lovers: Temple Sculptures from North India AD 800–1200*, New York: Asia Society Galleries, 1993, pp. 166–170; Arts Council of Great Britain, *In the Image of Man: The Indian perception of the universe through 2000 years of painting and sculpture*, London: Arts Council of Great Britain/Weidenfeld & Nicolson, 1982, p. 223.

3. Maspero, Henri, *Taosim and Chinese Religion*, Amherst: The University of Massachusetts Press, 1981.

4. This is presently in the British Museum collection. Ayers, John, 'Blanc De Chine: Some Reflections', in *Blanc de Chine Porcelain from Dehua*, edited by Kenson Kwok and Heidi Tan, Singapore: National Heritage Board and Landmark Books, 2002, p. 27.

5. Fong, Mary H., 'Dehua Figures: A Type of Chinese Popular Sculpture', *Orientations*, January 1990, pp. 43–44.

6. Kwok, Kenson & Tan, Heidi (eds.), *Blanc de Chine Porcelain from Dehua*, Singapore: National Heritage Board and Landmark Books, 2002, p. 60.

7. David, Sir Percival, *Chinese Connoisseurship: The Ko Ku Yao Lun, The Essential Criteria of Antiquities*, London: Faber and Faber, 1971, p. 141.

8. A dish with motifs similar to this can be found in the Cleveland Museum of Art. See Wirgin, Jan, *Sung Ceramic Designs*, London: Han-Shan Tang Ltd, 1979, p. 144, pl. 78b.

9. There are no surviving examples of Malay written in another script before the use of the Arabic script. Aside from the script, the Arabic language also had

an impact on Malay. About 15 to 18 per cent of the vocabulary in the Malay language is derived from Arabic.

10. Richter, Anne, *The Jewelry of Southeast Asia*, London: Thames & Hudson Ltd, 2000, p. 230.

11. Ibid.

12. The two-eyed motif is more commonly known as the *taotie* motif. However, scholars such as Wang Tao have urged the use of the term 'two-eyed motif', citing textual evidence of non-equivalence between the term and the actual motif itself. Whitfield, Roderick (ed.), *The Problem of Meaning in Early Chinese Ritual Bronzes*, Colloquies on Art and Archaelogy in Asia, no. 15, London: Percival David Foundation of Chinese Art, 1990.

13. Ma Chengyuan, *Ancient Chinese Bronzes*, New York: Oxford University Press, 1986, p. 40.

E

1. See examples of ancient gold jewellery from the collections of the Cleveland Museum of Art in Untracht, Oppi, *Traditional Jewellery of India*, Cleveland and Metropolitan Museum of Art, London: Thames & Hudson Ltd, 1997, pp. 289 & 292.

F

1. Wood, Nigel, *Chinese Glazes*, London: A. & C. Black (Publishers) Ltd, 1999, p. 238.

2. The white enamel owes its colour to the colourant lead arsenate white. Ibid., p. 242.

3. The yellow enamel owes its colour to the colourant lead stannate yellow. Ibid.

4. Pal, Pratapaditya, *The Sensuous Immortals: A Selection of Sculptures from the Pan-Asian Collection*, Los Angeles: Los Angeles County Museum of Art, 1978, p. 249.

5. Ibid.

6. Woodward cites an early example dated

to the late 11th to early 12th century, which is thought to have been used as an official insignia that was carried like a banner. Woodward, Hiram J., *The Sacred Sculpture of Thailand: The Alexander B. Griswold Collection, The Walters Art Gallery*, London: Thames & Hudson Ltd, 1997, p. 88.

7. Zhou Daguan, *The Customs of Cambodia*, translated by Michael Smithies, Bangkok: The Siam Society, 2001, p. 27.

8. Hall, Kenneth R., *Maritime Trade and State Development in Early Southeast Asia*, Honolulu: University of Hawaii Press, 1985, p. 49.

9. Jessup, Helen Ibbitson & Zephir, Thierry (eds.), *Millennium of Glory: Sculpture of Angkor and Ancient Cambodia*, Washington D.C.: National Gallery of Art, 1997, p. 36.

10. Ibid.

11. Ibid., p. 37.

12. Ibid., pp. 37–38.

G

1. Instruments have been depicted at central Javanese Hindu Buddhist monuments such as Dieng plateau temples and Borobudur (dating to the 8th and 9th centuries) and east Javanese reliefs on Majapahit temples (dating to 13th–15th centuries). Sutton, R. Anderson et al., 'Java', *The Garland Encyclopedia of World Music, Southeast Asia*, vol. 4, edited by Terry E. Miller and Sean Williams, New York: Garland, 1998, p. 632.

2. For a similar example see Lerner, Martin & Kossak, Steven, *The Lotus Transcendent: Indian and Southeast Asian Art from the Samuel Eilenberg Collection*, New York: The Metropolitan Museum of Art, 1991, p. 74.

3. Mitra, Debala, *Buddhist Monuments*, Calcutta: Sahitya Samsad, 1971, pp. 21–23.

4. Banerjea, J. N., *The Development of Hindu Iconography*, New Delhi: Munshiram Manoharlal, 1974, pp. 255–259.

5. This gateway was identified based on a photograph by Dr R. Nath, retired professor and Head of the Department of History and Indian Culture, University of Rajasthan, Jaipur, which altered the museum's earlier assumption that it came from an Islamic building. Dr Nath believes that the gateway is an outcome of a patronage soon after the death of Shah Jahan (1628–1658) when artisans began working for the nobility around Uttar Pradesh in a slightly vernacular style.

6. In conversation and written report on the gateway by Dr R. Nath (unpublished).

7. This does not mean that porcelain was not used by the Ottomans prior to the 16th century. Its use in Turkey was noted from the 14th century onwards.

8. Krahl, Regina et al., *Chinese Ceramics in the Topkapı Saray Museum, Istanbul: A Complete Catalogue,* vol. II, London: Sotheby's, 1986, pp. 833–834. The collection has a large number of ceramics as the court dined on Chinese porcelain.

H

1. Mani, Vettam, *Puranic Encyclopaedia*, New Delhi: Motilal Banarasidass, 1975, pp. 308–309.

2. Cooper, Robert (ed.), *The Hmong: A Guide to Traditional Lifestyles*, Singapore: Times Editions, 1998, p. 58.

3. Pourret, Jess G., *The Yao: The Mien and Mun Yao in China, Vietnam, Laos and Thailand*, London: Thames & Hudson Ltd, 2002, p. 150.

4. The batik technique is practiced by the sub-group called the Green Hmong, whose women decorate their pleated skirts in this way. Cooper, op. cit., p. 51.

5. Cohen, Erik, *The Commercialized Crafts of Thailand: Hill Tribes and Lowland Villages*, Richmond, Surrey: Curzon Press, 2000, p. 100.

6. The earliest record of suppression is found in the Chinese annals of 2679 BCE. They record the banishment of a tribal group called the Miao from the central Yangzi plains to northwestern Gansu. Cooper, op. cit., p. 14.

7. Fraser-Lu, Sylvia, *Burmese Lacquerware*, Bangkok: Orchid Press, 2000, p. 122.

I

1. Maxwell, Robyn, *Textiles of Southeast Asia: Tradition, Trade and Transformation*, Melbourne: Oxford University Press, 1990.

2. Guy, John, *Woven Cargoes: Indian Textiles in the East*, London: Thames & Hudson Ltd, 1998, p. 90.

3. The Qur'anic text could also be divided into 30 equal parts and bound into 30 separate volumes.

J

1. Sheets of gold, silver and bronze with engraved sacred formulas have been found inside some bronze images. Lunsingh Scheurleer, P. C. M. & Klokke, Marijke J., *Ancient Indonesian Bronzes: A Catalogue of the Exhibition in the Rijksmuseum Amsterdam With a General Introduction*, Leiden: E. J. Brill, 1988, pp. 15–16.

2. It is thought that the demand declined firstly for Hindu then Buddhist images during the 10th and 11th centuries respectively. Ibid., p. 39.

3. Miksic, John N., *Old Javanese Gold*, Singapore: Ideation, 1990, p. 63.

4. Richter, Anne, *The Jewelry of Southeast Asia*. London: Thames & Hudson Ltd, 2000, p. 7.

K

1. Brownrigg, Henry, *Betel Cutters: From the Samuel Eilenberg Collection*, London: Thames & Hudson Ltd, 1992, p. 41.

2. The body of this bowl is made of an artificial material known as stone-paste or fritware. Persian potters first used

Endnotes

stone-paste, which is a synthetic mixture of clay and ground quartz, in the 12th century. The stone-paste body was easier to fashion than earthenware, which was used previously, thus enabling a greater variety of shapes to be made.

3. Muthiah, S., Meyappan, Meenakshi & Ramaswamy, Visalakshi, *The Chettiar Heritage*, Chennai, 2000, pp. 230–231.

4. Wales, H. G. Quaritch, 'Archaeological Researches on Ancient Indian Colonization in Malaya', *Journal of the Malayan Branch of the Royal Asiatic Society*, vol. 18, part 1, 1940, pp. 1–85.

5. Wales, H. G. Quaritch, 'Further Work on Indian Sites in Malaya', *Journal of the Malayan Branch of the Royal Asiatic Society*, vol. 20, part 1, 1947, pp. 7–8.

6. Interview with Dr Gauri Krishnan, October 2002.

7. This idea has been further elaborated in Parimoo, Ratan, 'Khajuraho: The Chandella Sculptor's Paradise, Is there a Chandella Style of Medieval Indian Sculpture? Its Sources and Characteristics', in *Essays on New Art History*, vol. I, *Studies in Indian Sculpture (Regional Genres and Interpretations)*, New Delhi: Book & Books, 2000, pp. 324–370.

8. According to Purana, Vishnu, *Dvitiya Amsa*, Bombay: Oriental Press, 1899.

9. The subject of *apsara-devangana* has been explored by me some ten years ago, culminating in a Ph.D. thesis, *A Study of Medieval Western Indian Devangana Sculptures on Nagara Temple Architecture*, submitted to the M. S. University of Baroda, Vadodara in 1993 (unpublished).

10. Malleret reported that rock crystal occurs naturally in Cambodia and suggested that there was an important precious stone industry in Cambodia during this early period. Spink, Michael, *A Divine Art: Sculpture of Southeast Asia*, London: Spink, 1997, p. 99.

11. Ibid., p. 98.

12. Ibid.

13. Middleton, Sheila E. Hoey, 'Two Engraved Gems with Combination Monsters from Southeast Asia', *The Journal of the Siam Society*, vol. 85, parts 1 & 2, 1997, p. 96.

14. Ibid.

15. Roveda, Vittorio, *Sacred Angkor: The Carved Reliefs of Angkor Wat*, Bangkok: River Books, 2002, pp. 81 & 197.

16. Rinaldi, Maura, *Kraak Porcelain: A Moment in the History of Trade*, London: Bamboo Publishing Ltd, 1989, p. 60.

17. This particular Qur'an is interesting as it is probably from the same Qur'an of which a third is kept in Tashkent, Uzbekistan. The Qur'an in Tashkent is believed to have arrived there via the Silk Route.

18. This should not be taken to mean that the revelations were not written down during the lifetime of the Prophet. The gathering of the revelations into sheets was said to have been done during the time of Abu Bakr while the compilation of the Qur'an into a single volume is believed to have been done during the time of the third caliph 'Uthman.

19. Déroche, F., *The Abbasid Tradition: Qur'ans of the 8th to 10th centuries*, U.K.: The Nour Foundation, 1992.

20. Once stored, usually in mosques, the Qur'ans were generally left unattended.

21. The five known dated *kapardin* Buddhas are in the following collections: Kimbell Art Museum, Ft. Worth, 4th year (82); Mathura Museum, Sonkh, 23rd year (101); Dusseldorf, Private Collection, 31st year (109); Ahicchatra Buddha, National Museum, 32nd year (110); Palikhera, Indian Museum, Calcutta, 39th year (117). Dr Don Stadtner (unpublished).

L

1. Phim, Toni Samantha & Thompson, Ashley, *Dance in Cambodia*, Kuala Lumpur: Oxford University Press, 1999, p. 4.

2. Maxwell, Robyn, *Textiles of Southeast Asia: Tradition, Trade and Transformation*, Melbourne: Oxford

University Press, 1990, p. 321.

3. Parimoo, Ratan, *Life of Buddha in Indian Sculpture*, New Delhi, 1982, p. 78.

4. This artefact was displayed and published in the exhibition and catalogue: Desai, Vishakha & Mason, Darielle (eds.), *Gods, Guardians and Lovers: Temple Sculptures from North India AD 700–1200*, New York: Asia Society Galleries, 1993, pp. 234–235.

5. Not much is known about metalwork during the Fatimid period in Egypt. Most metalwork with animal figures is usually attributed to Fatimid Egypt, but could have been produced in Iran, Spain or Sicily. See Contadini, A., *Fatimid Art at the Victoria and Albert Museum,* U.K.: Victoria & Albert Museum, 1998.

6. Nguyen Van Huy, *The Cultural Mosaic of Ethnic Groups in Vietnam*, Hanoi: Education Publishing House, 2001, pp. 117–119.

M

1. This motif also suggests that this basin could have been used to hold water.

2. See Baer, Eva, *Islamic Ornament*, New York: New York University Press, 1998. She suggests that the design could have referred to the sun because if not for the rays of sun, which make water visible, would water be drinkable?

3. Allan, James, *Islamic Metalwork: The Nuhad Es-Said Collection*, London: Sotheby's, 1999.

4. Taylor, P. M. & Aragon, Lorraine V., *Beyond the Java Sea: Art of Indonesia's Outer Islands*, Washington D.C.: Smithsonian Institution, 1991, p. 210.

5. According to the *Markandeya Purana*, vol. 12, chp. 88, from Banerjea, J. N., *Development of Hindu Iconography,* New Delhi: Munshiram Manoharlal, p. 505.

6. Summerfield, Ann & John (eds.), *Walk in Splendor: Ceremonial Dress and the Minangkabau*, Los Angeles: University of California, 1999, p. 138.

7. Calligraphers were aided by eyeglasses for writing *ghubar* script as early as the 16th century.

8. See James, David, *Qur'ans of the Mamluks*, U.K.: Alexandria Press, 1988, pp. 170–177.

9. Guy, John, 'The Kosa Masks of Champa: New Evidence', *Southeast Asian Archaeology*, 1998, p. 52.

10. Ibid., p. 51.

11. Ibid., p. 53.

N

1. Brand, Michael & Phoeurn, Chuch, *The Age of Angkor: Treasures from the National Museum of Cambodia*, Canberra: Australian National Gallery, 1992, p. 84.

2. Jessup, Helen Ibbitson et al. (eds.), *Millennium of Glory: Sculpture of Angkor and Ancient Cambodia*, Washington D.C.: National Gallery of Art, 1997, p. 268.

3. Ibid., p. 272.

4. Many calligraphic pieces contain Sufi poetry, the meaning of which would have been much appreciated by the beholder.

5. Ghosh, Manmohan (ed.), *Abhinaya Darpana*, Calcutta: Manisha Granthalaya Private Ltd, 1975.

P

1. Hasibuan, Jamaludin S., *Batak: Art et Culture/Seni Budaya*, Jakarta: Jayakarta Agung Offset, 1985, p. 276.

2. Richter, Anne, *The Jewelry of Southeast Asia*, London: Thames & Hudson Ltd, 2000, p. 160.

3. van Brakel, J. H., *Budaya Indonesia: Art and Crafts in Indonesia*, Amsterdam: Royal Tropical Institute, 1987, p. 274.

4. Lee Chor Lin, *Ancestral Ships: Fabric Impressions of Old Lampung Culture*, Singapore: National Museum, 1987, p. 3.

5. There is another paper-cut calligraphy, which is in the collection of the Topkapı Palace Museum in Istanbul, that features the work of the same two artists.

6. Stadtner, Donald M. (ed.), & Herbert, Patricia M., 'Burmese Court Manuscripts',

The Art of Burma: New Studies, vol. 50, no. 4, June 1999, Mumbai: Marg Publications, pp. 10 & 92.

7. Welch, Stuart Cary, *India: Art and Culture, 1300–1900*, New York: The Metropolitan Museum of Art, 1985, catalogue entries 223 & 260.

8. See similar cloud pattern in Skelton, Robert, *Rajasthani Temple Hangings of the Krishna Cult*, New York: The American Federation of Arts, 1973, p. 35.

Q

1. Other panels from the same set are found in the Metropolitan Museum of Art, New York (five panels); Calico Museum, Ahmedabad (single panel); A.E.D.T.A., Paris (single panel); Victoria & Albert Museum, London (single panel without the border) and several other private collections.

2. Beach, Milo Cleveland, 'Mughal Tents', *Orientations*, January 1985.

3. Welch, Stuart Cary, *India: Art and Culture 1300–1900*, New York: The Metropolitan Museum of Art, 1985, pp. 252–256.

4. Translation quoted from Schimmel, Annemarie, *And Muhammad is His Messenger—The Veneration of the Prophet in Islamic Piety*, Chapel Hill: University of North Carolina Press, 1985, p.186.

5. For Muslims Adam is the first man and all humans are his progeny. For the complete translation of the text, please refer to Safwat, Nabil, *The Harmony of Letters: Islamic Calligraphy from the Tareq Rajab Museum*, Singapore: Asian Civilisations Museum, 1997.

6. Arabic is read from right to left.

7. Hue-Tam, Ho Tai, 'Religion in Vietnam: A World of Gods and Spirits', *Vietnam: Essays on History, Culture and Society*, New York: The Asia Society, 1985, p. 29.

8. Yaqut Musta'simi survived the destruction of Baghdad under the Mongols in 1258, after which he worked as a librarian in a *madrasah* (theological

college) and taught calligraphy.

9. Bayezid II (r. 1481–1512) was the first known Ottoman sultan to have learnt calligraphy.

10. The system of rules is based on diamond-shaped dots, formed by pressing the reed pen on the paper diagonally. The length of the letter *'alif'* (equivalent to the letter 'A' in English) was used as a standard and related to other letters. These diamond dots thus help guide the calligraphers as to the right proportions for each letter.

11. Before Yaqut al-Musta'simi, the Six Pens of Ibn Muqlah were made more beautiful by a famous 11th-century calligrapher, Ibn Bawwab, who was taught by Ibn Muqlah's daughter.

12. Décroche, François, *The Abbasid Tradition: Qur'ans of the 8th to 10th centuries*, London: The Nour Foundation and Oxford University Press, 1992.

13. The battle in Samarqand, near the borders with China in 751, has usually been cited by historians as the point in time when the Islamic world learnt the secret of paper-making from the capture of Chinese paper-makers. A scholar, Jonathan Bloom, has put forward the argument that paper-making was already present in Central Asia before the Muslim conquest. In the Islamic world paper was initially used only for everyday purposes.

14. Safwat, Nabil, *The Art of the Pen: Calligraphy of the 14th to 20th centuries*, U.K.: The Nour Foundation, 1996.

15. This composition is believed to have first developed in the 10th century.

16. Aside from the opening text pages, some Qur'ans have, for example, illuminated frontispieces and endpages.

R

1. *Rgveda*, book X, chp. 82, verses 5 & 6.

2. Kerr, Rose, *Chinese Ceramics: Porcelain of the Qing Dynasty 1644–1911*, London: Victoria & Albert Museum Publications, 1998, p. 88.

3. Nguyen Huy Hong & Tran Trung Chinh, *Vietnamese Traditional Water Puppetry*, Hanoi: The Gioi Publishers, 1996, p. 51.

4. Nguyen, Phong T., 'Vietnam', *The Garland Encyclopedia of World Music, Southeast Asia*, vol. 4, edited by Terry E. Miller and Sean Williams, New York: Garland, 1998, p. 444.

5. Nguyen & Tran, op. cit., p. 52.

6. Ibid., p. 66.

7. Untracht, Oppi, *Traditional Jewellery of India*, London: Thames & Hudson Ltd, 1997, p. 39.

8. Muthiah, S., Meyappan, Meenakshi & Ramaswamy, Visalakshi, *The Chettiar Heritage*, Chennai, 2000, pp. 232–233.

S

1. Guy, John, 'The Ceramics of Central Thailand', *Thai Ceramics. The James and Elaine Connell Collection/Asian Art Museum of San Francisco*, Kuala Lumpur: Oxford University Press, 1993, pp. 4–6.

2. Guy, John, 'Thai Ceramics in Southeast Asian Trade', *Thai Ceramics. The James and Elaine Connell Collection/Asian Art Museum of San Francisco*, Kuala Lumpur: Oxford University Press, 1993, p. 10.

3. Brown, Roxana & Sjostrand, Sten Turiang, *A Fourteenth Century Wreck in Southeast Asian Waters*, Pasadena: Pacific, 2000.

4. Guy, John, 'Thai Ceramics in Southeast Asian Trade', op. cit., p. 12.

5. Ibid.

6. Cort, Louise, 'Buried and Treasured in Japan: Another Source for Thai Ceramic History', *Thai Ceramics. The James and Elaine Connell Collection/Asian Art Museum of San Francisco*, Kuala Lumpur: Oxford University Press, 1993, p. 34.

7. Leigh, Barbara, *Hands of Time: The Crafts of Aceh*, Jakarta: Jambatan, 1989, p. 96.

8. This piece has been published before in the following books: Sastri, H. Krishna, *South Indian Images of Gods and Goddesses*, Ootacamund, 1916, fig. 67; Chandra, Pramod et al., *Master Bronzes*

of India, Chicago: Art Institute of Chicago, 1965, no. 54; Czuma, Stanislaw, *Indian Art from the George P. Bickford Collection*, Cleveland: Cleveland Museum of Art, 1975, no. 19.

9. Formerly in the George P. Bickford Collection, U.S.A.

10. For elaboration on this identification and of the *shraddha* ceremony, see Krishnan, Gauri Parimoo, *An Unusual Cloth Painting from the Pahari Region in the Collection of the Asian Civilisations Museum, Singapore* (unpublished).

11. There are unfortunately no reliable statistics. According to R. Bulliet, a scholar who specialises in Middle Eastern History, by the 9th century about 40 per cent of the population in Iran were Muslims, and this increased to 70–80 per cent by the 10th century.

12. Andaya, Barbara Watson, 'From Rum to Tokyo: Riau's Search for Anti-colonial Allies, 1899–1914', *Indonesia,* vol. 24, 1977, pp. 125–156.

13. Miksic, John N., 'A Lead Statue Recently Discovered at a Majapahit-Period Site in Singapore', presented at the Eighth Archaeological Scientific Conference, 15–18 February 1999, Yogyakarta, Indonesia.

14. The kingdom of Sukhothai is usually thought to have flourished from the mid-13th to the mid-15th centuries, although the dating of the inscription attributed to the founder, King Ram Khamhaeng, has now been revised to the mid-19th century. Krairiksh, Piriya, 'A Reassessment of the Sukhothai Walking Buddha', *A Divine Art: Sculpture of Southeast Asia*, London: Spink, 1997.

15. Fluidity of line and supple modelling are features that have been attributed to the influence of southern Indian art styles by earlier scholars such as Griswold. Woodward, Hiram J., *The Sacred Sculpture of Thailand: The Alexander B. Griswold Collection, The Walters Art Gallery*, London: Thames & Hudson Ltd, 1997, p. 148.

16. Indeed through their iconography,

Endnotes

images of the Buddha express important aspects of the dharma and may be considered to have a life force of their own. Ibid., p. 19.

17. One of the oldest of Buddhist narratives, depictions can also be found in a Sri Lankan mural painting. Ibid., p. 160.

18. Ibid.

19. Ibid., pp. 138 &155.

20. Krairiksh, op. cit.

21. Snellgrove, David, *Indo-Tibetan Buddhism: Indian Buddhists and Their Tibetan Successors*, London: Serindia Publications, 1987, pp. 312 & 315.

T

1. Contractor, Meher R., *The Shadow Puppets of India*, Ahmedabad: Darpana Academy of the Performing Arts, 1984, pp. 5–17.

2. Asian Civilisations Museum, *Ramayana: A Living Tradition*, introduction by Gauri Parimoo Krishnan, Singapore: Asian Civilisations Museum, 1997.

3. Persian tiles, on the other hand, were made from a man-made white clay body known as stone-paste or fritware.

4. The use of scripts with human and animal heads is found only on some metalwork from the 12th to 14th centuries.

5. The European traveller Tome Pires recorded its popularity during the early 16th century. Jessup, Helen Ibbetson, *Court Arts of Indonesia*, New York: Asia Society Galleries in association with H. M. Abrams, 1990, p. 164.

6. Although Cirebon is an important centre for *wayang topeng* there are also troupes in rural areas of Java such as Klaten, central Java, Malang and east Java, as well as on the island of Madura. Sutton, R. Anderson et al., 'Java', *The Garland Encyclopedia of World Music, Southeast Asia*, vol. 4, edited by Terry E. Miller and Sean Williams, New York: Garland, 1998, p. 654.

7. Jessup, op. cit., pp. 164–166.

V

1. Snellgrove, David, *Indo-Tibetan Buddhism: Indian Buddhists and Their Tibetan Successors*, London: Serindia Publications, 1987, pp. 333–336, 346 & 351.

2. Mani, Vettam, *Puranic Encyclopaedia*, New Delhi: Motilal Banarasidass, 1975, pp. 488–489.

3. Rao, S. R., & Sastry, Sri B. V. K., *Traditional Painting in Karnataka*, Bangalore: Karnataka Chitrakala Parishath, 1980, p. 35.

4. Krahl, Regina, 'Vietnamese Blue-and-White and Related Wares', *Vietnamese Ceramics: A Separate Tradition*, Chicago: Art Media Resources, 1997, p. 149.

5. Stevenson, John, 'The Evolution of Vietnamese Ceramics', *Vietnamese Ceramics: A Separate Tradition*, Chicago: Art Media Resources, 1997, p. 43.

6. Krahl, op. cit., p. 149.

7. Ibid., p. 153.

8. Guy, John, 'Vietnamese Ceramics: New Discoveries', *Treasures from the Hoi An Hoard*, Butterfields, 2000, p. xvi.

9. Krahl, op. cit., p. 148.

10. Guy, John, 'Vietnamese Ceramics in International Trade', *Vietnamese Ceramics: A Separate Tradition*, Chicago: Art Media Resources, 1997, p. 50.

11. Lead glazes tend to produce brighter colours than ash glazes such as celadon. They also tend to run during the firing. Stevenson, John et al., *Vietnamese Ceramics: A Separate Tradition*, Chicago: Art Media Resources, 1997, p. 276.

12. Krahl, op. cit., pp. 148–149.

13. Vietnamese ceramics are usually termed stoneware rather than porcelain as they do not have the pure white, translucent quality of porcelain.

14. Stevenson, op. cit., p. 247.

15. Lam, Peter, 'Vietnamese Celadons and their Relationships to the Celadons of Southern China', *Vietnamese Ceramics: A Separate Tradition*, Chicago: Art Media Resources, 1997, p. 136.

16. The greyish-green tone of celadon glaze was the result of naturally occurring

386

iron-oxide in the clay, which together with wood-ash were used to make the glaze. Ho, Chuimei (ed.), *New Light on Chinese Yue and Longquan Wares*, Hong Kong: Centre of Asian Studies, University of Hong Kong, 1994.

17. Stevenson, op. cit., p. 14.

18. Krahl, Regina, 'Plant Motifs on Chinese Porcelain', *Orientations*, vol. 18, May 1987, p. 52.

19. Stevenson, op. cit., p. 139. Figure C24 is a Longquan example with carved lotus petals on the exterior.

20. Ibid., pp. 135 & 139.

21. Region south of Mathura in southern Uttar Pradesh which was influenced by the Imperial Pratihara style.

22. For comparison with examples of Surya see Desai, Vishakha & Mason, Darielle (eds.), *Gods, Guardians and Lovers: Temple Sculptures from North India AD 700-1200*, New York: Asia Society Galleries, 1993, pp. 187–188, fig. 28 & pp. 262–263, fig. 70.

23. Banerjea, J. N., *The Development of Hindu Iconography*, New Delhi: Munshiram Manoharlal, 1974, p. 385.

24. Bechert, Heinz & Gombrich, Richard (eds.), *The World of Buddhism: Buddhist Monks and Nuns in Society and Culture*, London: Thames & Hudson Ltd, 1984.

W

1. *Kendis, A Guide to the Collections of the National Museum of Singapore*, Singapore: National Museum, 1984, p. 5.

2. Reid, Anthony, *Southeast Asia in the Age of Commerce, 1450–1680*, vol. 2, *Expansion and Crisis*, New Haven: Yale University Press, 1993, pp. 36–38.

3. Wood, Nigel, *Chinese Glazes*, London: A. & C. Black (Publishers) Ltd, 1999, p. 182.

4. Brandon, James R., *The Cambridge Guide to Asian Theatre*, Cambridge: Cambridge University Press, 1993, p. 121.

5. Sutton, R. Anderson et al., 'Java', *The Garland Encyclopedia of World Music, Southeast Asia*, vol. 4, edited by Terry E. Miller and Sean Williams, New York:

Garland, 1998, pp. 651 & 681.

6. Djajasoebrata, Alit, *Shadow Theatre in Java: The Puppets, Performance and Repertoire*, Amsterdam: The Pepin Press, 1999, p. 127.

7. Matusky, Patricia, *Malaysian Shadow Play and Music: Continuity and Oral Tradition*, Kuala Lumpur: Oxford University Press, 1993, p. 10.

8. Ibid., p. 24.

9. Maxwell, Robyn, *Textiles of Southeast Asia: Tradition, Trade and Transformation*, Melbourne: Oxford University Press, 1990, pp. 167 & 174.

10. Sheares, Constance, 'Ikat Patterns from Kampuchea: Stylistic Influences', *Heritage*, vol. 7, 1984, p. 49.

11. Maxwell, op. cit., p. 199.

12. Green, Gillian, 'Indic Impetus?: Innovations in Textile Usage in Angkorian Period Cambodia', *Journal of the Economic and Social History of the Orient*, vol. 43, no. 3, 2000, p. 305.

13. Maxwell, op. cit., pp. 158–159.

14. Sheares, op. cit., p. 45.

15. Maxwell, op. cit., p. 162.

16. Mullerova, Petra, *Pictures from the Land of the Dragon King*, Prague: Narodni Museum, 2000, pp. 33 & 38.

17. Interview with Le Ding Nghien.

18. Summerfield, Ann & Summerfield, John, *Walk in Splendor: Ceremonial Dress and the Minangkabau*, Los Angeles: University of California, 1999.

Y

1. The *qiblah* determined through folk astronomy (a popular method used by religious scholars) corresponds roughly with that determined by the astronomers.

2. Raphals, Lisa, *Sharing the Light: Representations of Women and Virtue in Early China*, Albany, New York: State University of New York Press, 1988.

3. This Yogini from Bijamandal was brought on loan to Singapore during the first visit of India's president, Mr K. R. Narayanan, in October 2000.

Neolithic period	c. 6500–1900 BCE
Xia dynasty	c. 2100–1600 BCE
Shang dynasty	c. 1600–1027 BCE
Zhou dynasty	c. 1027–256 BCE
Western Zhou dynasty	1027–770 BCE
Eastern Zhou dynasty	770–256 BCE
Spring and Autumn period	722–481 BCE
Warring States period	481–256 BCE
Qin dynasty	221–207 BCE
Han dynasty	206 BCE–220 CE
Western Han dynasty	206 BCE–8 CE
Xin dynasty	8–25
Eastern Han dynasty	25–220
Six Dynasties period	220–589
Sui dynasty	589–618
Tang dynasty	618–906
Liao dynasty	916–1125
Song dynasty	960–1279
Northern Song dynasty	960–1126
Southern Song dynasty	1127–1279
Jin dynasty	1115–1234
Yuan dynasty	1279–1368
Ming dynasty	1368–1644
Hongwu	1368–1398
Yongle	1403–1424
Hongxi	1425–1426
Xuande	1426–1435
Zhengtong	1436–1449
Jingtai	1450–1456
Tianshun	1457–1464
Chenghua	1465–1487
Hongzhi	1488–1505
Zhengde	1506–1521
Jiajing	1522–1566
Longqing	1567–1572
Wanli	1573–1619
Taichang	1619–1620
Tianqi	1621–1627
Chongzhen	1628–1643
Qing dynasty	1644–1911
Shunzhi	1644–1661
Kangxi	1662–1722
Yongzheng	1723–1735
Qianlong	1736–1795
Jiaqing	1796–1820
Daoguang	1821–1850
Xianfeng	1851–1861
Tongzhi	1862–1874
Guangxu	1875–1908
Xuantong	1909–1911
Republican period	1912–1949
People's Republic of China	From 1949

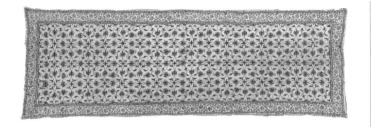

Antecedents of Indic civilisation	8000–2500 BCE
Indus and Saraswati civilisations	2300–1750 BCE
Vedic and Upanishadic periods	1500–450 BCE
Mauryan period	323–185 BCE
Sunga period	4th–2nd centuries BCE
Kushana period	1st–4th centuries
Satavahana and Ikshvaku periods	1st–4th centuries
Gupta period	4th–6th centuries
Early Chalukya period	6th–8th centuries
Pallava period	7th–9th centuries
Maitraka and Solanki periods	7th–12th centuries
Gurjara-Pratihara period	8th–10th centuries
Late Chalukya, Rashtrakuta and Western Ganga periods	8th–12th centuries
Pala and Sena periods	8th–12th centuries
Chola period	9th–13th centuries
Chandella and Paramara periods	10th–11th centuries
Eastern Ganga period	11th–14th centuries
Hoyasala and Kakatiya period	12th–14th centuries
Sultanate period	14th–16th centuries
Vijayanagara and Nayaka period	14th–18th centuries
Mughal period	15th–17th centuries
Bhakti revivalism	15th–19th centuries
Rajput period	15th–19th centuries
Sikh period	17th–19th centuries
Maratha period	18th–19th centuries
Company period	18th–19th centuries
Colonial India	mid 18th century–1947
Independence	1947

Chronology

Hoabinhian Period	4500–1300 BCE
Neolithic Period	3600–500 BCE
Ban Chiang Cultural Tradition (northeast Thailand)	3600 BCE–300 CE
Early period	3600–900 BCE
Middle period	1100–200 BCE
Late period	300 BCE–300 CE
Bronze Age	1500 BCE–500 CE
Gua Cha (north Peninsular Malaysia)	1300–500 BCE
Dong Son (north Vietnam)	500 BCE–300 CE
Island Dong Son	1000 BCE–500 CE
Pyu (Burma)	100–900
Funan (Cambodia and Vietnam)	200–500
Champa (Vietnam)	500–1450
Dvaravati (Burma, and central and south Thailand)	500–800
Chenla (Cambodia)	550–800
Srivijaya (Island Southeast Asia, southern Thailand)	600–1100
Angkor (Cambodia)	800–1450
Pagan (Burma)	900–1300
Pegu (Burma)	1000–1281
Ly Dynasty (Vietnam)	1009–1225
Janggala and Kediri (Java)	1049–1222
Sukhothai (Thailand)	1200–1350
Singhasari (Java)	1222–1292
Tran Dynasty (Vietnam)	1225–1400
Lanna (northern Thailand)	1281–1762
Majapahit (Java)	1293–1528
Rise of Pre-Modern Islamic Malay States	1297–1699
Ayutthaya (Thailand)	1351–late 1700s
Lan Xang (Laos)	1353–mid 1600s
Colonial Era	1511–1945
Classical Javanese Kindoms	1528–1830
Le Dynasty (Vietnam)	1539–1682
Nguyen Empire (Vietnam)	1682–1820
Chakri Dynasty (Thailand)	Late 1700s–present
Period of decolonisation	1945–1983

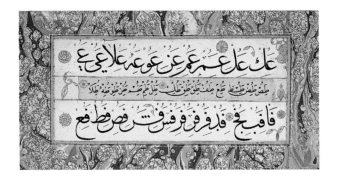

Orthodox caliphs	632–661
Umayyad caliphate	661–750
'Abbasid caliphate	749–1258
Samanids	819–999
Fatimids	969–1171
Ghaznavids	977–1186
Seljuks	1038–1194
Ghurids	1150–1212
Ayyubids	1169–1260
Rasulids	1228–1454
Mamluks	1250–1517
Ilkhanids	1256–1353
Ottomans	1281–1924
Timurids	1370–1506
Safavids	1501–1732
Qajars	1779–1925

abaca Hard fibre obtained from the leaf sheaths of a wild banana plant, *Musa textilis.*

Abbasids Second dynasty of caliphs that ruled from 750 to 1258; its main capital was Baghdad in 762–836 and 892–1258, and Samarra in 836–892. At its peak, the areas ruled spanned from north Africa to the borders of India. By the 9th century, rulers who had grown increasingly powerful in the various provinces established local dynasties. From the 10th century, the Abbasids fell under the control of military dynasties. The dynasty ended with the invasion of the Mongols.

abhaya mudra (gesture of fearlessness) In Hinduism and Buddhism, a hand gesture where the right hand is held upright with the palm facing outward; it is often depicted in sculptural representations of Hindu gods, Buddha and bodhisattvas.

abhaya and **katisama mudra** In Hinduism, south Indian Hindu deities are generally represented standing in this pose with their right hand in *abhaya mudra* and their left hand resting on the waist.

acharya A religious teacher or preceptor according to Hindu tradition.

adat In Malay societies, a set of customs and traditions.

al-aqlam al-sittah (six scripts) Cursive scripts which were codified by Abbasid vizier Ibn Muqlah in the 10th century and became an important part of a calligrapher's repertoire. The six scripts are *muhaqqaq, rayhan, thulth, naskh, tawqi', riqa'.* See **muhaqqaq**, **naskh** and **thulth**.

alamkarapriya A Sanskrit term used to address the Hindu god Vishnu for his fondness of being adorned.

alaya In Hindu architecture, a niche for lamps at the entrance or doorway of a house.

Ananda Tandava According to south Indian Shaiva tradition, a dance performed by Shiva in which he kills Mara, the demon representing ignorance.

antarala The conjoint or linking area between the sanctum sanctorum and the hall in any Hindu and Jain temple.

appliqué A decorative technique in which accessory pieces of fabric are applied to the ground fabric, usually by stitching.

apsara In Hinduism and Cambodian mythology, a beautiful celestial nymph who is born of the water and lives in the heavens, although she may choose to take birth on earth from time to time. Adept in dance and music, she is also regarded as a seductress, bestower of good luck, fertility and auspiciousness, and is written about in the *Vedas* and *Puranas* and is often depicted on temples.

arabesque A stylised floral motif with intertwined leaf stems.

ardhaparyankasana In Hinduism and Buddhism, the royal stance of sitting on a throne with one leg bent at the knee and the other leg touching the ground.

Asma al-husna In Islam, the divine Names or beautiful Names of God; reciting them is considered a source of blessing. There are believed to be 99 names in all.

Au Co A female spirit of the mountains whose union with the dragon king of the sea saw the mythical origins of the Vietnamese people.

ayah (sign) A term used to refer to a verse in the Qur'an. See **Qur'an**.

basmalah An abbreviation of *Bismillah ar-Rahman ar-Rahim*, meaning 'In the Name of God, the Gracious and the Merciful'; it is recited by Muslims before undertaking any task and usually written as the preface of any text.

batik A resist dyeing process in which a substance such as hot wax or rice paste is applied on a fabric surface. The substance acts as a resist to dyes, leaving patterns in the fabric's original colour. The resist is removed by boiling, melting or scraping after dyeing.

bhumisparsha mudra (earth-witnessing gesture) In Hinduism and Buddhism, a hand gesture symbolising Buddha calling the earth to witness his victory over the evil Mara, the demon representing ignorance. Buddha's right hand hangs over his right knee with his fingertips pointing downwards, while his left hand rests on his lap with his palm facing upwards.

bidri A technique of metal inlay that was very popular in Deccani and Mughal courts for making decorative arts.

bihari In Islamic calligraphy, the script developed in Sultanate India for writing Arabic, especially Qur'ans. See **Qur'an** and **Sultanate**.

blanc de Chine In Chinese ceramics, white porcelain made in Dehua kilns in Fujian province; the best examples were produced in the late Ming (16th–17th centuries) and early Qing (17th–18th centuries) dynasties. Also known as Dehua porcelain.

Bodhi Tree The tree under which Gautama Siddhartha attained enlightenment and became Buddha; a symbol used in Buddhist art to denote this event in the Life of Buddha.

bodhisattva In Mahayana Buddhism, a Sanskrit term referring to one who has achieved salvation but chooses to forgo entering nirvana out of compassion for the suffering of others.

brocade A textile weaving technique in which yarns of different materials or colours are woven into the base weave, usually monochrome, to create patterns. The most commonly used speciality yarns are metallic.

burnish In Chinese ceramics, a technique in which a stone is used to polish ceramic wares to a shiny finish, thereby providing a good surface for painted decoration.

caliph Derived from the Arabic word *khalifah*, which means successor; a title given to the supreme leaders of the Muslim community after the death of Prophet Muhammad.

cartouche A rounded oblong or oval panel that usually contains incised inscriptions.

celadon In Chinese ceramics, a generic European term for green-glazed wares; it encompasses the green stoneware of Yue, Yaozhou and Longquan kilns in China. The green colour is attributed to iron oxide in the glaze and firing in a reducing atmosphere. Celadon wares were also produced at northern Vietnamese and Thai kilns and competed for export markets during the 15th century. See **reducing atmosphere**.

chadma nataka (shadow puppetry) An ancient Hindu tradition that is still practised in different parts of India today.

chakravartin Sanskrit for Universal Monarch, a title that was adopted by early Hindu-Buddhist rulers in Southeast Asia.

chasing A metalwork technique that creates the appearance of a raised surface decoration, done by depressing the background of the image.

chedi Thai word for *cetiya* (Pali) or stupa (Sanskrit); a commemorative structure that represents the Buddhist universe, built to contain relics of Buddha or an important monk. See **stupa**.

chi dragon In Chinese symbolism, a type of dragon without horns.

chine de commande In Chinese ceramics, a European term referring to Chinese porcelain that was commissioned around the 18th century by Europeans actively engaged in trade with China.

City God In Chinese religions, literally the 'God of the Wall and Moat'; he is responsible for the peace and prosperity of his territory and for meting out justice in the underworld.

classic scroll In Chinese ceramics, a stylised band of recurring vines and leaves.

cloisonné A decorative technique involving the use of cloisons to form outlines on a metal surface. Powdered enamels are used to fill the spaces, and after firing, they are polished to a level surface with the cloisons. See **cloisons**.

cloisons Copper or bronze strips that are first bent into the required shape before they are glued or soldered onto metal vessels to form enclosures for enamels. This is part of the cloisonné technique. See **cloisonné**.

colophon An inscription usually found at the end of a manuscript giving the name of the copyist and the date and place where the manuscript was written.

crackles In Chinese ceramics, these are cracks that result when the glazes contract more than the clay bodies during cooling; a similar effect as crazing. It has been suggested that use of this term implies the effect is intentional and is therefore appreciated aesthetically.

danava In Hinduism, a Sanskrit term referring to ogres and demons.

darshana In Hinduism, a religious term used to mean a view of the main deity that is placed in a temple sanctum; a vision of the supreme divinity.

Dawenkou culture In China's Neolithic history, the main sites of this culture (4300–2400 BCE) are located in central and southern Shandong Peninsula and northern Jiangsu province of China. Dawenkou culture is characterised by millet cultivation, finely polished stone axes, highly varied forms of painted pottery and pottery with impressed and reticulated designs, and even jade and ivory objects.

Deepavali The Festival of Lights; it is celebrated in India and wherever Indians have settled abroad. Deepavali celebrates the victory of Rama over Ravana and Krishna killing Narakasura, an ogre from Hindu mythological tales. The festival falls on the last day of the month of Ashvin, which is a new moon day according to the Hindu calendar.

deva In Hinduism, a generic term used to refer to gods or divine beings.

devadasi In ancient India until the beginning of the 20th century, some women were married to a deity, especially in a Shiva temple. The women, called *devadasi*, performed daily rituals which included worshipping the deity with singing and dancing. *Devadasi* were considered ever auspicious and were held in good social standing. However, this practice became degenerate as time went by and the women were soon reduced to mere dancing girls.

dharma In Buddhism, the Law of the Universe; discovered and taught by Buddha, it is one of the Three Jewels, the other being Buddha and Sangha. See **Triratna**.

dhoti A lower garment of unstitched cloth tied around the waist; it is worn by men in India even today.

dhyanasana (meditation posture) A sitting posture used by yogis for meditation; Buddha is represented in this posture.

Dhyani Buddha In Mahayana Buddhism, there are five Dhyani Buddhas representing the different ages and cardinal directions.

diacritical dots Used in writing Arabic, these are added to the basic letter forms so that one can tell what letter is being represented. For example, the letter 'nun' shares the same 'u'-shape as the letter 'ba'. What distinguishes the two letters is a dot above the 'u' for 'nun' and a dot below the 'u' for 'ba'. Also known as *i'jam* in Arabic.

diaper In Chinese ceramics, a repeated geometric design either in the form of a decorative band or background; it first appeared as a decorative band on the earthenware of the Shang dynasty.

dikpala A directional deity who protects Hindu and Jain temples; there are eight directional deities representing the eight cardinal directions.

Ding In Chinese ceramics, the name of the monochrome white, purple, black, brown and green wares produced at the Ding kilns in Hebei province in China during the Northern Song dynasty.

diwani In Islamic calligraphy, a script devised by the Ottoman imperial chancery for official documents. See **Ottoman**.

Dong Son An agricultural culture in north Vietnam that was based on wet rice cultivation. Social stratification was high, as indicated by the marked difference in the burial items of some compared to the general population. Dong Son culture is particularly famous for its bronze drums, believed to be one of the earliest sophisticated bronze forms that independently evolved in Southeast Asia. Many Dong Son-type drums have been excavated in many different locations in mainland and island Southeast Asia, suggesting ancient trade links and transfers of technology.

Dvaravati A kingdom in central Thailand that emerged during the 7th century and was centred in Nakhon Pathom. It had a predominantly Mon population and had strong connections with Cambodia.

Eight Buddhist Emblems (Ba Ji Xiang) In Chinese symbolism, these refer to the eight auspicious Buddhist symbols: a vase (representing good fortune), an umbrella (dignity), a lotus flower (perfection and progeny), a pair of fish (domestic harmony and marital bliss), a conch shell (good fortune), a canopy (official status), the wheel of the law (truth and order), and an endless knot (longevity). Use of this group emerged during the Yuan dynasty and gained popularity during the Ming and Qing dynasties, as evident on textiles and ceramics of those periods.

ekavali A single strand necklace worn by deities in Hindu sculptures; probably an ancient Indian fashion.

electrum An alloy of silver and gold used for jewellery.

enamel In Chinese art, this glassy paste is a type of lead-rich glaze coloured by mineral pigments. It is used for overglaze decoration as it matures around a low temperature of 800 degrees Celsius. See also **cloisonné** and **iron red enamel**.

fahua In Chinese ceramics, a type of enamelled ware in which the designs are bounded by a raised trail of slip in deep blue, turquoise, purple, yellow, green and white glazes.

farashkhana (royal art studio) A rental shop for tents in north India; this was the artists' workshop during Mughal times.

Fatimids Dynasty of caliphs ruling in north Africa and Egypt from 909 to 1171. The Fatimids claimed descent from Fatimah, Prophet Muhammad's daughter.

filigree A decorative technique often used in jewellery-making in which twisted wire is welded or attached to an object.

five pillars of Islam In Islam, these comprise the *shahadah* (profession of faith), *salat* (five daily obligatory prayers), *sawm* (fasting during the Islamic month of Ramadan), *zakat* (giving of obligatory alms) and *haj* (pilgrimage to Mecca). See **haj**, **salat** and **shahadah**.

four Orthodox caliphs The four companions and immediate successors to Prophet Muhammad: Abu Bakr, 'Umar, 'Uthman and 'Ali. Also known as *Rashidun* or 'rightly guided' caliphs. See **caliph**.

fritting In Chinese ceramics, a technique in which two or more materials are heated so that they fuse together. After cooling, they are then ground. A technique normally used in the preparation of glazes.

gandharava In Hinduism, celestial or heavenly beings who are the spouses of *apsara*. They are believed to be endowed with great power and artistic talent. See **apsara**.

Ge Gu Yao Lun (The Essential Criteria for Chinese Antiquities) A Chinese manual or encyclopaedia on Chinese art and archaeology written by Cao Zhao in 1388. It was later translated into English by Sir Percival David, a prominent Chinese ceramics collector and published in 1971 under the title *Chinese Connoisseurship*.

gilding A decorative technique in which a thin layer of gold is overlaid on an object.

gopi Cowherdesses who, according to Indian tradition, are devotees of Krishna.

granulation Tiny metal granules or balls applied to plain surfaces to create a decorative effect.

Guanyin The Chinese equivalent of Avalokiteshvara, or Bodhisattva of Compassion, who emerged as a popular female deity during the Song dynasty. Also called Goddess of Mercy by Jesuit missionaries to China, and Quan Am in Vietnam. In Mahayana Buddhism, Guanyin is an enlightened being who postpones entering nirvana to remain with lay people to help them.

guldasta (flower vase) An Urdu term referring to a decorative motif often used in Mughal art.

gvala Cowherds who, according to Indian tradition, were the playmates of Krishna.

haj In Islam, a pilgrimage to Mecca that is performed during the Islamic month of Zu'l Hijah. One of the five pillars of Islam, it is to be undertaken by a Muslim at least once in a lifetime, if he/she is financially and physically able. See **five pillars of Islam**.

halus (refinement) A virtue espoused by noble heroes of the Hindu epics in the performing arts of the Malay world, or the aesthetic notion of high-quality workmanship in the material culture of the Malay world.

hat cheo Literally 'singing' (*hat*) and 'oar theatre' (*cheo*); a folk theatre tradition from the Goi area near Hanoi, which includes dance, mime, acting and singing. It is closely associated with the cult of the heroines, the Trung Sisters, who fought the Chinese during the Han period. The dances also contain remnants of the ancient maritime communities whose boats are depicted on bronze drums.

haveli A nobleman's mansion according to north Indian tradition.

Hinayana Sanskrit for the 'Lesser Vehicle' school of Buddhism.

hiranyagarbha (primodial egg) A Sanskrit term found in the *Vedas*, the ancient Hindu scriptures; it refers to the cosmic golden egg or the womb from which all creation takes place.

hman-zi shwei chá In Burmese lacquer, the process of placing glass fragments (coloured mirror glass or mica which had been cut into various geometric shapes) on the surface of relief-moulded designs.

hsun ok A Burmese votive lacquer vessel with a tapering cover, used for presenting food to the monastery as offerings. It has a wide bowl-shaped base with fitted trays and plates. Also sometimes referred to as *ok kwet*.

huanghuali In Chinese furniture, a type of wood (*Dalbergia odorifera*) often used for furniture from the mid Ming to early Qing dynasties.

Hungry Ghost Month In Chinese religions, a festival celebrated by Buddhists and Daoists on the seventh lunar month when ghosts are released from the gates of hell and allowed to roam on earth.

ikat A resist dyeing process in which warp or weft yarns are reserved to prevent dye from penetrating into the fabric. This is done by tying small bundles of yarns with strips of palm leaf or similar materials. Additional tying or partial removal of the bindings is required for each different colour. After the last dyeing, all the bindings are removed and the yarns are ready for weaving. See **warp** and **weft**.

ikat **technique** The oldest and most tedious of all traditional methods used in the making of textiles, it involves preparing the warp, tying, dyeing and weaving, plus sorting and counting threads based on a special numerical classification and counting technique that requires considerable skill and experience. The preparation of the warp and folding is a highly complex process. Also known as the tie and dye method. See **warp**.

imam In Islam, one who leads in communal prayers. Also used by Shi'a Muslims to denote Prophet Muhammad's descendants through his daughter Fatimah and her husband 'Ali ibn abi Talib, who are considered the true rulers of the Muslim community. See **Shi'a**.

intaglio Literally 'engraved'; it is the result of carving a design on gems, glass or ceramics such that the design is sunken or depressed below the surface.

iron red enamel In Chinese ceramics, lead glaze containing iron oxide. When fired in an oxidising atmosphere, the colour red is produced. See also **enamel**.

jali (monumental) In Islamic calligraphy, this denotes scripts written larger than their normal size, the exception being *jali diwani*. See **jali diwani**.

jali diwani In Islamic calligraphy, a version of *diwani* script which contains decorative devices; only used during the Ottoman period for important state documents. Also known as *celi divani* in Turkish. See **diwani** and **Ottoman**.

Janmashtami A festival celebrating Krishna's birth; according to the Hindu calendar, it falls on the eighth day of the dark half of the month of Shravan, which is also the rainy season.

jatabhara In Hinduism, a Sanskrit term referring to the matted hair of Shiva.

Jataka A Pali term for the 547 stories of Buddha's former lives. The stories illustrate particular virtues through Buddha's actions, which the laity can use as a model for their own lives.

jatamukuta (crown of matted hair) A Sanskrit term referring to the piled up tiara-like hairdo worn by Hindu-Buddhist deities. Also known as *jatabandha*.

jawi Malay written in a modified Arabic script.

jhankhi A tableau, generally of Hindu deities.

Justice Bao In Chinese history, a senior magistrate who lived in the Northern Song dynasty and was famous as an incorruptible upholder of justice. Also known as Bao Zheng or Bao Qingtian.

juz' The Qur'anic text can be divided equally into 30 sections. One-thirtieth of the text is known as a *juz'*. See **Qur'an**.

jyotirlingam According to Hindu tradition, a *lingam* that is believed to have evolved naturally from the earth; it is considered the most sacred of all *lingam*. There are traditionally 12 *jyotirlingam*. See **lingam**.

Ka'bah A cube-like building in Mecca— the focus of the *haj* and the direction for Muslim prayers. Muslims consider the Ka'bah the first holy sanctuary built on earth and its foundations laid down by prophets Ibrahim (Abraham) and Isma'il. See **haj** and **qiblah**.

Kadamba In Hinduism, the name of a flowering tree in the Vraja area where Krishna frolicked with the *gopi*. See **gopi**.

kala Sanskrit for *kirtimukha* (face of glory); a mask with the features of a human and lion, it represents life-giving powers, prosperity, time and death. See **kirtimukha**.

kammavaca A Pali term for Buddhist loose-leaf manuscripts containing the *Pali Vinaya* (rules and regulations of the monastery).

kapitha mudra (clasping gesture) In Hinduism, a hand gesture in which the thumb and the index fingers are joined together; it is used in classical Indian dance and held by deities, especially to hold a flower or a fly whisk.

Kartikai The full moon festival in the month of Kartikai (November–December) according to the Tamil calendar.

kasar (coarse, unrefined) A term used to describe the qualities of evil characters in shadow puppet play and other performing arts traditions of the Malay world.

Kathina A ceremony held at the end of the monks' rainy season retreat in Thailand and other mainland Theravada Buddhist countries, in which the monks are presented with new robes.

kavadi A wooden pole carried on the shoulder with milk pots on either ends, usually used by worshippers of Murugan, a popular Hindu deity in south India, Singapore and Malaysia.

kendi A vessel with a bulbous body, straight neck and a spout set at an angle on the body. It derived its name from an old Sanskrit term for a water pot and is used in Southeast Asia for drinking and for water storage; the porcelain ones from China serve as ceremonial vessels or display objects.

Glossary

key-fret A schematised cloud swirl probably adapted from Chinese bronzes in as early as the Shang dynasty.

kinnara A mythical bird with a human body; it is represented in Hindu-Buddhist art in India and Southeast Asia.

kirtimukha (face of glory) A decorative motif represented on Hindu temples.

klapmuts A bowl with rounded walls and flattened rim. Its Dutch name is derived from its close resemblance to an upside-down woollen cap with an upturned edge; it is used for soup or stews in Europe.

kosha A Sanskrit term referring to a cover for something precious.

kudumi A Tamil term referring to a tuft of hair on a shaven head.

Kufic-Abbasid In this publication, a term used to refer to a group of early angular scripts that were used for copying early Qur'ans as well as inscribed on objects and architecture. Also known as *kufic*.

lakshana A Sanskrit term for one of the 32 marks by which the Buddha is recognised as a *mahapurusha* (Great Person).

lalitasana (relaxed posture) Also known as the sitting posture of ease, it is depicted in Indian and southeast Asian sculptures of Hindu-Buddhist deities.

lasara A mythical Nias creature with a dragon-like head and bird-like tail. The head has horns, a strong open jaw with heavy lips, a forked tongue and diamond-shaped eyes. Sculptures of these creatures were traditionally commissioned, either in wood or stone, for great feasts and were believed to be symbolic protectors of the feast-giver and his family.

lead glaze In Chinese ceramics, a type of low-firing glaze that contains lead as its flux (any material that allows both glaze and body material to melt). When fired in an oxidising atmosphere, bright colours like green and amber are produced. It was commonly used during the Han and Tang dynasties.

lingam A Sanskrit term for 'sign, mark'. In Hinduism, a phallic symbol representing Shiva. It is worshipped by Hindus as a symbolic representation of Shiva. Also known as *linga* in north India.

Lingodbhavamurti In Hinduism, an image depicting Shiva emerging from the *lingam*, which is a phallic symbol representing Shiva. See **lingam**.

liuli In Chinese ceramics, a glaze made from a fired silicic composition of aluminium and sodium, usually used to glaze tiles.

lokapala In East Asian (namely Chinese, Japanese and Korean) and Tibetan Buddhism, the guardian kings of the four cardinal directions.

luting In Chinese ceramics, a method of joining unfired ceramic parts using a slip. See **slip**.

Maghribi In Islamic calligraphy, a script that developed from Kufic-Abbasid. It was developed and used in Islamic Spain and North Africa. See **Kufic-Abbasid**.

Mahabharata The epic of the great battle between descendants of Bharata, with one side of the nobility trying to recover authority from the other. It deals essentially with morality and the emergence of good over evil. The epic dates to the period between 1500 and 1000 BCE and consists of 106,000 verses in 18 books.

Mahayana (great vehicle) A Buddhist school of thought that developed during the early centuries of the Common Era in India when the sutras or written sayings of Buddha and his relics were worshipped as substitutes for the body and speech of Buddha. Mahayana Buddhism became the dominant form of Buddhism in the northern areas of Asia (East Asia, Mongolia and Tibet) although it also prevailed in northern Vietnam and at earlier Southeast Asian centres such as Shrivijaya in Sumatra and Borobudur in Central Java.

makara A sea monster, usually with the head of an elephant and the body of a fish. It is associated with water as a source of life and power and symbolises abundance and strength. The Hindu-Buddhist *makara* motif is usually placed on doorframes, lintels, gateways and thresholds of north Indian temples. The Thai version is described as crocodile-like in appearance.

makara kundala Crocodile-design earrings; it is a typical iconographical feature of the popular Hindu deity Krishna. See **makara**.

makara torana The entrance archway of a Hindu temple that has amphibian-like composite figures placed on two sides of the archway. See **makara**.

Mamluks Military slave dynasty that ruled Egypt, Syria, Arabia and Iraq from 1250 to 1517; its main capital was Cairo. The word *'mamluk'* is Arabic, which means 'taken into possession or owned'.

mandala (circular) In Hinduism and Buddhism, a Sanskrit term referring to a geometric or pictorial representation of the entire universe.

mandapam In Hinduism, the audience hall of any temple; it is routinely used for congregation, ceremonies, performances and celebrations. It can be big or small depending on the size of the temple.

mandorla In Hindu-Buddhist art, the framing device or aureole surrounding the image of a deity.

mandovara A technical Sanskrit term found in north Indian architectural texts; it refers to a temple wall.

mantou kiln In Chinese ceramics, a kiln used in north China, either dug into the earth or built of bricks. It is small and easily supports a higher firing temperature of around 1,350 degrees Celsius. Its name is derived from the bread rolls eaten in north China.

mihrab (prayer niche) A niche in the wall of a mosque denoting the *qiblah*. See **qiblah**.

mingqi (burial ware) In Chinese ceramics, an image or model used for burial in tombs.

moulding In Chinese ceramics, a technique that uses a stoneware mould to transfer relief decoration onto a ceramic ware. The mould is put on a turntable with its decoration facing upwards, then a lump of clay is beaten over it while it is turned.

Muchalinda The mythical serpent or *naga* King who offered Buddha protection during the storm after his enlightenment.

mudra Sacred hand gestures indicating the various stages of the life of Buddha; used in Hindu-Buddhist iconography, classical Indian dance and Tantric rituals. There are five basic *mudra* in most Buddhist images, although more *mudra* have developed in the Vajrayana or Tibetan Buddhist tradition.

muhaqqaq In Islamic calligraphy, a script with shallow downward sweeping strokes with flat endings resembling swords or daggers; it is one of the *al-aqlam al-sittah*. See **al-aqlam al-sittah**.

mukhalinga Literally 'face' (*mukha*) and 'sign' (*linga*) in Sanskrit; it is a *lingam* with the face of Shiva, a central god in the Hindu trinity together with Brahma and Vishnu. Shiva assumes many forms; in this form he is the God of Creation. See **lingam**.

mulavar (main immobile deity) In Hinduism, this is the main deity that is carved in stone and placed in the sanctum sanctorum of any Hindu temple in south India, especially in Tamil Nadu. It is immobile, in contrast to the bronze icons which are decorated and taken out during processions around the temple and the city.

naga (mythical serpent) In Hindu-Buddhist mythology, a prominent figure of the underworld or waters; it is worshipped as a spirit of the earth in many parts of Southeast Asia.

nagara A Sanskrit term referring to the north Indian region.

nagari Short for Devanagari, the script in which the Sanskrit language is written; a north Indian script.

naskh In Islamic calligraphy, a cursive script used widely for scribal purposes; one of the *al-aqlam al-sittah*. Also known as *nesih* in Turkish. See **al-aqlam al-sittah**.

nasta'liq In Islamic calligraphy, a script known for its rounded and sweeping curves. Favoured for copying poetry and literary epics, it was developed by the Persians in the 15th century.

navagraha (nine planets) In Hinduism, planetary deities including the sun and the moon. In a north Indian temple, images of the deities are usually carved on the frame of a sanctum door. In south India, the *navagraha* are placed on a platform in nearly every temple and worshipped daily to avert planetary misfortunes.

Ottoman Turkish dynasty that ruled Anatolia and much of the Mediterranean from 1281 to 1922. One of the longest lasting Islamic empires, its main capitals were Bursa from 1326, Edirne from 1366 and Istanbul from 1453.

overglaze blue enamel In Chinese ceramics, a low-fired lead-based blue used in limited amounts during Jiajing's reign and later revived during the 17th century in Jingdezhen.

oxidising atmosphere In Chinese ceramics, a kiln atmosphere rich in oxygen; a clean atmosphere tends to produce warm glaze colours.

padmasana (lotus posture) In Hindu-Buddhist tradition, the posture of sitting cross-legged in meditation. It is practised by yogis; Buddha in meditation is also depicted in this posture.

palmette A heart-shaped stylised floral motif.

panakawan A group of servant clowns—Semar, Petruk, Gareng and Bagong—thought to have been indigenous Javanese deities whose identities were adapted during the Hindu-Buddhist period.

panchayatana In Hindu tradition, this refers to the concept of five deities: Shiva (God of Creation and Dissolution), Vishnu (God of Preservation), Durga (Mother Goddess), Surya (Sun God) and Ganesha (Remover of Obstacles and God of Good Luck). They are placed in a temple complex. In general, Shiva, Vishnu and Durga are considered the central gods while the rest are subsidiary.

Panguni Uttiram A festival in honour of Murugan, it falls on the day of the Uttiram star in the month of Panguni (March–April) according to the Tamil calendar. The festival is celebrated as Murugan's wedding festival in south India, Singapore and Malaysia.

Panji stories A cycle of stories in which Prince Panji is the idealised hero. Created in east Java during the Majapahit dynasty, the stories had spread to Bali and other regions of Southeast Asia by the end of the 14th century.

patachitra A cloth-painting tradition prevalent in India.

patola An Indian double-*ikat* textile in which the warp and weft threads are resist-dyed prior to being woven together. See ***ikat***, **warp** and **weft**.

pin peat A Khmer musical ensemble comprising up to 20 musicians who play gongs and metallophones and accompany court dances; similar to other percussive ensembles such as the *gamelan*.

prada A term widely used in Southeast Asia to refer to gold leaf gluework—the application of gold leaf or gold dust to a cloth surface. Also known as *telepok*.

prajnaparamita In Buddhism, a term used to mean Perfect or Transcendental Wisdom, the most important mental power. It is personified as the Goddess of Wisdom, a manifestation of Avalokiteshvara or Guanyin. In Tantric Buddhism, it is the female counterpart of Avalokiteshvara. One of the most popular sacred Buddhist scriptures in China is the *Prajnaparamita Sutra*. See **Guanyin**.

Press-moulding In Chinese ceramics, a technique where clay is pressed into moulds and then luted together to form a ceramic piece with a hollow internal cavity; mostly used on *blanc de Chine* figurines. See ***blanc de Chine*** and **luting**.

puja In Hinduism, ritual worship performed in the temple by the priest or by a devotee at home, to venerate the deity through singing or chanting and offerings of flowers, fruit, lamps and incense.

pusaka A sacred heirloom associated with the spirits of ancestors. They are passed from generation to generation and are believed to contain great magical and spiritual power in the Malay world.

Pushti Marga In Hinduism, a sect of Vaishnavism started by Vallabhacharya in the 15th century. It became popular in Gujarat and Rajasthan. Followers of this sect address Krishna as Shrinathji or Thakorji.

Qajars Dynasty of shahs of Iran ruling from 1779 to 1925; from 1786, its main capital was Tehran. See **shah**.

qiblah The direction towards the Ka'bah in Mecca, it is faced by Muslims during prayers. See **Ka'bah**.

qingbai In Chinese ceramics, literally 'bluish-white' wares; this icy blue glaze was developed at kilns in Zhejiang province in China around the 10th century. *Qingbai* wares were exported in large quantities to Southeast Asia. Also known as *yingqing* or 'shadow-blue' wares.

Qur'an In Islam, the final message from God to mankind. It was revealed in Arabic to Prophet Muhammad in the 7th century. Derived from the Arabic verb, *qara'a*, which means 'to read' or 'to recite'. See also *ayah* and *surah*.

rakshasa A generic Sanskrit term referring to demons. See also *danava*.

Ramayana Believed to be the oldest Sanskrit poem written by the sage Valmiki, the earliest version dates to 1500–1000 BCE. It was transmitted to and adapted in many parts of Asia. The *Ramayana* arrived in Java as part of the Hindu oral tradition together with the *Mahabharata*. See **Mahabharata**.

Reamker The Khmer version of the *Ramayana* and one of the earliest Khmer literary works composed during the 16th or 17th century. See **Ramayana**.

reducing atmosphere In Chinese ceramics, a kiln atmosphere without oxygen; a dark and smoky atmosphere produces cool glaze colours.

repoussé A process in which decorative protrusions are created in sheet metal by beating, stretching and pushing using punches and a hammer from the rear of the metal sheet.

rishi (sage) In Hindu tradition, a holy man or mendicant.

rishipatni (wife of a seer) In Hindu tradition, the wife of a holy man.

rumah gadang The traditional matrilineal clan house of the Minangkabau people of Indonesia.

ruyi Literally 'having everything you wish for'; this form resembles a cloud or leaf and is often used as a decorative motif in Chinese art such as textiles and ceramics. It can be seen on the head of the *ruyi* sceptre, a ceremonial object which was also presented as a birthday gift in China.

Sadakopan In Hinduism, an *alvar* or Vaishnava saint whose devotion so touched Sri Ranganathaswami, chief deity of the famous Vishnu temple at Sri Rangam, that the latter named him Nammalwar, which means 'my devotee'.

Safavids Dynasty of shahs which ruled Iran from 1501 to 1732; its main capitals were Tabriz, Qazvin in 1548 and Isfahan from 1598 onwards. The Safavids adopted Shi'ism as a state religion. See **shah** and **Shi'as**.

saggar In Chinese ceramics, an earthenware or stoneware box used to keep ceramic pieces clean during firing and to enable a more even temperature; it also allows the pieces to be stacked.

salat In Islam, the five daily obligatory prayers; they are to be performed before sunrise (*subuh*), at midday (*zuhur*), mid-afternoon (*asar*), sunset (*maghrib*) and in early evening (*isyak*). One of the five pillars of Islam. See **five pillars of Islam**.

samadhi A Sanskrit term referring to the state of meditative concentration.

Samanids Dynasty ruling Transoxiana and parts of Iran and Afghanistan from 819 to 999; its main capital was Bukhara.

Glossary

sangha A Sanskrit term referring to a community of Buddhist monks or a monastery.

sarpech A head ornament worn by kings and noblemen, it was made popular during the Mughal period.

seal script (*zhuanshu*) In Chinese calligraphy, the earliest form used during the Zhou and Qin dynasties. It was used mainly for seals and other inscriptions but was revived as a medium during the 18th century.

Senai Mudaliar In Hinduism, the Chief of Hosts of Vishnu; the Hosts are liberated souls or devotees of Vishnu. The *alvar* saint Nammalvar is considered an *avatara* (incarnation) of Senai Mudaliar.

shah The ancient Persian title for a king.

shahadah In Islam, the profession of faith which states that 'There is no God but Allah and Muhammad is the Messenger of God.' One of the five pillars of Islam. See **five pillars of Islam**.

Shakyamuni In Mahayana Buddhism, an Indian prince who renounced worldly life and embarked on a religious journey. He gained enlightenment and spread his teachings, most notably the concepts of rebirth and *karma*, and the four noble truths, to the lay people. Also known as Gautama Buddha.

Sheshashayi Vishnu In Hinduism, the form of Vishnu which depicts him reclining on the *sheshanaga* (coiled serpent) and floating in the ocean. According to Vishnu *Purana* text, Vishnu began the creation of the universe when a lotus stalk appeared from his navel with Brahma on it.

Shi'as In Islam, Muslims who belong to *Shi'at 'Ali* (Party of 'Ali); also known as Shi'ites. They believe that leadership of the Muslim community after the death of the Prophet Muhammad rightfully belongs to 'Ali, the Prophet's son-in-law, and his descendants. Their difference with the Sunnis is basically political. See **Sunnis**.

shiraspata The halo behind the head of a deity in Hindu-Buddhist artistic traditions.

Shivaratri A festival in honour of Shiva, it is celebrated during the Spring season in March in India.

Shiwan In Chinese ceramics, these are kilns located southwest of Foshan near Guangzhou in Guangdong province. They have been in operation since the Tang dynasty and are renowned for their production of thickly glazed wares, which include popular and religious figurines and models and roof tiles.

Shravan The tenth month according to the Indian calendar; it occurs during the rainy season.

shukanasa In Hindu architecture, a term referring to the semicircular structure surmounting the entrance doorway of a north Indian Hindu temple; it identifies the temple's main deity.

shwei-zawa In Burmese lacquer, the production of lacquerware embellished with gold leaf designs.

singa Derived from the Sanskrit word for lion. In Southeast Asia, the *singa* is a mythical creature of the Bataks and has the features of the water buffalo, horse and *naga*. It is associated with fertility, abundance and protection. See **naga**.

Sino-Tibetan One of the three main language families in mainland Southeast Asia, together with Austroasiatic and Tai-Kadai language families. It includes the Chinese and Tibeto-Burman sub-groups of languages.

Skanda Shashti A festival celebrating the birthday of Skanda (also known as Murugan in Tamil Nadu). According to the Tamil calendar, it falls on the sixth day after Deepavali in October/November.

slip A diluted clay mixture applied to a ceramic ware so as to smoothen its surface and disguise the colour of its body. The lighter-coloured slip coating enhances the colour of the glazes which are later applied on top. Chocolate-coloured slip was used particularly by Vietnamese potters as a finish for the base of the vessel. Also used for luting. See **luting**.

slip-casting In Chinese ceramics, a technique in which liquid clay slip is poured into a plaster piece mould, taking the shape of the mould when all the water is absorbed. The parts are then luted before firing. See **luting** and **slip**.

smashana The burning grounds where Hindus cremate their dead.

songket A decorative weaving technique in which extra ornamental weft threads are woven into a textile between two regular wefts to create patterns additional to the ground weave. It usually denotes metallic threads as the major supplementary weft element. See **weft**.

stoneware A pale buff-coloured clay capable of being fired to 1,250 degrees Celsius. It is less porous than earthenware but not as translucent and durable as porcelain.

stupa The mound-like structure in which Buddha Shakyamuni asked to be interred after he expired. Widely accepted by Buddhists as the symbol of Buddha's enlightenment, it is the form from which such architectural types as the pagoda developed. See *chedi* and *Shakyamuni*.

suasa An ornamental alloy of gold and copper.

Sufism A mystical tradition of Islam; a Sufi is a mystic with a personal approach to religion.

sultan An Islamic title adopted from the 10th century by independent rulers no longer under the control of the caliphs. It was adopted by the Ottoman rulers and was officially recognised in the 11th century when it was adopted by the Turkish Seljuk dynasty. See **caliph** and **Ottoman**.

Sultanate A term denoting Muslim Turkish rule of northern India from 1206 to 1526. There were five dynasties—the 'Slave', Khalji, Tugluq, Sayyid and Lodi.

Sunnis In Islam, Muslims who accept the historic succession of caliphs after Prophet Muhammad's death. This is in contrast to the Shi'as who believe that 'Ali should have rightly succeeded Prophet Muhammad. See **four Orthodox caliphs** and **Shi'as**.

surah (chapter) The Qur'an is divided into 114 *surah*, generally arranged according to length. See **Qur'an**.

svayamvara In Hindu tradition, a wedding procedure where a woman chooses her own life partner; this has been in practice since ancient times in India.

swastika sthana (posture of good fortune) A standing posture in which one leg crosses over the other. Generally, Krishna playing the flute is depicted striking this pose. Also used in classical Bharatanatyam dance in India.

Swatow wares In Chinese ceramics, these are wares mostly decorated in underglaze blue, or red, black and turquoise enamels; these rough ceramics were produced around the 16th and 17th centuries and mostly exported from the port at Swatow (Shantou), Guangzhou province, to Southeast Asia and Japan. Also known as Zhangzhou wares as recent excavations in Zhangzhou kilns have revealed a huge quantity of these wares.

tabby weave A basic form of weaving where sets of warp (vertical yarns set on the loom), usually in twos or threes, float over sets of weft (horizontally running yarns being woven into the warps), to form diagonal patterns such as diamonds and herringbone. Also called twill. See **warp** and **weft**.

tangka An image or icon to aid concentration during meditation; this includes paintings, in various sizes, of deities or spiritual guiding figures in the Tibetan Buddhist tradition.

thape These refer to marks made with the palms on the walls of a house in rural and urban India on festive occasions such as weddings. It is still practised among the Hindus.

Theravada Doctrine of the Elders (*thera*); an early school of Buddhists who followed Buddha's teachings more closely than later schools. It is the institutional religion of Sri Lanka and mainland Southeast Asia except for northern Vietnam and is also the only surviving Hinayana school of Buddhism. See **Hinayana** and **Mahayana**.

thikana A principality; a colloquial term used in Rajasthan, western India to refer to a small kingdom.

Three Friends of Winter (*suihan sanyou*) In Chinese symbolism, pine represents longevity, prunus perseverance and bamboo flexibility. These plants either bloom in early spring or remain evergreen in winter, thus they also symbolise immutability and strength. This theme first emerged in Song poetry and later in paintings and ceramics.

thulth In Islamic calligraphy, a cursive script with deep downward sweeping strokes; it is favoured for monumental inscriptions. One of the *al-aqlam al-sittah*. Also known as *sls* in Turkish. See **al-aqlam al-sittah**.

tianbai In Chinese ceramics, literally 'sweet white', a pure white glaze with a sugary look mainly made up of porcelain stone with little or almost no glaze ash. It was produced during the early 15th century.

Timurid Dynasty which ruled Iran and central Asia from 1370 to 1501; its main capitals were Samarqand and Herat from 1450. It was established by descendants of the great conqueror Timur.

Tirthankara (holy teacher) A title referring to the 24 holy men of Jainism who, like Buddhist bodhisattvas, attained enlightenment and perfection in their mortal lives. Tirthankaras help ford the gulf between the mortal world and the world of perfection by guiding the laity. Mahavir, who was the last in the line, was also the most important. All 24 Tirthankaras were later deified.

topeng A mask worn in *wayang topeng* or masked dance. The classical Javanese masked dance repertoire is usually based on the Hindu epics as well as the stories of Prince Panji. See **Panji stories**.

Transitional period In Chinese ceramics, the 64-year period after Wanli's death in 1619, before the appointment of Cang Yingxuan as Superintendent of the imperial kilns in 1683.

tribhanga (three bends) A graceful bending of the waist in Hindu-Buddhist iconography.

Triratna Literally 'Three Jewels', it refers to the concept of Buddha, Dharma (his teachings) and Sangha (the assembly of monks), which Buddhists invoke in their prayers. See **dharma**.

tritik A resist-dye process in which the cloth is stitched, gathered and tucked tightly before dyestuffs are applied so that the dye cannot penetrate the reserved areas. Also known as stitch-resist dyeing.

Tughluqs Turkish dynasty that was established by Ghiyas-ud din Tughluq Shah and ruled north India and the Deccan from 1320 to 1414; its main capitals were Dehli and Daulatabad. It was one of the Islamic dynasties that ruled India from 1210 to 1526, known collectively as the Sultanate of Delhi.

umrah In Islam, a pilgrimage to Mecca which can be performed anytime other than the period of the *haj*; it is not as meritorious an act as performing the *haj*. Also known as the 'lesser pilgrimage'. See **haj**.

upavita In Hinduism, a Sanskrit term referring to the sacred cord which passes over the left shoulder and around the right waist of a deity. It symbolises spiritual rebirth and is another term for *yagnopavita*. See **yagnopavita**.

ushnisha (protuberance) In Buddhism, this symbolises enlightenment and is found on the head of Buddha.

utsavara (mobile image) In Hinduism, the processional image of a deity in south Indian temples. On festive occasions, the *utsavara* is specially decorated with flowers, garments and jewellery.

vahana (mount) In Hinduism, this refers to the vehicle of the gods.

vajra According to Hinduism, it is a symbolic thunderbolt and an attribute of the Vedic deity Indra. In Buddhism, it is an attribute of Vajrapani Avalokiteshvara. In Tibetan Buddhism, it refers to a sceptre used by a priest during rituals, representing wisdom which destroys passion.

vitarka mudra (gesture of argumentation) In Hinduism and Buddhism, a hand gesture in which the right hand is raised with the forefinger and thumb forming a circle.

vocalisation marks In the Arabic script, these are marks used to indicate parts of speech, such as short vowels, that are not represented by letters. Known as *tashkil* in Arabic.

Vraja An area around Mathura and Vrindavan in north India famous for the spread of the Krishna cult.

vyala In Hinduism, a composite rampant animal of great strength; it has a lion face and is represented in Hindu temples in north India.

warp Parallel threads that run longitudinally on the loom or cloth.

wayang purwa The oldest cycle of stories including pre-Hindu stories and those related to the Hindu epics such as the *Ramayana* and *Mahabharata*, found in the performing arts traditions of Malaysia and Indonesia.

weft Traverse threads in a fabric that cross and interlace with the warp elements. See **warp**.

whiteware Ceramic wares with white glaze decoration with a glaze recipe based on wood-ash; the naturally occurring iron oxide in the ash results in a warm ivory-white tone. Increasing the iron oxide content produces darker colours. Thus a wide spectrum of colours—ranging from ivory to green (also known as celadon) and brown—is obtainable from wood-ash glazes. See **celadon**.

Xing wares In Chinese ceramics, white stoneware produced around the 7th century in the Neiqiu and Lincheng counties in Hebei province.

yagnopavita In Hinduism, a sacred thread made of cotton; it is worn from the left shoulder across the chest by brahmins and priests. See **upavita**.

yaksha (male vegetation spirits) According to ancient Buddhist, Jain and Hindu traditions, these are nature spirits who are worshipped for their guardianship and for bestowing luck.

yakshi (female vegetation spirits) Like the *yaksha*, these are also nature spirits, images of which are usually placed on pillars and doorways of Buddhist monuments. They suggest fertility and abundance.

yaobian (transmutation glaze) In Chinese ceramics, a change in colour that takes place in the kiln as a result of chemical reactions during the firing process, leading to unexpected effects on a ceramic piece.

Yixing Located on the shore of Taihu (Lake Tai) in Jiangsu province, Yixing is known for the purple clay excavated there and is most well-known for the numerous teapot forms produced from the Ming dynasty until today.

Yoganidra In Hinduism, the goddess who emerged from the eyes of Vishnu when he awoke from cosmic slumber.

yoni In Hinduism, the symbol for the female principle; it is generally worshipped in conjunction with the *lingam*, a phallic symbol referring to the male principle. See **lingam**.

yuga According to the Hindu calendar, an age of the world. There are four yugas, each spanning 1,728,000 years.

Zhang Daoling In Chinese religion, the founder of the Wudoumi Dao (Five Bushels of Rice Movement) which later developed into the first Daoist sect, the Celestial Masters school. Zhang lived during the Han Dynasty and was said to have received religious mandate from Laozi himself.

Zhangzhou wares See **Swatow wares**.

anhua	暗花	Dayunsi (Temple of the Great Clouds)	大云寺
Anhui	安徽	Dehua	德化
Ba Ji Xiang (Eight Buddhist Emblems)	八吉祥	di (Emperor)	帝
Ba ye (Eighth Lord)	八爷	ding (food vessel)	鼎
Bao'ensi (Bao'en Temple)	报恩寺	Ding yao (Ding wares)	定窑
Baxian (Eight Immortals)	八仙	Dingling	定陵
bayan jueju (eight-character quartet)	八言绝句	Dizang Pusa Benyuan Jing (Original Vow	地藏菩萨
biantong (argumentative skills)	辩通	of the Bodhisattva Kshitigarbha Sutra)	本愿经
bingyin	丙寅	Dizang wang	地藏王
Bo Gu	博古	Dong Qichang	董其昌
bodi yangwen (shallow relief carving)	薄地阳文	Dong Yingke	董应科
buzi (badge)	补子	doucai (fitted colours)	斗彩
Cai Zhao	蔡照	Duan	段
Caishen (God of Wealth)	财神	dunwu chengfo (enlightenment)	顿悟成佛
Cang Yingxuan	藏应选	Duobao fo	多宝佛
Cao Guojiu	曹国舅	Erlitou	二里头
Cao Sugong	曹素功	Ershui	二水
Cao Zhao	曹昭	fahua	法花
Chang'an	长安	Famensi (Famen Monastery)	法门寺
Chen Hongshou	陈洪绶	Fan Jiangjun (General Fan)	范将军
Chen Hu (Lake Chen)	陈湖	fangyi (vessel)	方彝
Chen Sheng	陈升	fanlian (Indian lotuses)	蕃莲
Cheng Huang (City God)	城隍	fenbo	分箔
Cheng Junfang	程君房	fencai (famille rose)	粉彩
Chenghua	成化	Fengshen yanyi (Investiture of the Gods)	封神演义
chengxin (integrity)	诚信	fengshui (geomancy)	风水
Chengziya	城子崖	Foshan (Fo mountain)	佛山
chilong (chi dragon)	螭龙	fou (vessel)	缶
Cixi	慈喜	Fu Xi	伏義
Cizhou	磁州	Fufeng	扶风
Da Ming Chenghua Nianzhi	大明成化	Fujian	福建
(Made during the Ming dynasty,	年制	Gansu	甘肃
Chenghua's reign)		Gao Lian	高濂
Dabao Fawang (Great Precious	大宝法王	Ge Gu Yao Lun (The Essential Criteria	格古要论
Dharma King)		for Chinese Antiquities)	
Dadu	大都	Gengzhi tu (Illustrations on Agriculture	耕织图
Daode Tianzun (Celestial Worthy of	道德天尊	and Sericulture)	
the Way and its Power)		gu	觚
Daweide mingwang	大威德明王	Gu Lienüzhuan (The Ancient	古列女传
Dawenkou	大汶口	Biographies of Exemplary Women)	

Guan Sanlang	关三郎	jinzhong	浸种
Guan Yan	关严	Jiuhua shan (Jiuhua mountain)	九华山
Guan Yunchang	关云长	kaishu (regular script)	楷书
guangai (irrigation)	灌溉	Kangxi	康熙
Guangdong	广东	kesi (tapestry textile)	缂丝
Guangong	关公	kuilong (kui dragon)	夔龙
Guangxi	广西	Kunlun shan (Kunlun mountains)	昆仑山
Guangxu	光绪	Lan Caihe	蓝采和
Guanyin Pusa	观音菩萨	Laozi	老子
Guanyu	关羽	lei (vessel)	垒
gui (food vessel)	簋	Leng Mei	冷梅
Guo Ju	郭巨	Li Bai	李白
Guo Yu (Sayings of the State)	国语	Li Tieguai (Iron Crutch Li)	李铁拐
Han Xiangzi	韩湘子	Liao	辽
Han Zhongli	汉锺离	Liaoning shen	辽宁省
Hangzhou	杭州	Lienüzhuan (Biographies of Exemplary Women)	列女传
He Chaozong	何朝宗		
He Xiangu	何仙姑	liexian jiupai (Immortal Drinking Cards)	列仙酒牌
Hebei	河北	Lin Guangyi (Lin Kuang-I)	林泷沂
Heibai Wuchang (Black and White Faces of Impermanence)	黑白无常	Lincheng	临城
		Lingbao Tianzun (Celestial Worthy of Numinous Treasure)	灵宝天尊
Henan	河南		
Hongwu	洪武	Liu Haichan	刘海蟾
hu (drinking vessel)	壶	Liu Xiang	刘向
huanghuali	黄花梨	Liu Xiaoyun	刘筱云
huangyang mu (boxwood)	黄杨木	Liu Yong	刘墉
Huizhou	徽州	liuli	琉璃
ji (small table)	几	Long Nü	龙女
jia	斝	longjiuzi (nine dragon sons)	龙九子
Jia Qilüe	贾奇略	Longquan	龙泉
Jiading	嘉定	Longshan	龙山
jian (bronze basin)	鑑	longyan mu (Longyan wood)	龙眼木
jiang guo hong (peach bloom glaze)	豇果红	Lü Dongbin	吕洞冰
Jiangnan	江南	Lu Zhen	鲁珍
Jiangsu	江苏	Luo Guanzhong	罗贯中
Jiao Bingzhen	焦秉贞	luohan (great adepts)	罗汉
Jiaozhi tao (Jiaozhi ceramic)	交趾陶	Ma Chengyuan	马承源
Jiechuan	解川	mang kou (coarse rim)	芒口
jieyi (purity and righteousness)	洁义	mantou yao (mantou kiln)	馒头窑
Jingdezhen	景德镇	meiping (vase)	梅瓶

Mi Wanzhong	米万钟	Sanqing (Three Pure Ones)	三清
Miaofa Lianhua Jing (Lotus Sutra)	妙法莲华经	Shaanxi	陕西
Miaoshan Gongzhu	妙善公主	Shancai Tongzi	善才童子
(Princess Miaoshan)		Shandong	山东
Ming wucai (Ming five-coloured wares)	明五彩	Shantou (Swatow)	汕头
mingqi (burial objects)	明器	Shanxi	山西
minyao (folk ceramic)	民窑	Shaoxing	绍兴
Mulan	木兰	She	歙
muyi (maternal rectitude)	母仪	Shexian	歙县
Nanji laoren (God of the South Pole)	南极老人	Shi Chang	世昌
Neiqiu	内丘	Shijiamoni fo (Shakyamuni)	释迦摩尼佛
Niutou Mamian (Cow- and Horse-Face	牛头马面	Shiwan	石湾
Generals)		shou (longevity)	寿
panchi	蟠螭	Shuihu zhuan	水浒传
panlong	盘龙	Sichuan	四川
Putuo	普陀	Song Shi (Song Annals)	宋史
Qi ye (Seventh Lord)	七爷	Song Zhiwen	宋之问
Qian Hui'an	钱慧安	Songhua shi (Songhua inkstone)	松花石
qiankun xiang (portraits of Heaven	乾坤像	suanzhi (blackwood)	酸枝
and Earth)		suihan sanyou (Three Friends of Winter)	岁寒三友
Qianlong	乾隆	ta (day bed)	榻
Qie Lanshen	伽蓝神	Tai Yin	太阴
qilin (dragon)	麒麟	Taihu (Lake Tai)	太湖
qin (zither)	琴	Tang sancai (Tang dynasty	唐三彩
qingbai	青白	tri-coloured wares)	
qingtan (discourse)	清谈	tianbai (sweet white)	甜白
Qisha	碛沙	Tianqi	天启
Qiuying	仇英	tianwang (heavenly king)	天王
qiyi (extraordinary)	奇逸	Tongchuan	铜川
Quanzhou	泉州	Tongzhi	同治
Quyang	曲阳	wan (ten thousand)	万
Ren Bonian	任伯年	wandai jixiang (eternal prosperity)	万代吉祥
Ren Xiong	任熊	Wang Jinsheng	汪近圣
Ren Xun	任熏	Wang Shaoping	王少平
Ren Yi	任颐	Wang Wei	王维
Ren Yu	任预	Wang Xizhi	王羲之
renzhi (benevolence and wisdom)	仁智	Wang Xuiceng	王学曾
ruyi	如意	wangxiu (needleloop embroidery)	网绣
Sanguo Yanyi (Romance of the Three	三国演义	Wanli	万历
Kingdoms)		wanshou wujiang (boundless longevity)	万寿无疆

Wei Tuo	韦陀	yin	阴
Wei Zhongxian	魏忠贤	yingqing (bluish-green)	影青
Wen	文	Yisu	艺粟
Wen Nongheng	文农亨	Yixing	宜兴
Wen Zhengming	文征明	Yongle Nianzhi (Made during	永乐年制
Wen Zhenheng	文震亨	Yongle's reign)	
Wenchang (God of Literature)	文昌	Yongzheng	雍正
Weng Tonghe	翁同龢	Yu Huang (Jade Emperor)	玉皇
Wu Shuda	吴叔大	Yuan Shi (Yuan History)	元史
Wu Zhifan	吴之璠	Yuanshi Tianzun (Celestial Worthy of	元始天尊
Wufang ling (Five-Directions Spirit)	五方灵	Primordial Beginnings)	
Wuliangshou	无量寿	Yue yao (Yue wares)	越窑
Wuxian	吴县	Yungang	云岗
xiangzhu (spotted bamboo)	湘竹	Zhang Daoling	张道凌
xianming (sagacity)	贤明	Zhang Gongming	赵公明
xiao (filial piety)	孝	Zhang Guolao	张国老
Xiaoduan	孝端	Zhang Ruitu	张瑞图
Xiaojing	孝靖	Zhang Tianshi	张天师
Xiaolou	小楼	Zhang Zhenglong	张正龙
Xie Jiangjun (General Xie)	谢将军	Zhangwuzhi	长物志
Xiling	西陵	Zhangzhou	漳州
Xing Tong	邢侗	Zhao Lang	赵郎
Xing yao (Xing wares)	邢窑	Zhao Yuanshuai (Marshall Zhao)	赵元帅
Xiwangmu (Queen Mother of the West)	西王母	Zhejiang	浙江
Xizong	喜宗	Zheng Guanniang	郑观娘
Xuanhe	宣和	Zhenghe	政和
Xuansu	玄粟	zhenmushou (earth spirit)	镇墓兽
xuantan	玄坛	zhenshun (chastity and obedience)	贞顺
Xuanzong	玄宗	zhu sansong (Three Pines in Bamboo	朱三松
Xugu	虚谷	Carving)	
ya dan (refined and simple)	雅淡	Zhu Songlin	朱松邻
Yan Luo (Yan Lo)	阎罗	Zhu Xiaosong	朱小松
yang	阳	zhuanshu (seal script)	篆书
Yanshengyuan (Yansheng Monastery)	延圣院	zhuoji (ramie-splicing process)	捉绩
yaobian (transmutation glaze)	窑变	Zhushan	珠山
Yaozhou	耀州	zitan	紫檀
Ye Wang	叶王	zu (vessel)	尊
yijing weiyong, shiyi yongnian	以静为用,	Zuo Zhuan (Zuo's Tradition)	左传
(quiet is the quality leading to	是以永年		
strength and eternal)			

Bibliography

CHINA

Beurdeley, Michel & Raindre, Guy, *Qing Porcelain: Famille Verte, Famille Rose*, London: Thames & Hudson Ltd, 1987.

Cahill, James, *The Distant Mountains: Chinese Painting of the Late Ming Dynasty, 1570–1644*, New York: John Weatherhill Inc., 1982.

Caroselli, Susan L. (ed.), *The Quest for Eternity: Chinese Ceramic Sculptures from the People's Republic of China*, Los Angeles: Los Angeles County Museum of Art and Chronicle Books, 1987.

Carswell, John, *Blue and White Chinese Porcelain and Its Impact on the Western World*, Chicago: David and Alfred Smart Gallery, 1985.

Carswell, John, *Blue and White Chinese Porcelain Around the World*, London: British Museum Press, 2000.

Ch'en, Kenneth, *Buddhism in China, A Historical Survey*, New Jersey: Princeton University Press, 1964.

Chang Kwang-chih, *The Archaeology of Ancient China*, London and New Haven: Yale University Press, 1986.

De Meyer, Jan A. M. & Engelfriet, Peter M. (ed.), *Linked Faiths: Essays on Chinese religions and traditional culture in honor of Kristofer Schipper*, Leiden: Brill, 2000.

Fédéric, Louis, *Flammarion Iconographic Guides: Buddhism*, Paris: Flammarion. 1995.

Feuchtwang, Stephen, *Popular Religion in China: The Imperial Metaphor*, Surrey: Curzon Press, 2001.

Fung, Yu-lan, *A Short History of Chinese Philosophy*, New York: Macmillan, 1948.

Gao Lian, *Zunsheng baqian*, a 17th-century text.

Ge Wanzhang, 'You Ya Wenhan luohan lianzuo kan zangchuan fojiao yishu zai Qinggong de fazhan', *The National Palace Museum Monthly of Chinese Art*, no. 130, Taipei National Palace Museum, January 1994.

Graham, A. C., *Disputers of the Tao*, Illinois: Open Court Publishing, 1989.

Graham, A. C., *Yin-Yang and the Nature of Correlative Thinking*, Singapore: Institute of East Asian Philosophies, 1986.

Harrist, Robert E. & Fong, Wen C., *The Embodied Image: Chinese Calligraphy from the John B. Elliott Collection*, Princeton, New Jersey: Princeton University Press, 1999.

Hong Kong Museum of Art, *Heavens' Embroidered Cloths, One Thousand Years of Chinese Textiles*, Hong Kong: Hong Kong Museum of Art, 1995.

The Jingdezhen Institute of Ceramic Archaeology and The Tsui Museum of Art, *A Legacy of Chenghua: Imperial Porcelain of the Chenghua Reign Excavated from Zhushan, Jingdezhen*, Jingdezhen: The Jingdezhen Institute of Ceramic Archaeology, and Hong Kong: Tsui Museum of Art, 1993.

Krahl, Regina (ed.), *The Emperor's Broken China: Reconstructing Chenghua Porcelain*, London: Sotheby's, 1995.

Kuhn, Dieter, *Science and Civilisation in China*, vol. 5, *Chemistry and Chemical Technology*, part IX, *Textile Technology: Spinning and Reeling*, Cambridge: Cambridge University Press, 1986.

Lang Shaojun, 'Traditional Chinese Painting in the Twentieth Century', *Three Thousand Years of Chinese Painting*, Hong Kong: Yale University and Foreign Language Press, 1997.

Lau, Aileen (ed.), *Spirit of Han*, Singapore: Sun Tree Publishing Ltd, 1991.

Little, Stephen & Eichman, Shawn, *Taoism and the Arts of China*, Chicago: Art Institute of Chicago, 2000.

Li Zhaoru, 'Leishi yuxiang: Beijing gugong boyuan cangzhenpin Qingmo', *The National Palace Museum Monthly of Chinese Art*, no. 116, Taipei National Palace Museum, November 1992.

Lo Kai-yin (ed.), *Bright As Silver White As Snow: Chinese Ceramics from Late Tang to Yuan Dynasty*, Hong Kong: Yungmingtang, 1998.

Loewe, Michael & Shaughnessy, Edward L. (eds.), *The Cambridge History of Ancient China: From the Origins of Civilization to 221 BC*, Cambridge: Cambridge University Press, 1999.

Lu Yaw (ed.), *Song Ceramics*, Singapore: Southeast Asian Ceramic Society, 1983.

Ma Chengyuan, *Ancient Chinese Bronzes*, New York: Oxford University Press, 1986.

Ma Guojun & Ma Shuyun, *Zhongguo jiuling daguan*, Beijing: Biejing chubanshe, 1993.

Maspero, Henri, *Taoism and Chinese Religion*, Amherst: The University of Massachusetts Press, 1981.

Medley, Margaret, *Chinese Paintings and the Decorative Style*, London: Percival David Foundation, 1976.

Medley, Margaret, *The Chinese Potter*, London: Phaidon Press Ltd, 1999.

Mino, Yutaka & Tsiang, Katherine R., *Ice and Green Clouds Traditions of Chinese Celadon*, Indiana: Indianapolis Museum of Art, 1986.

Mou, Sherry J. (ed.), *Presence and Presentation. Women in the Chinese Literati Tradition*, New York: St. Martin's Press, 1999.

National Museum of History, *The Splendour of Buddhist Statuaries: Buddhist Stone Carvings in the Northern Dynasties*, Taipei: National Museum of History, 1997.

National Palace Museum, *Catalogue of a Special Exhibition of Illustrations of the Lotus Sutra*, Taipei: National Palace Museum, 1995.

The Oriental Ceramic Society of Hong Kong, *Jingdezhen Wares: The Yuan Evolution*, Hong Kong: The Oriental Ceramic Society of Hong Kong, 1984.

Peterson, Babara Bennett (ed.), *Notable Women of China: Shang dynasty to the early twentieth century*, New York: East Gate, 2000.

Raphals, Lisa, *Sharing the Light: Representations of Women and Virtue in Early China*, Albany, New York: State University of New York Press, 1998.

Rhie, Marilyn M. & Thurman, Robert A. F., *Wisdom and Compassion: The Sacred Art of Tibet* (expanded edition), London: Thames & Hudson Ltd, 1996.

Sang Xingzhi et al., *Shuo mo*, Shanghai: Shanghai keji jiaoyu chubanshe, 1994.

Scott, Rosemary E. (ed.), *The Porcelains of Jingdezhen*, Colloquies on Art and Archaeology in Asia, no. 16, London: Percival David Foundation of Chinese Art, 1993.

Scott, Rosemary E. & Guy, John (ed.), *Southeast Asia and China: Art, Interaction and Commerce*, Colloquies on Art and Archaeology in Asia, no. 17, London: Percival David Foundation of Chinese Art, 1994.

Shahar, Meir & Weller, Robert P. (eds.), *Unruly Gods. Divinity and Society in China*, Honolulu: University of Hawaii Press, 1996.

Shangraw, Clarence F., *Origins of Chinese Ceramics*, New York: China House Gallery, 1978.

Soothill, William Edward, *The Lotus of the Wonderful Law, or The Lotus Gospel: Saddharma Pundarika Sutra Miao-fa Lien Hua Ching*, Richmond, Surrey: Curzon Press, 1987.

Soothill, William Edward & Hodous, Lewis, *A Dictionary of Chinese Buddhist Terms*, Richmond, Surrey: Curzon Press, 1995.

Stuart, Jan & Rawski, Evelyn S., *Worshipping the Ancestors. Chinese Commemorative Portraits*, Washington D.C.: Smithsonian Institution, 2001.

Tan, Rita C. et al., *Chinese and Southeast Asian White Ware Found in the Philippines*, Singapore: Oxford University Press, 1993.

Teiser, Stephen, *The Scripture of the Ten Kings and the Making of Purgatory in Medieval Chinese Buddhism*, Honolulu: University of Hawaii Press, 1994.

Vainker, S. J., *Chinese Pottery and Porcelain from Prehistory to the Present*, London: British Museum Press, 1991.

Valenstein, Suzanne G., *A Handbook of Chinese Ceramics*, New York: Metropolitan Museum of Art, 1975.

Wang Gungwu & Lee Chor Lin et al., *The Chinese Collections: Asian Civilisations Museum*, Singapore: National Heritage Board, 1997.

Wang,Tao, 'A Textual Investigation of the Taotie' in Whitfield, Roderick (ed.), *The Problem of Meaning in Early Chinese Ritual Bronzes*, Colloquies on Art and Archaeology in Asia, no.15, London: Percival David Foundation of Chinese Art, 1990.

Wang Yuhu, *Wang Zhen Nongshu*, Beijing: Nongye chubanshe, 1981.

Watson, William, *Pre-Tang Ceramics of China: Chinese Pottery from 4000 BC to 600 AD*, Boston: Faber and Faber, 1991.

Watt, James C. Y. & Wardwell, Anne E., *When Silk Was Gold*, New York: The Metropolitan Museum of Art, 1997.

Weidner, Marsha (ed.), *Latter Days of the Law: Images of Chinese Buddhism, 850–1850*, Lawrence, Kansas: Spencer Museum of Art, University of Kansas, 1994.

Wen Zhenheng, *Zhangwu zhi (Treatise on superfluous things)*, a 17th-century text, Taipei: Yiwen Press, 1966.

Whitfield, Roderick & Farrer, Anne, *Caves of the Thousand Buddhas: Chinese art from the Silk Route*, London: The British Museum Press, 1990.

Wolf, Arthur P. (ed.), *Religion and Ritual in Chinese Society*, Stanford: Stanford University Press, 1974.

Wood, Nigel, *Chinese Glazes*, London: A. & C. Black (Publishers) Ltd, 1999.

Wu Shan (ed.), *Zhongguo gongyi meishu cidian (Encyclopaedia of the Arts of China)*, Taipei: Hsiung Shih Art Books Co. Ltd, 1991.

Xie Deping & Sun Dunxiu, *Wenfang sibao zongheng tan (The Four Treasures)*, Beijing: Wenjin Press, 1990.

Yang Boda, *Qingdai yuanhua (Imperial Paintings of the Qing Dynasty)*, Beijing: Zijincheng Press, 1993.

Yang Xiaoneng (ed.), *The Golden Age of Chinese Archaeology*, London: Yale University Press, 1999.

Bibliography

Zhao Feng, *Sichou yishushi (A History of Silk Art)*, Hangzhou: Zhejiang meishu xueyuan chubanshe, 1992.
Zhou Xinhui et al., *Zhongguo fojiao banhua (Buddhist Prints of China)*, Hangzhou: Zhejiang wenyi chubanshe, 1996.
Zhu Qiqian, *Sixiu biji (Notes on Silks and Embroideries)*.

SOUTH ASIA

Anand, Mulk Raj (ed.), *Homage to Kalamkari*, Mumbai: Marg Publications, 1979.
Arasaratnam, Sinnappah, *Indians in Malaysia and Singapore*, Kuala Lumpur, New York: Oxford University Press, 1979.
Art Institute of Chicago, *Master Bronzes of India*, Chicago: Art Institute of Chicago, 1965.
Arts Council of Great Britain, *In the Image of Man: The Indian perception of the universe through 2000 years of painting and sculpture*, London: Arts Council of Great Britain/Weidenfeld & Nicolson, 1982.
Banerjee, P., *The Life of Krishna in Indian Art*, New Delhi: National Museum, 1978.
Brand, Michael, *The Vision of Kings*, Canberra: National Gallery of Australia, 1995.
Bussabarger, Robert F. & Robins, Betty D., *The Everyday Art of India*, New York: Dover Publications Inc., 1968.
Chattopadhyay, Kamaladevi, *Handicrafts of India*, New Delhi: Indraprastha Press, 1975.
Crill, Rosemary, *Indian Embroidery*, London: Victoria & Albert Museum, 2000.
Czuma, Stanislaw, *Indian Art from the George P. Bickford Collection*, Cleveland: Cleveland Museum of Art, 1975.
Desai, Vishakha, & Mason, Darielle (eds.), *Gods, Guardians and Lovers: Temple Sculptures from North India AD 700–1200*, New York: Asia Society Galleries, 1993.
Goswamy, K. N. et al., *Krishna, the Divine Lover*, London: Serindia Publicatons, 1982.
Guy, John & Swallow, Deborah (eds.), *Arts of India: 1550–1900*, London: Victoria & Albert Museum, 1990.
Huntington, Susan & Huntington, John, *The Art of Ancient India: Buddhist, Hindu, Jain*, New York: Weatherhill, 1985.
Huntington, Susan & Huntington, John, *Leaves from the Bodhi Tree: The Art of Pala India (8th–12th centuries) and Its International Legacy*, Seattle, London: Dayton Art Institute, 1990.

Irwin, John & Hall, Margaret, *Indian Painted and Printed Fabrics*, vol. I, *Historical Textiles of India at the Calico Museum*, Ahmedabad: Calico Museum of Textiles, 1971.
Jaitly, Jaya, *The Craft Traditions of India*, New Delhi: Lustre Press Pvt. Ltd, 1990.
Kersenboom-Story, Saskia C., *Nityasumangali: Devadasi Tradition in South India*, Delhi: Montilal Banarsidass, 1987.
Kramrisch, Stella, *The Hindu Temple*, Calcutta: University of Calcutta, 1946, reprint New Delhi: Motilal Banarasidass, 1976.
Leidy, Denise Patry, *Treasures of Asian Art: Selections from the Mr and Mrs John D. Rockefeller 3rd Collection*, New York: Asia Society Galleries, 1994.
Lerner, Martin, *The Flame and the Lotus: Indian and Southeast Asian Art from the Kronos Collection*, New York: The Metropolitan Museum of Art, 1984.
Lerner, Martin & Kossak, Steven, *The Lotus Transcendent: Indian and Southeast Asian Art from the Samuel Eilenberg Collection*, New York: The Metropolitan Museum of Art, 1991.
Mani, Vettam, *Puranic Encyclopaedia*, New Delhi: Motilal Banarasidass, 1975.
Michell, George (ed.), *Living Wood: Sculptural Traditions of Southern India*, Mumbai: Marg Publications, 1992.
Michell, George (ed.), *Temple Towns of Tamil Nadu*, Mumbai: Marg Publications, 1993.
Mitra, Debala, *Buddhist Monuments*, Calcutta: Sahitya Samsad, 1971.
Muthiah, S., Meyappan, Meenakshi & Ramaswamy, Visalakshi, *The Chettiar Heritage*, Chennai, 2000.
Nigam, M. L. (ed.), *Decorative Arts of India*, Madras: Kalakshetra Publication, 1987.
Pal, M. K., *Crafts and Craftsmen in Traditional India*, New Delhi: Kanak Publications, 1978.
Pal, Pratapaditya et al., *Dancing to the Flute: Music and Dance in Indian Art*, Sydney: Art Gallery of New South Wales, 1997.
Pal, Pratapaditya, *The Peaceful Liberators, Jain Art from India*, Los Angeles: Los Angeles County Museum of Art, 1994.
Parimoo, Ratan, *Essays on New Art History*, vol. I, *Studies in Indian Sculpture (Regional Genres and Interpretations)*, New Delhi: Book & Books, 2000.
Reynolds, Valrae, *From the Sacred Realm: Treasures of Tibetan Art from the Newark Museum*, London: Laurence King Publishing, 1999.

412

Sandhu, K. S. & Mani, A. (eds.), *Indian Communities in Southeast Asia*, Singapore: Times Academic Press & Institute of Southeast Asian Studies, 1993.

Sastri, H. Krishna, *South Indian Images of Gods and Goddesses*, Ootacamund, 1916.

Singer, Jane Casey & Denwood, Philip, *Tibetan Art: Towards Definition of a Style*, London: Laurence King Publishing, 1997.

Skelton, Robert, *The Indian Heritage: Court Life and Arts under Mughal Rule*, London: Victoria & Albert Museum, 1982.

Snellgrove, David, *Indo-Tibetan Buddhism: Indian Buddhists and Their Tibetan Successors*, London: Serindia Publications, 1987.

Talwar, Kay & Krishna, Kalyan, *Indian Pigment Paintings on Cloth*, vol. III, *Historical Textiles of India at the Calico Museum*, Ahmedabad: Calico Museum of Textiles, 1979.

Untracht, Oppi, *Traditional Jewellery of India*, London: Thames & Hudson Ltd, 1997.

Viswanathan, Lakshmi, *Bharatanatyam: The Tamil Heritage*, Madras: United Printers' Syndicate (P) Ltd, 1991.

Welch, Stuart Cary, *India: Art and Culture, 1300–1900*, New York: The Metropolitan Museum of Art, 1985.

SOUTHEAST ASIA

Abdul Halim Nasir, *Traditional Malay Wood Carving*, Kuala Lumpur: Dewan Bahasa dan Pustaka, 1987.

Ahmad Fathy al-Fatani, *Pengantar Sejarah Patani*, Alor Setar: Pustaka Darussalam, 1994.

Andaya, Barbara Watson, 'From Rum to Tokyo: Riau's Search for Anti-colonial Allies, 1899–1914', *Indonesia*, vol. 24, 1977, pp. 125–156.

Andaya, Barbara Watson & Ishii, Yoneo, 'Religious Developments in Southeast Asia c. 1500–1800', *The Cambridge History of Southeast Asia*, vol. 1, part 2, *From c. 1500 to c. 1800*, Cambridge: Cambridge University Press, 1999.

Barbier, Jean P. & Newton, Douglas (eds.), *Islands and Ancestors: Indigenous Styles of Southeast Asia*, Munich: Prestel, 1988.

Barbier, Jean P. (ed.), *Messages in Stone: Statues and Sculptures from Tribal Indonesia in the Collections of the Barbier-Mueller Museum*, Milan: Skira, 1998.

Bechert, Heinz & Gombrich, Richard (eds.), *The World of Buddhism: Buddhist Monks and Nuns in Society and Culture*, London: Thames & Hudson Ltd, 1984.

Bechert, Heinz et al. (comp.), *Burmese Manuscripts*, Wiesbaden: Steiner, 1979.

Bhattacharya, Kamaleswar, *Millennium of Glory: Sculpture of Angkor and Ancient Cambodia*, edited by Helen Ibbitson Jessup and Thierry Zephir, Washington, D.C.: National Gallery of Art, 1997.

Blurton, Richard & Isaacs, Ralph, *Visions from the Golden Land: Burma and the Art of Lacquer*, Chicago: Art Media Resources, 2000.

Brand, Michael, & Phoeurn, Chuch, *The Age of Angkor: Treasures from the National Museum of Cambodia*, Canberra: Australian National Gallery, 1992.

Brandon, James R., *The Cambridge Guide to Asian Theatre*, Cambridge: Cambridge University Press, 1993.

Brown, Roxana, *The Ceramics of South-East Asia: Their Dating and Identification*, 2nd edition, Singapore: Oxford University Press, 1988.

Brown, Roxana & Sjostrand, Sten Turiang, *A Fourteenth Century Wreck in Southeast Asian Waters*, Pasadena: Pacific, 2000.

Brownrigg, Henry, *Betel Cutters: From the Samuel Eilenberg Collection*, London: Thames & Hudson Ltd, 1992.

Capistrano-Baker, Florina H., *Art of Island South-east Asia: The Fred and Rita Richman Collection in the Metropolitan Museum of Art*, New York: The Metropolitan Museum of Art, 1994.

Chin, Lucas & Mashman, Valerie (eds.), *Sarawak Cultural Legacy: a living tradition*, Kuching: Society Atelier Sarawak, 1991.

Cohen, Erik, *The Commercialized Crafts of Thailand: Hill Tribes and Lowland Villages*, Richmond, Surrey: Curzon Press, 2000.

Conway, Susan, *Thai Textiles*, London: British Museum Press, 1992.

Cooper, Robert (ed.), *The Hmong: A Guide to Traditional Lifestyles*, Singapore: Times Editions, 1998.

Cort, Louise, 'Buried and Treasured in Japan: Another Source for Thai Ceramic History', *Thai Ceramics. The James and Elaine Connell Collection/Asian Art Museum of San Francisco*, Kuala Lumpur: Oxford University Press, 1993.

Bibliography

Daravuth, Ly et al., *Lakhaoun Khaol and Khmer Lacquer Making*, Phnom Penh: Reyum Gallery, 1999.

Djajasoebrata, Alit, *Shadow Theatre in Java: The Puppets, Performance and Repertoire*, Amsterdam: Pepin Press, 1999.

Durand, Maurice, *Imagerie Populaire Vietnamienne*, vol. XLVII, Paris: Ecole Francaise d'Extreme-Orient, 1960.

Feldman, Jerome (ed.), *The Eloquent Dead: Ancestral Sculpture of Indonesia and Southeast Asia*, Los Angeles: UCLA Museum of Cultural History, 1985.

Feldman, Jerome, *Nias Tribal Treasures*, Delft: Volkenkundig Museum Nusantara, 1990.

Fischer, Joseph, *The Folk Art of Java*, Kuala Lumpur: Oxford University Press, 1994.

Fraser-Lu, Sylvia, 'Buddha Images from Burma', *Arts of Asia*, vol. 11, no. 2, January–February 1981, pp. 72–82.

Fraser-Lu, Sylvia, *Burmese Lacquerware*, Bangkok: Orchid Press, 2000.

Freeman, Michael & Jacques, Claude, *Ancient Angkor*, London: Thames & Hudson Ltd, 1999.

Frey, Edward, *The Kris: Mystic Weapon of the Malay World*, Singapore: Oxford University Press, 1988.

Gardner, G. B., *Keris and other Malay Weapons*, Singapore: Progressive Publishing Co., 1936.

Green, Gillian, 'Indic Impetus?: Innovations in Textile Usage in Angkorian Period Cambodia', *Journal of the Economic and Social History of the Orient*, vol. 43, no. 3, 2000.

Guillon, Emmanuel, *Hindu-Buddhist Art of Vietnam. Treasures from Champa*, English translation by Tom White, Trumbull, Conn.: Weatherhill, 2001.

Guy, John, 'The Ceramics of Central Thailand', *Thai Ceramics. The James and Elaine Connell Collection/Asian Art Museum of San Francisco*, Kuala Lumpur: Oxford University Press, 1993.

Guy, John, 'Vietnamese Ceramics and Cultural Identity', *Vietnamese Ceramics: A Separate Tradition*, Chicago: Art Media Resources, 1997.

Guy, John, 'Vietnamese Ceramics in International Trade', *Vietnamese Ceramics: A Separate Tradition*, Chicago: Art Media Resources, 1997.

Guy, John, 'The Kosa Masks of Champa: New Evidence', *Southeast Asian Archaeology*, 1998, pp. 51–60.

Guy, John, *Woven Cargoes: Indian Textiles in the East*, London: Thames & Hudson Ltd, 1998.

Guy, John, 'Vietnamese Ceramics. New Discoveries', *Treasures from the Hoi An Hoard*, Butterfields, 2000.

Ha Thuc Can (ed.), *The Bronze Dong Son Drums*, Saigon: T. C. Ha, 1989.

Hall, Kenneth R., *Maritime Trade and State Development in Early Southeast Asia*, Honolulu: University of Hawaii Press, 1985.

Hasibuan, Jamaludin S., *Batak: Art et Culture/Seni Budaya*, Jakarta: Jayakarta Agung Offset, 1985.

Herbert, Patricia M., *The Life of the Buddha*, London: The British Library, 1993.

Higham, Charles, *The Archaeology of Mainland Southeast Asia*, Cambridge: Cambridge University Press, 1989.

Higham, Charles, *The Bronze Age of Southeast Asia*, Cambridge: Cambridge University Press, 1996.

Ho, Chuimei (ed.), *New Light on Chinese Yue and Longquan Wares: Archaeological Ceramics Found in Eastern and Southern Asia, AD 800–1400*, Hong Kong: Centre of Asian Studies, University of Hong Kong, 1994.

Hue-Tam, Ho Tai, 'Religion in Vietnam: A World of Gods and Spirits', *Vietnam: Essays on History, Culture and Society*, New York: The Asia Society, 1985.

Inpam Selvanayagam, Grace, *Songket: Malaysia's Woven Treasure*, Singapore: Oxford University Press, 1990.

Irvine, David, *Leather Gods and Wooden Heroes: Java's Classical Wayang*, Singapore: Times Editions, 1996.

Jessup, Helen Ibbitson, *Court Arts of Indonesia*, New York: Asia Society Galleries in association with H. M. Abrams, 1990.

Jessup, Helen Ibbitson & Zephir, Thierry (eds.), *Millennium of Glory: Sculpture of Angkor and Ancient Cambodia*, Washington, D.C.: National Gallery of Art, 1997.

Keeler, Ward, *Javanese Shadow Plays, Javanese Selves*, Princeton, N.J.: Princeton University Press, 1987.

Kempers, A. J. Bernet, *The Kettledrums of Southeast Asia: A Bronze Age World and its Aftermath*, Rotterdam: A. A. Balkema, 1988.

Kendis: A Guide to the Collections of the National Museum of Singapore, Singapore: National Museum, 1984.

Krahl, Regina, 'Plant Motifs on Chinese Porcelain', *Orientations*, vol. 18, May 1987.

Krahl, Regina, 'Vietnamese Blue-and-White and Related Wares', *Vietnamese Ceramics: A Separate Tradition*, Chicago: Art Media Resources, 1997.

Krairiksh, Piriya, 'A Reassessment of the Sukhothai Walking Buddhas', *A Divine Art: Sculpture of Southeast Asia*, London: Spink, 1997.

Krishnan, Gauri Parimoo et al., *Ramayana: A Living Tradition*, Singapore: National Heritage Board, 1997.

Lam, Peter, 'Vietnamese Celadons and their Relationships to the Celadons of Southern China', *Vietnamese Ceramics: A Separate Tradition*, Chicago: Art Media Resources, 1997.

Lee Chor Lin, *Ancestral Ships: Fabric Impressions of Old Lampung Culture*, Singapore: National Museum, 1987.

Lee Chor Lin, *Batik: Creating an Identity*, Singapore: National Museum, 1991.

Leigh, Barbara, *Hands of Time: The Crafts of Aceh*, Jakarta: Jambatan, 1989.

Lerner, Martin & Kossak, Steven, *The Lotus Transcendent: Indian and Southeast Asian Art from the Samuel Eilenberg Collection*, New York: Metropolitan Museum of Art, 1991.

Lewis, Paul & Lewis, Elaine, *Peoples of the Golden Triangle: Six Tribes of Thailand*, London: Thames & Hudson Ltd, 1984.

Linggi, Amar Margaret (Datin), *Tun Jugah Pua Gallery*, Kuching: The Tun Jugah Foundation, 2000.

Lunsingh Scheurleer, P. C. M. & Klokke, Marijke J., *Ancient Indonesian Bronzes: A Catalogue of the Exhibition in the Rijksmuseum Amsterdam With a General Introduction*, Leiden: E. J. Brill, 1988.

Mabbett, Ian & Chandler, David, *The Khmers*, Cambridge, Mass.: Blackwell, 1995.

Matusky, Patricia, *Malaysian Shadow Play and Music: Continuity and Oral Tradition*, Kuala Lumpur: Oxford University Press, 1993.

Maxwell, Robyn, *Textiles of Southeast Asia: Tradition, Trade and Transformation*, Melbourne: Oxford University Press, 1990.

Middleton, Sheila E. Hoey, 'Two Engraved Gems with Combination Monsters from Southeast Asia', *The Journal of the Siam Society*, vol. 85, parts 1 & 2, 1997.

Miettenen, Jukka O., *Classical Dance and Theatre in South-East Asia*, Singapore: Oxford University Press, 1992.

Miksic, John N., *Old Javanese Gold*, Singapore: Ideation, 1990.

Miller, Terry E. & Williams, Sean (eds.), *The Garland Encyclopedia of World Music, Southeast Asia*, vol. 4, New York: Garland, 1998.

Mohd. Kassim Hj. Ali, *Barang Kemas Melayu Tradisi*, Kuala Lumpur: Dewan Bahasa dan Pustaka, 1990.

Moore, Elizabeth H. et al., *Ancient Capitals of Thailand*, London: Thames & Hudson Ltd, 1996.

Mullerova, Petra, *Pictures from the Land of the Dragon King*, Prague: Narodni Museum, 2000.

Newton, Douglas, (ed.), *Arts of the South Seas*, Munich: Prestel, 1999.

Nguyen Huy Hong & Tran Trung Chinh, *Vietnamese Traditional Water Puppetry*, Hanoi: The Gioi Publishers, 1996.

Nguyen Van Huy, *The Cultural Mosaic of Ethnic Groups in Vietnam*, Hanoi: Education Publishing House, 2001.

Pal, Pratapaditya, *The Sensuous Immortals: A Selection of Sculptures from the Pan-Asian Collection*, Los Angeles: Los Angeles County Museum of Art, 1978.

Pham Huy Thong (ed.), *Dong Son drums in Vietnam*, Hanoi: The Viet Nam Social Science Publishing House, 1990.

Phim, Toni Samantha & Thompson, Ashley, *Dance in Cambodia*, Kuala Lumpur: Oxford University Press, 1999.

Piper, Jacqueline M., *Rice in South-East Asia: Cultures and Landscapes*, Oxford: Oxford University Press, 1993.

Pourret, Jess G., *The Yao: The Mien and Mun Yao in China, Vietnam, Laos and Thailand*, London: Thames & Hudson Ltd, 2002.

Puranananda, Jane, 'Mahayana Votive Tablets', *Heritage*, vol. 6, 1984, pp. 33–38.

Quigley, Sam, 'Gong smithing in Twentieth-century Surakarta', *Asian Art and Culture*, vol. 8, Fall 1995.

Raja Ali Haji ibn Ahmad, *The Precious Gift (Tuhfat al-Nafis)*, annotated translation by Virginia Matheson & Barbara Watson Andaya, Kuala Lumpur: Oxford University Press, 1982.

Rajadhon, Phya Anuman, *Thet Maha Chat*, Thai Culture, new series, no. 21, Bangkok: Fine Arts Department, 1990.

Reid, Anthony, *Southeast Asia in the Age of Commerce, 1450–1680*, vol. 2, *Expansion and Crisis*, New Haven: Yale University Press, 1993.

Richter, Anne, *The Jewelry of Southeast Asia*, London: Thames & Hudson Ltd, 2000.

Roth, Henry L., *The Natives of Sarawak and British North Borneo*, Singapore: University of Malaya Press, 1968.

Roveda, Vittorio, *Sacred Angkor: The Carved Reliefs of Angkor Wat*, Bangkok: River Books, 2002.

Scott-Kemball, Jeune, *Javanese Shadow Puppets: The Raffles Collection in the British Museum*, London: British Museum, 1970.

Sheares, Constance, 'Ikat Patterns from Kampuchea: Stylistic Influences', *Heritage*, vol. 7, 1984, pp. 45–53.

Sibeth, Achim, *The Batak: Peoples of the Island of Sumatra*, London: Thames & Hudson Ltd, 1991.

Singer, Noel, 'Kammavaca texts: Their covers and binding ribbons', *Arts of Asia*, vol. 23, no. 3, May–June 1993.

Sorrell, Neil, *A Guide to the Gamelan*, London: Faber and Faber, 1990.

Spink, Michael, *A Divine Art: Sculpture of Southeast Asia*, London: Spink, 1997.

Stadtner, Donald M. (ed.), *The Art of Burma: New Studies*, Mumbai: Marg Publications on behalf of the National Centre for the Performing Arts, 1999.

Stevenson, John et al., *Vietnamese Ceramics: A Separate Tradition*, Chicago: Art Media Resources, 1997.

Sulaiman Othman, *The Crafts of Malaysia*, Singapore: Editions Didier Millet, 1994.

Summerfield, Ann & Summerfield, John, *Walk in Splendor: Ceremonial Dress and the Minangkabau*, Los Angeles: University of California, 1999.

Sweeney, P. L. Amin, *Ramayana and the Malay Shadow-Play*, Kuala Lumpur: Penerbit Universiti Kebangsaan Malaysia, 1972.

Tambiah, S. J., *Buddhism and the Spirit Cults of North-east Thailand*, London: Cambridge University Press, 1970.

Tarling, Nicholas (ed.), *The Cambridge History of Southeast Asia*, Cambridge: Cambridge University Press, 1992.

Tate, D. J. M. (comp.), *Rajah Brooke's Borneo: The Nineteenth Century World of Pirates and Head-hunters, Orang Utan and Hornbills, and other rarities*, Hong Kong: John Nicholson, 1988.

Taylor, Keith Weller, *The Birth of Vietnam*, Berkeley: University of California Press, 1983.

Taylor, P. M. & Aragon, Lorraine V., *Beyond the Java Sea: Art of Indonesia's Outer Islands*, Washington, D.C.: Smithsonian Institution, 1991.

Tooker, Deborah, 'Putting the Mandala in its Place: A Practice-based Approach to the Spatialization of Power on the Southeast Asian 'Periphery' – The Case of the Akha', *The Journal of Southeast Asian Studies*, vol. 55, no. 2, May 1996.

Tran Van Khe, 'Water Puppets of Vietnam', *Asian Art and Culture*, vol. 8, Spring–Summer 1995.

van Brakel, J. H., *Budaya Indonesia: Art and Crafts in Indonesia*, Amsterdam: Royal Tropical Institute, 1987.

van Duuren, David, *The Kris: An Earthly Approach to a Cosmic Symbol*, Wijk en Aalburg, The Netherlands: Pictures Publishers, 1998.

van Zonneveld, Albert G., *Traditional Weapons of the Indonesian Archipelago*, Leiden: C. Zwartenkot, Art Books, 2001.

Wales, H. G. Quaritch, 'Archaeological Researches on Ancient Indian Colonization in Malaya', *Journal of the Malayan Branch of the Royal Asiatic Society*, vol. 18, part 1, 1940, pp. 1–85.

Wales, H. G. Quaritch, 'Further Work on Indian Sites in Malaya', *Journal of the Malayan Branch of the Royal Asiatic Society*, vol. 20, part 1, 1947, pp. 7–8.

White, Joyce, *Ban Chiang: Discovery of a Lost Bronze Age*, Philadelphia: The University Museum, University of Pennsylvania, 1982.

Woodside, Alexander, 'Vietnamese History: Confucianism, Colonialism and the Struggle for Independence', *Vietnam: Essays on History, Culture and Society*, New York: The Asia Society, 1985.

Woodward, Hiram J., *The Sacred Sculpture of Thailand: The Alexander B. Griswold Collection, the Walters Art Gallery*, London: Thames & Hudson Ltd, 1997.

Zhou Daguan, *The Customs of Cambodia*, translated by Michael Smithies, Bangkok: The Siam Society, 2001.

Zwalf, W. (ed.), *Buddhism Art and Faith*, London: British Museum Publications Ltd for the Trustees of the British Museum and the British Library Board, 1985.

WEST ASIA/ISLAMIC

Alexander, David, *Arts of War: Arms and Armour of the 7th to 19th centuries*, London: The Nour Foundation, 1993.

Allan, James, *Islamic Metalwork: The Nuhad Es-Said Collection*, 2nd edition, London: Sotheby's, 1999.

Atil, Esin (ed.), *Renaissance of Islam: Art of the Mamluks*, exhibition catalogue, Washington: Smithsonian Institution, 1981.

Baer, Eva, *Islamic Ornament*, New York: New York University Press, 1998.

Baker, Patricia, *Islamic Textiles*, London: British Museum Publications, 1999.

Bayani, Manijeh, & Contadini, Anna, *The Decorated Word: Qur'ans of the 17th to 19th centuries*, London: The Nour Foundation and Oxford University Press, 1999.

Blair, Sheila, *Islamic Inscriptions*, New York: New York University Press, 1998.

Bloom, Jonathan & Blair, Sheila, *Islamic Art*, London: Phaidon Press, 1997.

Bloom, Jonathan M., *Paper before Print: The History and Impact of Paper in the Islamic World*, New Haven and London: Yale University Press, 2001.

Brend, Barbara, *Islamic Art*, London: British Museum Publications, 1991.

Derman, Uğur, *Letters in Gold: Ottoman calligraphy from the Sakip Sabancı collection, Istanbul,* translated by M. Zakariya, New York: The Metropolitan Museum of Art, 1998.

Déroche, François, *The Abbasid Tradition: Qur'ans of the 8th to the 10th centuries,* London: The Nour Foundation and Oxford University Press, 1992.

Encyclopaedia of Islam, 2nd edition; Leiden, Netherlands: E.J. Brill, 1979.

Frishman, Martin & Khan, Hasan-Uddin (eds.), *The Mosque: History, Architectural Development and Regional Diversity*, London: Thames & Hudson Ltd, 1994.

Grube, Ernst, *Cobalt and Lustre: The first centuries of Islamic pottery*, U.K.: The Nour Foundation, 1994.

Hillenbrand, Robert, *Islamic Architecture: Form, Function and Meaning*, Edinburgh: Edinburgh University Press, 1994.

James, David, *After Timur, Qur'ans of the 15th and 16th centuries,* London: The Nour Foundation and Oxford University Press, 1992.

James, David, *Qur'ans of the Mamluks,* London: Alexandria Press, 1988.

James, David, *The Master Scribes. Qur'ans of the 11th to 14th centuries,* London: The Nour Foundation and Oxford University Press, 1992.

King, David, *World maps for finding the direction and distance to Mecca,* Leiden, The Netherlands; Boston: Brill, 1999.

Lewis, Bernard (ed.), *The World of Islam,* London: Thames and Hudson Ltd, 1976.

Maddison, Francis & Savage-Smith, Emilie, *Science, Tools and Magic*, U.K.: The Nour Foundation, 1997.

Melikian-Chirvani, A. S., *Islamic Metalwork from the Iranian World: 8th to 18th centuries,* London: Victoria & Albert Museum, 1982.

Minorsky, Vladimir, *Calligraphers and Painters: A Treatise by Qadi Ahmad, Son of Mir Munshi,* Washington: Smithsonian Institution, 1959.

Mitchell, George (ed.), *Architecture of the Islamic World,* London: Thames and Hudson Ltd, 1978.

Mohamed Zakariya, *Brocade of the Pen: The Art of Islamic Writing,* East Lansing, Michigan: Kresge Art Museum, Michigan State University, 1991.

Porter, Venetia, *Islamic Tiles,* London: British Museum Publications, 1995.

Robinson, Francis (ed.), *The Cambridge Illustrated History of the Islamic World,* Melbourne: Cambridge University Press, 1996.

Rogers, J. Michael & Ward, Rachel M., *Süleyman the Magnificent,* London: British Museum Publications, 1988.

Rogers, J. Michael, *Empire of the Sultans: Ottoman Art from the Collection of Nasser D. Khalili,* London: The Nour Foundation, 1996.

Safwat, Nabil, *The Art of the Pen: Calligraphy of the 14th to 20th centuries*, U.K.: The Nour Foundation, 1996.

Safwat, Nabil, *The Harmony of Letters: Islamic calligraphy from the Tareq Rajab Museum,* Singapore: Asian Civilisations Museum, 1997.

Schimmel, Annemarie, *Calligraphy and Islamic Culture,* New York: New York University, 1984.

Schimmel, Annemarie, *And Muhammad is His Messenger—The Veneration of the Prophet in Islamic Piety,* Chapel Hill: University of North Carolina Press, 1985.

Soucek, Priscilla P. (ed.), *Content and Context of the Visual Arts in the Islamic World,* Pennsylvania University Park: Pennsylvania University Press, 1988.

Turner, Howard, *Science in Medieval Islam: An Illustrated Introduction*, Austin: University of Texas Press, 1995.

Vernoit, Stephen, *Occidentalism. Islamic Art in the 19th century,* London: The Nour Foundation and Oxford University Press, 1997.

Ward, Rachel, *Islamic Metalwork,* London: British Museum Publications, 1993.

Watson, Oliver, *Persian Lustre Ware,* London: Faber and Faber, 1985.

CHINA

Ancestor Portraits
China
Late Qing dynasty
Chinese ink and colour on silk
(EACH) 179.6 x 86.9 cm

Ancestral Figurines
China
Qing dynasty
Boxwood
(FEMALE) h. 28.5 cm; (MALE) h. 29 cm

Ancestral Tablet Shrine
Fujian province, China
Late Qing dynasty
Longyan wood
71.5 x 54 x 24.8 cm

Bamboo Brush Holder
Jiading, China
17th century
Bamboo
h. 15 cm, diam. 8.3 cm

Black and White Faces of Impermanence
Taiwan, Republic of China
Contemporary
Silk, satin, metal and wood
(GENERAL FAN) 220 x 93 x 68 cm;
(GENERAL XIE) 298 x 108 x 70 cm

Blue and White Stemcup
China
Yuan dynasty
Ceramic
h. 9.7 cm, diam. 10.8 cm

Dehua Circular Covered Box
Dehua, China
12th–14th centuries
Ceramic
diam. 15 cm

Bronze Silkworm
China
Han dynasty
Gilt bronze
7 x 21.6 x 1 cm

Limestone Stele Depicting Buddha, Avalokiteshvara and Maitreya
China
Eastern Wei dynasty, 534–550
Limestone
84.5 x 47.7 cm

Cards for Drinking Game
China
1854
Paper, woodblock print
17.3 x 7.1 cm

A Section from a Chinese Qur'an
China
17th century
Ink, colours and gold on paper
(FOLIO) 29.7 x 21.5 cm

Cizhou Pillow
China
Song dynasty
Ceramic
22 x 34 x 11 cm

Cornelis Pronk Dishes
BLUE AND WHITE CORNELIS PRONK DISH
China
18th century
Ceramic
h. 2.9 cm, diam. 23.4 cm

ENAMELLED CORNELIS PRONK DISH
China
18th century
Ceramic
h. 2.7 cm, diam. 25.9 cm

Crowned Buddha
China
Ming dynasty
Gilt bronze
40 x 27.5 x 25.5 cm

Daoist Pantheon on Robe
China
Late Ming dynasty, 17th century
Embroidery on silk
130 x 206 cm

Dehua Enamelled Wares
TEAPOT WITH ZHANGZHOU-STYLE ENAMELS
Dehua, China
17th century
Ceramic
h. 8.5 cm

VASE WITH ZHANGZHOU-STYLE ENAMELS
Dehua, China
17th century
Ceramic
h. 17.8 cm

Dehua Figurines
SEATED WENCHANG WITH POTTER'S MARK
Dehua, China
Early 17th century
Ceramic
h. 34 cm

SHAKYAMUNI SEATED IN MEDITATION
Dehua, China
Early 17th century
Ceramic
h. 21.3 cm

SEATED GUANYIN
Dehua, China
Late 18th century or later
Ceramic
h. 20.6 cm

Dharani Mantra
Jiangsu, China
Yuan dynasty, early 14th century
Paper, woodblock print
(FOLIO) l. 975 cm;
(FRONTISPIECE) 30.2 x 11.5 cm

Ding Dishes
DING DISH WITH MOULDED FLORAL DECORATION
China
Song dynasty
Ceramic
h. 6 cm, diam. 30 cm

DING DISH WITH INCISED FLORAL DECORATION
China
Song dynasty
Ceramic
h. 3.5 cm, diam. 17.3 cm

DING DISH WITH INCISED TWIN FISH DECORATION
China
Song dynasty
Ceramic
h. 5.8 cm, diam. 20.9 cm

Dizang
China
Tang dynasty, 7th–8th centuries
Stone
104.7 x 52 x 30.5 cm

Doucai Cup
Jingdezhen, China
Ming dynasty, Chenghua period
Ceramic
h. 3.8 cm, diam. 6 cm

Drinking Vessels

JIA
China
Early Shang dynasty, Erlitou period,
c. 2000–1500 BCE
Bronze
h. 22.7 cm, diam. 15.6 cm

GU
China
Late Shang dynasty
Bronze
h. 30.3 cm, diam. 16.4 cm

Eight Immortals on Hanging
China
Ming dynasty, c. 1600
Silk, *kesi*
224 x 172 cm

Famille Noire Dish
Jingdezhen, China
Qing dynasty, Guangxu period
Ceramic
h. 5.3 cm, diam. 28 cm

Famille Rose Dish
Jingdezhen, China
Qing dynasty, Yongzheng period
Ceramic
h. 8.8 cm, diam. 50 cm

Festival Badge
China
Ming dynasty, Wanli period
Silk, gold thread, embroidery
34.5 x 36.5 cm

Filial Piety Scenes on Funerary Stele
China
Six Dynasties
Stone
(ENTIRE PANEL OF FOUR SCENES)
76 x 163 x 2.7 cm

Guangong
China
Late Ming–early Qing dynasties
Gilt bronze
32 x 22 x 15 cm

Guanyin
China
Tang dynasty, 7th–8th centuries
Limestone carving
43 x 19 cm

Guanyin with Acolytes
China
13th–14th centuries
Gilt bronze with silver inlay
48 x 29 cm

Heart Sutra
China
Jiaqing period, 1796
Blue-dyed paper, gold paint
22.2 x 11.3 cm

Ten Courts of Hell
Taiwan, Republic of China
Late Qing dynasty
Chinese ink and colour on paper, mounted
(EACH) Approx. 135.7 x 66.9 cm

Ink Cake by Cao Sugong
Shexian, Anhui province, China
17th century
Ink
h. 1.5 cm, diam. 8.8 cm

Ink Sticks
Huizhou, Anhui province, China
Qing dynasty, Kangxi period
Ink
18.2 x 18 x 9 cm

Jian
China
Spring and Autumn period
Bronze
h. 24.3 cm, diam. 56.1 cm

Jiaozhi Ceramic
Taiwan, Republic of China
Contemporary
Enamelled pottery
Approx. 36 x 25 x 12 cm

Kesi Fragment
China, Tibet
Mid Ming dynasty, 15th century
Silk
124 x 92.2 cm

Kraak Porcelain
KRAAK DISH WITH PERSIAN LADIES
Jingdezhen, China
Mid 17th century
Ceramic
h. 10 cm, diam. 48.3 cm

KRAAK KENDI
Jingdezhen, China
Mid 17th century
Ceramic
h. 23.5 cm

KRAAK KLAPMUTS WITH BIRD MOTIF
Jingdezhen, China
17th century
Ceramic
h. 4.7 cm, diam. 15 cm

Lead-glazed Model Stove
China
Eastern Han dynasty
Ceramic
18 x 18.2 x 9 cm

Liao-Jin Dynasty Silk
Northeast China
12th century
Silk and gold
32.5 x 95.5 cm

Lienüzhuan
China
1779
Paper
(FOLIO) 21.9 x 15.3 cm

Longyan Wood Day Bed
Fujian, China
Early 19th century
Longyan wood
203 x 110 x 87.5 cm; (SEAT) h. 51.5 cm

Lotus Sutra
China
Qianlong period, 18th century
Paper, woodblock printing
h. 26.5 cm

Marshall Zhao
China
Late Ming dynasty
Polychrome and gilt on silk
150.5 x 77.5 cm

Monk's Cap Ewer
Jingdezhen, China
Ming dynasty, Yongle period
Ceramic
(WITH LID) h. 20.8 cm

Neolithic Black Stemcup
Shandong province, China
Longshan culture (2400–2000 BCE)
Ceramic
h. 17 cm, diam. (MOUTH) 7.5 cm

Qingbai Porcelain

QINGBAI BELIMBING JARLET
WITH IRON SPOTS
China
Yuan dynasty
Ceramic
h. 6.6 cm, diam. (MOUTH) 6.5 cm

WATER DROPPER IN THE FORM
OF A BOY SEATED ON A BUFFALO
China
Yuan dynasty
Ceramic
9.3 x 8.3 cm

QINGBAI EWER WITH IRON SPOTS
China
Yuan dynasty
Ceramic
h. 11 cm, diam. (MOUTH) 2.3 cm

QINGBAI JARLET WITH
COPPER RED MOTIFS
China
Yuan dynasty
Ceramic
6.5 x 6 x 5.8 cm, l. (MOUTH) 1.8 cm

Rabbit Dish

Jingdezhen, China
Early–mid 17th century
Ceramic
3.5 x 17.8 x 9.3 cm

Reliquary Box

China
8th century
Gold foil on silver
3.8 x 7.2 x 4.6 cm

Ren Bonian's 'Birds, Pine and Prunus'

China
1882
Chinese ink and colours on paper
242 x 121 cm

Robin's Egg Glazed Vase

China
Qing dynasty, Qianlong period
Ceramic
h. 17.1 cm, diam. (MOUTH) 10 cm

Round Ink Cake by Cheng Junfang

Huizhou, Anhui Province, China
Second half of 16th century
Ink
9 x 18 x 18.2 cm

Roundel

China
Ming dynasty, Wanli period
Silk and gold thread
diam. 36 cm

Stele Depicting Shakyamuni and Prabhutaratna

China
Northern Qi dynasty (549–577)
White marble
57 x 35 cm

Songkhua Inkstone

China
Qing dynasty, Kangxi period
Green Songhua stone
16.9 x 12.1 x 1.5 cm

Sui Buddhist Triad

China
Sui dynasty
Gilt bronze
25.5 x 13.4 x 10.5 cm

Tang Sancai Tomb Guardians

A PAIR OF EARTH SPIRITS
China
Tang Dynasty
Ceramic
h. 76 cm, diam. 20 cm; h. 80 cm, diam. 20 cm

A PAIR OF BUDDHIST LOKAPALA
China
Tang Dynasty
Ceramic
h. 84.5 cm, diam. 14 cm;
h. 80 cm, diam. 17 cm

A PAIR OF CIVIL OFFICIALS
China
Tang Dynasty
Ceramic
h. 76 cm, diam. 13.5 cm;
h. 76 cm, diam. 14 cm

Tangka

China
Qing dynasty, Qianlong period, 18th century; (SILK FRAGMENTS) Qing dynasty, Wanli period, early 17th century
Silk
265 x 512 cm

Thousand Buddha Robe

China
Ming dynasty, 15th century
Silk
116.5 x 271.5 cm

Votive Paintings of Luohan

China
1795
Silk
(WITHOUT FRAME) 122 x 67.5 cm

Water Dropper

China
Qing dynasty, Kangxi period
Ceramic
h. 8.7 cm, diam. (BASE) 12.5 cm, diam. (RIM) 3.5 cm

Wine Container

China
Warring States
Bronze
h. 38 cm, diam. 18.4 cm

Yaozhou Bowl

China
Song dynasty
Ceramic
h. 9 cm, diam. 14.5 cm

Yin and Yang Zodiac Signs

North China
Liao dynasty
Wood
26.5 x 20.5 cm

Zhang Ruitu's Calligraphy

Fujian, China
1626 *bingyin* year of Tianqi reign
Ink on paper, hardwood covers
33.5 x 19.9 cm

SOUTH ASIA

Akshobhya

East India
Pala period, 12th century
Schist
60 x 35.5 x 12.5 cm

Ankusha

Mysore or Tanjore, India
17th–18th centuries
Steel and gold
h. 39 cm

A Section from a Baluster

Mathura area, Uttar Pradesh, north India
Kushana period, c. 2nd century
Red spotted sandstone
h. 102.2 cm

Bhairava
Uttar Pradesh, Haryana area, India
c. 10th century
Red sandstone
h. 61.6 cm

Standing Bhairava
Chola, Tamil Nadu, south India
Late 11th century
Granite
108.5 x 59 cm, diam. 20.5 cm

Brahma
Tamil Nadu, south India
12th century
Granite
h. 105 cm

Seated Buddha
Sri Lanka
Late Anuradhapura period, 10th century
Bronze with traces of gilding
10.5 x 9 x 5 cm

Buddhist Vajra and Ghanta
Tibet
15th century
Cast and gilt bronze
(VAJRA) 18 x 4.5 cm;
(GHANTA) h. 23 cm, diam. 10 cm

Chamunda in Dancing Pose
Rajasthan or Madhya Pradesh, India
c. 10th century
Sandstone
86.5 x 45 x 23 cm

Ancient Indian Gold Coins
India
Mauryan, Sunga, Kushana
and Gupta periods
Gold
Av. diam. 1.5 cm,
weight 4.08–8.07 g

Colonial Palanquin
Bengal, India
1820s
Wood, cane floor and iron attachments
l. 506 cm;
(CABIN) 97 x 174 x 76 cm

Cosmic Being
Mewar, Rajasthan, west India
Painted cotton cloth
19th century
183 x 94.5 cm

Daggers and Hilts
JADE DAGGER HILT (KHANJAR)
India
Aurangzeb period (1659–1707)
White nephrite jade with silver inlay
hilt and steel watered blade with
silver inlay
36.6 x 6 cm

JADE HILTED DAGGER WITH
RAM-HEADED POMMEL
India
Aurangzeb period (1659–1707)
Spinach-green jade inlaid with rubies
37.5 x 6.4 cm

JADE INLAID DAGGER HILT
India
19th century
White nephrite jade inlaid with
semi-precious stones and gold
13 x 6 cm

Dancing Ganesha
Central or east Madhya Pradesh, India
First half of the 10th century
Buff sandstone
46.4 x 35.5 cm

Deepalakshmi
Vijayanagara, India
15th century
Bronze
h. 34 cm

Earrings
Kushana, northwest India
1st century
Gold
3.5 x 3.5 cm

**Europeans Visiting the
Vishnupada Temple**
Patna or Murshidabad, India
Colonial period, 19th century
Paper and pigment
(WITH FRAME) 74.8 x 66.5 cm;
(WITHOUT FRAME) 52.2 x 45.2 cm

Foundation Stone
Probably Gujarat, west India
15 Muharram AH 775/7 July 1373 CE
Marble
61 x 137 cm

Gandhara Stupa
Gandhara or Mathura, India
Kushana period, 3rd–4th centuries
Sandstone
56.6 x 30 x 29.5 cm

Seated Ganesha
Halebid, Karnataka, south India
12th century
Schist
105 x 55 x 35 cm

The Gateway
West Uttar Pradesh or
east Rajasthan, Vraja area,
north India
Post-Shah Jahan period,
late 17th to early 18th century
Pink sandstone
350 x 365 x 70 cm

Gauri Mask
Maharashtra, India
19th century
Brass
40 x 23 cm

Hanuman
Tamil Nadu, south India
Late Chola period, c. 1200
Bronze
63.5 x 22 x 19 cm

Huqqa
North India
19th century
Silver
h. 66 cm

A Pair of Jali Screens
Agra area, Uttar Pradesh, India
Late 17th century
Red sandstone
128.5 x 92.5 x 9 cm;
128.5 x 96.5 x 9 cm

Kavacam
KAVACAM FOR A MALE DEITY
Tamil Nadu, south India
18th century
Gold
12.5 x 7.5 cm

KAVACAM FOR A FEMALE DEITY
Tamil Nadu, south India
18th century
Gold
9.7 x 6.8 cm

Kazhuththu Uru
Tamil Nadu, south India
19th century
Gold
94.5 cm

Keshanistoyakarini
Madhya Pradesh or Rajasthan, India
11th century
Sandstone
h. 99 cm

Krishnalila
Tamil Nadu, south India
19th century
Kalamkari, cotton painted and printed
256 x 506 cm

Kushana Buddha
Mathura, Uttar Pradesh, India
96–97
Red spotted sandstone
84 x 78 cm

Relief Fragment Depicting the
Life of **Buddha**
Gandhara, northwest India
3rd–4th centuries
Grey schist
h. 59.4 cm

**Lintel from Entrance to a
Vishnu or Durga Temple**
Central Madhya Pradesh, India
Mid 9th century
Sandstone
40 x 127 cm

Seated **Lokeshvara**
Northeast India
Sena dynasty, 12th century
Bronze with copper and silver alloy
h. 30 cm

A Page from the **Mahabharata**
Kangra, Himachal Pradesh, north India
Late 18th–early 19th centuries
Paper
30.4 x 41.5 cm

Relief Fragment of
Three **Matrika**
Uttar Pradesh, India
10th century
Buff sandstone
45 x 62.9 cm

Mughal Sword Hilt
India
18th century
Gold and silver on steel
17.5 x 8.5 cm

Nataraja
Halebid, Karnataka, south India
12th century
Schist
102 x 70 x 40 cm

**Picchavai Depicting Gopi
Under a Tree**
Rajasthan, northwest India
19th century
Dyed cotton, painted and gilded
196 x 209 cm

Qanat
Rajasthan, possibly Jaipur, India
18th century
Velvet, stencilled and painted
with gold leaf
439 x 268 cm

Ramayana Manuscript
Maharashtra or Tamil Nadu, India
Maratha period, 18th century
Natural colours on paper
20 x 40 cm

Ranganatha
Tamil Nadu, south India
Tanjore style, 18th century
Ink on paper
21.3 x 15.6 cm

Rudraksha Malai
Tamil Nadu, south India
19th century
Bronze
circ. 39 cm,
h. (LINGAM BOX) 7 cm

Shatari
Tamil Nadu, south India
19th century
Gilt copper
h. 14 cm,
diam. (BASE) 18.4 cm

Shiva, Parvati and Skanda
Tamil Nadu, south India
Late Chola period, c. 1200
Bronze
(SHIVA) h. 54.9 cm;
(PARVATI) h. 51.4 cm

Shri Chakra
Tamil Nadu, probably Thanjavour,
south India
c. 1700
Bronze
h. 48.9 cm

Shri Yantra on Kurma
Tamil Nadu, south India
19th century
Copper
9.5 x 22.8 x 16 cm

Painting Depicting **Shrines
to Lord Shiva**
Pahari region, Himachal Pradesh,
India
Late 17th–early 18th centuries
Cotton, painted and inscribed
90 x 198 cm

South Indian Lingam Boxes
CHAUKA LINGAM BOX
Karnataka, south India
18th–19th centuries
Silver
5.9 x 10.5 x 4 cm

LINGAM BOX WITH STUPA SHAPE
Andhra Pradesh,
south India
18th–19th centuries
Silver
10.5 x 14.2 x 4.2 cm

CYLINDRICAL LINGAM BOX
South India
18th–19th centuries
Silver
3.8 x 13 x 14.3 cm

Subrahmanya
Tamil Nadu, south India
Late Chola, 12th century
Granite
116 x 56 x 26 cm

Summer Carpet
Gujarat, west India
c. 1800
Quilted cotton with
silk thread embroidery
135 x 401 cm

Syamatara
Bihar, east India
10th–11th centuries
Schist
h. 49.9 cm

Talismanic Jama
India
17th century
Ink and colours on cotton
66 x 96 cm

Tholubomalattam
Andhra Pradesh or Karnataka,
south India
19th century
Goat or deer skin
(ARM TO ARM) 110.5 x 137 cm

Tibetan Book Covers
Tibet
12th–13th centuries
Painted and gilded wood
10.7 x 61 cm

**Tile Panel Containing
the Shahadah**
Multan, central Pakistan
18th century
Earthenware
53.5 x 120 cm

Vaishravana
Tibet
18th century
Gilt bronze and copper repoussé
h. 44.4 cm

Vatapatrashayi
South India
Vijayanagara style
(15th–16th centuries)
Bronze
14 x 10 cm

Venugopala
Tamil Nadu, south India
Early 19th century
Painting on wood with
semi-precious stones
(INCLUDING FRAME) 118 x 93 x 5.5 cm

Standing **Vishnu as Trivikrama**
Uttar Pradesh, India
9th century
Red-beige sandstone
107 x 55 x 18 cm

**Yakshi Capital Depicting
Four Shalabhanjika**
Northwest India
Kushana period, 2nd century
Red spotted sandstone
50 x 49 cm

Yogini
Bijamandal, Vidisha district,
Madhya Pradesh, India
c. 11th–12th centuries
Pink sandstone
138 x 78 x 40 cm

SOUTHEAST ASIA

Akha Accessories
HEADDRESS
North Thailand
Early 20th century
Cloth, silver and feathers
58 x 30 x 13 cm

BAG WITH GREEN BEETLES
North Thailand
Early 20th century
Embroidered cotton, buttons, wool
and dried green beetles
92 x 31 cm

JACKET AND SKIRT
North Thailand
Early 20th century
Indigo-dyed cotton with embroidery
and appliqué
(JACKET) 64 x 130 cm;
(SKIRT) 40 x 69 cm

Angkor Borei Buddha
Lower Mekong Delta, Cambodia
7th–8th centuries
Bronze
43.5 x 12 cm

Aso Carvings
Sarawak, Malaysia
c. 1900s
Wood
(EACH) 75 x 35 cm

Ayutthaya Buddha
Thailand
Late Ayutthaya period,
second half of 18th century
Gilt bronze
h. 112 cm

Badik
Sumbawa, east Nusa Tenggara,
Indonesia
19th century
Iron, silver, wood, horn
35.1 x 8.4 cm

Baju and Seluar Melayu
Riau-Lingga Archipelago, Indonesia
c. 1860–1870
Silk, cotton, gold thread
(TUNIC) 160 x 60 cm;
(TROUSERS) 140 x 110 cm

Baju Kurung
Riau-Lingga Archipelago,
Indonesia
19th century
Silk, gold thread
150 x 103 cm

Ban Chiang Earthenware
Khorat Plateau, northeast Thailand
300 BCE–200 CE
Earthenware
38 x 25.5 cm

Batak Carved Singa
North Sumatra, Indonesia
c.1930s
Wood
80 x 35 x 63 cm

Batak Ritual Buffalo Bones
North Sumatra, Indonesia
c.1930s
Bone
18 x 2.5 cm

Batik
BATIK FROM YOGYAKARTA
Surakarta, Java, Indonesia
20th century
Cotton, natural dyes
140 x 245 cm

BATIK FROM CIREBON
Cirebon, Java, Indonesia
20th century
Cotton, natural dyes
75.1 x 174 cm

Bronze Blade
Probably east Java or Bali, Indonesia
600–300 BCE
Bronze
28 x 19 cm

Bronze Drum in Pejeng Style
East Java, Indonesia
600 BCE–300 CE
Bronze
h. 161 cm, diam. 81 cm

Burial Bronze Bangles
Northeast Thailand
300 BCE–200 CE
Bronze
h. 6 cm, diam. 10 cm

Burmese Buddha
Shan State, Burma
c. 18th century
Alabaster
64 x 44 cm

Chedi
Central Thailand
Lopburi style, 12th–13th centuries
Bronze
38.4 cm

Chettiar Documents
Singapore
1920s–1940s
Paper
25 x 19 cm

Dayak Baskets
Sarawak, Malaysia
Early 20th century
Plant fibre and wood
h. 23 cm, diam. 18 cm;
h. 20.5 cm, diam. 13.5 cm;
h. 17.5 cm, diam. 13.5 cm

Dayak Carved Human Skull
Sarawak, Malaysia
c. 1900s
Human bone
h. 16 cm, diam. 17.5 cm

Dayak Shield
Sarawak, Malaysia
c. 1900s
Wood
123 x 39 cm

Divination Manual
North coast of Java, Indonesia
c. 1824
Ink and colours on paper
(FOLIO) 33.1 x 20.8 cm

Dokoh
Kelantan, Malaysia
Late 19th–early 20th centuries
Gold, *suasa*, diamonds
circ. 42 cm; circ. 34 cm

Dong Son Drum
North Vietnam
180–100 BCE
Bronze
h. 36 cm, diam. 55 cm

Finger Bowls
Riau-Lingga Archipelago, Indonesia
19th century
Silver
h. 4.3 cm, diam. 8.5 cm; h. 4.5 cm, diam. 9.9 cm

Finial
Cambodia
Bayon period, 12th–13th centuries
Bronze
7.1 x 3.4 x 3.4 cm

Funan Female Deity
Reportedly from Mekong Delta, Vietnam
c. 5th century
Wood
79 x 19.5 x 9 cm

Gamelan
Yogyakarta, Java, Indonesia
Probably mid 20th century
Bronze, wood

Garuda Headdress
Kutai, east coast of Borneo
1920s
Gold
15 x 17 cm

Hilltribe Silver
NECKRING, CHAIN AND SOUL LOCK
Hmong and Yao people, north Thailand
Early 20th century
Silver
diam. 15.4 cm

BRACELETS
Lahu and Akha people, north Thailand
Early 20th century
Silver
diam. 6–8.8 cm

EARRINGS
Hmong and Yao people, north Thailand
Early 20th century
Silver
diam. 3.4 cm

Hmong Accessories
BABY CARRIER
North Thailand
Early 20th century
Batik and cotton embroidery
69 x 64 cm

EMBROIDERED COLLARS
North Thailand
Early 20th century
Batik and cotton embroidery
9–12 x 5–7 cm

Hornbill Carving
Sarawak, Malaysia
Early 20th century
Wood
100 x 20 x 80 cm

Hsun Ok
Burma
Early 20th century
Bamboo, wood, lacquer
h. 20 cm, diam. 36.6 cm

Hudoq
Sarawak, Malaysia
c. 1900s
Wood
33 x 39 cm

Ikat
T'BOLI WARP IKAT
South Central Mindanao, the Philippines
20th century
Abaca
168 x 50 cm

GUJARATI DOUBLE IKAT (PATOLU)
Gujarat, India
Probably 19th century
Silk
99 x 400 cm

Indonesian Qur'an
Indonesia
AH 1237–1238/1822–1823 CE
Ink, colours and gold on paper
(FOLIO) 40.4 x 25.8 cm

Jataka Stories
North Thailand
c. 1950s
Painted cotton
l. 33 m

Javanese Bronzes
SEATED FIGURE OF KUBERA
Central Java, Indonesia
8th–9th centuries
Bronze
11.7 x 5 x 4 cm

SEATED FIGURE OF VAJRAPANI
Central Java, Indonesia
8th–9th centuries
Bronze
12.5 x 5 x 5 cm

Javanese Proto-Classic Jewellery
Java, Indonesia
Proto-Classic period
(3rd–8th centuries)
Gold
w. 2.5–3 cm

Kacip
KACIP FROM BALI
Bali, Indonesia
c. late 19th–early 20th centuries
Silver
17 x 4.7 cm

KACIP FROM SUMATRA
Palembang, south Sumatra,
Indonesia
c. late 19th–early 20th centuries
Iron, gold, *suasa*
18.5 x 4.3 cm

KACIP FROM JAVA
Solo, central Java, Indonesia
c. late 19th–early 20th centuries
Iron
19 x 6 cm

Kammavaca Manuscript
Burma
Early 20th century
Ivory, cinnabar and gold leaf
8.9 x 55⁊ cm

Kedah Buddha
Kedah, Malaysia
5th–9th centuries
Bronze
h. 20.6 cm

Keris
BUGIS KERIS
Riau-Lingga Archipelago, Indonesia
Late 19th century
Iron, brass, wood
31.5 cm

JAVANESE KERIS
Solo, central Java, Indonesia
19th century
Iron, ivory, brass, wood
45 cm

Khmer Crystals
SEAL WITH IMAGE OF HANUMAN
Ta Kev region, Cambodia
7th–13th centuries
Crystal
3 x 2.3 x 2 cm

SEAL WITH IMAGE OF
A FEMALE FIGURE
Ta Kev region, Cambodia
7th–13th centuries
Crystal
6.5 x 2.6 x 4.3 cm

SEAL WITH IMAGE OF
A FEMALE FIGURE
Ta Kev region, Cambodia
7th–13th centuries
Crystal
4.3 x 2.6 x 2.2 cm

Khmer Stone Lintel
Cambodia
Banteay Srei style,
12th–13th centuries
Sandstone
23.5 x 153.5 cm

Lakhaoun Khaol Masks
LAKHAOUN KHAOL MASK
FOR NEANG SEDA
Phnom Penh, Cambodia
1999–2000
Papier-mâché
h. 47 cm, diam. 24 cm

LAKHAOUN KHAOL MASK
FOR HANUMAN
Phnom Penh, Cambodia
1999–2000
Papier-mâché
h. 26 cm, diam. 27 cm

LAKHAOUN KHAOL MASK
FOR KRONG REAP
Phnom Penh, Cambodia
1999–2000
Papier-mâché
h. 58 cm, diam. 28.5 cm

LAKHAOUN KHAOL MASK
FOR EYSEI AKANEAT
Phnom Penh, Cambodia
1999–2000
Papier-mâché
h. 83 cm, diam. 34 cm

Lawon Prada
Palembang, south Sumatra,
Indonesia
19th century
Silk, gold
83 x 184 cm

Lolo Garments
Ha Giang province,
north Vietnam
Early 20th century
Embroidered and appliquéd cotton
(JACKET) 132 x 47 cm;
(HEADCLOTH) 260 x 33 cm;
(TROUSERS) 97 x 87 cm

Mamuli Ornaments
East Sumba, Indonesia
Late 19th–early 20th centuries
Gold
6.5 x 5.7 cm; 7.3 x 6.8 cm;
7.5 x 8 cm

Mandau Hilt
Sarawak, Malaysia
c. 1900s
Deer antler
17.5 x 10 cm

Minangkabau Jewellery
MINANGKABAU BRACELETS
West Sumatra
1930s
Gold with red staining, gems
and copper plate
24 x 18 cm

HEADDRESS
West Sumatra
1930s
Gold and copper plate
73 x 48 cm, diam. 14 cm

Mukhalinga
Cham, reportedly from
south Vietnam
c. 11th–12th centuries
Silver and gold
15.5 x 8 cm

Naga Muchalinda
Cambodia
11th–12th centuries
Sandstone
h. 101 cm

Nias Ancestral Carvings
Nias Island, Indonesia
c. 1900
Wood
30 x 20 ɔʀɪ

Osa Osa
Nias Island, Indonesia
c. 1900s
Stone
130 x 80 x 115 cm

Ox-shaped Vessel
Lopburi, Thailand
300 BCE–200 CE
Earthenware
33.5 x 10.8 x 21.6 cm

Padung-padung
North Sumatra, Indonesia
c. late 19th–early 20th centuries
Gold, silver and *suasa*
17 x 16.5 cm

Palembang Lacquerware
TENONG
Palembang, south Sumatra, Indonesia
c. 1900
Wood, lacquer, gold leaf and paint
h. 51 cm, diam. 37 cm

PADDLE
Palembang, south Sumatra,
Indonesia
c. 1900
Wood, lacquer, gold leaf and paint
99.8 x 20 cm

Palepai
Lampung, south Sumatra, Indonesia
Late 19th century
Cotton and vegetable dyes
50 x 245 cm

Panakawan
Java, Indonesia
20th century
Leather
h. 50–60 cm

Panel Carved with the Shahadah
Cirebon, north coast Java, Indonesia
Mid 20th century
Wood
51 x 75 x 3.5 cm

Parabaik
Burma
Late 19th century
Paper and water-soluble paints
59.7 cm x 12.65 m

Pending
Riau-Lingga Archipelago, Indonesia
19th century
Gold, diamonds and rubies
19 x 11.5 cm

Pinggan
Riau-Lingga Archipelago, Indonesia
c. 1900
Silver
h. 1.6 cm, diam. 16.3 cm

Pua Kumbu
Sarawak, Malaysia
c. 1900s
Cotton
255 x 120 cm

Pustaha
North Sumatra, Indonesia
c. 1930s
Bark
32 x 25 x 8 cm

Quan Am
North Vietnam
18th century or later
Bronze, painted and gilded lacquer
107 x 135 x 60 cm

Roi Nuoc
LION WATER PUPPET
Hanoi, Vietnam
c. 1995
Wood
57 x 29 cm

FAIRY WATER PUPPET
Hanoi, Vietnam
c. 1995
Wood
59 x 21 cm

BOY ON A BUFFALO WATER PUPPET
Hanoi, Vietnam
c. 1995
Wood
56 x 25 x 31 cm

Royal Malay Seal
Kelantan, Malaysia
AH 1310–1311/1892–1893 CE
Tin, copper alloy
h. 1.2 cm, diam. 3.9 cm

Sarung Featuring Camels and Tents
Possibly Pekalongan,
north coast of Java, Indonesia
Early 20th century
Cotton
(FOLDED) 107.2 x 88.9 cm

Sawankhalok Ceramics
BROWN AND WHITE COVERED JARS
North-central Thailand
13th–15th centuries
Stoneware
diam. 9.7 cm; diam. 8.5 cm;
diam. 14 cm

DISH WITH FISH MOTIF
North-central Thailand
13th–15th centuries
Stoneware
diam. 24.5 cm

CELADON BOWL
Si Satchanalai,
north-central Thailand
Mid 15th century
Stoneware
h. 8.5 cm, diam. 24.5 cm

POURING VESSEL IN THE SHAPE
OF A KNEELING FIGURE
North-central Thailand
13th–15th centuries
Stoneware
18 x 8 x 9 cm

SCULPTURAL FIGURES
North-central Thailand
13th–15th centuries
Stoneware
h. 10.3 cm; h. 10.5 cm

MAKARA FINIAL
North-central Thailand
13th–15th centuries
Stoneware
64 x 26 x 27 cm

Seurapi
Aceh, north Sumatra, Indonesia
Late 19th century
Gold
35 x 11.3 cm

Sewar
South Sumatra, Indonesia
19th century
Silver, horn, wood, iron
34 cm

Sireh Sets
KOTAK SIREH
Riau-Lingga Archipelago,
Indonesia
19th century
Silver, gilt silver,
lacquer, wood
15 x 32 x 19 cm

PUAN SIREH
Kedah, Malaysia
1900–1950
Silver, brass, iron
h. 14.5 cm, diam. 23.5 cm

Songket
Riau-Lingga Archipelago,
Indonesia
Mid–late 19th century
Silk, gold threads
150 x 103 cm

Staff of Authority
North Sumatra, Indonesia
c.1930s
Wood and feathers
l. 106 cm

Majapahit-style Statue
Possibly from Java, Indonesia
Majapahit era, c. 14th century
Lead
5.5 x 5.6 x 1.9 cm

Sukhothai Walking Buddha
Sukhothai, north-central Thailand
15th–16th centuries
Bronze
h. 117 cm

Syair
Pattani, Thailand
AH 1250/1835 CE
Paper, pigment
(FOLIO) 17.5 x 8.5 cm

Topeng
Java, Indonesia
Early 20th century
Wood
14–20 x 14–16.5 cm

Tripod Vessel
North Vietnam
100
Bronze
h. 43 cm, diam. 40 cm

Tung Thieu
Yasothorn Province,
northeast Thailand
c. 1930s
Silk and cotton
384 x 54 cm

**Vietnamese Blue
and White Ware**
BLUE AND WHITE EWER
Vietnam
16th century
Stoneware
h. 23.5 cm, diam. 13.5 cm

DISH WITH UNDERGLAZED BLUE
LANDSCAPE DESIGN
North Vietnam
15th–16th centuries
Stoneware
diam. 33 cm

SHARDS OF ARCHITECTURAL TILES
Vietnam
15th–16th centuries
Stoneware
l. 9–20 cm, w. 8–12 cm

**Vietnamese Green-glazed
Wares**
GREEN-GLAZED DISH, JARLET AND CUP
North Vietnam
14th–15th centuries
Stoneware
(DISH) h. 5 cm, diam. 23 cm;
(JARLET) h. 7 cm, diam. 8 cm;
(CUP) h. 5.5 cm, diam. 9.5 cm

CELADON JAR WITH COVER
North Vietnam
14th century
Stoneware
diam. 15.5 cm

Vietnamese Whiteware
OIL LAMP IN THE SHAPE OF A PARROT
Vietnam
11th–12th centuries
Stoneware
11.5 x 18.2 x 8 cm

CONICAL BOWL
Vietnam
13th–14th centuries
Stoneware
h. 9.4 cm, diam. 19.5 cm

Votive Tablets
Malay Peninsula
8th–10th centuries
Clay
h. 5–7 cm; w. 3–4 cm

Water Containers
LABU
Kuala Kangsar, Perak, Malay Peninsula
c. late 19th–early 20th centuries
Earthenware, silver
29 x 55 cm

KENDI
West Sumatra, Indonesia
c. 1900
Brass
30 x 21.5 cm

Wayang Kulit
Java, Indonesia
20th century
Leather
h. 50–60 cm

Weft Ikat
DETAIL FROM A PIDAN
Cambodia
19th century
Silk
87 x 230 cm

KAIN LIMAR (WEFT IKAT
SHOULDER CLOTH)
Bangka Island, south Sumatra,
Indonesia
19th century
Silk
500 x 90 cm

Woodblock Print
Hanoi, Vietnam
Late 20th century
Paper and inks
32 x 65 cm

Woodcarving
MINANGKABAU ARCHITECTURAL PANEL
West Sumatra, Indonesia
20th century
Wood, pigments
50 x 156 cm

MALAY ARCHITECTURAL PANEL
Northeast Malay Peninsula
20th century
Wood
79 x 20 cm

Yao Accessories
TROUSERS
North Thailand
Early 20th century
Embroidered and appliquéd cotton
80 x 132 cm

CHILDREN'S HATS
North Thailand
Early 20th century
Embroidered and appliquéd cotton
h. 13–18 cm, diam. 18–20 cm

APRON
North Thailand
Early 20th century
Embroidered and appliquéd cotton
79 x 88 cm

SHOES
North Thailand
Early 20th century
Embroidered and appliquéd cotton
24 x 11.5 cm

WEST ASIA

Astrolabe
Isfahan, Iran
c. 1700
Copper alloy
diam. 15 cm

Bowl with Foliated Kufic-Abbasid Script
Khurasan, northwest Iran
10th century
Earthenware
h. 10 cm, diam. 34 cm

Burmese Qur'an Box
Myanmar
Late 19th century or early 20th century
Wood
33 x 33 x 25 cm

Calligraphic Lion
Probably from Iran
19th century
Gold ink on paper
27.4 x 38 cm

Cenotaph Cover
Turkey
18th century
Silk
93.7 x 64.8 cm

Dala'il al-Khayrat
DALA'IL AL-KHAYRAT FROM INDIA
Kashmir, India
18th–19th centuries
Ink, colours and gold on paper
(FOLIO) 21.2 x 14 cm

DALA'IL AL-KHAYRAT FROM
NORTH AFRICA
North Africa
18th century
Ink, colours and gold on paper
(FOLIO) 11.8 x 11 cm

DALA'IL AL-KHAYRAT FROM TURKEY
Turkey
Ottoman period, AH 1294/1880 CE
Ink, colours and gold on paper
(FOLIO) 22 x 14 cm

Firman of Sultan Abdülhamid II
Turkey
AH 1311/July 1893 CE
Ink and gold on paper
131.5 x 68 cm

Folio from a Maghribi Qur'an
Islamic Spain
13th century
Ink, colours and gold on paper
33.8 x 26.2 cm

Fragments from a Minbar
Turkey
19th–20th centuries
Walnut wood
290 x 320 cm

Gem-set Chinese Porcelain for Turkish Market
(BOWL) China; (MOUNT) Turkey
Late 16th century
Emerald, gilt copper on porcelain
h. 6 cm, diam. 11.7 cm

Kashan Lustre Bowl
Kashan, central Iran
13th century
Stone-paste
h. 10.1 cm, diam. 22 cm

Khurasan Jug
Khurasan, northeast Iran
Late 12th century
Silver and copper inlay
on copper alloy
h. 27.2 cm

Kiswah Fragments from the Holy Ka'bah
Egypt
Early 20th century
Gilded silver and silver threads on silk
89 x 538 cm

Kitab al-Shihab
Valencia, Spain
Dated AH 568/1172–1173 CE
Ink, colours and gold on parchment
(FOLIO) 29 x 17.5 cm

Kufic-Abbasid Qur'an Folio
North Africa
Early 8th century
Ink on parchment
55 x 70 cm

Lajvardina Tile
Kashan, central Iran
13th century
Stone-paste
33.5 x 32.5 cm

Lion-shaped Incense Burner
Egypt
11th–12th centuries
Copper alloy
h. 22 cm, w. 15 cm

Mamluk Basin
Egypt
1342–1345 or 1351–1354
Silver inlay on copper alloy
diam. 34.5 cm

Mihrab Tile
Northeast Iran
c. 11th century
Earthenware
43 x 28.3 cm

Miniature Qur'an
Western Persia (Iran) or
Anatolia (Turkey)
14th century
Ink, colours and gold on paper
(FOLIO) 7 x 4.9 cm

Moroccan Wooden Panels
North Africa
19th century
Colours and silver on wood
163.2 x 86.3 cm

Mosque Candlesticks
Turkey
Ottoman period
Tinned copper alloy
h. 76 cm, diam. 51 cm

Mufradat by Hafiz Osman
MUFRADAT WITH EBRU MARGINS
Turkey
Ottoman period, late 17th century
Ink, colours and gold on paper
(FOLIO) 15.2 x 27 cm

MUFRADAT ON GOLD-SPRINKLED PAPER
Turkey
AH 1095/1658 CE
Ink, colours and gold on paper
(FOLIO) 17 x 24.5 cm

Fragments from a
Muhaqqaq Qur'an
Anatolia (Turkey)
c. 1300–1335
Ink, colours and gold on paper
(FOLIOS) 28 x 18.5 cm; 28.9 x 18.5 cm

Nasta'liq Calligraphy by
'Imad al-Hassini
Safavid, Persia
Late 16th century
Ink, colours and gold on paper
16.7 x 26 cm

Ottoman Stele
Turkey
Ottoman period, 18th–19th centuries
Stone
161 x 51 cm

Paper-cut Nasta'liq Calligraphy
Iran
Early 16th century
Paper
18.5 x 28 cm

Penboxes
IVORY PENBOX
India
18th century
Ivory
7.5 x 28 x 11.3 cm

GOLD DAMASCENED STEEL PENBOX
Turkey
Ottoman period, 1876
Gold on steel
3.7 x 28.5 x 5.9 cm

LACQUERED PENBOX
Qajar, Iran
AH 1318/1900 CE
Wood
3 x 20.5 x 3.3 cm

Qajar Standard
Iran
AH 1262/1845–6 CE
Ink and colours on cotton
122 x 191 cm

Qasidat al-Burdah
Turkey
AH 1121/1709 CE
Ink, colours and gold on paper
(FOLIO) 31 x 27 cm

Qit'ah Written by Ahmet
Al-Karahisar
Turkey
16th century
Ink and gold on paper
(TEXT AREA) 11.5 x 23.2 cm

Qur'an
Baghdad, Iraq
AH 681/1282 CE
Ink, colours and gold on paper
(FOLIO) 17.4 x 12 cm

Qur'an in Naskh
Turkey
AH 907/1501 CE
Ink, colours and gold on paper
(FOLIO) 35 x 24 cm

Qur'an Leaf
Iran
11th–12th centuries
Ink, colours and gold on paper
(FOLIO) 28.2 x 18.2 cm

Qur'an Scroll
Turkey
Ottoman period, 15th century
Ink, colours and gold on paper
14 x 112 cm

Qur'an Stands
QUR'AN STAND WITH TORTOISESHELL
AND MOTHER-OF-PEARL INLAY
Turkey
Ottoman period, 18th century
Wood
(OPEN) h. 56.5 cm, w. (BASE) 61 cm,
(TOP) 30 cm

WOODEN QUR'AN STAND
Anatolia (Turkey)
19th century
Wood
(OPEN) h. 24 cm, w. (BASE) 37.5 cm,
(TOP) 35.5 cm

JASPER QUR'AN STAND
North India
Late Mughal period, early 19th century
Jasper
(OPEN) h. 28 cm, w. (BASE) 31.5 cm,
(TOP) 27 cm

Qur'an Written by
'Abd Allah Al-Sayrafi
Iran
14th century
Ink, colours and gold on paper
(FOLIO) 29 x 19 cm

Safavid Qur'an Case
Iran
17th–18th centuries
Gold on steel
5.9 x 4.6 cm

Scribe's Table
Turkey
Ottoman period,
17th century
Wood
35.5 x 56 x 33 cm

Slip-painted Bowl
Samarqand (Uzbekistan)
AH 300/912 CE
Earthenware
diam. 36 cm

Timurid Kufic-Abbasid Tile
Iran
c. 1450
Glaze and gold on stone-paste
15.2 x 14.5 cm

Yemeni Manuscript
Yemen
Muharram AH 758/
25 December 1356–23 January 1357 CE
Ink and colours on paper
(FOLIO) 26.5 x 17.5 cm

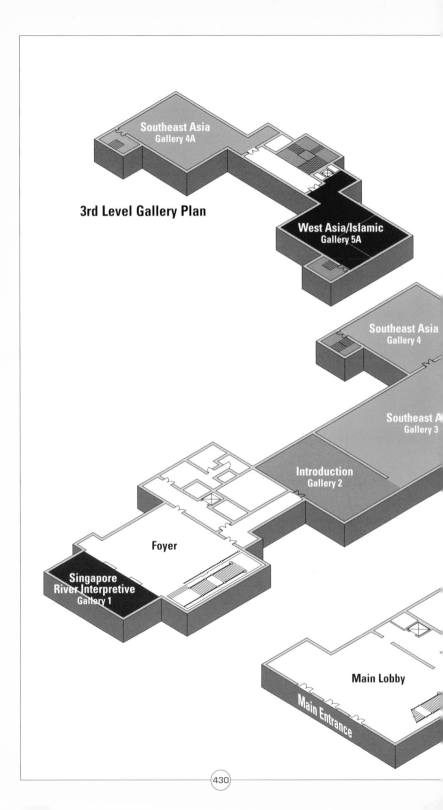

3rd Level Gallery Plan

Southeast Asia
Gallery 4A

West Asia/Islamic
Gallery 5A

Southeast Asia
Gallery 4

Southeast Asia
Gallery 3

Introduction
Gallery 2

Foyer

Singapore
River Interpretive
Gallery 1

Main Lobby

Main Entrance

Gallery Plans
Asian Civilisations Museum
Empress Place

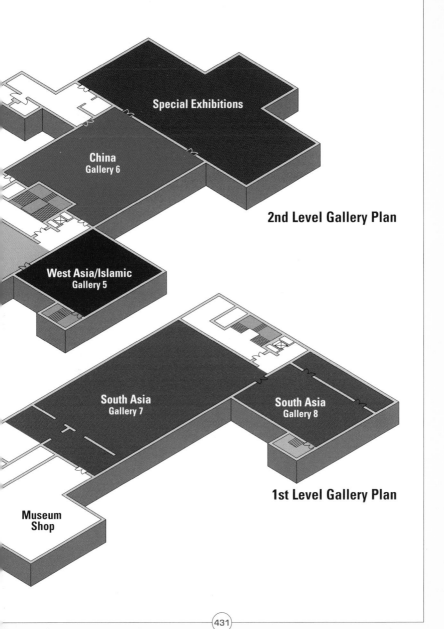

Special Exhibitions

China
Gallery 6

2nd Level Gallery Plan

West Asia/Islamic
Gallery 5

South Asia
Gallery 7

South Asia
Gallery 8

1st Level Gallery Plan

Museum
Shop